Live Respected, Die Regretted

GERALD MILNER'S WAR
Letters to Eva from a "Desert Rat"

Part 1:
June 1941– December 1942

Written by
'Desert Rat' Gerald Milner
Compiled by John Milner

Live Respected, Die Regretted: Gerald Milner's War, Part 1
John Milner

Published by Aspect Design 2012
Malvern, Worcestershire, United Kingdom.

Designed and Printed by Aspect Design
89 Newtown Road, Malvern, Worcs. WR14 1PD
United Kingdom
Tel: 01684 561567
E-mail: books@aspect-design.net
Website: www.aspect-design.net

ISBN 978-1-908832-03-0

Live Respected, Die Regretted

To: Tony

Best Wishes

[signature]

ACKNOWLEDGEMENTS

I would like to thank:

- My wife Kim and family Robert, Elsa, and James for putting up with me while I prepared this book and for their help in reading it an pointing out errors.
- My cousin, John Stephens, and his wife Sylvia for their help and encouragement and for supplying some photographs.
- Dilip Sarkar MBE, Bob Cotes, Francis Smith, Alan Hyde, and Margaret Woodward for their help and encouragement
- Stuart Millward for help with transcribing and word processing the letters.
- Harry and Judy Needham for their help in reading it and pointing out errors.
- Peter Harrington of Ivanhoe Photography for help in copying many of the photos included in this book.
- The National Archive, Kew for the passages from the War Diaries.
- Joanne Milner, Paul Milner, and their families, Tony Wilkes, Margaret Boxley, Gerald & Anne Butler and Jessie Payze for allowing me to use the photographs of their family members.
- The Stourbridge News (Newsquest Media Group).
- The Daily Mail.
- The Birmingham Mail
- Desert Rat Website
- Ian Paterson
- Jon.
- The Imperial War Museum.
- Hugh Harrison-Allen www.cresselly.com.
- Raymond E G Seale DL, Grenadier Guards .
- www.desertrats.memorialassoc.btinternet.co.uk/.

The letters in this book tell the story of an ordinary soldier's thoughts and feelings as he went through the war. I have not changed the letters and there are, in today's terms, one or two politically incorrect passages. I spent sometime wondering whether I should delete or censor them but decided to leave them as written. If this causes offence, it is not meant to. Even after the war Gerald still shot straight from the hip and told people what he thought, whoever they were, and he usually made his assumptions as to people's character on merit.

He also wrote a few letters to family members, a personal diary throughout the desert war and in later life wrote several pages on his experiences. I have included these along with transcriptions of the War Diaries courtesy of the National Archives, one letter from my mother, an extract of a letter from a comrade in 287 Coy and hundreds of photos and memorabilia of the time. I hope you enjoy reading them.

JOHN MILNER 2011

Contents

Part 1: June 1941 – December 1942

Part 2: January 1943 – March 1946

FOREWORD

I sat there holding his hand. He said, "You'd better call your Mother now. I don't know how you're going to cope with her". I reassured him, made the call and waited. Eva eventually arrived with my wife Kim. I whispered to him that Mom was here and told him I loved him. He said to his beloved, "I'll be waiting for you. I've got to go now. Bye Bye", and was gone. He died as he had lived with courage and fortitude.

The church was packed for the funeral. I had been close to this man who had been there for me all my life. He was a lifelong Aston Villa fan but most of all I will remember him as a true 'Desert Rat'[1]. I knew so much about him and yet so little. He was respected by everyone who knew him.

> Raymond E. G. Seale DL, Grenadier Guards wrote, *"Gerald Milner was my close friend and mentor. We first met in 1953 and from that first meeting remained close associates for the next 45 years. Gerald was a man of honour and of the highest integrity. Regardless of personal inconvenience he was fearless in declaring his strong feelings for truth and justice. He would not give in to intimidation. He met his death with the same philosophy he had lived his entire life with fortitude and courage, giving words of comfort to his family and friends interwoven with little jokes even as the end drew near."*

At the beginning of 1997 Gerald had a prostrate problem and had some investigative work done. After attending the doctor's surgery in September he informed me that there was nothing to worry about and that it was a benign condition and then went with his beloved Eva on a fishing trip to Wales. My son Robert took them and they had a good time. Shortly after returning Gerald was rushed to Russells Hall Hospital and two weeks later he was dead. I was told in a room adjoining the Heron Ward that he had no chance. Questioning the doctor as to why he had been told the cancer was benign I received the reply that sometimes the test results were not accurate. I will never know whether this brave man knew far more than he had told me, but do know that his compassion and thoughtfulness lasted until the end. He insisted that my wife's 40th birthday party go ahead a few days before his death and arranged for his friends in three Masonic Lodges to donate a nebuliser to the hospital.

Mother struggled on for five and a half lonely years without him before she passed away on 25th August 2003. I knew that Mom had a collection of letters from Dad when he was overseas which she kept in an old suitcase. She always said that they were private and that they were love letters. Having collected dust for years Mom wanted to burn them after my father's death. I looked at some of them and realised that they formed a fantastic historical record of the time. I persuaded her not to destroy them and began typing. Reading them again seemed to give Mother great comfort and she said she was happy for me to show them to other people after she had gone. Oh how I wished I had read them while my father was still alive and listened more intently to his stories, because they posed so many unanswered questions. He had always wanted to write a book and had produced several short stories about his life as a boy on Worcestershire, yet here in these letters was the book he had already written.

He was born on 10th October 1910, to Walter and Eunice Milner at Kings Norton. My grandfather was a policeman stationed in Kings Norton at the time of Gerald's birth. During

---

[1] Following a visit to Cairo Zoo the wife of General Creagh (the Divisional Commander) produced a design of a Jerboa (desert rat), which was approved by the officers and men of the 7th Armoured Division and was then drawn up by Trooper Ken Hill of RTR. The men took to the Jerboa and adopted the name of 'The Desert Rats'. It is worth pointing out that the term 'Desert Rats' is often used to describe any soldier of the desert army or any soldier who fought at Tobruk but the only true 'Desert Rats' are the men who served in the 7th Armoured Division, whose shoulders or vehicles carried the Jerboa emblem.

his police career he was posted to several different villages in Worcestershire until he finally arrived in Stourbridge and became the town's policeman No. 7. En route Gerald had gained a sister Margery who was just two years younger than him. The family lived in Clark Street, Stourbridge, where Roma, the baby of the family, was born in 1921.

It was at Brook Street School (later called Longlands) that he first met the love of his life Eva Williams. After a childhood illness, Gerald sat the entrance examination for Stourbridge Grammar School, but failed by a couple of marks. Walter offered to pay for him to go, but he refused the offer and stayed at Brook Street until he was apprenticed, at 15 years of age, to The International Tea Company in Stourbridge for three years. When qualified he was sent, in 1930, to work at their shop in Tenbury Wells. While there he lodged at 33 Cross Street. (I found it fascinating that the company paid for digs for their junior employees but expected them to sleep in the same bed!) During the few months he was there electricity was, for the first time, installed at his lodgings.

At this time he was already courting my mother and during his time away, constantly wrote letters (many by candle light) to her, professing his love for her. Unable to see her because of the 30 mile distance and an unhelpful train timetable, he eventually persuaded his father to buy him a motor bike. That Ariel was his pride and joy and enabled him to come home on Saturday nights after work and spend time with my mother until early on Monday morning when he would make the, often arduous, journey back to Tenbury. He rode home most weekends and constantly had his leg pulled by other members of staff about his devotion to her.

In March 1931 Gerald was moved to the stores in Broadway, Worcestershire and lodged with a Mr & Mrs Payne at 2, Bibsworth Avenue, later renamed New Avenue. Although this increased his journey time considerably, he still continued to ride home, such was his love. Wind snow and ice were no deterrent. During his time there he was sent to many other shops, never being sure whether he would be working in Cheltenham, Evesham, Dursley or Broadway and eventually becoming a relief manager. In October 1931 he came off his motor cycle while delivering groceries and severely damaged the tendons and ligaments of his ankle. He wrote to my mother saying that it could take many weeks or months to heal. At some point between then and late 1932 he had fallen out with his employers, given in his notice and set up his own shop at 52 Brook Street, Stourbridge, where the family were then living in rented accommodation. I assume he must have had permission from the landlord, a Mr Titley because the front room (some 12 feet x 12 feet) was converted into a grocery shop.

My mother Eva Williams was the daughter of a railwayman and was a couple of years younger than Gerald. After leaving Brook Street School, she went into service, and then got a job in Stourbridge High Street at The Royal Turf Cafe. It was here that Gerald started to court her seriously. She later worked at Lewis's department store in Birmingham commuting by train every day. It was at Lewis's that she met her friend and 'bundle of fun', Lucy Goddard who came from Elsmere in Shropshire, and who later stayed with her and kept her company through all those lonely war years. Her mother passed away in June 1932 and her father died of a broken heart five months later. She lived with her parents at 43 Hatfield Road Stourbridge but was now on her own at 19 years of age. Gerald continued to support her and they eventually married on August the 5th 1940 at St Mary's Church, Oldswinford, Stourbridge, less than a month after he applied to join the Worcestershire Defence Volunteers, otherwise known as The Home Guard, or 'Dad's Army'. George Veal was the best man. Gerald was accepted for service in the WDV on 30th August 1940. During the war his sister Roma worked in a munitions factory and there met and fell in love with 'Steve' (Horace Reginald Stephens), who had cycled to Stourbridge from Newport in Wales to seek his fortune with only £2 in his pocket. They married in 1942 and Steve was to eventually became Mayor of

Stourbridge in 1966. They had one child, John born in 1945. Sister Margery married Martin C. Hogan and they had three children; Michael and Peter were born before the war and Patricia was born in 1941 just after Gerald left for Egypt.

Walter's brother, Bert Milner lived in Norton Road and was a police Sergeant in Stourbridge. He had three sons; Stanley, Eric, and Dennis, and a daughter, Gladys. All three sons went to fight. Eric became a Lieutenant in the Navy while Dennis remained a rating and was taken prisoner. Stanley joined the army.

A month after war had broken out in September 1939 the government announced that all men between the ages of 18 and 49 who were not working in reserved occupations could be called upon to join the armed services and could chose between Army, Navy or Air force. Conscription was by age and initially only those between 20 and 23 were conscripted. Gerald joined the Stourbridge home guard for a while and then decided to volunteer in 1941. Thus less than a year after marrying Eva he left her for four and a half years to fight for King and country. During that time he endured both hardship and comradeship and became one of the famous 'Desert Rats.'

> *"In days to come when people ask you what you did in the Second World war*
> *it will be enough to say, 'I marched with the 8th Army'"*.

These words were spoken by Winston Churchill when he addressed the men in the North African desert. My father Gerald Milner was one of those men. He was in the Royal Army Service Corps, HQ Platoon, 287 Coy, attached to the famous 7th Armoured Division. After the desert battles he caught Diphtheria from the enemy's practice of dropping dead bodies into wells in order to pollute them. He was however a survivor and after several weeks in a South African Field Hospital was posted to 804 Veterinary & Remount Conducting Section which took him through Italy and eventually to Austria. His desire to return to his wife and sweetheart never wavered and he wrote to her constantly. Before big battles he destroyed all of her letters to him by burning them. He eventually returned home for a months' leave in 1945 but had to wait well into the following year to be demobbed and finally return to days with Eva. I don't know whether he actually took the holiday he promised himself with her, but he did find a peaceful spot in England.

NOTES ON THE RASC

In 1794 the Royal Waggoners were formed, they were the first British Army uniformed transport corps. It changed its name a couple of times and was eventually disbanded in 1833. During the Crimea War, the Land Transport Corps was formed which later changed its name to the Military Train. Over the years there were various other changes, until in 1888 a new Army Service Corps emerged. At the end of the First World War it became the Royal Army Service Corps and was divided into Supply and Transport branches. During the Second World War the RASC were organised into companies and RASC units of a division were collected under the Commander Royal Army Service Corps (CRASC). Their duties included transporting troops, ammunition, petrol and other supplies. They were considered to be combatant personnel. After the war there were various other mergings and today they are known as the Royal Logistics Corps.

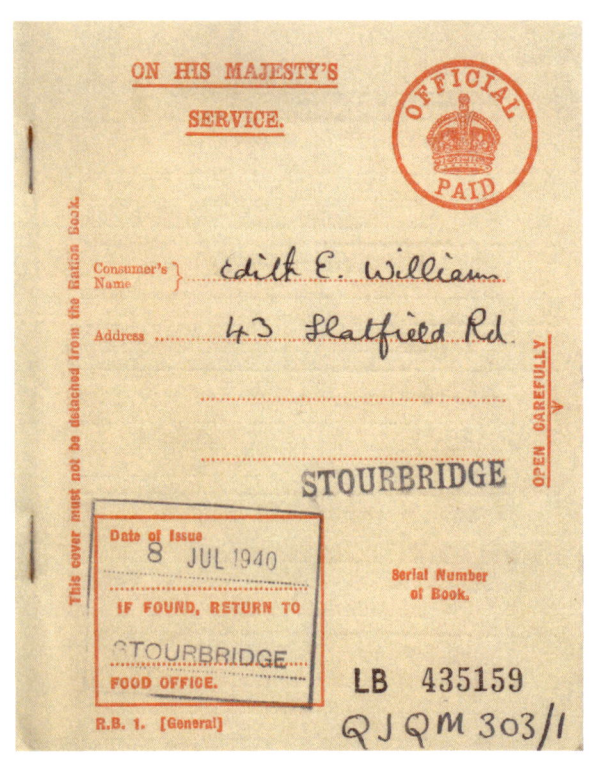

ON HIS MAJESTY'S SERVICE.

OFFICIAL PAID

This cover must not be detached from the Ration Book.

Consumer's Name .... *Edith E. William*

Address .... *43 Hatfield Rd*

....

....

STOURBRIDGE

OPEN CAREFULLY

Date of Issue
8 JUL 1940

IF FOUND, RETURN TO

STOURBRIDGE

FOOD OFFICE.

R.B. 1. [General]

Serial Number of Book.

LB 435159

QJQM 303/1

WORCESTERSHIRE CONSTABULARY.

THIS IS TO CERTIFY that the Bearer

Gerald Milner

is a Member of the

WORCESTERSHIRE DEFENCE VOLUNTEERS.

W. H. Wiggin

Colonel.

County Sub-Area Commander

Food and goods were being rationed.

Gerald had joined the Worcestershire Defence Volunteers, otherwise known as the Home Guard or 'Dad's Army'.

NATIONAL SERVICE (ARMED FORCES) ACT, 1939

GRADE CARD

Registration No. *STG. 3680*

Mr. *Gerald Milner*

whose address on his registration card is ....

52 Brook St. Stourbridge

WOLVERHAMPTON

was medically examined at ....

on **15 JUL 1940**

WOLVERHAMPTON MEDICAL BOARD (No.1)

and placed in

GRADE* *I (one)*

E.D. Until* .... (Medical Board stamp.)

Chairman of Board *W. J. S. Bythell*

Man's Signature *G. Milner*

*The roman numeral denoting the man's Grade (with number also spelt out) will be entered in RED ink by the Chairman himself, e.g., Grade I (one), Grade II (two) (a) (Vision). If the examination is deferred the Chairman will enter a date after the words " E.D. Until ", and cross out " Grade " ; alternatively, the words " E.D. Until " will be struck out.

N.S. 55

[P.T.O.

DESCRIPTION OF MAN

Age *29*

Height .... *5* ft. *10 3/4* ins.

Colour of eyes .... *Blue*

Colour of hair .... *L/Brown*

If this Certificate is lost or mislaid, the fact must be at once reported

The finder should send it to the nearest Local Office of the Ministry of Labour and National Service.

[77752] 9228/4099 500m 4/40 M&C Ltd. 705

My Impressions of the War,
Commencing Nov 25th 1940.

Gerald Milner

It is my strong belief that Hitler has missed a number of chances with regard to the attack on this country. His greatest chance was immediately after Dunkirk. Many experts expressed the opinion that he was uncertain about the reserve strength of our forces. My own opinion is that he himself was very short of the necessary first class material for such a venture immediately after the exhausting continental battles. Time will tell. Then came the battle of London. The people of that City refused to panic, but just when the services were at the end of their resources with regard to water, gas and electricity he transferred his activity elsewhere. Then came the blitz on Birmingham and district. Then the terror was rained for one unforgettable night on the City of Coventry. Then Birmingham was reported by the Nazis to have been concentrated. Two nights later the attack was resumed with increased violence. Then came Southampton (Nazi report). After that came Bristol (Still Nazi report). Now two quiet nights. To my mind his one great mistake has been to transfer his energies elsewhere just as he had the defences of these Cities strained severely. One night of quiet is sufficient to put new life into the population, and the clearing up and repairs to vital services in 24 hours has been extraordinary.

His dear friend and accomplice has just about cooked the goose for Adolf. He has tried to catch Greece on the hop, severely burnt his fingers, and now he wants Hitler to pull the chestnuts out of the fire for him. Once again experts predict that Hitler will move in a certain manner.

My own view of the matter is that a large percentage of Italians did not want war. Mussolini had entered it on promises of great gains to Italy. These promises proved to be typical of all others made by Hitler. The Italian public wanted to know a few things, and explanations were hard to find. To sum up briefly Italy was up to the neck in the war, but had not gained one square yard of the promised territory. Mussolini had to do something pretty quickly, so all on his own initiative he decided to turn the propaganda machine on Greece. Zero hour came and his troops marched. Instead of the expected victory against a small nation the cream of the Italian Army received the best smack in the eye that any major power has received for many years. Not only did the Greeks rise to defend their soil, but the Italians have been and are still being pushed back through Albania by the raging torrent of Greek troops. And in the midst of it all – TARANTO. The blackest day of Mussolini's regime. And now the RAF are giving the Greeks great assistance.

In face of all opinions I predict that Hitler will not and indeed dare not move to the assistance of his partner of convenience. Hitler knows better than anyone that if he eases up in his attack on Britain, even for one moment, it is as good as putting a whole fleet of aircraft in our possession. On top of all this it is essential that if he did decide to move his troops to aid the Italians it would be necessary for him to move through Jugo Slavia. This country is standing up well to Axis pressure, and German troops would probably receive a very doubtful welcome.

The nature of the Jugo Slav country is very mountainous and the mechanised army of the Nazis would in all probability meet the same fate as the army of Mussolini. Distance is another factor. If German troops move through Hungary or directly through Jugo Slavia they must travel nearly a thousand miles. And when they get to the eastern end of Slav country they have to face the Greeks holding a bottleneck of territory through which invading troops must pass. This bottleneck was made possible by the Greeks driving the Italians out of Northern Albania and retaining the command of their own territory on the other side of Jugo Slavia; I cannot see the German army falling into this death trap. He cannot move by sea as there is still a British Navy. Should he try to push through Bulgaria he would inevitably have Turkey at his throat, and the inscrutable Stalin may be forced to take a hand. And what of all the countries of Europe? If only Hitler moved and reduced his troop concentrations what a chance for sabotage, revolution, strikes etc. and for the RAF to strike with ever increasing violence at the vital parts of his machine.

The war of 1939-40 will certainly be decided by the financial power of the countries concerned. At the commencement of the war Germany, Italy & Japan formed the Anti Communist pact and each country was according to financial experts, bankrupt. If this was the case the first question asked by many people is "How did Germany manage such a gigantic attack through Europe if they had no money".

To my mind the financial stability of my country is dictated not so much by money itself, but by the industrial capacity of that particular country. Early in 1939 Hitler said any country must "Export or die. Export we must".

Since May his industrial output has been badly hampered by the RAF. This together with the naval blockade and consequent rusting of many of his cargo boats in ports scattered throughout the world has confined his exports to the continent of Europe. In spite of this he has carried on. As far as I can see the only way he has carried on the war on the present scale is by plundering each country in rotation and using the gains to supplement his losses. After Austria, Poland, Denmark, Norway, Belgium, Holland, France, Rumania and Hungary a glance at the map will show that he has no other countries completely under his heel with the single exception of Switzerland.

On that basis he will now have to manage on what he already possesses. He cannot expect Italy to help him as they are already in need of help themselves. In addition to this many countries occupied by German troops are beginning to prove a source of trouble. Any sign of weakness on his part now will serve to aggravate his difficulties. For instance what do the people residing in the Channel ports think of his inability to invade this country.

And what do they think of the work of the RAF. A censorship may be imposed for a time, but as the devastation goes on those people must certainly be sent further inland. And the Gestapo cannot close every mouth.

While on the subject of export and finance, a few remarks and criticisms would seem to be in order. Why is it that when England is at war, our experts can almost immediately formulate a plan for export, which involve a foreign market for practically every article we can produce, while in peace time we have to be the witnesses of nearly two and a half million men and women on the "dole"? Will the old order reign after this war is over? Will the financial powers that be demand the interest on their money and securities invested abroad?

And if these countries default in cash will they say "Well we will have the value in machinery etc. and put our machine makers on the "dole". In simple language will they flood our country with imports to pay their interest and let the men who are producing the materials to win the war get on as best they can?

Russia

Russia to all intents and purposes is tied up hand and foot with Nazi Germany. Hitler in his speeches and in Mein Kampf has vilified everything communist. Even his rise to power was based on his preachings against and hatred of Communism. The fire at the Reichstag was purported to be caused by Communists and the poor Dutch half wit, Van der Lubbe was made the scapegoat in an elaborate trial and attempt to fix the blame. To have been able to do this would have been a feat worthy of the most skilful diplomat. He had tramped across Germany and on the day of his arrival in Berlin the great fire occurred. Therefore if the Nazi charges were correct, he must have immediately found out the secret quarters of the Communists, gained their complete confidence, been promoted to high rank in the organisation and personally conducted the outrage. Yet in spite of all this hatred the two countries have signed a number of pacts, treaties etc. since early 1939. The eventual value of these pacts remains for the future to tell. A large section of opinion in this country is of the opinion that the pacts are of very frail substance and that this country should endeavour to make a more friendly relationship between Britain and Russia.

Definitely this would strengthen our hand against Germany, but what of the other side of the question? In 1938 Mr Chamberlain signed an agreement with Poland that if that country should be the subject of unprovoked attack, we would go immediately to her aid. On many occasions since then we have been told that we are fighting aggression and the perpetrators of this form of war. But Russia stabbed Poland in the back and my opinion is that she is as bad as Germany. We are not fighting countries, we are fighting for principles. Russian policy or what is known of it seems to be "What I have I hold." Stalin has said very little on the subject of the second European War, but we can rest assured that he is watching the situation and all the moves of each side with the eyes of a hawk. The great danger from Russia is not the present but the future. My guess is that Stalin is sitting tight until both Germany and Britain are exhausted by their efforts and then he will step in and try to take exactly what he wants with the minimum of inconvenience to himself. That is what I judge to be his present policy, but I do not think his judgement will eventually gain him anything. There is a strong possibility that Britain will emerge from this war far stronger than ever before. All the dictators are watching the Balkan countries with great anxiety. Even mighty Germany is being politely snubbed by neighbours who until recently were ripe for the nazi jackboot. However the success of Greece and the fiasco of Taranto have entirely altered the outlook of many small countries. Unless Stalin is very careful he will find that instead of taking what he wants he will be in grave danger of being economically strangled.

England

It is a popular idea that after any war ends a great trade slump is bound to follow. Well, I think this war is going to prove the exception. My own view is that the prosperity or otherwise of the building trades is the barometer to the prosperity of a nation. Can anyone doubt the colossal task that will present itself to the bricklaying fraternity of this country when the war ends? I do not wish to infer that everything will be rosy immediately after the cease fire. It is inevitable that a certain amount of time must elapse before the machines and men engaged on war production can readjust themselves to peace time necessities, but if the situation is handled properly it should be possible to do this in a short space of time. The working class people are saving hard. £475,000,000 saved by small investors in one year testifies to this. Apparently we are to be denied the pleasure of purchasing a new car for the duration of the war. Imagine the demand that will be made for all the latest models to replace the vehicles that have had to be used for several years. Even now the demand is so great that second hand cars in good condition are fetching more money than the original price when brand new. The same applies to hundreds of other articles such as bicycles, wireless sets, and even children's toys. We are obliged to carry on with what we already have and the demand for replacements will in my opinion exceed the supply for a long time to come. And the ready cash is now being saved to pay for them.

Charlie Boxley, unknown, Gerald Milner, Eva Williams, George Veal, Walter Milner at the wedding August 5th 1940 St Mary's Church, Oldswinford.

Eva Milner on Kinver Edge, Staffordshire, 1935

Lucy whose family came from Oswestry, was a lifelong friend of Eva's. This picture was taken a couple of years before the outbreak of war, whilst they were on holiday in Jersey.

CHAPTER 1

50 days at No1 Military Training Camp, No4 Training Battalion,
Sutton Veny Camp, Nr. Warminster, Wilts.

NOTES ON MY ARMY SERVICE BY GERALD MILNER

I joined the Army on June 12th 1941 at Sutton Veny, Salisbury Plain and the German Luftwaffe gave us a pretty warm reception. Tents were scattered around the square and the cooking and serving were on the edge of the square. Our first orders were to keep well apart and approach the serving benches one at a time. Over came long range Me-109s, rat-a-tat went the machine guns, down came a long range fuel tank and seconds later I found that I had jam, cheese and herrings in my mess tin. A very good introduction. I was soon on a draft for an unknown destination. It turned out to be Bradford and there formed into groups, marched to the railway station and so on to Liverpool where we boarded the troopship *Strathnaver.*

First letter from Sutton Veny Thursday June 12th 1941

Sutton Veny Camp
Warminster
Wilts
Thursday Night

My Dear Wife,

Just a line to let you know that I arrived here quite safely at about 7.15 p.m. We have been put under canvas for the present. It all seems very strange at present but I suppose I shall soon get used to it. I cannot tell you my number yet so I should advise you to wait patiently until you hear from me before you write to me. Just enjoy your holiday and don't worry too much about me as I shall be quite alright. We have a decent lot in our tent. I don't know yet how long we shall be here but I am told it is preliminary training. I have given the necessary information for your allowance, and if you do not receive any notification within about a week please let me know at once. Well dear, I think this is all for now, as it is getting dark and we are not allowed any lights. Just keep your pecker up. Please

All my love
Remember me to Lucy[1]
Gerald XXXXXXXXXX

Undated letter. *Probably Friday 13th June 1941*

Recruit Milner G.
271347
No. 2 Squad,
No. 1, Military Training Company
No. 4 Training Battalion,
R.A.S.C.
Sutton Veny Camp,
Nr Warminster
Wilts

My Dear Wife,

Well, dear, you see my short address opposite. I think we move in about three weeks to another camp for advanced training. We are under canvas now and it is not too bad as

---

[1] Lucy was a lifelong friend of Eva, see photo opposite.

long as it does not rain. I don't know what sort of a mess it will be then. We did not sleep to well last night. Our lads in blue up above made too much noise. We all have cause to remember Friday the thirteenth of June 1941. We have been lined up, stripped in a bitter wind for a medical exam this morning. Admitted we were in a tent but it did not afford much protection as we had already been waiting an hour to see the Commanding officer. He seems alright. Then we had a lieutenant (Dental) to examine teeth. I think I shall have to have 2 out. If the Stourbridge H.G. could see the kit I have been issued with they would think it was to supply a company. By the way I was again grade 1 in the medical, although some of the men were placed in a lower grade than at the previous exam. Then we had to strip to the waist again after dinner. We lined up outside this time and had to file in to the M.O. He gave us a good vaccination. When we came out we had to line up again just as we were. Then we filed in again and received a splendid jab

Eva Milner in the Civil Defence

in the left arm for inoculation. As we came out we had to line up again for another dose in the other arm. A general came to talk to us. Told us that what we had had was worth 48 hours without duties, so that is what we now have. The way we all feel now is that we need it. I can hardly move my right arm. The food here is quite decent so far. That is something to be thankful for. Well darling, I hope you are enjoying your holidays. I wish I was with you. We are not allowed to leave camp so can you please send me a writing pad, envelopes and stamps.

Think this is all for now sweetheart so I will close with all my love,

Gerald XXXXXXXXXX

Undated letter. *Probably 17th 18th & 19th June 1941*

Wednesday

My Dear Wife,

Just a few lines in haste for you to receive on your return home, as I did not know how long you were staying at Oswestry. Well dear I am not doing too badly so far. But I shall be glad when the time comes for me to return to you permanently. The life here is healthy but terribly hard after civilian life. Still we are all determined to stick it, come what may. We have already been congratulated by the major for our enthusiasm. He tells us that he and all the N.C.O.s are agreed that we are the best bunch of fellows they have yet had to train, and we are all very proud of that. But when we get on the square in the boiling sun it is absolute hell. I feel sorry for some of the poor devils but they refuse to go sick until they drop, and that seems to happen quite often. We dare not even bat our eyes. Still we know that it is for our own good eventually and we have only just over three weeks to go here. Those chaps in the H.G. picture we saw would look tame against us already. We are putting in 16 hrs per day so far so if I don't write for a week or two you will know the reason. One chap has gone balmy and been taken away. Two more have been taken ill. One or two more have fainted temporarily but it is all in the days work. If you could see me now I would lay you every penny I have that you would not know me. We had a tidy old raid round here last night. I thought I had left all that behind. I have been told that all the machine gunning and bombing we heard resulted in a German coming down to his doom a few fields away. I don't know definitely, but anyway he went over us in pretty serious trouble. I hope his whole outfit was smashed to smithereens.

Well my dear, I started to write the foregoing in bed on Tuesday night but I did not have time to finish it so I am continuing the episode in bed. Wednesday night now. The hard work in the boiling sun has been hell again today, but we can take it. The N.C.O.s are hooting and bawling at us all the time and they use beautiful language, both rude and sarcastic. If a chap gets caught moving a finger etc. he usually gets told he looks like a little girl who has wet herself. We have a pro Boxer in our squad. He threatened to punch the corporal's something nose today while on parade. They were <u>nice</u> to him. I know I shall keep my mouth shut whatever happens. The food is quite decent so far. I don't know whether we shall always find it so. The sergeant cook has a good laugh out of us but we don't mind. He says "Look at them coming for more, and when they came in their nice clean collars & ties they said we don't want this and we don't want that". He is right too. I am fitter now than I have ever been in my life. My face is now like the top of the dining table at home. And the N.C.O.s say that we have to sweat blood yet before they finish with us. I reckon we can take even that. My H.G. training has stood me in good stead so far as it goes although this is ten times harder. I have already been picked out as No. 1 in our rank, but I can assure you it is no picnic. We have not been allowed out yet. I don't know how long that will last. Well my darling I don't think there is much else to write about now as it is getting dark again now. I wish I could be with you again if only for a few hours, but we cannot find out anything about leave at present.

I have not broken into my 10/- note yet. I have spent a few shillings altogether. Some in Bristol on periodicals to read most of the rest on cleaning equipment at the NAAFI, but it is a very poor show here. About 2 dozen cups of tea, a few dusters, tins of polish, cigarettes per day; to serve scores of troops.

They are trying to alter it, but not very hard by the look of things. Good night darling, and just think of me when you retire.

Remember me to Lucy. All for now with all my love

Gerald XXXXXXXXX

PTO

As I did not get time to finish addressing the foregoing epistle last night I have decided to write a little more tonight. It will be posted on Friday at the Guard room and I expect you will receive it on Sat or Monday. Well dear we have had another hard day of sweat & toil. As soon as we finish drill we have to run up the hill to our tents, change into gym dress in about five minutes, run back, and immediately start an hours physical training. It is pretty stiff too at our ages. Throwing ourselves forward on head & hands and doing a complete forward somersault, coming back to standing position immediately. Then straight on to jerks and body bends running, lying flat on stomach and raising body to full extent of arms. All this usually without so much as a breather and in this weather too. I've never seen so much honest sweat. And after all that they paid me 10/- today. It is the hardest ten bob I ever earned in my life. Still it does not seem so hard now as it did at first, and I know most of us will carry on to the best of our ability. I have had an extremely pleasant surprise today. Can you guess what it is? To me it seems a terrific release. The N.C.O. in charge of the camp came round to the chief instructors & told them to pick out seven men. They were to be the hardest working and most enthusiastic men and the best at drill. No slackers allowed. And those seven can have 10 hours off on Saturday and a pass into Warminster with a bus to take us and bring us back. I was no3. "ex army chaps" were the only ones to lick me for 1st place, and that only by a short head. I was pleased, and darling I know you will be. Then I had another surprise. I received your letter. I am glad you are having a good time.

We have had rifle aiming practice for three quarters of an hour today. They have a special device to tell you (without actually firing) how far you would be off the bull each time you take aim and pull the trigger. I never missed dead centre bull once. The instructor told me it was the most remarkable aiming he has known for a beginner, and I did not enlighten him[1]. There will be 10/- for the highest score on the range on Wednesday, and he thinks I should have a cake walk. I hope I do get it as if we do well in our squad he may get another stripe in preference to other instructors. I hope he does. We think he is the best man we have met yet. And he is in our tent too. Not that that makes much difference when we are on parade. Darling, please don't forget my cigarettes as we can't get any here. I will write again on Sunday. Good night dear, God bless you.

All my love from

Gerald XXXXXXXXX

Sunday June 22nd 41

My Dear Wife,

Many thanks for parcel which I received quite safely just as I was finishing the last letter to you. Well dear, I have a little more time to spare today as I have been selected for 12 hrs Military Police duties. 1½ hrs on and 1½ hrs in the Guard Room to write to you, and have a read. Of course writing to you comes first. I don't know whether I can wangle it to post this today but I will try. My tent is half a mile away over the plains, and my envelopes and stamps are up there. I stuck the writing pad inside my shirt to come down as we are now working in shirt sleeve order owing to the terrific heat. My arms are swollen with sun effects until I cannot get my wrist watch on. It has been awful, and we have to stick it. There is not a solitary tree near the camp to give us a little shade. The Guard Tent I am in now is the coolest place I have found for a week. I got my pass to Warminster alright yesterday. It was a breath of freedom, but all too short. I am told that if I pass out here alright it will be easier for me at the next camp. It almost joins this one. If it were not for the heat and hell of this "square" I would not mind staying here. The rest of the work is very hard but I don't mind that. I am very glad you did not shed too many tears on my departure. It made me feel miserable but it just has to be done so I shan't worry to much about it now. I am in a tent with some very decent fellows, for which I am thankful. And what do you think of this. I went for breakfast this morning at 7a.m. I was almost last because of the M.P. job I am doing today. The sergeant cook took me in and gave me <u>six</u> slices of <u>fat smoked bacon</u> and 3 rounds of bread dipped in fat, and three Pints of scalding hot tea. I shifted the lot and <u>enjoyed</u> it. The food so far has been excellent. Everyone says the same so it must be right. Our drill sergeant is quite decent. Also 2 of the corporals. The other corporal is a Jew boy, and I will say no more. He says "Vat is the matter wit chew". Don't the lads love him? Like poison they do. They are already deciding their respective places in the queue when the war is over. To punch his nose I mean. He has not interfered with me so far. Perhaps as well for both of us. Well 10 hours have gone by and I have been too busy to write any more so I am having to continue in my tent. I received a parcel from home late last night. I was very pleased with the contents thereof.

Quite a lot of nice girls in summer array have gone by here today while I was on duty. Made me wish you were here. The heat has been worse than ever today. I have hundreds of small blisters on my fore arms, and the pain is lousy. My face has peeled entirely. Not in bits either. Pieces ½ inch square came off. Some of the men are raw from the chin up. Just like pro boxers. A lot of new lads have been bowled right over. One chap has been to

---

[1] Gerald was already good with a shotgun with his family all being country people. He also used to shoot rabbits on Guy Butler's farm.

see the Medical Officer, but he couldn't see him. His eyes were closed, and the swelling protruded beyond the bridge of his nose, so you can tell what we are having to contend with. Sweetheart, it is getting late now, so I must close or I shall be too late for 7.30 a.m. post as I don't have any spare time in the morning. Just carry on thinking you have me there as I am doing this end.

Good night my dear and God bless you and keep you safe until I can return. All my love from your loving husband

Gerald XXXXXXXXX

Remember me to Lucy. Tell here to be careful of the colour her nose gets on Saturday nights.

Received about 27ᵗʰ of June 41 *Undated letter. Probably Tuesday 24ᵗʰ June 1941*

Tuesday Night.

Just a few lines again before lights out at 10.15 p.m. It has been another terrible day. Sun hotter than ever. I have never known anything like it. It is no exaggeration to say it was like holding red hot irons on our arms and faces. No protection from it all day long. We are getting used to it now we have our second skin, but I shall be very thankful when it gets cooler. We are having to carry on with the drill whatever happens. I am counting the days until I finish here. We are told it is a lot easier up the road when we move. I sincerely hope I pass out. I think I shall, although we are expected to approach the standard nearing miraculous. The motor cycle test will be like Rushmere trials. None of us have ridden yet but I have every confidence about that part of it. Very few men here can ride a motor cycle, but they all have to learn. We go to Bulford tomorrow to try and pass our firing test. In gas masks too. I will write and let you know how I get on. One thing, it will be a few precious hours off the square. The more I see of it the more I hate it, and yet I know it is for my own good. If it were not for the terrible effects of the sun it would not be too bad. I have put on nearly a stone in weight since I have been here, and most of it is sheer muscle. We don't have a chance to get flabby. Darling I am longing for the time when I shall see you again. We have almost lost count of time here. I expect I shall have some teeth out soon. I hope I can carry on when they come out. If we go sick when we are due to pass out we have to go through this lot again right from the beginning. And I'm not having that if I can help it. How is work going down? Rough I'll bet. By the way have you heard anything about your allowance yet? If not, let me know immediately. Time to close now, so good night sweet heart, sleep well.

All my love from

Gerald XXXXXXXXX

Remember me to Lucy, Mrs Taylor² and Billy

Wednesday Night 25.6.41

Darling,

You are now being addressed by the champion shot of No1 Military training Company. And what a hell of a shoot it was. My rifle jammed with every shot. They tried to put it right in-between times of firing but all to no avail. In the rapid firing I had to work and think like the devil. I loaded and fired each cartridge separately and got every one on target in 60 secs. (Stop watch time) Of course there was the usual swindle. One of the novices just

---

² Mrs Taylor & Billie were neighbours

beat me. It turns out that he was firing well away from the officer, so one of the instructors stepped in beside him and fired his shots. Trying to pull his squad's average up, but it won't wash. Some one detected who was firing and I am almost certain to get the first prize. Anyway every one is agreed that it belongs to your humble. That means a week extra as Bren Gunner <u>without</u> going on the square. I think I am going to enjoy that. The Scots Sergeant Brodie's "Pipes" are playing "Old Faithful", just behind me as I write, and he <u>can</u> play them too. By the way we have seen Stonehenge today. Also dozens of tanks, armoured cars & motor cycles manoeuvring on Salisbury Plain. That is where we have been firing today. I will give you a demonstration of how to keep a cool head in the British Army. A chap in our tent was 8 points behind me on the range. We did not know our scores until we got back to camp. Well he got so pleased & excited at his good performance, that he thoroughly cleaned <u>my</u> rifle in mistake. That is the second time that has happened. Someone was cleaning a pair of boots too on Monday morning. When they finished I told them I did not mind them cleaning them for me, but I did object to them wearing them for me. They keep leaving stuff about for me to make a mistake. They will have to get up earlier. I don't think there is much else I can write about now as time is short. Good night dearest and write often. I have not received many letters since I have been here. One from you and a parcel from home is all in two weeks. And please don't forget to ask Vic Watkins[1] or Stan Haynes for some cigarettes. I have only had 5 in 4 days and most of the lads are the same. They give us 5 minutes break from drill every hour, so that we can have a smoke. Just imagine about 400 men sat on the edge of the square and not a smoke between them. Same on the range today. And we can't get out to try & get any. I really must close now darling, as it is getting late. Good night, all my love,

From your straight shooting husband

Gerald XXXXXXXXXX

Received on June 29th 1941

Wednesday night 26.6.41

My Dear Wife,

Darling I have received your letter tonight. I was very pleased to hear from you. It seems years since I left home. The time is going more quickly now though. When we came we were the only ones in camp and they had no one else to knock the stuffing out of. There are hundreds more new recruits coming in regularly and that makes it a little bit better for us.

We feel like "old sweats" already. I told you in my last letter about my shooting achievements. Well I am pleased to say that No. 2 Squad, that is my own squad, scored the highest percentage recorded at this camp. Nearly doubled the scores of the previous crowd. Today I have been in the lorry to Warminster. Been through the military gas Chamber test once with respirator and once without. Came through alright. Tonight I have been to Sheerwater Lake[2] with officers and N.C.O.'s 19 of us passed our swimming test. I seem to be doing well in the Army. We all have to have another inoculation this week. In the left breast, and I'll bet that won't be so good. Teeth to come out any day now too. Still I have gained quite a lot of weight, and that is something. When I get to the other camp I have been told by one of the senior N.C.O.'s that I could pass out on driving and other tests in a week. He advised me to crash the gears a bit so I can stick with the rest of the squad and get posted together. Well sweetheart I must close now as it is getting late now. All my love from

Gerald XXXXXXXXXX

---

[1] Vic Watkins was the men's hairdresser in Stourbridge just after the war.
[2] Sheerwater Lake is at Crockerton near Warminster

Received July 2nd 1941 Undated letter. *Probably Sunday 29th June 1941*

Sunday

My Dear Wife,

Thanks for your letter which I received safely yesterday. Also the next which I received last night. First of all darling, please write address as above. It is to quicken postal service from here which is lousy at present. I received parcel from home last night. I can tell you it could not have reached a better place. I was picked again for guard duties last night, and you are lucky to be hearing from me again. Guard Commander had an accident with a rifle. The bullet missed me by about 4 inches. It went off in the guardroom and I was the only one stood on that side. The officers came running in and there was the devil to pay. I expect I shall have to give evidence at the inquiry. After dark, the guard commander was continuously receiving complimentary reports on my efficiency as a sentry. From all but the captain. When he did not halt properly I nicked his throat with the point of the bayonet. He played hell up. The other officers told him politely that he should obey the sentry's orders or take the consequences. He will know better next time. Well dear I am glad you and Lucy enjoyed your holidays. And good weather too. I thought about you often when I was being tortured by the sun. it is just a little cooler here now. According to the paper it is the hottest weather here for over 100 years. I can believe it too. My arms, neck and throat are in a terrible state, although not quite so bad as they were two days ago. New chaps coming in can't understand how we stood it all to get in such a state. I'm sure I don't know. My arms from elbow to wrist have blistered, skinned blistered again with the heat, burst again, dried, fallen off in little pieces and then started off afresh. Throat and neck the same, but we are getting used to it now. I suppose if the sun does not come out one of these days we shall think we are back in winter. Well sweetheart I have not much time to write any more now, except to endorse all you wrote in your last letter so I will close now with all my love

Gerald XXXXXXXXXX

Undated letter. *Probably Monday 30th June 1941*

Monday night

My Dear Youngster,

Well dear, I am feeling much better today. I have had a gruelling day again. The power of the sun is as strong as ever. We have not seen a drop of rain since we have been here with the exception of a sharp shower in the middle of one night a week ago. I wish you could see my arms. However they are drying up a little now, so they may get alright soon. Five hours bayonet fighting again today and the rest of the day Guards drill ready for Wednesday has made mincemeat of my inoculation. I can hardly feel it now. I won't tell you what it felt like at first. Still badly swollen but I will soon get rid of that. I'm exasperated now. I have just seen Battalion orders. I have to visit the dentist again tomorrow. Only a day before the big event. Just my luck. Never mind I shall be on parade whatever happens. I have just received your letter, also a card from Lucy. Surely she does not think that men of our calibre shoot when we hear a rabbit. There are plenty of better targets than that in Germany. If the peas have gone like you say, pull them up and put leek plants in the same places. No dear, I have not passed out yet. As you see from the first part of my letter, that is an ordeal to come. We have put up a show tonight that has never been equalled on this square. If one man makes a mistake it is all "U.P." The most enthusiastic people were the officers and N.C.O.'s Samples of what we got. Sergeant Major:- "Oh! Bloody fine show. I'm proud of you. Officers:- "Keep it up lads, it's the best marching we've seen yet." Instructors:- "Splendid, but you can expect it harder on Wednesday." Why we can expect that is because the congratulations of General Beale OBE will be more lengthy now. And believe me, the hardest thing a soldier has to do is to stand rigid in a blazing sun, and not blink an eyelid! There is no escape. The swarm of Officers and N.C.O.'s buzzing around spot everything. I shall not write to you until Wednesday night, and then I can tell you how I get on. If the extraction does not affect me too much it is a certainty. Good night darling. God Bless you. Sleep well.

All the best from your loving husband

Gerald XXXXXXXXXX

PTO

One of our fighters has just made a forced landing in our camp. I've never seen anything like it. Nearly took our tent with him just as I was putting the crosses on the bottom of the page. I don't know what is the matter with it, but he landed perfectly and the pilot appears alright. I'll let you know more next time I write.

Gerald

Undated letter. *Probably Wednesday July 2nd 1941.*

Wednesday night.

My Dear Youngster,

Just a few more lines to let you know that I am now feeling OK again. My gums bled like a tap for 22 hours. Had to report sick this morning. Dental officer soon stopped it. Said I should have been sent to him yesterday. No duties at all today. He gave me a note ordering a complete rest after the loss of blood. It has done me the world of good. I have been lying in the tent watching the lads doing their stuff in the terrific heat. How I wished I could be with them. I could not take the risk of bleeding starting afresh however. We have a grand parade on Wednesday next. Generals etc. to examine, inspect and otherwise criticise, and pass or fail us. I think most of us will come through alright. From all I hear the new lot are not as good as we were at the same stage, and their shooting today was very disappointing. My corporal instructor has just instructed me that I am to shout out and let all the world know "Sir, 2 Squad" when I go before the major for my prize this week. And I shall for his sake. I am having any amount of laughs here at the expense of different chaps. Not that I am the only one to laugh. Some of the expressions will live in our memories for ever. Some are crude, some vulgar and others genuinely witty. For instance 20 men sat in a line on the latrines. In walked a corporal. His words in drill tones, "Forward No. 1, 2, 3, steady 4, 5, 6. A little to the rear No. 12, 13, 14 etc Rear Rank STEADY". That is what we get when we line up on parade. It was amusing in the other place. A chap named Gibbs was on parade. Sergeant asked him what the next order should be. He gave the wrong answer. He asked what his name was. He answered "Gibbs". The sergeant immediately replied "Well I've heard of Einstein's theory, but I'm buggered if I ever heard of Gibbs theory before". We get that all day. And when we get to our tents it is added to, multiplied, subtracted and divided until the poor devil's life is not worth living. The orderly Officer is round shouting now, so I must close now.

Thursday night. *Continuation.*

Well darling I have had another awful day today. On the square everything went well for a time, and then we got a little bit slack. We really deserved all we got. The sergeant laughed like the devil, and we did the sweating for half an hour. I had to peel my shirt off after, but we took it in good part. To top it up we had a fair dose of bayonet charging. Then a period of bayonet drill at dummies. My wrists are getting raw. The instructors are not satisfied until your wrists are bleeding and the more blood the better they like it. That is why our lads are feared throughout the world in bayonet charges. Then PT Drill. Oh dear! It was hot. We shall have to be more careful tomorrow. I got your parcel today. Thanks very much for cigarettes etc. if you see Stan Haynes tell him I will write to him in a few days and thank him for the cigarettes. I shall have more time for correspondence when I get out on the Bren gun.

There is a notice on Battn. Orders for me to parade before the major at 10.15 in the morning. The proudest day of my army life. My Army pay Book is also being signed as a proficient rifle shot. When I am passed out I hear it makes a difference of 3d per day to my pay. I myself am not certain, but I hope it is correct. Now for that Bren. Have been to the other camp tonight for a haircut, and on the way back saw a nasty accident. Despatch Rider came off his Norton and broke his arm. Red Cross soon took him off. Glad to hear George is alright[1]. Remember me to him if he has not gone back. Also to all at Palfrey Road. Vic Watkins too if you see him. I will write him soon. I wish I had Jane's Fighting Ships here, but I have no place for it. We are sleeping seven in a bell tent. Feet against. Must end now. Will write on Sunday. All my love

Gerald XXXXXXXXX

P.S. Don't worry about washing etc. Could do with a few new handkerchiefs though. Remember me to Lucy

Undated letter. *Probably 6th July 1941. Note says received about June 12th but I think there is an error there. May be July 12th*

My Dear Wife,

Just a few lines to let you know that I am now getting over my big dose of the needle. If I have many more I shall be feeling like a gramophone record. Well dear, it really got me that time towards night yesterday being the worst kind of feeling I have ever had. By the way please excuse writing as I am lying on my back to try and write these few lines. Well, to continue the epistle, as Saturday evening wore by, I got worse and worse until towards 10 p.m. I knew the fever had me properly in its grip. I turned and twisted in my bed, puffed and blew, sweat poured out of me and yet I was shivering. All the time I knew I was on the verge of hysteria or something similar, so I asked the corporal in our tent to keep his eye on me for a bit. I was wishing something would happen to give me relief. I can verify all I have heard that it makes you feel as though Death itself would be sweet when it really gets you. Anyway, there I was stretched out helpless, when something happened. Do you know what it was? You came to me and took my hand. All I remember is that I stiffened, clung on to you, at the same time knowing the crisis was past. When I woke this morning I was terribly weak, no energy, and my brain seemed clouded. My left arm where I had the injection is swollen very badly and I can hardly move it, but whatever happens I am determined on one thing. When the brigadier comes on Wednesday, that arm is going to swing enough for half an hour to pass me out. I am not spending another period here under any circumstances if I can avoid it. And if you are unfortunate enough to be ill on that particular day you have to go through it all again. One chap here is having his third month here. Was cut badly and taken to hospital on the first occasion, then went down with tonsillitis second time. He is hoping Wednesday will be luckier for him. I think I told you I shall stay on Bren gun. My wits are still a bit scattered. I keep drying off too. It is nearly tea time now and I feel a lot better. If only my arm wasn't so painful I should feel almost normal. A lot of fellows here have had relations to see them on week end. They have been granted passes to go out for Sat afternoon or Sunday. How I have silently wished I could get back to you for a few hours. I'm afraid there is not much chance of that yet though as travelling would take 24 hrs, even if the trains ran fairly frequently. You must still wait patiently. Darling I will close now with all my love

Gerald XXXXXXXXX

---

[1] "George" is a friend, George Calver, who was Gerald's best man.

Undated letter. *Probably Wednesday 9ᵗʰ July 1941*

T/271347
DRIVER Milner G.
L.M.G. Squad,
No. 1, Military Training Company
No. 4 Training Battalion (Drivers),
R.A.S.C.
Sutton Veny
Nr Warminster
Wilts

My Dear Youngster,

Oh yes, it is quite true. DRIVER class now. The Brigadier General was really amazed. The words he said were a credit to us all. He came here prepared to make his usual stereotyped speech but after what he saw he altered it all. And Whoopee! He has done something that has not happened before. He ordered that every man on the parade be given a pass out to go where he liked until MIDNIGHT. That shows how good we were. Women from various parts had got to hear of the parade, and lined the low hedges on the road. And we could hear them saying how wonderful it all was. Darling how I wished you had been among them. I wish I was near enough to get home with my pass. But I must get those ideas out of my head.

Well it is Thursday night now dear. I just went into the village a mile down the road with my pass. The rest of the lads emptied the pub and went into Warminster to make merry. I went for a stroll by a trout stream. It is absolutely alive with 3 & 4 pounders. I have never seen so many trout. Well after a quiet stroll, I went back to camp early to finish my letter to you. I was wishing you were with me all the time. Imagine my surprise on returning to find my name on the list of men posted. Only up the road, but the name was there. So I just had to wade in and pack my kit right away and so I could not finish my letter. They were bawling for me to go with the machine gun squad at 6.30 this morning, but I came up here instead. Therefore I was booked to stay and move at the same time. Much as I wanted the gun course I think I have done the right thing.

Well sweetheart I have not said anything before, but in addition to the terrific work I have been putting in on the square etc I have been going to school, and I have come through everything OK. And up here I am doing the same. It takes some doing but I have already been placed (after one day only) in a class that will pass out of here in three weeks instead of nearly six. It means splitting the lads up then, but I am looking after number one.

We have been for another medical tonight. Passed A1 again. Had my teeth done too. Afternoon before the big parade but I got through it with flying colours. Stood motionless for nearly an hour, then came the Brigadier. Everyone was anxious to do the right thing. Then the band struck up "Annie Laurie", "Loch Lomond" and then I thought of you when it came to "Home sweet Home". Then Killarney. I lost all nerves. We are in huts now. What a change from the hardships we have endured. What are those did you say? Well a few. Shaving at 5.30 with cold water. Sleeping on the damp earth every night. Hauling and trying to place your bed and entire kit every morning and evening. Walking 600 yds each way to meals, in the short time at your disposal. A hundred and one other things when we might have been writing home.

Darling now for a few requests. First will you please send me Fighting Ships. Registered. Will you also write to Phoenix and ask them to send me "Notes on Map Reading" published by the Stationery office. About 3/6 I think it is. Ask them to send it as soon as possible. Also required: - One pair of scissors.

Will you also try and see Jim Hughes[1], or as he is at work, leave a note asking him to call on you. Ask him if he can lend me the watch I had before until I can get on leave. My other has

---

[1] Jim Hughes was a friend from Stourbridge.

stopped since I have been here and the strap has broken. I could do with one urgently. I can then split my spare time up into separate parts. Cleaning equipment. Personal cleanliness. Writing letters. Studying.

Every second counts when you have to be on parades to the second. I think I shall be lorry driving tomorrow. My new address is now T/271347 Driver G. Milner. Room 19 No. 3 Company No. 4 Training Bn. <u>RASC</u> Sutton Veny nr Warminster. Could you possibly let Stan Harper[2] and George Calver know my new address? Sorry to have to ask you to run about so much. I know you won't mind really. They are getting very hot on V disease here. Have to take our trousers down any old time for the M.O. I am getting a bit suspicious that something is not as it might be. Get lectures on it now too. Our reputation earned yesterday has gone before us. The greatest show ever put up by the RASC training Coy. The other chaps in training are told to try and <u>equal</u> the standard we set. The NCO's say it is impossible to beat it. And we have been treated with respect because of it since we came here. It is quite a change to be treated as human beings.

Remember me to Lucy and next door. Also to Mildred and Arthur[3] if you write. I am still sleeping next to Edward Round[4] up here. Well I must close now as I have my cleaning to do. Just keep warm until I can act as hot water bottle. And behave yourself too. I know you will do that. Good night sweetheart. God bless you and keep you safe. All for now.

Your loving husband

Gerald XXXXXXXXXX

Thursday night and Friday

T/271347
Driver Milner G.
Room 19, No. 3, Specialist Training Company
No. 4 Training Battalion
R.A.S.C. (Drivers)
Sutton Veny
Nr Warminster
Wilts

Please address letters exactly as opposite.

My Dear Youngster,

Just a few lines while I have time. I am on the main guard at the camp at present. I have to remain on duty for 24 hours on the old system. 2 hours on duty and four in the guard room. It is no picnic having to salute and present arms continually to officers walking about the camp. I am meeting quite a lot of interesting fellows here. We have just had a pilot of R.A.F. attached to our squad. He asked for a transfer to a different Fighter Squadron but got transferred to the Army. He is trying to get back to the R.A.F. They want him back but the Army won't release him. I have been driving from 7.30am until 12.30, a big left handed 3 tonner. My corporal whom I have mentioned previously was with me all the time. I asked him if he could not find anyone else to pick on for a change. He said he was interested in my progress. He cross questioned me on all the lessons I have had at school and it was very rarely he caught me out. He told me he thinks I have great possibilities as a *lecturer*. That comes in the dim future when I have squeezed past the officers exam. They are the chaps who question us at the actual passing out. I have already been asked some pretty ticklish questions with regard to engines. One was, *"if your tappet clearance fell in the sump of the engine how would you get it out"*.

Well dear for your information the tappet clearance is the *space* between two parts of the engine. It would be very difficult to get a bit of space out of the engine. Some chaps said they would use a bit of wire. I won't tell you what the officer said.

---

[2] Stan Harper swas a friend from Stourbridge
[3] Mildred & Arthur Millward were long standing friends
[4] Edward Round was a friend from home

With regard to the books you mention at the shop I should not bother too much about it. They have mentioned it in a letter to me. I think if they require some of the books from home I should let them have what they require. I can't say I am too enthusiastic myself but with the other goods being in short supply it is a source of income and after all without their assistance it could not be carried on. I think they are doing it for my benefit. Darling I don't want any bad feeling as I shall be worrying more about that than anything. The only thing I am concerned about at present is the settling up of outstanding a/cs. How are you doing about my allowance to you. If you can manage as we arranged I expect mother can do with some money to help along. She has only told me that B.H.& G[1] is now £13 and that she has paid the current a/c of other firms. I am working hard here to get promotion so that I can square up everything and also have some coppers when this lot is over. As soon as I get on as a Driving Instructor (if and when) I am in line for a stripe as soon as I can pass the technical side. The difference in pay will be about 15/6 per week, split between you and me. It is well worth going after. How is work going down after the holiday? You have not mentioned it yet. Don't forget to remember me to Lucy. I will write her a private note on a wife's etiquette and how to see it is carried out when I have a bit of time to spare. I hope it won't be needed. Roma writes that Dad has bought me a cigarette lighter. It will be one of my greatest assets as we can't get many matches now. I have 3 to last me until Saturday. That is if I can get any then at the N.A.A.F.I. I may get a pass out and go into Warminster on Sat afternoon. I have stayed in camp ever since I came here so think a change will do me good. It is grand when you go by lorry (free) and meals only cost a few coppers at the Y.M.C.A. They are doing grand work there. A rice salad and bread and butter 3d. Cups of tea with plenty of sugar 1d. Lovely cakes 1d I am a bit disappointed having to do this guard. It means I have to miss a whole days lessons. However have brought my precious books here so I shall have to "get cracking" as they say in the Army.

Well it is now late Friday night. I have ended the guard ordeal. What a night and day. Poured in torrents all the time. I never had a chance to finish my letter. I have been told now that I am to have the driving part of my examinations on Monday or Tuesday. It was booked for today but as I was on guard it had to be cancelled. I have been told I am far too good a driver to keep wasting the instructor's valuable time and petrol. I hope I don't get nerves when the officer gets in the cab. Fancy in only 7 day instead of 21. I shall then have more time for the other side of the test. I thought about you at midnight. I was just seeing that vacant pillow. At 6.30 I could just imagine you looking at the clock and having another 5 minutes. At 4.30 am I was wishing I was in the HG again so that I could creep upstairs and put my cold feet on you. I will bet you would like even that to come true. The other crowd from the tents down the road have arrived now. They seem a pretty middling sample. I suppose we shall again be held up as an example. The standard of our chaps is considered to be a very high average. I am glad in a way that I missed that gun course. I may have been stuck in the rut here now. We are now being issued with coupons for cigarettes. Five a day for five days. None at all on Saturday and Sundays. We have had our first egg today since we have been in the Army. The food is not too bad really. The only fault is it is all mixed up on one plate. Still we must be thankful to get any at all. There is a parcel at the stores for me. From home I expect. I have not been able to collect it as we are not allowed to leave the guard room. I shall have to get it tomorrow now. I feel too tired to go to Warminster tomorrow so I shall keep up my good reputation. I shall invest my coppers in another book on map reading. They have just put one on sale at 2/6 in the camp. We get them cost price. Retail price for them is about 3/6.

Excitement in the camp. One of the prisoners helped me on with my kit for inspection by the officer before we were dismissed. A few minutes after, the new guard missed him and

---

[1] BH&G were food wholesalers Brown Hopwood & Gilbert and supplied the shop.

no trace of him has been found yet. He has already been at large for 90 days before being recaptured. I should not like to be in the guard commanders shoes.

It is now nearly lights out so I really must close. God bless you and keep you safe. Just keep plenty of room on my side the bed as I am now fighting fit after all the work and I shall need more space. I am losing a bit of my sun burn now I am in barracks, but I would sooner do that than get flooded out. That is what happened at the other camp. They have brought the men up here for the time being.

Good night dear

All my love from

Gerald XXXXXXXXX

Received July 4th 1941 *Undated letter. Probably Tuesday July 1st 1941*

My Dear YOUNGSTER,

Many thanks for your letter and cigarettes. I am always glad to hear from you. I can imagine how you felt when you heard of my shooting. Well darling our officer has chosen me together with a few others to stay for another week. Nothing but instruction on various weapons. He has promised us a good easy time and from what I know of him he will be as good as his word. I shall not write a very long epistle tonight as I feel a bit under the weather at present. I have been to visit the Dental officer this morning. One tooth came out before I knew anything about it. I won't mention the other "b". It has been bleeding for 11 hours now, and no signs of ceasing just at present. I am reporting sick at reveille in the morning; as if I don't I shall be marked absent from parade. I have been excused all duties since my return this morning. I don't know which was the worst. This or the square. Darling I must confess to vanity. I am beginning to like the square. And it is all to show the men who keep coming here from "Civvy Street" what we can do. And when they realise the short time we have been here they can hardly believe it. We have been through the burning fires of Hell itself, but how proud the men of our squad are. And honestly we deserve the praise we are reaping now because we know we have worked for it. The sergeant instructor told myself and four others yesterday that the Guards themselves have never tuned out any better soldiers. He also immediately informed us in Army language that if we let it swell our something heads he would knock our something blocks off. That is how we get spoken to on parade, but off parade our N.C.O.'s say they will be very sorry to loose us when our training finishes. And it makes me feel a bit more miserable to think I shan't be swanking with the lads on the square in the morning. Well sweetheart it is getting late now and my face is feeling a bit better. I feel a bit better myself too. I shall still report sick in the morning as drill will be liable to make me bleed again. I still have another tooth to come out yet. The sooner it is over the better. I also have another stiff inoculation soon. The other lads have already had theirs, but as I had to do guard duties on Saturday night the Medical Officer refused to give me an injection. If you should not hear from me for a day or two in the near future, you will know the reasons as the effects on the arms are pretty severe and I may not be able to write much. I am expecting it on Saturday, but cannot be sure. Went to Sheerwater last night. I'm doing well, am I not. Well dear, remember me to Lucy and "next door", for I must close now with all my love from

Yours ever

Gerald XXXXXXXXX

(The following is the end of a letter. It is difficult to place in order)

From you which I could not understand, and then I got the previous one which cleared the air a bit. So if I should not refer to your letters you will know that I have failed to receive them up to the time of writing. Darling I think our name will live for ever in the RASC. The company down the road at the other camp I so recently left had to do their stuff before the Brigadier this afternoon. He said something he has never been known to say before. That is that they were <u>fairly</u> good. Also that they should have tried to approach the shining example set by us a week ago. He hopes that every man left in the camp who has to pass out at a later date will use our example as an objective to be attained by themselves. The chaps in this room all know one another and trained together at the other camp and we get on well together. But when it comes to work I just go my own way, and refuse to be led astray in the slightest degree by anyone. I got severely censured on parade this morning however. I just set my teeth and said nothing. By an officer too. An instructor came to my rescue like a man, and it blew over very quietly. My dear please believe me when I say I did no wrong. It was the fault of the instructor, and as soon as he explained to the officer no more was said. It was the talk of the squad that I of all people should be spoken to like that. They all know that I was in the right though. When I went on the lorry driving the D.I. apologised profusely so I told him to forget it. Anyway he gave me top marks again for driving. I have had my chart signed, "Very good driver" every time I have been out yet. I am pretty certain of getting an instructor's job when I finish my training. I have already been approached <u>officially</u>. It all depends on how I pass on the technical side. I can pass anytime on the driving side and I have been told I have the right temperament. You ask what I am learning at school. Well I have been studying Anti Gas, Map Reading at which I have become quite good, Weapons and most vital and also most difficult Technical Engineering in the Army manner. I have been "taken to" by my corporal, and he has given me all the information he can on "the quiet". The sergeant has also lent me some books which my pay will hardly stand after I have bought the other books and a few personal requirements. After buying soap, tooth paste, dusters, Blanco, cotton, shaving cream, Brasso, boot polish etc I have not much to throw about. If it will bring me promotion within the stipulated six month I shall consider it to have been worth the sacrifice. I did so well yesterday that the corporal smuggled me to my room (in amongst the guard marching down the road) at just turned 3.30. I was very glad of the chance to get to my books. We start on parade at just turned 7.15 a.m. here and we finish before 5 p.m. It makes a nice evening and quite a change from the rigors of the other camp. Since we have talked it over everyone is agreed that he only kept going to the square because all the others seemed to be sticking it. I know that is my only explanation. Well sweetheart I will close now, thanking you for the contents of parcel and sending you all my love

Gerald XXXXXXXXXX

P.S. Vacant pillow will be filled as soon as possible. With regard to the watch I think it will be advisable for me to keep it for the present. There is nowhere here for me to register a parcel and I have told you what the postal service is like. Please remember me to Jim Hughes, Lucy and Mr Taylor and Billy. All for now

Gerald

Undated letter. *Probably 12th & 13th July 1941 A note on the letter says June? 41*

My Dear Youngster,

Well darling, I have a little more time to write to you now. I have to go on guard tonight at 5.45 p.m. until 6 a.m. but I am free otherwise from noon today until Monday morning. What a holiday. I am afraid this letter will be a bit mixed. Past and present I mean. I did not get much time to write you any coherent letters before. I no sooner started to write than I had to knock off for something or other and then forgot what I was going to write. So if my letters of the past have not been too interesting please forgive me. I want to try and give you a true picture of what I have been through, and believe me when I look back on it all there are no pleasant memories. First of all we arrived at the station. We were met by a whole host of Officers, sergeants etc. They started hooting as soon as we got off the train. We were lined up and sorted out like cattle, then bundled into lorries and whisked away. Eventually we arrived at a big field with many tents, a few corrugated iron buildings, and last but not least a square. We were marched up to the tents and told which one we were to sleep in. Then we were marched down for something to eat. I had a job to eat mine. I've got over that now however. Then the corporal known universally as "The Bastard Jew" took us in for equipment. It was just thrown at us. No fitting or anything else. We then marched off again under all out kit, and were then shown how to make our beds. 7 in a tent. I slept only a bit though. Next morning they were after us for breakfast. Hooting and bawling before we had had time to finish washing and shaving. That procedure happened every day. 20 minutes to get across the field, queue up, wash shave, teeth cleaned and get to the latrines and back ready to march. And we had to go about as far as you would to get to the junction. As soon as we had breakfast we had to race back and get our beds and kit outside. Groundsheet laid out, blankets folded properly, Army stile, and everything else laid out neatly as per regulations. Then on the square. And all the time whatever we were doing the N.C.O.s were hooting us to hurry up. It was very nice for them. As soon as a drill instructor finished with us he handed us over to someone else. But the drill instructor himself had very likely finished his job for several hours. We just had to keep going. On the square we had to parade for inspection each morning. We were examined in every minute detail by Lance Corporals, Corporals and sergeant, then very likely the sergeant major before the officers came to do the job. And no matter how carefully the N.C.O.s had inspected us, the officers could always find something wrong. I think it is to my everlasting credit that during more than 100 inspections as a recruit I was never once pulled up for anything. I think I was about the only one. I often had to sacrifice the time in which I should have been writing to you, but I know you will not mind now. If faults are found, it means extra duties after everyone else has finished, and I did not want that. Then came drill. 2 hours of it in the burning sun. Then we were handed over for rifle instruction, bayonet practice, Physical training etc. to make up the day. Out in the open all the time, and working continually. And then school. After that changing the size of any misfitting equipment, or marching a mile for a haircut. Or being inspected by the M.O. or dentist, or being injected or teeth extracted. The only change was the reversal of the programmes. Then we got a few night guards thrown in just to fill our time in. The worst torture a man can have is to stand to attention for half an hour, head up, chins in, shoulders back, and arms rigid. Just try it for 10 minutes without turning a hair. The first thing you will notice is the breathing strain. That is the worst part. The Brigadier compliments us on that part of out parade. He said very few men can stand it for long. Where he finds it he knows he will find discipline. That is what he told us. I am on guard now. Have been inspected by Lieut. Nares and found OK Owen Nares' son. I have met some well known people here. Footballers, actors, musicians, County cricketers, dirt track riders and hosts of others. The life here at this camp is very interesting but they are exceptionally strict on discipline. Boots must be like mirrors, and no excuses taken. Nearly all the men get checked for them although they clean them regularly. I walk like a cissy to the parade ground. It is the only way. Darling I wish you were here with me now. I am sitting in the middle of the Plain. Not a house in sight. The scenery is grand and it is the cool of the evening now. I have just had a big meat pie and a quart of cocoa so I feel very contented at present.

I had a grand day yesterday. School of mechanics in the morning. My pay nearly gone on books again. Still I shall get that back on promotion if I keep up my reputation. I am going to keep hunting that stripe. Six months is usually the time before any promotion is considered. I am going to beat that. I'll just bet you sixpence. The stripes here are given on driving ability and brain work on engines. I drove a 3 ton Bedford 70 miles over Salisbury plains yesterday. I should have gone on a van to start, but they made a mistake and I did not tell them. The instructor said I was the best pupil he has had for months, and after 10 miles he just sat back and had a joy ride. I had a job with the gears at first, but he said it was amazing how I dropped into it. These instructors get sick of it, and are lucky to get an easy afternoon. He marked every part of my driving chart with 3 stars, which is very good. A personal note to finish signed by him "Extremely good all round". Signed F Lake Cpl. I could have had 4 stars and passed out with the Bedford this week, but if I had that I should not have any more trips out so he put 3. I expect I shall be on the big left hand drives in the morning. We have to drive every type. As far as I can see there is nothing but a line of lorries. We are part of the guard on them tonight.

There is a faint possibility that when I pass out I may have to stay here as an instructor without extra pay. Still that will be a start. I am in a special squad here now. 17 of us have been picked from the company, and we are having classes which will pass us out in 21 days instead of 6 weeks. I think I shall do it. Although the exam is pretty stiff. If I don't pass it, I can never get promotion. I have decided to take the risk of 21 days although I could have backed out and gone among the six week class. What happens a fortnight on Wednesday if I pass out is in the lap of the Gods. Set your mind at rest, for I feel confidant I can pass. The camp here is now almost empty as a great number of men have been sent to working units. Another big lot come up next week from our old camp. That is if they pass out. We are told they are a very poor lot. Their drill is miles behind the standard we set. Well sweetheart, it is getting dusk now, and I am feeling like a trussed up duck with all this equipment on. Ordinary uniform, steel helmet, respirator at the alert, gas cape, 50 rounds of ammo, a rifle, overcoat on shoulders, large pack on back, belt and bayonet, haversack full of kit strapped over left hip, water bottle on right hip. Everything except a lorry under my arm.

The squad commander has just seen my record card and says I stand a good chance of getting an instructor's job. I hope he is right. What an army record if I can get it and work hard for one stripe. I shall get an extra ⅓ per day. It's worth going after. Watch my smoke. Please remember me to Arthur and Mildred, Lucy and Mrs Taylor and Billy. Well darling it is nearly dark now, so I really must close. I wish I was with you tonight. Just think of me at about 11 o'clock tomorrow, stretched out sleeping off my guard. I can't get any leave for 3 months if I get away then. I shall try my hardest but I must wait for the results of all my studies first. Roll on the next fortnight. I wish you could see the country round here. I will make you a promise. If I come through this lot safely, I will bring you to see this section of England.

Good night. Sleep well

God bless you and keep you safe until I return.

All my love,

Gerald

Undated letter. *Probably Monday 14th July 1941*   Monday night

My Dear Youngster,

Just a few more lines hoping you are keeping well and that you have managed to wade through my last epistle. I am much happier here. I think we all are. They are exceptionally strict on discipline and personal cleanliness, but it is only as it should be. One chap who was here before us strikes me as a proper lead swinger. They are on him continually. Had to report at Company office clean tonight. He is cleaner now than he has been since the midwife washed him. Several others have had to be smartened up too. They don't mind dirty uniforms. It cannot be avoided. And we have a working suit and a battle dress for driving in and a battle dress for best. After messing with lorries we can't help grease on our clothes, but they will take no excuse whatever for dirty boots, cap badges, arms, necks and feet. I am in a tight corner at present. The laundry have not returned my clean underclothes. The quartermaster has taken the matter up pretty strongly, but nothing has been returned yet. He says if they do not return the articles he will see that they replace them. That does not give me a change of clothing though. I have been out for five hours driving this morning. One of those very big LEFT hand drive "No Signals" lorries. I got on very well with it too. I can tell you I had a bit of a sinking feeling inside me before I got in the cab. Everything is just the opposite to what I have been used to. After 5 minutes I had complete confidence in my own ability to handle it in any emergency. The instructor said I took to it like a duck takes to water. To show his confidence he had a nap and left me to it. He has starred my card for this trip and marked it "Expert driver". Then this afternoon we paraded and marched on to the square. I thought we were for a dose of drill. But no. Pleasant surprise. We had a lorry each with an expert instructor and learned all about petrol systems. How to clean, find faults, service, dismantle and re-assemble them and everything in general to do with that part of the engine. Then we went to school for pretty severe examination on what we had learned. The sergeant could not ask us a question we could not answer. It is surprising what I have learned about :- Thermo syphonics, Centrifugals, Impeller Thermostats, A.C. systems, Gravity systems and Autovac Systems. I did not know such things existed until I got here. Now I know all about them. It would be impossible to get a course like this anywhere else outside the Army. By the way have you noticed how desperate Hitler has got since I joined the R.A.S.C. I told you before I came what he would do when I was called up. You may be interested to know that the new nickname given to our unit by the rest of the Army is the "Royal Army Suicide Corps". That is after Greece, Libya and Crete. Darling we are finishing training at 4.45 p.m. in our specialist squad. It is wonderful to have a few hours to ourselves in the evening. We do little but cleaning, studying and writing. Do you know that I have not had a game of cards yet. Shows the amount of work we put in when we don't get time for that. I thought the camp had been attacked last night. I woke up at 1.30 a.m. to find our hut a hive of activity. It turned out that all the guard had been found asleep on duty. They were immediately arrested and our chaps were routed out to take their places. I was lucky. I had been on the night before, so they left me alone. Well sweetheart I must get on with my studies so I will close now. Remember me to the usual people.

Good night. Sleep well.

All my love

Gerald XXXXXXXXXX

Received July 23rd 1941. *Undated letter. Probably around 17th July 1941*

Just a few lines after a pretty stiff time of it. We are having nothing but guards here at present. I have put in over 60 hours guard this week, in addition to training and school. I feel dog tired just at present. In an addition to the duties mentioned we have had 3 hours trench digging after work, one air raid alarm when we all had to get in the trenches at midnight, and one escaped prisoner hunt in addition to parading for pay, one church parade and two lectures by officers. "Otherwise our spare time is our own" is now a regular saying in the hut. Oh! I forgot a parade for haircutting, and a bath & showers parade. Some of the chaps have gone sick. I don't wonder at it. We have to parade one hour before we are due to go on guard. In full marching order. That is with everything but our own beds. Fully laden we have somewhere in the region of 3/4 cwt strapped about us. Then we have to stand motionless on the parade ground for the officer. Then he inspects us, which takes nearly half an hour. And it is woe betide anyone who has a button undone or one speck of dust on his equipment. The standing and waiting is heart and backbreaking. The men who have been here nearly a week have done no extra duties at all yet. After complaints, and what the medical Officer has said, (that one guard a week is sufficient in addition to our training) it is being altered

Everyone of the new squad is on duty tomorrow night. Before going on guard yesterday my meals were as follows:-

Breakfast	½ slice of bacon, ½ round of bread; little lump of butter and mug of tea.
Dinner	one rissole
Sweet	4 prunes, one spoonful of custard
Tea	one round of bread, one small portion of butter and one spoonful of jam

And they had the cheek to tell us not to waste any. We have to go and spend our money at the NAFFI then. It cost me 10d yesterday. Today has been a little better, but I still had to spend 6d on food at the NAFFI. I wonder what the majority of civilians would say if they had that to do a day's work on. The chaps have not much money left after buying extra food and cleaning equipment. I know if I went out regularly I would soon be in debt. I am not going to let that happen. Some of the chaps here brought as much as £20 with them and they have hardly a copper left. They are in the fortunate position of having fairly wealthy relatives however.

It was bitterly cold on guard last night. I was wishing I was occupying my lawful pillow. I think you had better sell the bed now for after sleeping on a bag of straw placed next to mother earth for nearly two months, I think I shall feel uncomfortable in a proper bed. Did I hear you say a straw bed suits you alright.

All the fellows here are discussing the **second** thing they will do when they get home on leave. The first seems to be unanimous. What an army! They all seem to be intent on holding a flare up. They are going all over the place. They can't understand me when I say I will be quite content to sit by the fireside and talk to you for hours in an evening. They also cannot understand me not going out at every opportunity I get. I have not been out of camp yet. If they go out and blue in their pay they are miserable having to wait for pay day. They send home for money every week, and even then some of them try to borrow. They never ask me a second time.

I am quite content to stay in and study my books. I have set my mind on reaching the required standard of efficiency and I am getting on quite well. I only hope I don't get tongue tied when it comes to the actual examination. I cannot afford to fail, and I know how you will feel if I go under.

Many times during the day, especially when I feel tired, my mind wanders and I think of you and wonder what you are doing, and suddenly a loud voice somewhere in the vicinity brings me back to earth. At night I always think of you. At church on Sunday the Captain Padre made me think more than ever. His words, though kindly, were like a whiplash, and I know they caused quite a lot of soul searching.

He mentioned particularly wives, mothers, sweethearts. He said "They don't tell you everything but I am often told in confidence. They are not concerned so much with your personal safety. They worry as to whether life in the Army will <u>change you</u>. Whether it will make you a drunkard. Whether you will seek other company. Whether you will curse and swear when you never did it before" He gave many similar examples.

Darling, My thoughts were that I sincerely hope I never let you down. You know I have never cared for doubtful company. I can manage without it now. That is why, although I usually join in any fun in the hut I never hardly go out to be led into temptation. I hope that in the future, wherever I may be sent, I shall remain so. You said in one of your letters that you thought I was changing. Well that is my opinion. Through all my hardships my thoughts constantly turn to you, and the burdens seem lighter. I have just had my chart marked "Almost ready for test". I hope it will be delayed as long as possible towards the 21 days. It will give me a better chance. I can't afford to fail. I am certain in my own mind that if I had never met you my Army life would have been different. I am glad it is just exactly as it is. I had the disappointment of my life yesterday. One of our fellows got time off to go by car to Wolverhampton. I wanted to give you a surprise, <u>but</u> on Sat afternoon my name went up on the list for guard last night. Very little chance now. I have been on a lousy guard every weekend since I have been in the Army. Some chaps have not done a weekend guard at all yet. Just my luck. The trouble is I should have come by road. I cannot afford the railway fare, and in any case I should have 20 hours travelling out of 24. That would not be much good. Still it won't be so very long now before I am due for seven days. That is if I get it when it falls due. I can apply for it immediately I pass my exams (if and when) and my name will go on a rosta, from which I take my turn. Well my sweetheart don't forget the "remembers" as I must close now. All my love from

Gerald XXXXXXXXX

PS Can you let me have some stamps. I had some from home on Saturday. I was called out for a few minutes and when I returned they had been lifted from my parcel. I'll bet it does not happen again.

Undated letter. *Probably Monday 21ˢᵗ July 1941*

Monday night

My Dear Youngster,

Just a few lines to let you know that I have just received your parcel. Thank you very much for the cigarettes and the book. It was just what I wanted. I have something on my plate to get that lot into my head. I shall manage it somehow. Your letter and photo have cheered me up quite a lot. I have not been feeling too unhappy considering everything, until today. I was on another Sunday night vehicle guard last night. You remember me telling you about the prisoner escaping a few days ago. Well the "Yard" got him. He was brought here and not supposed to move anywhere without a guard with fixed bayonet with him. Anyway he did it again last night. He got out of his cell somehow, pinched a motor cycle, which no one heard, and vanished into the blue. The commander of the main guard is in trouble. All of us vehicle guards were confined to our room for routine inquiries, and after cross questioning we were allowed to go. We were driving etc all day. The Brigadier is coming tomorrow, and as soon as we finished training we had to turn round and do trench digging etc until nine o'clock. Every man in the camp had to do that. We knocked off then because it started raining like the very devil. We were then allowed to get out mail which had been there since morning. Your letter was just the tonic I needed. I am under a pretty big strain just at present what with all these guards and the studying. And what ever they do with me after, I am determined not to fail. I had a great compliment paid to me today. One of the driving instructors had to question us and give us a lecture on the Bedford engine etc . I seemed to be the only one who could answer every question he asked, and after a short time he asked me to give the lecture for the rest of the time as I knew more about his vehicle than he did. He told me that few men could have done it in the time I have been here, and that he certainly could not. I suppose some silly thing will trip me up and stop me getting full marks. Another squad have been tested today but I don't think any have equalled my score.

Well darling, to get onto more pleasant subjects. I am changing. I can feel it in my bones. But it is definitely for the better. I feel as though, hard as Army life is, I can settle down to home life and make you happy. I know that as soon as there is money in hand at the shop I shall have no worries whatever, and that my hobby from then on will be looking after you.

Perhaps then I shall be able to afford some of the small surprises which I know you appreciate. I hope you liked the souvenir of Aug 5th . Wherever I may be on that day, my heart will be with you.

Whatever I am doing lately you seem to be with me. Even tonight when I was feeling tired and miserable I had your letter. And I have been to church every Sunday. That seems to bring you very near to me. The time is travelling swiftly along in my mind. Pay-day seems to fly round and my reckoning says every one is a week nearer seeing you. Many times when big cars flash by filled with pleasure seekers, I feel very bitter that I have to leave you to come and defend their rights. I think some-day the lads of the Army will reap their reward.

Well darling it is Tuesday night now. I did not have time to finish my letter last night as it gets dark quickly now, and we are not allowed lights. I feel much better today. I feel, strange as it may seem to you that I have been talking to myself for about 5 hrs while driving the wagon this morning. The reason. Well I had a D.I. who has been telling me about himself and his wife. It is almost exactly the same as our past has been, and I should think she must be a great resemblance to you. It seems grand to find a fellow like that.

There are many other good lads here. They tell you sometimes what they have given up. It is amazing what is being done by these ordinary fellows to win this war. It is rarely you find one who growls at you when driving. Nearly every one is agreed on that point. They would be justified in growling very often. I have again been congratulated on my engine knowledge today. Tomorrow is the great day though. I am hoping to pass alright. I don't know yet whether I shall be kept on as a D.I.

Two other chaps have been asked before I came to this camp. They are on the last days of a motor cycle course and they have heard nothing. It is very annoying as I don't know whether I shall remain or be transferred to holding company over the road. If that happens then I shall shortly be transferred to a working or field unit. Whatever happens you can rely on me to look after myself.

Well sweetheart, there is a film show here tonight, and I may go. We get them often and free. I have not been to one at all in seven weeks as I have always had some duty to perform. I think it is "Hey Hey USA" The "Ghost train" was here at the week end. We also have professional dancers in our hut, and singers, while in the camp we have pro. Footballers, cricketers, boxers, musicians, etc. When they get going everything is free. Well dear, will close now, asking you to do the usual remembers and please don't forget the 5th. All my love from your husband

Gerald XXXXXXXXXX

Received July 24th

Tuesday Night

Sweetheart,

Just a few lines in reply to your letter and thanking you for contents of parcel which I have just received. It was quite a surprise to get a parcel at the beginning of the week.

Darling I do not want you to upset yourself about the book affair. The reason I did not mention it right away was because I had your first letter two days after the second. I could not understand what you meant in the second. When the first arrived however it became quite clear. At first I thought you were referring to ration books. Fancy thinking I would choose to ignore it. I thought you knew me much better than that. I also wrote about it in a letter last week. Evidently you have not yet received it.

With regard to the questions you want answered if I can get the job as a D.I. I shall take it. The chances of promotion are fairly good normally, but if I stick my back into it I should get on alright. The reason I shall take it is merely to gain as much experience as I can. As

I mentioned before, no civilian could hope to learn as much as we can here. They have everything relating to vehicles.

With regard to going overseas, I do not mind that, but I do not feel inclined to go as a more or less beginner.

The DI s here remain for 8 to 10 months and then get posted anywhere. If they do not like it they can ask for a transfer. I am very sorry I forgot to thank you for the handkerchiefs. I thought I had written that in one of my previous letters.

Please don't forget the "remembers"

Just cheer up and think that it won't be so very long now before I am due for my first 7 days leave. The time is flying. If I don't write to you for a day or two you will know why. I am on a long guard at the supply depot at Warminster. Commences tomorrow. That will be about 100 hours in 10 days. I shall soon be getting used to it. Sorry I forgot to fill in the beginning of your letters. That was because I was trying to catch the post I expect.

Glad to hear peas are doing well and that you are making the garden look so nice. I wonder if you would spend so much time in it if I were there now. I think I should see you did not. Thanks for letting them have the money. I know you are doing all you can for me. I shall make it up to you some day by trying to be a better husband. I know now I am away that you deserve it. That is another promise I intend to fulfil. Fancy writing to me like you did and then following up by informing me you did not intend to write like that.

Darling you know the last thing I wanted was awkwardness with those at home. Please don't make it any harder for me. Goodness knows I have gone through enough here without that to worry about. I know that you will do your best although I shall understand what is really in your heart.

I am looking patiently forward to seeing you again. I hope the time will not be long delayed. I am always thinking of you and many times if I have done well on any particular subject I wished you were here for me to tell you about it. I shall have such a lot of experiences to relate to you. I know you will want to hear them. The thing here that surprises me most is the lack of bad language. We hear it sometimes, but it is generally a laughing matter and not a "choking off". If I were at home some of the things I could tell you would drive all those blues away. What about this for an example.

We paraded for Physical Training at 7.30 a.m. in vests shorts pumps & socks. The instructor asked later on if anyone was wearing pumps too tight for him. Edward Round said his pinched him badly. Instructor examined them and said the quartermaster ought to be shot for issuing him with a pair like that. The next chap was marching in his socks. Edward had picked his up by mistake and the other poor devil could not find his so had to go without any. He will never hear the last of it. We have dozens of things like that happen. Still I must keep those for another day. Well my dear, shall have to close now and will write again at the first opportunity. All for now and keep your pecker up.

All my love from your husband

Gerald XXXXXXXXX

Undated letter. *Probably Wednesday & Thursday 23rd & 24th July 1941. A note says June 41 but I think it was added later when someone was trying to remember the date.*

June 1941

Wednesday & Thursday

My dear youngster,

Just a few lines thanking you for your letter which I have just received. I knew that even if you did not write and tell me, you would feel better after, and wish you had not written it. I have known you too long, and I was not really worrying too much about it. I was wishing I could be with you. I wrote yesterday but if you think I am annoyed, please alter your opinion. As long as you can make yourself reasonably happy and comfortable during my absence, I am determined to do the same. I want to write or talk to you all the time, and often there is little or nothing to write about. Often when I get something to write about I have to do it in odd moments, and that is why I am liable to forget something. Some days I have hours to write in and other times I can't find above ten minutes, and then something else is usually left undone.

I am developing habits, and with a watch it is much easier.

Rise and dress	10 mins.
Wash and shave	10 mins.
Make bed and lay out kit for inspection	10 mins
Parade for breakfast and return in about	25 minutes.
Give final clean and polish to shoes, brasses, get into full kit for work about	20 minutes.

The rest of the day is dictated by the Army.

I have been driving this week on the Exeter end. It is wonderful country. I saw rambler roses (one mass of bloom) trained to the top of a telegraph pole today. It was a magnificent sight. There are hundreds of beds of splendid onions everywhere I go. The corn is rapidly ripening and all over Salisbury plains it looks grand from the top of a hill. It makes me think of rabbit shooting in a few weeks time. Somewhere on my travels today I saw the most wonderful garden full of roses that ever I have seen. No painter ever born could do them justice. It was like looking into paradise when I caught the first glimpse of them. The cottages here give one the impression of living in a world of old. They are all built of stone and everything seems so clean and neat and tidy. The men, women, sons and daughters stand outside nearly every morning to greet us as we go by. That little feeling of welcome does us all good. Takes our mind off stern military matters for a time. Of course we are not allowed to stop and speak to them but we make "One hell of a row as we go by". Just imagine a couple of hundred 3 ton wagons going by slowly and war cries coming from every one. I have wished many times that you were somewhere near so that we could go roaming round. Trouble is so much of the country is out of bounds to troops on foot. I have not been out of this camp yet. I am keeping my reputation up.

You speak of coming to see me at August. Well darling I couldn't imagine anything I should like better. "But" That word always has to creep in when the Army is concerned. I am on guard unexpectedly now. As I mentioned in my last letter it will be 100 hours this week, and I never know when I shall be on again. There are a new lot of chaps coming up from the other camp tomorrow, so that should make it easier.

And of course there is always the question of how long I shall be here. I still have not had my test, but several of our chaps who have held heavy goods vehicle licences before joining the Army had their test today. They also were approached 2 days ago about being D.I.s. They scraped through the driving test, but only just, and failed in their test as D.I.s. That was today.

They go to holding company in the morning ready for posting to a working unit. So you see that what can happen in a day can easily happen in nearly two weeks. Anyway, my 21 days are up next Wednesday, sink or swim, so I will let you know immediately I have any definite information. I really do want to see you, but I know how disappointed you would be if you got to Warminster and then could not see me. If I do remain here I will see the sergeant major and see what I can do. If I do stay I think he will make it fairly easy if I tell him I want to see you with regard to my business. I should have been able to get 24 hours off before but it would take me nearly that long in travelling. And if we are late returning there is the devil to pay. Usually pack drill. Seeing others do it has put me off it.

Darling I am writing this while on guard so I don't know when I shall be able to post it as I can't leave the guard room. Especially after the escaped prisoner affair. Still I will post it at the first opportunity. With regard to the escaped prisoner, it is a very complicated affair and would take too long for me to write. | I shall have to keep that for when I see you again.

The same with the affair with the officer. I can tell you this. I have been to a devil of a lot of trouble to see it does not happen again. The officer concerned is the man to visit our guard in the morning. He has a habit of coming without his identity card. If he does that in the morning he will have the job of going back 6 miles and fetching it. He has already been stuck though the arm with a bayonet for trying to pass the guard without a pass. He will be asking for some more if he tries it again.

Well fancy trying to get another job and never telling me. If you feel you can carry on where you are, that is what I should advise you to do. I am glad the garden is looking all right, but don't over work yourself in it. I know it is a big job for you. I wish I could be there to help you.

Whatever toil you put into it, rest assured that every ounce of food you produce will be ample repayment. I wish we could get some of the produce here. We have had no veg at all for nearly a fortnight. When it is like that it makes you wish you could get the contents of a nice garden on your plate. I have not even *seen* a Strawberry, Rasp. or any other soft fruit in this area. That is the first season I can remember that happening.

Well darling if I keep writing like this I shan't have an envelope big enough so I must close for tonight and see what tomorrow brings.

Good night darling. God bless you and keep you safe. Sleep well.

Thursday now. Have done another night and morning. It is a grand day. It has been very hot on sentry duty. We had a bit of an alarm last night. Movements heard in long grass etc. near petrol dump. Guard turned out. No reply to challenges. Rifles were ready to fire and two of us went to investigate. Found six cats doing their courting. I did say sweet words having to turn out at that time in the morning. In my four hours off too. I was still thinking of that vacant pillow during the night. Well dear, I am afraid there is not much else for me to add except that I was very pleased with Jane's Fighting Ships. I am going to try and sleep now, (on bare wooden planks) and make up for last night. I said try. It is most uncomfortable while I am awake, but I may not notice it so much if I can get to sleep.

Well I have just been "woken up" from a lovely sleep. That "b" lieutenant has just been. He tried to get in at a fast speed on his motor cycle. He would not stop on challenge so the lads tipped him off his bike. They all swore they would get one in for me if they had the chance. He was in a pretty state. However he was man enough to admit that he asked for it. I don't often bear grudges, but that is one wiped off.

Well sweetheart, it is nearly time for my last turn on guard, so I will close with all my love from your loving husband

Gerald XXXXXXXXX

Don't forget the remembers

Undated letter. *Probably Sat July 26ᵗʰ 1941*

Sat

Darling,

Just a line in great haste to let you know that I have passed the first part of my driving with the highest marks in the whole company. I'm feeling on top of the world. Will write again in detail tomorrow.

All for now love

Gerald XXXXXXXXX

Sat & Sunday

My dear youngster,

Well dear, I don't know whether you have received the few lines I wrote in such a hurry, but I just could not resist writing although I only had about 10 minutes to write it in. I told you I would write in detail later. Well, here goes. Yesterday afternoon, I was to have gone with the rest of the squad, driving by map. When we got on the 3 ton Bedfords we were told we were going for our test. Each wagon was to have an officer to pass or fail us. We waited anxiously for them to arrive. Suddenly they appeared, and walked towards their respective vehicles. Darling, can you imagine my dismay, when up to my wagon walked the "gent" who had said such "sweet words" to me a week before. I sat there with nothing but grim determination in my heart. He got in beside me, looked right through me and never spoke. After 5 minutes I got the curt order "Start". I did start, and he tried everything he knew to catch me. In the end "Jack was as good as his master" I never did wrong or even made a sound with the gears. And then my rotten luck came back. Just as I was stopping the lousy engine cuts out for a few seconds, and the wagon almost stopped in a narrow lane. For that I dropped two marks out of a possible hundred. I swore under my breath but I knew that could not alter the decision. I would have given a weeks pay to have been able to tell you I had got the hundred. Anyway, after it was all over he told me I was a "B. good driver", and that one change down I made into second gear while I was going down hill was bordering on the impossible. By the way every change and everything else I did was on his orders.

When I made that change, I set my teeth for the terrific clash of gears, but no one was more surprised than I was when it went in silently. He was surprised too, and told me so. I can assure you I was relieved when he did not ask me to repeat the dose. Then I had to turn in a narrow lane. My heart sank, but I managed it beautifully. I think the unseen hand guided me most of the time. Anyway I came through miles in front of the rest. Only one of the squad actually failed, although quite a number of them only just scraped through. After it was all over the Lieutenant became most affable. For a time I watched my step. He was not trying to catch me however and today he has been quite nice to me. Although he has not said so he knows that his first judgement was wrong.

He asked me if I would become an instructor. He did not know I had previously been approached. I did not enlighten him. He wanted to know how long I had held a licence, and where he could check it up. I told him. He told me that he knew I had been on the road for a long time by my driving. He seemed a bit anxious as he thought I should refuse. However I accepted. I told him I was keenly interested. He asked me quite a lot about myself and seemed quite interested. Gave me 2 hours off after, although he never even told me I had passed. Of course that is for the corporal and I suppose he did the proper thing.

Today he has been after me several times. Asked me once to go to his bedroom for a walk and fetch some papers for him. 3/4 of a mile each way. He told me not to rupture myself in my hurry as there was plenty of time. "Just have a nice walk and if anyone says anything to you, refer them to me" I've had several jobs like that this morning. Suits me nicely. But darling, when I was told how I had passed, I could not hold myself. I am sure your arms do not ache any more than mine did at that moment. I wanted you to share my success. My corporal was as proud as I was. That is only the first stage. I have another test with another officer which is pretty stiff, although not as severe as that one.

Sweetheart, I have promised myself another success for your sake. I will write to you immediately my ordeal is over. I will try to explain a few details of these tests. The one I have just passed ensures that I shall not keep the same rank during my Army career. If I had failed, I told you I could never have been promoted.

I am almost certain now of the D.I. position. But the next tests are grades ABC classes. It depends on what class I pass in as to how soon I get my first stripe.

I think I shall be alright on the technical side. As I have told you I have studied until I have felt like throwing up the sponge. The lads here however are just a little envious of my knowledge. Still, as I have told them, I have studied while they have been out or pleasure bent. What I have been doing this week, just for my own ends, is to let anyone have any one of my books, ask me any question and I try to answer. I have done it to such an extent that I can answer almost everything.

I went to Warminster Sat afternoon just as a bit of a change. I thoroughly enjoyed myself in my quiet way. One of the fellows in the tent at the other camp happened to be there. He is a fine chap. Owns a big hotel at Malvern.

He is expecting his commission soon. (By the way his income tax was just over £700 this time) He was waiting for his wife to arrive in his car. He asked me to stay and meet her. After a few minutes a luxurious car drew up outside the largest hotel in Warminster. Three beautiful young ladies got out. His wife and two cousins. They are staying a few days at the hotel. We went in for tea amongst a dining room full of officers.

Every officer's eyes goggled when we went into the room. They had cause to. We carried it through as though we were officers ourselves. The officers ladies were not in the one two three with the ones at our table. The waitress came in and asked if the teas on the tray were for us five *soldiers*. 3 ladies mind you. That started the ball rolling. Then we got down to the humours of camp life. Although the officers could not hear all we said they laughed as much as we did. Dear I wished you could have been there. I have promised to take you to see them some day. They would not hear of me paying a copper.

I was the guest of the ladies because the two of us had gone through so much together. I really appreciated the kind thought. I know you will feel the same. I know that I have made real friends. He is very much like Arthur in his ways. Anyway it was like being absolutely free again for a short time. After that I went and did a little bit of shopping, had a meal at the YMCA and walked back to camp almost "stony broke" except for what I had when I came. I am trying not to part with that. I am enclosing a little souvenir in remembrance of August 5th. I hope you will like it. I am sending it now as the post is very uncertain at present. I keep getting letters a week old, and then getting one only posted the previous night.

Sweetheart, I don't know whether you have seen the papers, but August Bank Holiday is definitely off. We have a holiday here, but we are confined to Barracks to relieve pressure on transport. The notice only went up on Friday while I was on guard. Still perhaps another opportunity will arise. In any case it should not be too long before I get leave now.

If I get through these exams fairly quickly and with success I can put my name down for it. I may get it quickly or it may be delayed. I shall take a chance. While I think about it, many thanks for the stamps. I have put them safe. We are only allowed one a day if the N.A.A.F.I. have any. You think I shall be a skeleton. Well I think you can leave that to me. As long as I can afford something to eat I shall have it, and I have nearly finished buying books now.

What do you think of Friday's tea. One cream cracker with jam on. ½ round of bread and butter, and a mug of tea. We are getting no veg or fruit. The tea is getting more like dishwater every day. I received the parcel from home yesterday. It was most welcome. I have just seen my name up again for guard tonight. That is every weekend since I have been in the Army. It is getting monotonous. I am beginning to think I am doing the job too well. Please remember me to Lucy, Mrs Taylor and Billy and George if you see him. Also can you let me have Arthur's address again as I have put it away too safe. Why has George got back home again. Is he for the water again. Oh! Don't forget to remember me to his people.

Well youngster, it is nearly time for Church parade, and my powers of letter writing are nearly exhausted so I will close now. All the best from your ever loving husband

Gerald XXXXXXXXX

Received about July 28th 1941. *Letter undated but probably July 30th 1941*

Address to follow
Wednesday night

My dear youngster,

Well I know now how my fate is being decided. I leave here at 8.45 am tomorrow. Several of us were booked in for D.I. but at the last minute we have been taken off the list. I came through all my exams quite well. I am in the top four for everything although in my view the exams were most unsatisfactory. I can tell you about that in greater detail when I see you. Let it suffice to say that we were examined in fours. The first man was questioned and if he passed, so did the others. Our four came out top. It was pure luck, as I did not have a chance to answer a question. On the other stuff I was quite OK. All the men at holding company were suddenly told to pack their kit today. All our chaps have been told to be ready to move over there tomorrow. It now transpires that they have been held back at holding company until tomorrow, as they have not enough fellows to transfer. I understand most of them are going to the Midlands and Yorkshire. Some of us are evidently to go with them. They seem to be getting desperately short of first class drivers. I have just been informed that several of the instructors here have to go over to H.C. too. I will write and let you know immediately I can tell you anything definite. Even the men who are in for commissions are to go now. So you see we are all anyhow. Darling I have just received your letter. I was in such a state the other night that I believe I forgot to mention your office job. Well dear, I am really glad you are staying on at the old place. I don't know why, but I don't think you will be really happy anywhere else, and somehow I feel contented to know that you are among people you are used to. Glad you made 4/3. Keep it up. Also pleased to hear you are OK at home again. The books seem to be doing well. It must be a good profit on them. Don't worry about B.H. & G. being paid in a week. I shall be quite satisfied as long as it is being reduced gradually. However if you can manage a lump sum so much the better. As I said before, once there is cash in hand, I am confident there will be no further troubles. And dear, I know that when that is achieved you will still save for when this lot is over. I know now that with your help I shall make a success of my life, and also make you happy. While I think of it, I got the ring OK but it broke again in the same place, so I shall have to wait for a leave and get it done with my watch. Tell Lucy I will try and earn her another drink as soon as possible. This sudden transfer of half the unit has complicated matters, but I will soon put that right. Tell her to save her money fast, as she might want several doses.

Well dear, I must close now as I have to pack my kit for morning.

Love

Gerald XXXXXXXXXX

CHAPTER 2
Somewhere in England…to somewhere else.

Somewhere in England (We hope)
Saturday August 2nd

My Dear Youngster,

Just a few lines to let you know I am quite alright at present, but very tired and weary. I don't know what is happening to us at present but we are certainly doing a bit of moving about. On Wednesday night I finished my training. On Thursday I was rushed to H.Q. and Holding Company with the rest of our specialist squad. Fourteen of us had passed out. We spent one night there in complete misery.

Have you ever tried sleeping on a bed consisting of a wooden frame with webbing stretched across, the webbing broken in the middle and your posterior dropping through and almost touching the floor while your feet are on the framework level. It is a splendid position.

Yesterday (Friday) we were fetched out of the NAAFI during our break, and paraded for making up any kit deficiencies. After a lot of messing about we were transferred to Bulford.

We were stuck in tents with no beds to lie on, and we had to make the best of it. There is an aerodrome 200 yds from where we (slept?) and the bombers were taking off and landing all night. It was lousy with that and no beds. My neck was like a poker this morning. Then they had us on parade before 6 am gave us 1/6 each, took us for another medical, (second in two days) and ordered to get in full marching order. There we stood on the square for 3 hours waiting for the Brigadier. Then we marched a mile to the station and I am writing this on the train. I think we are going somewhere near George. There are about 200 of us, all drivers on this train, but we don't know if we shall all get to the same destination. From all we hear there is a strong possibility that we are due to cross the water. Anyway, we have been measured for tropical kit. Don't worry dear, as we may never have to go. All these things are done in readiness. If it were not for you, I should not mind in the least. Some of the men here are worrying although they do not say a lot. Most of them have several children. If we are absent off any parade now, we are to be listed as deserters. We have a roll call every hour. That is just in case any of the "tough guys" slope.

Darling I don't know when I shall get any letters from you. They will send them on from Sutton Veny and they should follow me. I hope so anyway.

Well dear I will write and let you know what happens to me as soon as possible. Don't forget Aug 5th. I shall be thinking of you, wherever I am

All for the present.

All my love

Gerald XXXXXXXXXX

Received Aug 5th *Undated letter but probably Sunday 3rd August 1941*

Shipley
Yorkshire
August Sunday

My Dear Youngster,

Well at last I have reached somewhere for a few more fleeting moments. I wrote in the train yesterday of my movements and experiences up till mid day. Of all places, they brought us through Birmingham. I intended asking the officer if I could pay you a visit, but you can imagine my feelings when our train did not stop. Never mind, the Army seemed much better as we came through the country I know so well. My spirits were much higher than they have been since I last saw you. We arrived here at 10 p.m. We marched about in full kit (after roll call) trying to find billets. It so happened that hundreds of men from other parts had been brought here at the same time. At midnight, after many faintings and revivals etc we got stuck over a big hotel. Every available place is filled with troops.

We had no bed again, except bare boards and blankets.

We had only had two sandwiches and one cup of tea in 18 hours when we arrived.

We "painted the town red" until we got a good meal. The cooks took it very well. It is not very nice getting out of bed and starting work at 1 am

The people here are true Yorkshire, and treated us like conquering heroes. Many of the men are Dunkirk chaps. Others are Libya, Palestine and Middle East veterans. While I am thinking of it, please do not write to me until you hear a definite address from me. We have just been told we are expected to be on the move again before night. We are certainly seeing the country. Well darling, just as I finished that little piece our new sergeant has just informed us we may be staying here a few days as he has to find more billets.

Our address is:- T/271347 Driver Milner. Oddfellows Hotel Shipley Yorkshire.

Will you please let them know at Brook Street. I can't tell you any more as we know nothing at all. Many rumours keep floating round but I am ignoring them until I hear something more substantial. By the way the address should have read Shipley nr Bradford, Yorks.

Darling some of the burdens we have had since joining the Army have been almost too heavy to carry, but if it will enable us to settle down to a peaceful and happy home life afterwards we will continue to the end. Talk in civilian life is easy. Putting that talk into effect is very different. It means troops being moved like we are, and homes being broken up. No civilian can understand what these boys are giving up. I only hope it will be appreciated after this lot is over. I am afraid there is not much else to write about at present but I will let you know anything that happens to me. Somehow I can't get it out of my head that we are due for the Far East. How soon no one knows. I shall be thinking of a year ago on Tuesday. The happiest day of my life. I shall be glad when I can resume as before. I will close now. Don't worry about me. I can take all they can give me.

God bless you and keep you safe.

I am yours ever

Gerald XXXXXXXXXX

Tuesday August 5ᵗʰ

T/271347
Driver Milner G
R.A.S.C.
Oddfellows Hotel
Shipley
Yorks.

My Dear Youngster,

        Congratulations on the anniversary of a great occasion. I wish my thoughts today were as happy as those a year ago. The news concerning us is definitely bad at present. I, together with many hundreds of others, am on the draft for foreign lands. I may get leave before I go, but no one is getting more than 48 hrs. Some of the chaps have nearly 400 miles each way to travel. It is hopeless for them. Others are trying various methods of dodging the column. If I cannot get leave I know you will agree with me where my duty lies. From what I know and guess, I don't think it is going to be so very long before this show is over. That is all I am waiting for, and then you will be able to find out if the Army has really altered me. We have just been on parade and the sergeant has threatened Blood & Thunder if any man overstays his leave. From that I take it our section is due for 48 hrs. When it will come goodness only knows, as we are due out at almost any time in the next few days. I wanted desperately to get back on the 5th but it seems fate is still against me.

I have been treated with great kindness and consideration since I arrived here. The people are grand. Of course most of them know we are for overseas, but nothing seems too much trouble. One old lady gave me a drink of water which I shall always be thankful for. She gave it to me when we arrived at H.Q. on Sat night after 18 hrs without a drink. I was just getting to the stage where I did not trouble what happened when she arrived. Most people do not know what "Full Marching Order" means until they have had a few hours of it. The less I have to do with it the more I appreciate it.

I don't know whether there is anything else I have to write about or any questions I have left unanswered. I have had a lot to think about over these last few days. Somehow I know I shall come back to you before very long. Well my dearest I will close now hoping to see you for a few fleeting moments in the near future.

All my love
Gerald XXXXXXXXXX

August 5th 1940. Marriage of Gerald Milner and Eva Williams at St Mary's church Oldswinford Stourbridge.

Received August 9th 1941 after 48 hours leave. Last letter dated August 5th therefore leave must have been 6th & 7th

T/271347
Driver Milner G.
Draft R.H.F.G.F.
63, Kirkgate,
Shipley
Yorks.

Darling,

First of all let me thank you for the wonderful 48 hrs and all you did for me. I feel different altogether now. I can assure you from all I have heard since my return I was one of the lucky ones. Most of the men had to march quite good distances to get home, and then when they got there, their wives told them they were just unfortunate and that they should have gone a day or two earlier or later. The chap who travelled down with me was one of them. He has had something to put up with since he came back. When I was at home I made you a promise, and somehow I am glad. When I get mixed up with some of the fellows here I feel very thankful I am not that way inclined. Well I saw you waving as I went by. I did not feel as though I was leaving you. I felt and still feel you are very near me. I thought perhaps you would not be there and felt slightly disappointed, for the 4.30 never ran, and the one we caught was late.

Breaking in on what I was writing, a gust of wind has just blown across the room and blown my writing material about. Can you guess what else. Well I will tell you. It has turned your "snap" up in front of me. I think it must be that Guardian Angel still at work. We arrived at Snow Hill in time to make one terrific dash to New St. and catch the train for Leeds. Those people who had been asked not to travel, were there in force. For about 70 miles we stood in the corridor packed like sardines. I did not even have room to get my kit off. Anyway we arrived here and clocked in at two minutes to twelve. Nearly everyone is back on time or very near it. I was most surprised.

We have been fiddling about again all morning, and just received our pay. It takes quite a time to do that job! We cannot understand this pay business. We have all had £1 instead of 10/-. They told us that was the amount we should receive but no explanation has yet been given about the second 10/-. Without being pessimistic, I don't like the look of it.

On the other hand we have been given the new address, although we are still in the same old place. There is also a rumour that we may stay here another fortnight.

Since I wrote that little effort we have been on parade again. We finished for the day at 2 o'clock but we must keep close to barracks as we are being called up in rotation for our new rig out. Quite a number have already been fitted up.

Well I have found out what the pay is for. We all receive £1 per week until we land again. Then the difference will be stopped out of our wages, but living is cheap, cigarettes are supplied, and comforts are sent for the troops overseas. So at present I am 10/- in debt. This Army pay takes some understanding.

We are having an extra special clean up during the next two days. Another brigadier is expected any time now for inspection, but even that does not mean we are obliged to sail. From what I can learn of the procedure, we shall be out there 15 months even if the War finishes soon after we go. I don't mind half so much now I know a definite date is likely with regard to the time we stay.

Well darling, to get on to more pleasant subjects. The bed was very nice last night. I got frozen stiff. We had a ground frost, and everyone was shivering. Even thoughts of you did not warm me up. We have just found another man who has come back disappointed. He is going through it now.

The corporal in our room is a grand fellow. The men will do anything for him although we have not known him long. He is "John Bull", and no respecter of high officers. And he is not afraid to say so in their hearing. He lets us fall out to post letters, have a drink going to company office for parade, and he never forgets, to say, "Stand at ease, stand easy, have a smoke, and if you have no cigarettes, then go through all the motions in drill time". If there is any chance of doing us a good turn or giving advice then he will give it. He fought in the last war, and he has been abroad during most of this one. He has advised me to make you a voluntary allowance when I get East. 5/- per week if I can afford it. So if your pay is made up without word from me, you will know it is for my ultimate benefit. Whatever allowance I may be able to make, please put it in the bank.

Well my dear, it is almost time for post now so I must close now.

With all my love, and still more thanks for a glorious 48 hrs.

Your loving husband

Gerald Xxxxxxxx

Received Aug 12th 41. *Undated letter probably sent August 10th 1941*

My Dear Youngster,

Sunday

     Just a few more lines to let you know I am alright. Having plenty of pack drill, but I can stick it. I am in a section of (Scots crossed out) Kings Own Scottish Borderers who have been transferred to R.A.S.C. recently. I have a job to understand them but they are nice fellows. Have two officers to my section now. Fifty altogether. Our two are fine chaps. By the way with regard to what I spoke about it is the third letter. I could not just remember what I said.

    I have my tropical kit. About the best one in the unit. Made by Christies of London. I want to keep it when this war is over. The best shirts I have ever seen. I am having those when this war business is over.

    I don't know how soon we move, but I will write as soon as possible and let you know. I think ADOLF wants to know a few things and arrangements are being altered continually. I have not much time now as it is a big parade for the Brigadier tomorrow, so I will close now.

    All my love from your loving husband

Gerald Xxxxxxxxxxxx

My Dear Youngster,

     Just a few more lines in haste to let you know I am alright, except for a cold. We stood in full kit for 3 ½ hours in the pouring rain yesterday morning while the Brigadier inspected us. He was what is known as a 'Buggerooter' with a capital 'B' he called the officers everything but gentleman. It is a pity there are not more like him. He would liven any army up. He made men turn out everything in their pack to see if they had the articles inside which he had ordered. He pulled cords to see if gas capes would roll down immediately. I'm fact he asked every man to do something. I was ok. I am in new quarters now. I am in a big empty house almost in Bradford. I wish I lived in it in peace time. It would find you a job to furnish it. We still have boards to lie on. It is also very inconvenient as it is so far from the canteen. If you should get this letter in time on Wednesday I should be glad if you could send me a few coppers. I am not really short but it is costing me quite a lot more now. It will cost me 3/6 per week as long as I am here, to travel to meals. If we walk we are too late to parade. We have really 2 miles each way and only an hour for dinner etc. If we have meals out it is more expensive still. I can't weigh this lot up at all. If we are going away immediately as most people think why have we all had to change billets. Kitbags are to be ready for transport at 8 AM tomorrow (Thursday). I saw a fellow last night who knows George and I wrote a note asking him to come see and see me at 7 tonight and now I can't go out. Still we can have a good rattle in here if he turns up. We have the boat number painted on our kits so it seems as though the time is very near. I don't think we shall get any more leave now but I shall hope against hope until the last moment. If I do not I shall not grieve too much although I am always wanting to see you. I shall go with a memory that I will always remember, whatever part of the world I may be in. That is a memory of 48 brief hours including Aug 5th. And you say the next leave will be even better. I should love to know what you have planned out. You know I like the simple things of life and I am sure you know how to set about giving the reception. Well sweetheart if I do go without seeing you again, please look after yourself and place your trust in the Personage above to keep me safe. I know I will be alright and so do you, but it is a duty that must be carried out. From all I can gather, the time of service abroad is about 15 months so that is better than not knowing when we will get back. And look at the stories I will have to tell you. I hope you don't get used to going to bed and getting warm without me. It is an honour to feel you are really needed. Did you say you won't? That is alright then. While I am on the subject, I don't know how the post will be from now on, so if you should not hear from me for a time in the near future, please don't worry. While I have the opportunity I want to mention another distasteful subject.

That is if anything should happen to me. We are at war and no-one can tell. Well my darling, if I do go under, I want you to know this. I want you to carry on in the way you think is best for yourself. No matter what course you choose to take, think it over well first and do it with my best wishes! I do not regret a moment I have spent with you and I am certain you are worthy of all the happiness you can find. I feel obliged to write that little piece darling, morbid as it seems, but I want you to know that what I think or suffer is nothing to me compared to your happiness. I will write again just as soon as I can. God bless you and keep you safe always.

I am dearest, your loving husband

Gerald x x x x x x x x x x x x x x x x x x x x

Received around 21ˢᵗ Aug

Darling,

I have just received your letter together with one from Mr Digger which I should have received a fortnight ago. Well my dear I like the miniature very much. Where did you have that taken? I wish you would send me a really good photograph. I feel different since I have moved. I should like one or two to show these Highland laddies. We have now been reduced to live in my room. We get on very well together, but I feel I should like to be able to show them what you are really like. They treasure their photographs more than anything. They have many things in common with me. They don't drink, they have little interest in women and they think the world of their wives and their homes. I saw an exhibition this morning that I never want to see repeated. A bit of real highland work. A 'worm' who is stationed in a room below us went out last night and no more has been seen of him until this morning. We went for a wash and shave etc at 5:30am in the wash and bathroom appointed to us. I could not get in. The others tried. One of the Macs got in by force. Darling I hope you never see a prostitute taken naked from a 'soldiers' bed and held up by highlanders for all the world to see. They told her they hadn't seen a bath since the midwife did the job. They are wild devils but they are spotless in habit and morals and I would not be in that fellow's shoes for all the money in the world. They certainly won't stand for that sort of game in any

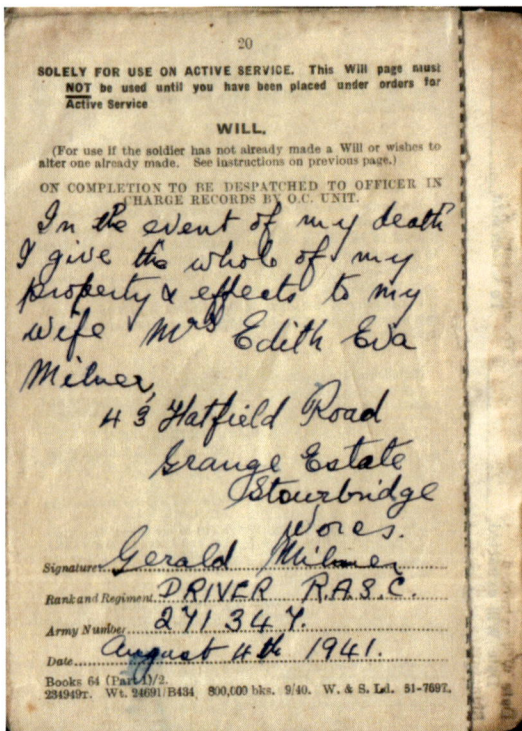

Walter William Milner. Gerald's father (Dad) when he was in the police force before the war

rooms. I feel glad they are like that. Darling it as though we are expecting to move at any minute. We are confined to billet again and the officers say there is no more time left for leave yet we are fiddling about here for hours doing nothing special. Everyone has been compelled to make a will. I have left all my humble possessions to you. If anything should ever happen to me I hope you will let Dad and Mother have any relics they may require, but no squabbling please, that is looking on the morbid side. What I really want you to have is my presence for the rest of our lives. I think that sounds more like the proper way to look at things. Well dear, I am really amongst a bit of Scotland now. They call our section the 'Macs'. I am doing quite well though. None of them will believe I have only been in the army 8 weeks. They think I am leg pulling, anyway I was congratulated by my new officers this morning as being the cleanest and smartest man on parade. Darling, I am writing this in my short dinner time so I shall have to close now or I shall miss the post. I am thinking of you continually so if your ears ever burn you will know what is the cause. I do hope I do not go without seeing you again if it is only for a few hours. I shall because my first leave all my life. The more I think of it the more I am determined to keep the promise I made you. God bless you and keep you safe until I see you again. I am your loving husband

Gerald x x x x x x x x x x x x x

About Aug 21ˢᵗ Undated letter but probably August 21ˢᵗ when written.   T/271347
   R.A.S.C.
   Draft R.H.F.G.F.
   Army Post Office 1000
   Thursday Dinner time

Darling,

       I feel I must write these few lines while I have a few moments to spare before going to dinner. I wrote you yesterday, but from now on my address will be as above unless you hear from me otherwise. The old address will still find me but the above will be much quicker. I am expecting to leave at any moment now. Breakfast is at 2.30 am in the morning so it seems like a long journey. My thoughts will be with you dear. Please don't worry about me. I realise all the dangers of the sea and the East that will face me but I have full confidence in the navy. One of our chaps shot himself yesterday. All some of the men think of seems to be torpedoes. I don't know whether he was one of them. I've just heard another one has followed suit. I don't know whether it is right or not. Anyway, they have taken all rifles and ammo from us. I reckon that is to prevent an epidemic. Had another V.D. inspection yesterday. I'm beginning to lose count of them now. We have to go through the gas chamber without respirators this afternoon. All kit is being collected today. Please do not pass on any of this to outsiders as we want a sporting chance to get there. I saw George last night. We went to the pictures, but it was poor, so we came out half way and went for supper. It only wanted you to complete the table. Army life was forgotten for a moment. I don't know if I shall see him again, but I will endeavour to let him know what happens to me as we shall not be allowed to write for some time according to orders just published.

     (Rumour we expect to be on the water 13 weeks)

Well, my darling, I really must close now although I could go on writing all day. If you don't hear from me again for a time, just keep that chin at the same angle and keep smiling the same as I shall. Will you let them know at home as I may not get a chance to write, Remember me to Lucy & all.

"Till we meet again" is just being played by one of the Scots

So I will close on those few notes. God bless you.

I remain your Ever loving husband

Gerald XXXXXXXXX

A letter missing written on Wednesday 13ᵗʰ or 20ᵗʰ August

Received August 25ᵗʰ 1941 *Only possible dates are August 14ᵗʰ or 21ˢᵗ 1941*

Please Write Address as opposite

T/271347
Driver Milner G.
No. 14 Section
R.A.S.C.
Draft R.H.F.G.F.
Army Post Office 1000
Friday afternoon

My Dear Wife,

        Well dearest, here I am at last, all set for foreign lands. I am writing this on board ship. I don't know how soon it will be delivered to you but I expect it will be delayed for a few days from what the officers have already told us. We are on a splendid ship. I don't know what the name of it is yet and in any case I don't expect I would be allowed to tell you. All the rules and regulations seem very vague to everyone just at present. If I did write it for you I suppose the censor would cross it all out so it is the same either way. Well my dear, I am awfully disappointed that we could not get than forty eight hours leave. At the finish it was just one mad rush. I know you will feel it keenly. I am sure I do. I have very mixed feelings just at the moment. It was alright until the lads started singing "There'll always be an England" and the Scots piped up with "Auld Lang Syne". When I got on board it was like being in a new world. How I wish you were here with me. I know what you would do. The same as I did. Examine and discover everything about your cabin. I have been like a child with a new toy. Everything inside is spotlessly clean. I think it must have been a luxury boat in peace time. I envy the people who could afford to travel in it regularly. There are only two of us in this cabin. Myself and one of the Scots boys I wrote and told you of. The rest of them are in the next cabin and we have just discovered a sliding panel that connects the two cabins. Our corporal is next door too. He is a Birmingham lad. There will be plenty of devilment going on before long. McCoy of Glasgow Rangers is in there too. We are lucky being in the same part of the boat. And darling what do you think I have found at long last. A <u>Real</u> bed. I think I shall be getting used to it soon. It seems years since I slept on feathers last. I hope I do not feel too uncomfortable after such a sudden surprise. I was resigning myself to sleeping on boards for weeks yet. I suppose the roll of the ship will about upset all that comfort though. I don't expect you will hear for some time after this letter reaches you whether the rolling affects me, but somehow I don't think it will. Well sweetheart, I have just been and had my tea. The mess room is about the size of the Town Hall. I never dreamt they had such affairs inside so plain looking exteriors. If it were not for leaving you behind after so many happy years, I think I should enjoy it all, torpedoes, bombs or anything else included. I used to think how brave it was of the men to go abroad, yet I have felt <u>no</u> tremor of personal fear so far. (Interrupting, we have just discovered HOT water. What a shave we'll have tonight). The men I have every respect for are the crew. They just have to keep on doing it time and time again. When I get back home, in the months to come, and I feel confident I shall, what tales I shall have to tell. I hope these lads who are with me will be lucky too. I want you to meet them when we get back. I know you won't fail to take an instant liking to them. When you come up with lads who will divide their cigarettes into portions so that they are equal for everyone concerned you know what to expect in an emergency. One of the boys, McCoy was "squirted in the arm" as he called it. One man took his kit bag in addition to his own while I felt compelled to carry two rifles. As long as we keep together we will be alright.

        Well dearest it seems like time for post aboard, so I must close wishing you all the best in every respect during my absence, and kindly wish them the same at home as I shan't have time to write at present.

Darling I send you all my love, and my only hope is that I can do it again for August 5th next year. What a celebration. Remember me to Lucy, Mrs Taylor, Billie and all our many friends who may ask after me. Farewell for the next few months dear, keep your chin high and I will do the same, whatever the coming dangers may be. I shall be thinking of you always. And my promise will be kept, never fear. I will write again as soon as possible. With regard to my business I know you will do your best to keep things going until my return. I think the supply situation should ease a little as winter approaches. Will you ask Mother if she can possibly come to some arrangement with Mr Butler in regard to the rabbits. Also please do not forget the letters I spoke to you about during my leave. It is just a reminder while I think of it although I should know better than have to remind you of anything. The boot is usually on the other foot.

Well youngster I really must close, although I feel like writing for hours. Good night sweetheart,

All my love from your husband

Gerald Xxxxxxxxxxx

Mr & Mrs Guy Butler of Church Farm, Churchill, Worcs. Taken in 1962 at his son Gerald's wedding to Ann. Eva made the button holes, dress sprays, and bouquets for the occasion. Gerald used to shoot rabbits on his farm before the war.

The SS Strathnaver

CHAPTER 3
At Sea

NOTES ON MY ARMY SERVICE BY GERALD MILNER
We sailed at a few seconds after midnight of the 13/14th August 1941

T/271347
Driver Milner G.
Address as before
At sea

My Dear Wife,

In days to come when memories are recalled by a good old English fireside I shall be able to tell you the full story of my adventures. Until then, unfortunately, the censor has the upper hand. You should already have had my first letter, and this will be a continuation. For days on end we saw nothing but water, but that same water was always a source of interest and very often of great surprise to all of us. We saw sharks trailing in the wake of our ship. Flying fish of all sizes came out of the sea in thousands. Then we stood on deck trying to get some indication of the direction we were travelling. Then at long last we reached a haven of comparative safety in the shape of land. We have travelled many miles of English countryside together in the past, but I can assure you there is nothing to touch this place for beauty and grandeur. As we sailed steadily along to find anchorage, the loveliness of this strange land was revealed. All our wonderings and expectations were shaken to the foundations. Blue mountains in the background. Then more mountains which could be plainly seen, all topped by fleecy white clouds as they floated by. These mountains were, surprisingly enough, covered by natural vegetation which was of an extremely dark green. I really think we had expected to find just plain rocks. A narrow strip of golden beach and water like a beautiful lagoon completed the picture (with the exception of scenes that would not pass the censor). To be a "globe trotter" has always been one of my weaknesses as you know. Well so far, I know my instincts have not been wrong. I am looking forward anxiously to the continuation of the story. There is an old fable that when a man reaches this country it "gets him". Somehow I feel it to be true in my case. Then all around the ship is further interest provided by men with tiny boats. The men throw pennies and they just leave their boat, dive into the sea and usually come up a long way off with the coins between their teeth.

At a Bank Holiday Fete in England they would draw a tremendous crowd. I wonder it has not been tried before. You should hear the lads teaching them to swear, and the speed with which they learn. If someone throws a ½d they come up again with disgust and say another "B Glasgow tanner". For the price of ½d one of the boatmen was persuaded to take his shorts off. You never heard anything like it was on deck. Then with a great smile the same fellow offered to bring his sister for sixpence. I have enjoyed myself so much lately that I can't bear to think of leaving this boat. I only wish you were here to see it all.

Since I wrote that last little piece the fun has got better and better. On a boat below us were three darkies who gloried in the names of Ajax, Amarah, and Sergeant John, ex Royal Navy and wise in the ways of British troops. He lined up the two youngsters, and started to give them drill instruction. I must say Sergeant John's drill was "Red hot" but I am afraid his two pupils were not very apt. Every time he was making progress with them the lads threw down a shower of coppers. I am afraid the drill was forgotten until all the coins were picked up. They kept up the same procedure for a long time and I for one was sorry when it was all over. They must have collected several £s. Another strange thing that occurs in this part of the globe is the change from day to night. You may not believe it, but if we look out of our porthole, then have a quarter of an hour for supper clear sunshine has gone and complete blackness has descended.

Well my dear, since I started the last two pages night has arrived, so I will turn to other subjects. There is a possibility that we shall get leave during the voyage. I don't know when of where, but I shall probably be enjoying it when this letter is being posted. Of course there are a lot of "ifs".

If we get into trouble on the ship we may get put on fatigues or on the other hand we may get leave and pay stopped. The most serious offences are blackout, late for parade, or smoking after hours or in prohibited places. I don't think it should be too difficult for one to keep out of those troubles. Then of course there is the financial side of the occasion. If I were in touch with home it would be alright, but that dream is smashed.

My pal and I are doing without everything except our tobacco and bare necessities in order to have a few pounds to spend. I think it will be worth the sacrifice. I must say however, that we have to keep a firm upper lip and eyes front as we walk past counters full of lemonade, chocolate, oranges, apples, confectionery etc. never mind, as long as we can get out cigarettes we shan't mind. While I think of it, please don't forget those photographs if you have not already sent then. I only have the small snap with me.

Since I ended the foregoing chapter, many hours have elapsed, and many leagues of water traversed. It has been a strange journey altogether and I suppose as time slips by, it will become still more strange. The ever changing picture is a source of continuous interest. If only we were permitted to use a camera and keep a diary. However, as I cannot afford to prejudice my leave, I must stick to wishful thinking. Our officers ran another "Bee" last week, between our section and that same one we competed against the last time. We won in grand style. I failed on one answer only, and I tipped up very badly on that one. As it is to do with our voyage, I shall have to keep it for a later date.

I have just read in a book that October born people are birds of travel. I think the fellow who wrote that must have known something.

We had a whist drive on board recently. I lost the last three hands and a prize. Two more are being held next week. I hope to make that 291 prize list into 300 before long. I have a ticket for another concert tonight. If it's half as good as the last I know I shall enjoy it.

During the last few days I have been running into trouble for some unknown reason. I got put on a police job for the rest of the voyage. I can tell you it is no picnic, and I was thankful when one of my officers got me off it. I went to bed that night and woke up to a strange event. I had evidently dropped the catch on my cabin door. Someone tried the door during the night, could not get in, and I was later told that I and my Scots pal would be on a charge. We had to report for trial, but after waiting quite a long time nothing happened except we were told to appear again the next morning. This we did. Still no charge. Our officer stood by us right through and we were eventually sent before the O.C. for a severe censuring. When we got before him, imagine our surprise when he congratulated us on the cleanliness of our cabin, told us to keep it up, and then gave us friendly advice on leaving the door open for hygiene purposes. There is an old saying that doubt is the worst torture of the mind. Well I know it to be true. I don't ever remember being so miserable in my life as I was in those two days. I always promised you I would keep out of any trouble, but I never imagined anything like that ever happening.

I have been to the concert previously mentioned and it was extremely good. If it were completely revised, I think it would just squeeze past the BBC censors. Any way the lads thoroughly enjoyed it and after all, that is all that matters. Up till now we have had quite a good voyage in regard to the sea. For several hours now we have been running through very heavy waters. Quite a lot of the lads who thought they had got used to it, are now finding their stomachs turning over. I am glad to say it has not affected me yet.

Please remember me to my many friends, and also find enclosed a few lines for Lucy. I think she deserves them. Just keep your chin up. God bless you and keep you safe until I return. All for now, from your loving husband

Gerald Xxxxxxxxxxxx

1941

My Dear Wife,

I owe you many apologies for this letter before it ends. I have already written one and crossed out most of it as the new censorship regulations come to my notice. It looked so bad eventually, that I have decided to start anew. You have previously told me that I have made my letters very interesting. Well this is where I begin to fail you. I am writing this very many miles from the old country, and up to present our voyage has been most interesting.

Shaving with hot water is one great asset to this ship. Plenty of good food is another. Tobacco is cheap. Fruit and confectionery are plentiful and quite reasonable. I have a real bed to sleep on. I don't have to rise until 6.30 am . No queuing up for meals, and only one and a half hours physical training and boat drill per day. What more can a soldier ask. Some of the lads are so pleased they say they won't worry if we never reach port. For myself it does not seem right that I should be on a trip like this by myself, after we have gone everywhere together for so many years. We have passed through the more dangerous waters now and we are allowed to sleep with our clothes off. We are running into hot weather now and we are wearing our tropical kit for the first time.

So far I have not been affected by either sea or sun. I must not cry too loud though, for we have a very long way to go yet. We get quite a lot of amusement from the Lascars who form part of the crew. They are all shapes and sizes, and their colour varies from light brown to ebony. The dresses they wear are gorgeous and flowery, and their hats would put any Paris model in the shade. I heard one of them bidding for a watch this morning. He appeared to have great difficulty in understanding the English language, but when the soldiers asked him £3 for it, the Lascar's scathing reply would have made any "old sweat" blush.

While I think of it, will you please see George Calver, or Bert Wilkes and ask them to start the Austin up occasionally during my absence. That is if no one else decides to try their hand at driving it. Remember me to Lucy, Mrs Taylor & Billy, Capt. Rigby R.A.S.C. if you see him. Just tell him to hurry up and come this way. Also Mrs Chapman[1] and all the rest of the folks. Tell Donald that if he does get out this way I shall expect to see a crown instead of "3 pips". I can give him a "present arms" then. What a situation I seem to be in. Donald a Captain, Ron Bate a Lieut. Len Cowley Second Lieut. Ken Heathcock 2nd /Lt[2] and

---

[1] Mrs Chapman was a neighbour who lived at 43 Brook Street.

[2] I believe Cpt. Rigby RASC, Donald, Ron Bate, Len Cowley and Ken Heathcock were all in the Stourbridge Home Guard.

myself with the least Army experience going overseas first to get a welcome ready for them. Somehow I think I shall meet them during my travels. The only trouble is, with the exception of Donald, I do not know what units they are in at present. If I am lucky enough to drop across only one of them I will let you know.

Well my dear, it is nearly time to go and draw a few coppers which have not been earned but are never the less badly needed. For the first time in my life I am nearly "on the rocks". I think you had better send me a few coppers by wireless or something equally as quick. It is hopeless for me to try and make any arrangements as I have not the foggiest notion what will happen when I reach my destination. As far as I can see the only thing to do is to continue as before and trust to luck that some of the parcels will catch up with me. I should think some of them should already be on their way, as you addressed them all to the draft.

Received 10/- to last me a week. I was almost ashamed to take it. I have one consolation however. It will help to balance up what I went through at Sutton Veny.

After that place, it is like a breath of spring to have Officers and N.C.O.s who treat you as a human being. I have seen one of my old corporals on board. He is a sergeant now. He tells me that the man who is afraid of his own shadow has wangled his way out of this trip after all. You know the one I mean. I wonder what you would have thought of me if I had done the same. Will you write and let George know I have gone abroad. As you know, I met him in Bradford. His officers are on a special course and he arranged to meet me on the evening after I left. I had no means of informing him what was happening and I expect he is wondering what it is all about. If you will do that for me he will understand. He was confident that I should not leave England for a very long time.

Well with all the many shoulder badges of rank among all my old friends I have a feeling of pride that I am the first one to blaze the trail to warmer climates. What an Aug 5th we will all have when this lot is over. I have promised myself I will break a 16 year old record and have a drink with the rest of them to celebrate. I would not mind betting that "Curly" will want an AMBULANCE instead of a car to get home on that night. Or should I have said morning. It is a long time to wait but if I should not be back home on that date, please don't forget to celebrate. I know I shall wherever I may be.

We have a fellow on board who must like soldiers. Anyway he gets jiggering about with the clock and about every other day we have an extra hour in bed. I hope we keep travelling in the same direction. Most of the things that happen on this ship are like Grimm's Fairy Tales. They certainly seem too good to last.

While I think of it will you let me know occasionally how the business is going on, also the poultry, pigs, ducks etc and the garden and allotments? I seem to have left such a tremendous lot of work behind, but I have no fears as to how it will be carried out in my absence. If you need any advice with regard to the gardening, ask Dad or Mr Calver senior. I know they will help you. Another day which must not be named has now arrived. My partner and I got up at 5.30 am cleaned sink, water pipes, five mirrors, dressing table, wardrobe and scrubbed floor. We made the beds, washed and showered and had breakfast at 8 am (anything but Greenwich Time). We had nothing else to do until 2 p.m. except take to the sea air and sun. How I wish I had my books here. I miss them more than anything. The only books we seem to be able to get on the ship are all fiction. Wish I had my "Seven pillars of Wisdom" to read on my wanderings. Please don't try to give me a surprise by sending it. I should hate to think of it being lost. We had a "knowledge contest" on deck today. I wrote about 150 questions and acted as "ref.". It went off quite well, but I am afraid the old brain box is getting a trifle rusty. I could not think of all the "hot ones" from memory. Still 150 is not too bad to begin with. I could almost see my old no's 2, 3, 4 &5 sat there. About half an hours P.T. has been our only parade today. The decks are a tremendous size. Some of the fellows get quite humorous about things. One said he was sure he took the wrong turning at the same corner yesterday. And then you see fellows looking at the water and calmly discussing a wave. Having a dispute as to whether it was the same one they saw yesterday. In the next cabin to mine we have a bald Scot. He says he will throw himself overboard when he hears a new joke about his hair. They told him today that it was love's labour lost to brush a bald head. They have just told him his name in German. (Herr) Hair von Missing. He has not gone over the side yet. Well I must soon end my letter as I am sending it for early censorship. I believe it will then be posted at port of call sometime in the near future. Before I left I made a voluntary promise. It still holds good. I will only add that the standard I set myself in civilian life will be maintained to the best of my ability during my Army career. As long as I keep to that straight and narrow path I do not think either of us will have undue cause for worry.

My only ambition is to work to get back the "tapes" I lost when I joined the Army. I do not think it will be for a long time yet though as everything is so uncertain, even when and where we eventually land. I will end now with all my love from your husband

Gerald Xxxxxxxxxxx
one of those for Lucy.

P.S. As incoming mail will probably be censored, please use your discretion as to what you write. I learn that if letters require to much censoring they are placed in the fire and I do not want that to happen to any of my mail.

The place this letter is written about is Cape Town

My Dear Wife,

No more can I say I am sad, lonely and far away from home. On the contrary I have had adventures that read like a fairy tale and I am certain I can tell you the story without any interference from my friend the censor.

First of all let me say that my previous letters have probably been subjected to considerable delay in the interests of the human cargo of this ship (including yours truly). I know that it is absolutely essential that this should happen, so please do not be too harsh in your judgement of the authorities.

Now for the rest of the story from wonderland. We arrived at a certain port, and after special lectures on various subjects including our behaviour, our personal smartness, and those eternal mysteries, the constant females, we went ashore. We were allowed ashore each day during our stay, and I can assure you it was with a deep feeling of regret that I left on the next part of my journey.

As I walked down the main street completely lost in wonder at what I saw, a voice suddenly broke into my dreams and asked me if I would like to go for a ride. Remembering all I had heard in the lectures, and realising that the voice belonged to a female, I gave the matter due consideration. As she was a middle aged person, I made up my mind, threw caution to the winds, and let valour become the better part of discretion by way of a change. What followed afterwards is about beyond my powers of description. I was taken through a very dangerous area and eventually after many suspicious thoughts ended up in a residential quarter.

First of all I was given a square meal. Almost too square for an appetite of my capacity. It started with a thick slice of ham, a nameless local savoury, new potatoes and just to finish it two real eggs. Fruit before and then afterwards they brought me fresh pineapple, oranges, fresh peaches and apricots. I had just enjoyed that lot when they brought me another plate of ham etc. Like a good soldier, I endeavoured to keep up the traditions of the Army, and as the news editor said, with great pressure on space I eventually succeeded. By this time the battle dress was getting fairly tight around the waist.

I was then taken to the pictures. After that a whirl of sight seeing and then the crowning episodes. Yes, luck was really with me. I was taken to the home of a young lady from whom you should have received a letter by the time this reaches you. The wife of a high ranking officer in the Middle East. We were later joined by the Governor of a large province, together with his wife, and I am now wondering if all that happened to me from that moment can still be true. In a very high powered car I have travelled hundreds of miles in this queer country. The usual speed is generally in the region of 70 mph.

In between deep breaths and violent shakings, at various intervals we stopped and examined the flora and fauna of our immediate surroundings. We saw arum lilies growing as profusely as blue bells in England. Miles on end of acacia woods in full bloom (mimosa as it is known at home). Great tufts of prickly cactus, giant tree ferns, and majestic palms.

As I got into country where white men are not to welcome, I came across wild canaries and budgies in thousands. Most marvellous of all was the tiny weaving bird. I watched them for a long time. One bird sits in a tree and weaves a nest slowly round itself and the tip of a slender branch while its mate brings the necessary material. When it is finished it is just large enough for the bird to enter. In one tree I saw several hundred nests hanging upside down, side by side, and looking for all the world like a great exhibition of Chinese lanterns. In years to come I know I shall class that scene as one of the most remarkable sights I have found during my travels.

Another amazing sight was hundreds of thousands of acres of peach trees in full bloom. It has to be seen to be believed. Then I saw in the shadow of a great mountain, nearly a million acres of grape vines. The fruit will not be ready for harvesting until January. I wish I could be here then. They are sold at four large bunches for one penny.

I could have bought oranges at fifty for one and sixpence, but I had eaten so many free ones that I just did not bother about them. Then they have a new fruit coming into production. It is a cross between an apple and a lemon, and strange as it may seem it is a first class article.

Still farther inland I came across dilapidated motor tractors drawing worn out ploughs across great tracts of country. Still farther and the nature of the surrounding country changed completely. I saw vast territories looking like a tremendous lawn. My curiosity aroused, I stopped. On examination I was very surprised to find it was wheat. About 18 inches high. Pasture land ran in a strip right down the centre and a flock of sheep and goats were feeding there. Before I could get back into the car a whole cloud of picaninnies appeared out of the blue yelling "big Soldier" continually. It seemed to be the only two English words they knew. It was all very amusing.

From there I travelled into more dangerous country. On the way I saw ploughs being drawn by teams of mules, and in the last place I visited the primitive oxen were being used. I must say that considering the means at their disposal, these people make a very neat appearance of their cultivated land.

In these parts I saw tiny crosses in all sorts of queer places. I was informed that they were graves. While living these people stake a claim anywhere they fancy, and when they die, they are buried in that particular spot.

On my way back I saw millions of beautiful daffodils, and just a few cannibal orchids. Geraniums of all shapes, colours and sizes were growing wild in profusion. A noticeable fact was the size of some of these geraniums. They were almost as large as a laurel bush. Then there were strange plants like large skeleton currant bushes. And on the very tip of each branch was a tuft of leaves exactly like the ice plants found in England.

Reaching a distant part of the sea shore I saw the local inhabitants wading about catching cray fish. As soon as they get a bag or basket full they take them to a place to be cooked and canned.

The sands on the beaches are of a glistening silver nature. As we came into port we saw them and from the distance we thought at first it was snow. Personally I prefer the beautiful golden sands at another port I wrote about. As we gradually got nearer the town again I noticed the differences in the plants and shrubs. At first glance everything seems to be the same as in England. Yet the hedges and trees are entirely different. Some of the immense bunches of flowers I had offered to me were magnificent. I wish I could get a boat load to my business at the present time. I think they would soon be doubling my bank a/c.

My keenest disappointment in a land which seems to produce everything was that the roses were not yet in bloom. I wanted to find a few more specials to go among my collection. By the way, please do not prune my trees until March 25th and cut them all back to within two buds of the stock. I think if you are careful they should be alright. With regard to the latest addition "Chieftain" please leave that until the 9th and 10th of April. Sorry to have to butt in with these instructions, but you know the value of the collection, and after all, there will not always be an armed conflict in progress.

After the first day was over, I managed to get back to the ship by the turn of midnight, highly elated though I have still kept strictly tee total, and wondering what the future held. Well my dear, quite a lot of the foregoing happened on different days, but I have written it as interestingly as I can.

In the middle of all that I had quite an unpleasant experience. I took a bus to visit my friends and the journey was about five miles. I asked the conductor to put me down by a certain well known store. Although I am a stranger on this dark continent of Africa, I had an idea that I was on unfamiliar territory. Eventually he told me I had reached my destination, and that the place I wanted was just round the corner. Imagine my consternation when I discovered I was in a forbidden area. I think it was about the most unsavoury looking place I have ever been in. At that moment I would have given all I possessed for "old faithful" with a bayonet on the end. I decided I had to make the best of a nasty job, so I stuck my chest out, marched resolutely forward, avoiding doorways and alleys as much as possible, and got into places growing even worse. I think the scenes I saw there are better left undescribed. After what seemed to be years, the miracle happened. A white man came to my rescue. He told me rather sorrowfully that he had degraded himself in the eyes of decent people, and that the least he could do was to lead a fellow countryman to safety. This he eventually did, much to my relief, and I arrived to keep my appointment exactly one hour late. When I look back on it all, it seems like a fiction, but every word is true. At least I have had a glimpse of Eastern life and native beggars as they really are.

It is all over now and I am very sorry. During my stay it did not cost me a farthing, and anything I wanted was mine for the asking. Luggage room had to be the deciding factor. And hung in our ship is a message "The conduct of the men was exemplary". We are proud of that. Do you remember the H.G. commander using similar words in his speech when I left to join the Army?

I am afraid however that my conduct at the moment is anything but exemplary. Sometime after we left port we ran into mountainous seas, and any loose articles were thrown all over the place. I was in a relay race team during that part of the voyage and as I was tearing along the deck, the ship heeled at a very steep angle, and I heeled with it. Result, a badly torn muscle above the right knee. The pain was very acute for a couple of days, but after attention by the M.O. I can hobble about now. I had to use all my powers of persuasion to keep out of hospital. The M.O. told me today that it should be alright again in a fortnight.

I must close now or the censor will be having a heart attack. Let Lucy read this letter to save me writing a further epistle and remember me to Mrs Taylor and young Billie. Please pay for the drinks I wrote about in the letter to Lucy, from my a/c. Also please give the usual party at Christmas on my behalf during my absence. Necessary cash to come from the same source. I shall be thinking of you all on that day wherever I may be. While on that subject,

"many happy returns" and if there is anything you need, get that at some time. If I don't stop I shall end in the bankruptcy court, so I will end with all my love from your husband
  Gerald Xxxxxxxxxx

LETTER FROM A FRIEND IN CAPETOWN

6 Leerhampton Court
Main Road
Kenilworth Cape
S.Africa

Dear Mrs Milner

    My friend Mrs Traill and I lately had the pleasure of entertaining your husband during his short stay here. Mine is a big organization called the Women's Auxiliary Services – of whom the members try to arrange some sort of entertainment to the men in any Convoy that calls at Capetown. We were so glad to have your husband and a friend of his called Booth to supper and to have some first hand news of home.

You may have another letter with news of your husband as I believe someone took him and friends of his for a drive before they came here – but in any case may I wish you many happy returns of the day for November 2nd – as perhaps your husband's letter may not arrive in time and he so wanted you to have the good wishes – your husband was looking very well – and was most cheerful – they had apparently had an excellent voyage – I can sympathise with you over the parting – I suppose we all have to go through it these days –

My husband is somewhere in the Desert in Egypt. – I was living in Cairo for 2½ years and was moved down here last spring – and have two small children – and most Army families have moved. People in S Africa are most kind and the country is beautiful, but it is hard to be really happy – with a husband in the war zone in one direction and my mother in a much bombed district at home – though it is grand for the children. We are full of admiration for all of you at home – and the wonderful spirit every where -- & wish we were there to take our share.

Let us hope the reward will come sooner than we think – with end to all these partings –

Your husband also gave me the address of his parents 52 Brook Street, Stourbridge- I wonder whether you would send them on this note – as I am sure they too would be glad to know he was well and in good spirits.

Your husband is sure to tell you about this short stay at the Cape so I shall leave the description to him. It certainly is a beautiful part of the world.

I hope that your business is doing well & that you will soon get very good news from your husband- when he has reached his destination.

Good luck to all

Yours sincerely

Patricia Saunders

I was particularly glad to meet your husband and his friend – as they both belong to my husband's corps Best of luck to them.

LETTER FROM A FRIEND IN CAPE TOWN

NORWAY
Ferguson St
Plumstead
Cape Town
S.Africa
Sept 15 1941

My dear Mrs Milner,

      I am sure this will come as a great surprise but having met your husband during his stay at Cape Town I am a war worker belonging to the Wifuberg Auxiliary we have many branches. It was at the Wifuberg Canteen I met him. It is our duty to help the boys when they arrive here. In the afternoon they were taken out for drives to homes for afternoon tea then they come back to the canteen for supper & in the evening there was a dance. I asked him to meet me the next day being a Saturday my hubby being home could take them for a run I arranged for four but only your hubby with his pal came so I asked another two. So off they went. I am sure your hubby will tell you all, they were able to pick arum lilies they grow wild in the millions although they are just about finishing & our country is just one blaze with wattle, we were hoping to meet the next day as I said to my chief I am having tomorrow off. Her reply was I don't know. So much about that but my hubby was going to take them for a 100 mile run in a different direction and they were to come to my home for supper. Being Sunday there is always a concert for the troops & from this he can be spared. My work is entertaining, canteen, knitting, visiting the sick & wounded. I am also a warden in the ARP (Air Raid Precaution) although we term ours as Civilian Protection Society CPS. I do a days work at the Soldiers Sailors & Airmen's Club. I am a cashier here. Now my dear I think you will agree with me it is just a little difficult to write somebody you haven't met, but being a wife & a mother I can just imagine the longing for a few lines from our loved one. I have one child a girl of 18 years. I'd be very pleased to hear from you at any time. May I say I will try to assure as I have many to assure back in their convoy. I have fifty two to write & receive from the boys up East & North but in due course everybody will be assured. My phone has just rung asking me to keep on Saturday afternoon at the Air Command display so you see dear I am doing my best for this war. May it soon come to an end enabling all the loved ones to be reunited, with our very best wishes from all at Norway Cheerio for the present
    I remain
    Yours very sincerely
    Frances George

CHAPTER 4
October 12th 1941 to December 31st 1941
Somewhere in the Desert

Egypt

03/10/1941 General Auchinleck was in charge of the 8th Army and his field commander was Sir Alan Cunningham. The Western Desert Air Force had 16 fighters, 8 bombers and 3 reconnaissance squadrons and they were to provide the air support for the soldiers on the ground. The army was equipped with 713 tanks armed with guns and had a further 200 in reserve. "Operation Crusader" was the name given for the planned attack on the 15th and 21st Panzer Division aimed at destroying the enemy tank strength. It was approved by Auchinleck on November 3rd 1941 and was scheduled to commence on 11th November. 30 Corps would then envelop the axis forces from the south and advance on Tobruk.

Meanwhile the Italians under the command of Italian Supreme Commander in North Africa, General Ettore Bastico had decided to attack and overthrow Tobruk and the Afrika Korps under Rommel were to engage and neutralise the British on the Sidi Omar front. Gerald Milner arrived in the Middle East just as these decisions were being taken.

NOTES ON MY ARMY SERVICE BY GERALD MILNER

We duly arrived in Egypt (known to most soldiers as Egg-Wiped) and went to a holding depot at *Geneifa*. Transferred to No. 2 Heavy Repair Shops for a few weeks to acclimatise, and finally "up the blue" to join 287 Coy R.A.S.C. where the vehicles bore the sign P (P ammunition) The Germans were "Stonking", (Desert term for steady shelling) This soon turned into a mighty enemy attack to drive a wedge between *Tobruk* and *Bir Hacheim*. Tobruk fell. Bir Hacheim held for nearly a fortnight and the great chess game began. The German Army knocking us back mile after mile, but always conscious of the thorn in their side at Bir Hacheim.

Date order 12 – 10 –41. Received 10 – 12 – 41

T/271347
Driver Milner G
No. 1 Company
R.A.S.C Base
Depot
M.E.F.

My Dearest Youngster,

Just a few more lines to keep your mind at rest in regard to my welfare. Just at the present moment I am feeling extremely well. The life here is pretty tough after life in England but I cannot say I dislike it. I am rapidly getting used to it and I suppose before long I shall be getting conceited and judging myself to be the veteran warrior. One good point out here is the great latitude allowed the men. As long as we behave ourselves we are allowed to do many things we could not do at home. I have my breakfast long before you are up and many times I have thought of you dreaming peacefully while I am marching across a sea of sand and dust. Those thoughts of home are a great consolation to me and I am only sorry I have no photographs with me. I hope you have remembered to send me a few. As soon as I get a chance I will get some snaps and send you. I can't afford a camera at the present so I shall have to try and borrow one or get to a photographer. Well darling, owing to the censorship you will have to be content with shorter letters than usual but I will endeavour to make them fairly regular. I am sitting on my kitbag in our tent to write this and in a very short space of time I am going for my afternoon swim in the briny. At present I am in with a very good crowd of fellows and if you could hear some of the evening sing song you would never think such a thing as war existed. We may be far from home but we are certainly not downhearted. How is everything at home? Alright I hope. And how is Lucy? Just see that she behaves herself while I am away. I suppose I shall be finding her married or something when I get back. I reckon the garden will be looking pretty bleak by the time you get this letter. Please don't neglect it in spring though. Make a good a job of it as you did this time and it will be alright. The only thing I am anxious for now is the end of all this war, so that I can get back to you and live as a peaceful citizen and a good husband. One other thing I want to say. Before I left England you had a feeling you would like to try and come out to me. My only remarks now are 'forget it'. These are no places for women. As I wrote before, if I should 'get a packet' I want you to do what you think is right. You know I shall look after myself to the best of my ability, but I am now on active service and the danger is always present. If I should be one of the unlucky ones, my best wishes and love go with you. Try and think kindly of me.

Those are morbid thoughts but they are bound to creep in when one thinks of a good home. I don't want you to brood on it but I feel it to be my duty to write it. A lot of the fellows are not even bothering to write home. I don't think they can have a wife like I have as they would want to write every day. Well youngster, I will close now, praying that I may soon be permitted to make a surprise return, and sending you all my love and kisses.

Your loving husband
Gerald

x x x x x x x x x x x x x x x x x x x x x x x x x x x x x x x x
A few of those are for Lucy

(On Reverse of letter)

Just going to enjoy a nice game of football. Pretty warm though.

Dated 13th Oct 41. *Received 11 – 12 – 41*

My Dear Youngster,

Just a few more pages just to let you know that I am still alive and kicking. You should have received some of my previous letters by now and today I have spent my last few coppers on a cable to you. As soon as I get paid again I shall send you an airgraph. You should have received both these and probably several later ones by the time you get this letter as I shall send it by sea. If I write fairly regularly by the various services available from here you should be sure of a fairly consistent flow of correspondence. To resume from where my last letter ended. My knee has now almost completely recovered, although it was very miserable for several weeks. I can assure you I do not want to travel through any more seas as rough as those were. You must please excuse my writing but I am drafting this letter under similar conditions to those existing when I did my first period of training. I have no grumbles about it so far. If I never get any worse treatment than this I shall be quite alright. My only regret is that I cannot tell you the full story of my travels. There are many things I have seen and done, but if I describe them I have great doubts whether the censor would pass them, as it is easy to give places away by description without actually naming them. One of my most exciting experiences was to be picked for the crew of a boat in a race. My unit raced against representative crews of every unit with the company. I hang my head in shame when I tell you we came in second, beaten by about two feet. I am just getting rid of the blisters but I thoroughly enjoyed every minute of it. You will understand the blisters when I tell you the crews raced in lifeboats with about four dozen men in each as passengers. It was most exciting

(sorry I missed a line in the darkness)

when the boat rode the crest of a wave, then dipped down and gave everyone a shower bath. I really appreciated the bath as the heat in that part of the world has been almost beyond endurance. Just after the race the weather broke and we had one of the worst thunderstorms I have ever experienced. I am writing this part of the letter just outside my tent in the cool of an eastern evening. .The light is failing rapidly and a splendid moon will be illuminating everything very shortly. There are two pictures in Jim Hughes window and they are very similar, except that I am a soldier and not a redskin brave. One thing I shall have to get used to is sand.

Another is the intense heat of the sun. Of course the greatest enemy to be fought out here is disease, and I can assure you it is remarkable how clean everything is kept considering the conditions. All the cooking utensils, the food and the mess tents are kept spotlessly clean. Before I landed, I can honestly say I expected to find very primitive conditions existing. I have altered my ideas. Of course I can't say I like using a razor at 5:30 AM with a cold water tap to do the lathering and I cannot truthfully say that sand is the best foundation for a bed but I suppose those are just minute discomforts. By the way I was told an amusing story on arrival here. It was 'If incendiary bombs fall, you run to the Company Office to get a bag of sand to put them out'. Another humorous story which is true. One of the men in my tent was being interviewed in front of me. The Cpl. asked him if he was interested in any sport. He said the only game he was interested in was getting back to London as soon as possible. The Cpl. marked him on his sport chart 'SWIMMING'. I don't think he will ever live that down. I am in with a crowd of very decent fellows at present. You should see us at night. It is just like the tent in 'Journeys End' only instead of drink it is just sober wit. When you get fellows from various counties all together there is bound to be plenty of leg pulling but so far they do not seem to have found much wrong with Worcs. The best fun we have in the daytime is trying to learn the native languages. The money is difficult to understand too. It is very easy for us to get 'twisted'. I suppose we shall learn by experience. Well my dear I don't think there is much more I can write about. Please remember me to all my friends. Also Lucy.

I have not received any news from home yet, but I am not worrying! If you keep writing I expect I shall get some of them eventually. Well, I will end now, wishing you all the best, also a prosperous New Year if it not too late. All my love from,

Your Husband

Gerald X X X X X X X X X X X X X X X X X X X X X X X X X X X

October 19ᵗʰ 1941

Well darling as you can see from the date my anniversary has come and gone. I hoped to receive some mail from home for that date but nothing arrived. I am still waiting patiently to hear from you. I sent you a cable on arrival in this country also airgraphs so you should have received my address at Base Depot. I think I shall be at the above address a little longer than most of the other places I have been in so far. It will be a pleasant change to be settled if it is only for a few months. I am getting a bit travel weary. I have met several local fellows out here. One is a cousin of Fred Malpass who lived opposite the shop. He was born there but lives in Manchester now or rather his wife does. While I think of it, my service pay will be due on 12ᵗʰ Dec so you will have to attend to it. I shall put in the necessary application at this end. You should receive 3/6 per week extra from that date.

Please do not try to send me any food or perishable articles if you send parcels, as the climate is most inhospitable. It will suit me far better if you just send the money instead. The articles for personal cleanliness make a big hole in my wages and I want to get as many snaps and souvenirs as possible while I am in Egypt. We are to get a week end every month to go to various places of interest. I can put in for a week end now, but I am waiting until I have a few more coppers so that I can get round on a good tour of sight seeing during one visit. That will leave the next week end to visit some other place. Some of the lads here have some splendid snaps and I am anxious to get similar collection. When this war is over and we are old and grey dear, I shall be able to sit by the fireside and tell you of my travels until you will be telling me to keep quiet about the East. Please give my love to Lucy. Also remember me

A smile for the camera man

to Mr Taylor and Billie. What about Arthur and Mildred? Has he had his leave yet? I hope he has been luckier than I have in that respect. We have quite a good crowd of fellows at the place in which I am now residing. Fred Lomas from Coventry is still with me. The only two of the old brigade left together now. Edward Round and Philip Rogerson were having a good dose of 'square bashing' at Base Depot when I left. I felt really sorry for them. I do not know why their section was on the square and mine had all the easy stuff. If you see Stan Haynes, tell him a lad named Smith is with me. He worked with George Wright. While I am writing, a whole pile of mail has arrived in the bays. Still none for me. We had a lovely sand storm at one camp I was in recently. The fellows there said it was only a mild one. It was like a wall of fog blowing up continuously. It got in your hair, teeth, eyes and food. I am anxious now to find what a real desert howler is like. I don't expect I shall have long to wait. Well my dear, it is evening now so I will close. All my love and best wishes for a speedy union from your loving husband.

Gerald X X X X X X X X X X X

October 21st 1941   *Somewhere in Egypt*

A few more lines hoping you are well at home. I am quite alright and taking good care of myself so far. The desert is a hard task master after life in the old country but I am getting used to it now. The scenes I have seen out here are most interesting. The thing that annoys me most is the way the native women carry the bundles of goods or pitchers of water on their heads. Even with such great loads they bend down and catch hold of a child's hand with as much care as I should do with a trilby hat on. We have a boy as a servant in our billet. He is one of the best lads I have come across yet. He is 17 years old and looks about 11. From him I have already learned quite a bit of Arabic language. I hope to be speaking it fluently before long. I have quite a good idea of the swear words at any rate and I suppose I shall have to bring the other ones in gradually. I do not know how we shall get on for the next couple of days.

The people here are to hold the feast of Ramadan. For a month they have been fasting. The only food or drink they had was between their hours of sunset and sunshine. Now they are going to the towns to celebrate with feasts and to buy new clothes and last but not least to visit the brothels. The waterways here are full of strange craft. It is a most interesting sight to watch the bargees climb an incredibly high mast and rig the sail. I will try and get you some snaps to give you some idea of the apparent top heaviness of the boats and yet they seem to do the job. Then the tiny asses have my entire sympathy. They carry great loads of grain or household goods and often a great Arab sits on top of the whole lot. Another strange thing I have seen regularly. The men who are rich enough to own an ass or a camel always ride while their women and children have to walk, often carrying a great load. To return to the subject of yours truly. Well darling, I am now back to my old love. In other words two wheels, an engine and me. Who would have thought an old veteran like myself returning to motor-cycling? The riding here is something similar to that at Astley where I pitched you off. If you happen to be on a road and you get in a tight spot, well you just turn into the desert and back again. Still, dear, as long as I have a bike I am not worrying. I am getting familiar with driving on the wrong side of the road now. I do not know what my driving will be like when I get back. By the way we have quite a decent wireless here and I listen to the news from London every night. Seems like old times to hear the voice of the announcer. Makes me feel like taking my collar and tie off and pottering off to bed. I hope the day will not be very distant when I shall be with you again, for good this time I hope. Well my darling I must close now or I shall be in bed at 5.30 AM. All my love. A small piece for Lucy too. Keep smiling. I remain,

Your Loving Husband

Gerald X X X X X X XX X X X X X X X

Sunday, Oct 26th 1941

My Dear Wife,

I still have not heard from you at the time of writing these few lines, but I shall continue to enquire for mail each day. You know the old saying 'While there is life.' Really I expect it will be some time before I get a letter, but I will assure you it will be a welcome surprise if I do hear from home. You will see from this page that I am numbering my letters so that you will know if any go astray. I am quite alright at present. My only worry is the well known pest mosquito. The little devils have played havoc with all of us here for the last two days. When I came in today I am sure I looked like a million lumps hanging together. Still I suppose I shall survive them. I am in with a very decent lot of men at present. I am grateful for that small mercy. The company of your fellow men can make life so much easier or harder out here. It all depends on good or bad tempers. We seem to have an abundance of the former.

Water carriers

As I have written in my previous letters, I can do with the 'sheckles and dimes' instead of goods. There is nothing I require otherwise. You know my wants are usually very simple. The only thing I want a fair amount of cash for is photography. It is rather expensive here but I think the result will be well worth the expense. Of course I can imagine you counting the £ notes over several times and then muttering, 'Well I suppose I shall have to send them.' Now smile my dear. What a trial it is for a poor soldier to have a hard headed business woman to manage his a/c during his absence. Well darling, all joking on one side, I can do with anything up to £10 during the next two or three months so that when I get my leave (if any) I can increase my travels very considerably. And I know that when I get home I shall have a very enthusiastic audience to see my pictures. I already have some fine specimens. Please do not send the money all at once. If you send it at intervals the chances of the majority of it vanishing are much greater. Remember me to Lucy and all next door I wish I could see you all again. That is too much to hope for yet, I suppose. Never mind that time will come. Good night my dear, keep smiling. Must close now with all my love from

Your Husband

Gerald X X X X

Nov 1 1941

My Dear Wife,

Just a few lines to let you know I am still alright. I still have not heard from you. I am wondering now if I shall have a surprise on your birthday. In any case, many happy returns. I wish I could be with you the same as in the past. I shall be thinking about you on the appropriate date while I am wandering about the desert.

It has been extremely hot here during the past few days. I must have lost quite a bit of weight according to the way I have been perspiring. I would not mind the heat so much if we could find a method of defeating the mosquito pest. They have been unusually active just recently.

How are you getting on over there? I suppose after being always together for so many years you are bound to miss my company but please do not let it worry you too much. The war will not last forever. I was so disappointed at having to leave England without seeing you again. What has happened about the car? Has any one tackled driving it yet? If not please ask George (Curly) or Bert Wilkes to give it the "once over" occasionally.

I am hoping to get a weekend off to get away from this desert home very soon. I shall get a few photographs taken then just to let you know what I look like now. I hope they will be alright considering they will be the first I have had taken. You should consider yourself highly honoured to know I have condescended to that stage just for you. Now smile.

I hope you have been receiving my letters and airgraphs fairly regularly. I should feel much easier in my own mind if I was certain of that. The only thing I have to add is look after yourself and entertain only in our own circle of friends.

Please remember me to Lucy and Mrs Taylor and Billie. Also Mrs Chapman. Well my dear, I do not know what else I can write about without the censor crossing it out. The only thing we are short of here is reading material. Please do not forget to try and send me some "filthy lucre" however. We can never have too much of that. By the way I am off the motor cycle now. I know that will ease your mind little. Of course I cannot very well tell you what I am doing now, but you have little cause to worry over me.

Well darling I will close now, once again Happy Birthday.

All the best from your loving husband

Gerald Xxxxxx

On November 3rd 1941 a month after the decision to adopt "Operation Crusader" General Auchinleck had to postpone the commencement of the operation by one week to allow the 1st South African Division to undergo more training.

Wed November 12 1941

My Dear Wife,

Many thanks for the cable which I received on Nov 7th. I do not think you can possibly realise how welcome it was. I came in that night very tired and weary and, I must confess it, extremely angry. That will surprise you. You often said you wish I had a temper to see what I looked like. I will not tell you what caused me to get in that state, but it was nothing to do with the Army. I think it was the first time since I have been out here that I did not go to see if there was any mail for me. Then someone told me I had a telegram at the office. I hope I shall continue to hear from you regularly now. It seems to make life out here a little happier. If any of the boys do not receive any letters while the rest of them get a stack of mail, there is very little said, but you know what the man is thinking.

Well darling, I have had a bit of a break from the desert. I must say it passed all too quickly, and I came back almost spent out but it was well worth the expenditure. I went to see the wonders of an ancient civilisation, the Great pyramid, the Lesser Pyramid and the Sphinx. To me it was a remarkable sight. Instead of just having a look round and then going away again, I went to the trouble to try and find out about things for myself. The Great pyramid is 4,500 years old, and it is an affair covering 30 acres of ground. It is about 870 feet in height and in the exact centre is the chamber and coffin of King Memphisis or some such name. It is just a honeycomb of passages and burial places of Kings and Queens. I have a few snaps of it and I have some more to be developed There is one (or should be) of me on the Alter of Sacrifice in the Temple of the Gods. I can hear you saying "What a place to have it taken",

In case the other letters should not reach you, I will ask you once again to send me "filthy lucre". Also it appears from other parcels arriving out here that it is alright to send almost anything except food.

13th now. I have just received a parcel in excellent condition from Roma. It should have reached me in England. Thank her very much for me. The desert was very cloudy with good old "Woodbine" smoke for quite a time. Chocolate good too after 3 months. That was because it was in a tin. Just afterwards I received your airmail card. I am beginning to feel on top of the world after all that.

Well darling I must close now. Will write again soon.

All my love from your husband

Gerald xxxxxxxxxxx

The Sweetwater Canal

The Sphinx

*Fred Lomas & Dick Chalk with second Pyramid
in the background. Snap taken from the top of
the Tomb of Memphisis. Remains of alabaster
still existing can be seen at top of pyramid*

*Dick Chalk & Gerald by the two
remaining pillars at the entrance
of the Temple of the Gods*

The Pyramid

On the Altar of Sacrifice

The Sphinx taken through the ruined walls of the Temple of the Gods. It was risky climbing up crumbling walls to required height to take the picture. Head of Dick Chalk in the foreground.

Sunday Nov 16 1941

Dear Youngster,

Many thanks for the card which I received quite safely 3 weeks and one day from the time you posted it. Considering the fact that I had moved twice since it was addressed and had to follow me round, it was excellent service. I hope they continue to arrive with the same degree of efficiency, but of course anything can happen to prevent that. I knew you would be pleased to hear I had landed safely. Just one little addition I would like to add to anything I may have written previously.

As long as I live I shall always have the deepest respect for the lads of the Royal Navy. More than that I will not write as information must not be given away. Anyway the fact remains that I am safe and in splendid health.

I am getting used to the climate now and it is a great relief to find the mosquito plague or pest or whatever you call it diminishing. Fancy receiving the cable on my birthday. And Arthur getting leave too. I hope you enjoyed the drinks at my expense. Also I hope you had those I mentioned in previous letters. How is Arthur getting on now? Alright I hope. And Mildred too. He used to think I was the lucky one, but the boot seems to be on the other foot now. I hope for his sake it continues so.

Really I am glad to hear someone has made a valiant effort and got my car on the road again. It seemed a great pity for it to lie idle when there was so much work for it to do. I sincerely hope you make a good job of it between you.

What of the pigs and all that poultry and the gardens and the allotment. I don't seem to be getting any news of all that. What I want to know is, "What sort of a crop came off those beans I was taking such great pains over". I hope the result was better than last year. If it was not I shall be getting a bad reputation as a seed agent.

Thank Dad very much for the kind offer to send me money. I have already told you in previous letters what I want it for. If one has the cash available there are so many opportunities of spending it wisely on things I may never have the chance to see again. I have to make the best of my rare escapes from the desert to get anything I want. All we have here is a picture house and a NAFFI so you can see there is not a great deal of competition. I have sent several snaps surface mail so you should be receiving those anytime now. I hope to send you one or two of myself next week. I tried to get a proper photograph taken during a recent visit to the Pyramids but all the photographers seemed to be closed. Anyway, I will send you one when I get my next weekend off, which if all goes well will be 3 weeks today.

In addition to the question of money you can if you wish send cigarettes or any non perishable articles, but please try not to send cakes or anything like that. I saw one last week. It was a splendid cake completely spoilt. I cannot say, but it may have been alright if it had been in a tin instead of a wooden box. I don't think the sender could get hold of a suitable tin.

Please remember me to Lucy. Tell her one of the crosses on the bottom is for Christmas if it is not too late. Also best wishes to Mrs Taylor & Billie. Congrats to the old City on raising £9,600,000. That is the way to hit back. Did you get that other £32? I hope so.

Well darling I am getting to the end of the paper, so I will close with all my love, and once again thank you for the card. I remain your loving husband

Gerald. Xxxxxxxxxxx

18/11/1941 'Operation Crusader', began at 6 am. Rommel who had just arrived back in the desert from Rome was caught by surprise and the 30 Corps were able to advance some 50 miles and capture one of his airfields some 10 miles south of Sidi Razegh. He sent his famous Afrika Korps on a wild goose chase believing that the British were about to encircle Bardia.

20/11/1941 The British garrison at Tobruk was ordered to break out and link up with 30 Corps

22/11/1941 Rommel realizing what was happening then sent the Afrika Korps to Sidi Rezegh where the 30 Corps were stopped from advancing towards Tobruk. It lost many tanks and the Tobruk break out had to be postponed. Sidi Omar and Capuzzo were however captured by the 12 Corps.

24/11/1941 Rommel "dashed for the wire" by moving towards the Egyptian frontier in order to cut off the British supply routes. At the end of this day he had caused complete confusion at the rear of the 8th Army.

Sunday 23rd Nov 1941

Somewhere in the desert

To my Dear Wife,

Just a few more lines to let you know I am quite safe and well. Many thanks for the mail which I have received quite safely. Up to the present I have received a cable from you, a parcel from Roma, an air mail card from you, an airgraph from Mother and last but not least a registered letter from you which I should have received in England. The £5 enclosed was very welcome, but in the future will you please make it Postal Orders or £ notes as silver is very difficult to change. The letter seemed rather gloomy at the time of writing, but a long time has elapsed since then so I will pass no comment until I learn more from you. I want you to do as you think best, but even now my wish is for my business to carry on in my absence. I am a long way from England now and you will appreciate the fact that it is very difficult to judge the amount of goods available but I do not think there is any need for pessimism now. The darkest clouds have a silver lining you know. Well darling, to return to the subject. I am still sorry to have to inform you that the snaps I mentioned in previous letters have not yet reached me from the printing shop. It is very difficult to arrange these things when you are parked in the middle of a desert. Still I think I shall manage them in my next letter. I was lucky enough to get a week end leave pass recently so 'hitch-hiked' to Cairo to have a look around. The city itself rather impressed me. Parts of it were quite like good old Brum. The best of it I must leave until another day. I was very interested to hear that George was expecting to sail. Fancy that after all this time. I thought he was on a permanent fixture. And how is old 'Curly' getting on. I hope he is getting the trout in good condition for when I return. Tell him I shall be expecting to find plenty of 2lb trout for Monday morning breakfast. I should like to see one on my plate out here. I think I should appreciate it even more than I did at home. As you know for a long time now I have had a great wanderlust, but I think that after this lot is over I shall settle down to home life, with just my trout rods and gun as hobbies. All that is, of course, providing I return home in one piece. As I look outside there is a glorious sunset. They appear to be different every night and the beauty of them has to be seen to be believed. The only trouble is they are a warning of rapidly approaching darkness. It is getting cooler in the day now, and at night it gets quite cold. I cannot say that it is unwelcome either. The mosquitoes are less numerous now too, so altogether, life is getting a little better. Please let me know if you have received the letters I wrote on the boat. My officers who came over with us told me they were quite in order but you have not mentioned them in your cards to me. The outgoing mail is censored from here but there does not appear to be any censorship of mail coming to the Middle East. If you get anything crossed out, please let me know, then I shall be able to avoid the same mistake next time. Please remember me to Lucy and all my friends. Will close now, all the best from your loving husband,

Gerald X X X X X X X X X X X X X X

Monday Nov 24th 1941

My Dear Wife,

Just a few more lines to let you know I am safe and well. I have already written several airmail letters and airgraphs and by the time you receive this you should have had quite a string of news.

You should by now have received a fairly good story of my long voyage, although we were in a very difficult position, in regard to censorship. I am afraid those days are far away now and to be perfectly honest, I cannot say I am sorry. It is no joke being on the water for weeks. The part I disliked about it was that I could not stretch my legs the same as on land. I have plenty of scope for that sort of exercise now. It seems a long time since I wrote those letters and I think the best thing to do is forget any parts of them that appear to be gloomy. When I reflect on the past, I think the worst part of it is the fear of the unknown. By that I mean that when I left England, I did not know what to expect at sea. I did not even know what the ship would be like until I was aboard. In that respect I was really fortunate as you know. Then when we got to sea, we had nothing but confidence in the lads of the Royal Navy. They saw us through in grand style. As long as I live I will never say a word against the navy. I sometimes wonder whether it is really appreciated in regard to the service they render.

Then there was the great welcome we received during our shore leave. Then the old recurring thought "What are we going to now". It is strange what thoughts you conjure up in your spare moments. I can't really say what I expected. Of one thing I am certain. I really expected the Middle East to be much worse than I have found it. By that statement, please do not run away with the idea that I am living in a bed of roses. Far from it, but conditions could be worse. I have good companions and when the day is done, there are very few moans. There is plenty of leg pulling, plenty of gaming in a friendly way, and always something or someone to laugh at.

Just one instance. One of the lads came in with a "great secret". He said the enemy had invented an armour piercing bullet which went through your pay book and killed your next of kin. The immediate reply from one of the beds was "That's nothing. We have a bullet that goes through your pay book and wiped your credits out". Those are the sort of things we have to say to keep us going. Then there is sometimes a contest in using "tall language". That goes on for a while, then we start a debate nearly every night. We discuss everything from engines to murder. We get some really interesting evenings in that respect and it is amazing what can be learned from the discussions.

You will find a snap enclosed showing a local young lady just about to fill a water pitcher. Did you ever see such a smile? There are scenes like that happening every day out here. The women go down to the waterside with the pitchers in the position shown in the snap, and return with it in the upright position when filled. In addition to water carrying it is the local method of carrying almost every article in this part of the world. As far as I can find out it is only the women who are able to perform these balancing feats. The men are content to look on. It is quite a common sight to see a native riding an ass while his wife carries a tremendous bundle on her head, and in many cases has several children to attend to at the same time.

Well darling I think that is about all for now so I will close. Please remember me to Lucy and all next door. Also to Jimmy King and the lads of H.G.

All my love from your husband

Gerald xxxxxxxxxx

26/11/1941 General Cunningham was feeling the strain and wanted to stop the offensive but General Auchinleck over ruled him and replaced him with General Ritchie as commander of the 8th Army. He later said. "My opinion was different from Cunningham's. I thought Rommel was probably in as bad shape as we were, especially with Tobruk unvanquished behind him, and I ordered the offensive to continue. I certainly gambled (in fact by going on we might have lost all) and Cunningham might very well have proved to be right, and I wrong."

27/11/1941 After a tough battle the last Italian town held in East Africa surrendered to the British forces.

Sunday Nov 30th 1941   Somewhere in the desert.

Just another small epistle to let you know a little more of the life I am leading in this part of the world. First of all I am in very good health and I have few worries or troubles. Of course the obvious thing every soldier wants to see is the end of the war and a speedy reunion with their wives and families. That however is an objective that must be worked for. I do not think it is revealing any military secret when I say that things are getting warm in this part of the globe, and I can say without any hesitation that everyone feels better for it. You have no idea how impatient fellows get when they know there is "something brewing" and they have to keep waiting for the word of command instead of going right in. Everyone is willing to work any number of hours without a murmur. Whatever the outcome, I can honestly assure you there is no pessimism in our camp. The lads I am with are a cheerful crowd, and as I have told you previously we have to make our own amusement, but we do not go very short of laughter when the work of the day is through.

One of the most comical sights I have seen here for a long time is a fellow 6ft 1in and with rather large feet enclosed by heavy army boots, learning to tap dance. I can't explain what he looks like, so I must leave it to your imagination.

Then we have a little fellow with a very serious expression who stands, on his bed and makes speeches. From all the beds come either cries of approval or loud "boos" as the case may be. Everyone seems to shout the right thing all at once. It is very rare to hear a "boo" among the "hurrahs". One example of his speeches begins "What we want is more milk for babies" or "What we want is higher ideals for the lower classes". You should be able to imagine what is added by the lads. If he gets "booed" too much he lies on the bed and calls out "Abdul, Abdul, bring in the dancing girls, I am tired of all this childish laughter".

There are many other items that happen everyday in camp life, but I will keep those until I am permitted to see you again.

How are you getting on at Birmingham? I saw in a M.E. periodical of today's date that all the shops are to close at 4 pm. I immediately wondered how it would affect you and Lucy. As far as I can judge it should prove to be very favourable. By the way, has Lucy had those drinks charged to my account? Those I wrote about on the boat, I refer to. I suppose you will be wondering what it was all about. Well darling keep wondering until I get home.

Somehow although I am thousands of miles away, home seems very near to me. Naturally I miss all the comforts of a good home, and above all I miss your company most, but those are things that must be tolerated until this job is concluded. I think of you every night and wonder what you are doing, and how all my friends are getting on, and it gives me a great feeling of comfort to know that I have a good wife and good friends.

Please remember me to Arthur and Mildred. I hope his unit of the R.A.F. will remain where they were when I last heard from you. I am glad he got leave just in time to celebrate my safe arrival out here. Tell him to keep on getting all the leave he can, but to be careful what he finds to celebrate over each time. While I think of it ask him to order a new pack of cards with plenty of aces in for the day I return. I don't know how long that will be but it should give him plenty of time to get a good stack of "filthy lucre" on his favourite Jack of Spades. He will be able to say it is a business man taking the hard earned coppers off a poor airman then.

I have tried in my spare moments to decide what sort of a "bust up" we shall have when that day arrives. I think it is going to be a little more boisterous than taking the "two Georges" home.

Well darling, you know those promises I made before I left you. They have been kept, and will not be broken now, whatever happens. The longer I am away from you the more I realise what your company meant to me. All I pray for is your safety, and that I may return as I left you. In your letter you said that whatever I do, or in whatever state I come back you will stand by me. I cannot tell you how much those few words mean to me. If I should be unlucky enough to get a "smack" before this lot is over I know I have someone on whose word I can rely. For that reason only, I have nothing but confidence for the future.

Please remember me to everyone at home. I will close now, with just one small request. Please send me all the snaps or photographs you can. Thank you. God bless you and keep you safe. Keep your chin up and do not worry over me. All for mow from your loving husband

Gerald Xxxxxxxxxxxxxx

07/12/1941 Japan attacks America at Pearl Harbour without declaring war.

BY AIR MAIL Date stamped '*Egypt 93 12 DEC 41. Free Xmas delivery***'**

Sunday Dec 7ᵗʰ 1941. Somewhere in the desert

Happy Christmas <u>to you all</u>

Darling,

Many thanks for telegram. It only took six days to reach me which I think is extremely good under present conditions. It was a remarkable coincidence that on that particular day I was detailed to go to Army Post Office and fetch the mail for the first time. The following day I went again and this time I got a wire from Edna and Syd. I hope I have to go regularly if the supply of telegrams does not run out.

Well darling how are you. I suppose you miss me just a little after being together for so many years. Still, keep smiling. The war will not last for ever. Of one thing I can assure you the lads here often think of home, but they get very little time for getting really home sick. That "terrible man with a bugle" comes round and disturbs our slumbers at 5.30 a.m. From that time onwards until 8.30 p.m. it is work and meals. Spare time is occupied by personal cleanliness and occasional letters home. So in the near future, if you do not get quite so many letters please do not think too badly of me. I shall certainly try to write as often as possible. This is being written while I am standing by. I am Duty Driver today. I started at 6 a.m. and tonight when I feel tired I shall wrap my blankets round me and sleep by the telephone. Still the job has to be done, and I make no complaint. I am only too anxious to get back to you with the knowledge that I did whatever was asked of me without a grumble.

I have several snaps of myself and also various places of interest which I have visited during my travels. I hope you will like them. Of course being just an amateur photographer I have had a few failures which I have discarded but some of them are very good. I hope you are keeping that album going. As my wages will not permit me to have too many prints, I shall send you some of the negatives in due course, and then you can have what amount you require. One of the fellows who sleep near me has taken up snapshot colouring as a hobby, and he is turning out some of the best specimens I have seen so I shall be sending you some very shortly.

Well darling, space is getting short so I must close. Please remember me to Mrs Taylor & Billie. Don't forget to thank Edna & Syd for the cable. I do not know their address. Also keep Mildred in order during her "Airman's" absence. Now smile. All my love darling from your husband

Gerald Xxxxxxxxxxxxxx

Sunday Dec 7ᵗʰ 1941

Somewhere in the desert

Darling,

I wrote three pages of a letter to you yesterday, and now I have to start all over again. You see it happened in this way. Two days ago I received a telegram from you. It arrived in six days. Yesterday I received another one from Edna and Syd. It seemed to good to be true. Now today I have received four letters so someone still thinks of me. Two letters were from you, one from Mother, and one from Roma. They all contained Christmas greetings. The one from you was especially welcome. In the letter I wrote yesterday I stated that I must be the only soldier serving in the Middle East who cannot produce a whole sheaf of photographs of his wife. Since I got your letter I am glad to say that state of affairs has now been remedied. I have had a small bet with myself if that is possible. It is that the postcard size head and shoulders of yourself is an enlargement of one of those miniatures that were on top of the stairs. Please let me know if I am right. One thing still puzzles me after receiving the letters. Up to the present I have now received ten from home, yet no mention has been made in any of them whether you are getting my letters alright. Of course I know you received the telegram I sent, but I have also been writing regularly for about 16 or 17 weeks. However, perhaps I shall know by the time you receive this as I am sending it by sea. I am enclosing a few more snaps to take their place in the album. I hope you will look after them for me, also the letters I write, as they will be a source of interest when I get back home. That brings me to another subject you mentioned in your letter. Someone has been telling you the war looks like lasting several years yet. I should judge those people as having financial benefits as a result of the war. I know they exist, but they are few and far between. My only advice to you is to take no notice whatsoever of that kind of talk and just let men like Churchill and Beaverbrook get on with deciding those sorts of things. If it should last for a long time even that does not mean that I shall stay here for the duration. Men came back from Norway and Belgium and France you know and we are still a long, long way from being defeated. I can certainly assure you that there is very little of that sort of talk out here, and if you could see the capers of some of the lads while I am writing this letter you would not think they had a care in the world. Now to the more serious side of affairs as it concerns us. I have already sent you an air graph asking you to give up all idea of trying to get near me. Please do not think I don't want you near me. That is the last thing I should dream of. But I told you I would try to give you my reasons after due consideration. To begin with I do not think you would ever settle down to life in the services, although I must confess I cannot class that as a very sound reason. Then again if you joined a nursing section I cannot be sure that I would be allowed to take you out. Out here it is only officers who are allowed to escort the nursing profession. Of course you will say that an exception might be made. But do you honestly think it is worth the risk. I certainly do not. Then again, have you thought what it would be like if you came out here and had to stay while I happened to be sent back home. It is impossible for me to say where my travels will take me. With the exception of fleeting visits to large cities I have seen about half a dozen white women in two months so you can see that the climate is most unsuitable for females. Most of those women who have been in the East have only seen life as it exists in the comparative comfort of the cities. I believe most of the girls in the hospitals near here come from cities that get a very high temperature during the summer so they are able to stand the heat. According to the few periodicals I receive, it has at times been almost too overpowering for those girls. I know you want to see me. I too would like to see you if only for a few hours, but I think it is best to put these thoughts resolutely behind us until we see how things are going to turn out. There are many more reasons I could give but I will end the subject for the present. I will just add that wherever I may go I shall always be thinking of you. Well darling I am pleased to hear that the beans did well in the garden. If you can, please give the same variety another trial this spring. Plant them about 23rd or 24th April. Another thing you mentioned in the letter was that Lucy was deputising for me in some respects. I hope she does not do me out of the job permanently. I can see I shall have to look to my laurels. Thanks for the heather. It is a real bit of "Old England". We only find stunted camel thorn out here, and there is not much of interest in that.

Please remember me to Mrs Taylor and Billie. What has happened to George? Has he sailed yet? He has been lucky getting all that leave, but somehow I don't think he will leave England after all. For his sake I hope not. Well darling I shall have to close now as it is getting dark and I have to be driving across the old dessert at dawn in the morning. Just one more item of interest. I discovered Philip Rogerson residing about 200 yds away from me and I did not know he was there. He is in a different unit to me, but I hope we can remain close together now. Goodnight darling. All my love from your husband

Gerald

XXXXXXXXXXXXXX

PS Please wish Arthur and Mildred all the best for the New Year

> **08/12/1941** America declares war on Japan.
> The Eighth Army relieves the Tobruk garrison.
>
> **11/12/1941** Germany and Fascist Italy declare war on America

December 10th 1941

Somewhere in the desert

My Darling,

Just a few lines in haste. I thought I had better not send you the enclosed snap without a few words. I hope you will like it alright. I am sending you some more of the same snaps at regular intervals. Then if old Hitler should have a bit of luck, some of them should reach you. I expect you will think it strange that I often repeat myself in my letters, but in the present conditions it is impossible to <u>guarantee</u> delivery. Of course the greater part of the mail arrives safely, but by repeating various items it certainly makes you more certain of getting what I want you to know.

The first and only thing I want you to know from every letter you receive is that I love you the same as I always have done. I may be a long way from you now, but that does not prevent me from working to bring nearer the day when I shall return to you, and try to make up for all the opportunities you have been denied by my stay in the Army. Rest assured sweetheart I have made up my mind to give a great deal more attention to the things that go to make up your happiness in the future. I have been analysing myself and being quite honest about it recently. I know my faults, I admit them to myself, and I am endeavouring to remedy them. I am writing this on two sides of the paper so that I can send as much as possible for you. I am afraid I cannot afford any more at present. My few snaps which I have sent are using up all my spare coppers. I have sent quite a lot by sea and you should be receiving the first of them at any time now. Once again I ask you to take great care of them in the album. I will also send you some negatives a bit later on. I received your telegram on Saturday. It took six days. Also I received one from Edna and Syd. Thank them very much. Received one today from Lucy. Also many thanks. Tell her I will save a nice kiss for her when I get home.

Eva

Photographs also received. They are very good but do not let that prevent you sending some more. I have received a letter from you. Also one from Mother, one from Roma and one from Dad. The latter three all containing Christmas cards. I have rigged the lot up (with your photograph in the centre) over my bed. They look alright too. I hope the orderly officer does not put me on the "hook" tomorrow, for having an unauthorised picture gallery in my residence.

By the way I have written and asked you not to join any of the services to try to get near to me. I have given my reasons in a letter which I have sent by surface mail. Please do not be annoyed with me. I don't know why but although I am I am in real earnest when I reply "No" I can't help feeling a great sense of amusement. Darling if only you realised what a week or two of life in this country is like. There is no glamour and as far as my experience goes nothing but discomfort. I am sitting on boards writing this for instance, by the light of a hurricane lamp. Later on I must wash and shave by the light of the moon. The days are hot, the nights bitterly cold, and at times those mosquitoes and gnat bites I have seen on your arms would look like a few odd spots by the side of what we go through. Add about 50 degrees to the hottest day you remember and you will know what the summer is like. Only there are no trees around this desert. No animals with the exception of camels, goats, sheep and water buffaloes. Very few birds. Plenty of sun and FLIES. Millions of them. Disease is a great enemy.

Darling forget it all for my sake. If I painted a true picture for you I do not think you would believe it.

Well my darling I will close now.

All the best from your loving husband

Gerald XXXXXXXXXXXXXXXXXXXXXXXXX

Thursday Dec 12th 1941

My Darling,

Just a few more lines to let you know I am quite safe and in the best of health. Well darling I hope you will take particular note of the date on which I am writing this. It is just six months since I left you and I have been thinking about you all day. I have one consolation now however which is rather difficult to explain. This week I received a certain letter from you which contained quite a bunch of photographs. The head and shoulders portrait was particularly good. I have made it a central point in the midst of a display of Christmas cards which I have received. I did the job in the dark, but the strange thing is that every time I go to my mansion, your eyes are turned on the entrance with a smile of welcome. So you see if I do not happen to be thinking of you at that moment, I soon realise with a jolt there is someone who wants me. I don't know why but it is in my opinion the best photograph I have seen of you. I won't tell you now what I think of when I look at it. You see, sweetheart, I <u>know how vain you</u> are and I think it is only fair for me to tease you in the same manner as this photograph .... all right. Enough said. Just use your own imagination until I get back.

All joking on one side just for a moment. I do not know whether you have received any extra allowance at the time you receive this letter, but I have been recommended for it today so you should be receiving it in the near future. It should be from 12th Dec 1941. Of course you will realise it may take a week or two before it is settled as it is being done from the Middle East.

Well back to more personal subjects once more. I am getting quite a lot of mail just recently. I had a telegram from you, one from Lucy and one from Edna and Syd. Please thank them all for me. I have also received a letter from you, another letter containing Christmas cards and photographs, a Christmas card from Mother, one from Roma and another from Dad. Today I received an airgraph from you, and another from Mother. Please accept my thanks for these letters. It seems as though there is quite a lot of money on the way for me. I am very grateful for the kind thoughts that prompt it. Oh no! I am not spent out but very often I have to go a little short of various little luxuries. All this is in order to give you what photographs I can. As I have told you in previous letters I want to send as many as I can, but I cannot afford too many of them out of my Army pay. As a driver I get quite a lot of opportunities that are denied to other soldiers. When I am out in the desert or along roads when such things exist I see scenes which would make wonderful snaps. I am making a mental note of all these things and as soon as I receive the filthy lucre to pay the charges for developing and printing, then you can look out for a whole flood of pictures of life and scenery as I find them. Of course I want you to realise this. Life out here is not as beautiful as that depicted in the snaps I have sent and shall continue to send. I may at times have to travel 30 of 40 miles to get a couple of snaps. One good thing is that I can usually get a lift on an Army wagon so that expense is minus.

There are a lot of big cities that I am enabled to visit periodically when finances permit, and I intend to take full opportunities at the earliest possible moment. As soon as I receive the necessary amount of money which I asked you about, I shall try to get to the Holy Land for leave. If circumstances permit I should be able to send you a good collection of snaps of my tour. We are entitled to seven days leave in every 3 months here but most of us cannot afford it regularly, so most of the lads save up during a six months sojourn in the desert and then go for a really interesting tour. I will assure you that they deserve their break.

In the airgraph from Mother she asks me what I am doing and I think she would also like me to tell her where I am. Well dear, I am afraid the latter part is not allowed until you see me in the flesh, so we must forget it. As for the former I have had several jobs since I have been in the Middle East.

The first part of it was quite an easy job at Base Depot. By the way I have just learned that

Edward is stationed there permanently. Sneaky fellow. On one parade here a small number of men were required to volunteer for a certain job. None of the N.C.O.'s in charge were certain what it was about, but they gave us a pretty good idea that it was going to be a dangerous job. The men to be accepted had to be medical category A.1. and all drivers of long experience. We had the opportunity of getting a bunch of pals together to go away. In any case we knew we would not be at Base Depot very long. Well dear, to cut a long story very short Fred Loman and myself are the only pals left together. Still I bear no ill will. We all have to make our own way in this world. The funny part of it all is that we ended up many miles from the place everyone "who knew someone who knew someone else" knew we were going to. As you know from the address sent some time ago I am now with No. 2 Heavy Repair Shops. I can tell you that there are no "cushy jobs" in this outfit. At first I did the dispatch riding as you know. After that I was on a job of which I must not write. Now I am on the regular driving staff. I was in a bit of a fix this week. I nearly got put on "the hook". A certain N.C.O. thought I was doing a certain thing which in reality I was not. He told me I was on a charge. A little later he told me he had a nice little trip across the desert for me at dawn the following morning. I told him I could not go as I was to appear on the charge. He swore black and white that he had never even spoken to me all that afternoon, so I think this Land of the East must be affecting me too. Anyway I am still out of "clink".

By the way dear, I am writing this while acting as Duty Driver. The second night in five. I have to sleep by the telephone all night in case of emergency. I finish at daybreak, have breakfast, and then away amongst the sand again. However I make no complaint. I know that when I go for my mess tins etc. in the morning, someone will still be looking at me with that smile of welcome as I go through the entrance. All the lads who live with me ask me "Why should a fellow like that be so lucky as to have a wife like that". I usually reply "She is as good as she looks, and in any case you have only seen the Army side of me. You should see me when I get all sentimental and you would not wonder then". I am afraid I had better not repeat the remarks that follow. They are trying hard to persuade me to give them a demonstration. I have told them as the Arabs say, "Bandin"

Well my darling, I don't know what else I am going to write about. I can't write about what I see and do and know as it would only be crossed out. I can't keep telling you that there is a lot of sand here or you will be starting to believe it. One thing I do want you to do for me. When you write another air mail card or graph please let me know approximately the amount of money that has been sent, also the dates of posting. It will be alright if you let me know approximately, but please let me know as soon as you can. According to the airgraph which I rec'd today George is still in "Blighty". I don't think it is his destiny to travel to these parts. In any case he can't grumble about leave. Wish him the best of luck for me and I sincerely hope he can stay where he is now. Also thank Lily for cigarettes, which are being sent. Please remember me to all their family. Also Mrs Taylor and Billie. Give my love to Lucy in return for hers as she puts it. What a thing it is when a poor old married man has two females to worry over. And I haven't even got a photograph.

Hope you enjoyed your Christmas. Happy new year to all. Oh! I have another thing to say. I don't even get grapefruit here. Lucky to get water. So you see I am still tee-total and I shall remain so. The 5 white women I have seen in 3 months were all travelling in cars so they do not interest me. In fact this place is "quite select".

Good night darling. God Bless you and keep you safe! All my love from your husband
Gerald XXXXXXXXX

15/12/1941 The German and Italian positions at Gazala are attacked by the Eight Army. Rommel ordered a retreat to stop the British outflanking him.

Monday Dec 21ˢᵗ 1941

My Dear Wife,

   Many thanks for air mail card which is numbered ten. It is strange that you should begin to number the letters you send with a number like that as it reached me in exactly ten days. Since you have been addressing my mail direct to 2 H.R.S. it has been arriving very quickly. I have received 23 letters and airgraphs during the last seven weeks. That is of course including those from Brook Street. I hope you are hearing from me more regularly now. I can assure you that I have written to you or to Brook Street at least four times a week. Some are air mail, some airgraph, and I have sent one or more by surface mail every week. So you should be receiving quite a supply when once they start to arrive. I sincerely hope you get all which I wrote on the ship, as I spent many hours writing them so that the censor would pass them. The censors were my own officers at that time, and they told me that there was nothing in them of any military value, so they will reach you exactly as I intended them to. I have been having a few daydreams of that voyage this evening, and I have come to the conclusion that, pleasant as most of it was, I am not in any way sorry to leave it all behind me. I cannot say why, but although I am a long way from civilisation as I know it at home, I would far sooner be in a sea of sand than on a sea of salt water. I have always led an active life, and I am sorry to say that as days rolled on into weeks and weeks into months, with just the same decks to stroll around, I got really sick of it all. For days we saw nothing but a vast expanse of water, and on two occasions on which we crossed the equator, how we longed for a cool dip in the briny. But that was not to be. We just kept going. The latter part of our voyage was accomplished quite well, but I often think of one thing which will always live in my memory. That was a sea of dolphins, and sharks. There seemed to be thousands of them, and I dread to think what fate would meet "a man overboard".

By the way dear, I caught a small shark during the voyage. I think you had better inform George of that performance. It was just under 2ft long, and a very nasty sort of customer. Anyway I am glad I did not have one of his ancestors to deal with.

I have heard to day that there are quite a lot of my old Army pals out here now, so I have a job trying to find them during my travels. Do you remember the day we went to the hotel and dined with the ladies who created the minor sensation at the time? Well I believe the lad who paid the bill is out here somewhere. If I can find him you can rest assured that something will be happening; only I am afraid the female element will be absent. I wish I could drop on him before Thursday. It would be a real Christmas then.

Philip has been in with me all afternoon and we have been having quite a chat about old times. He was very unfortunate a short time ago. He has just received a letter from Violet asking to listen to Sandy Macpherson's half hour on 28ᵗʰ Nov. of course he did not hear the message for him. Still better luck next time.

Well dear it is almost time to hang my stocking up, but for the first time, I think it is going to be rather empty. Still I must not grumble. We are at war, and those sorts of things have to be sacrificed. We are expecting to work most of Xmas day, although we are not certain, but in any case it will not worry me very much. I am still tea total and as regards revelry and riotous celebrations, well, I realise that work must come first. All I miss now will be saved up for when I get back home, so look out when that day arrives. Someone is going to need more than my car to get them home that night, and I do not think you will need any guesses who it will be. And you can promise them from me that they <u>won't</u> be found with mistletoe at strange angles in strange places next morning.

There is I know, a long way to go before that day arrives, but I am determined it shall come. According to your airmail card you are to spend Christmas at Digger's. I hope you have a good time. I am wondering how many of the old school will be left to attend. I suppose "Curly" will still be there. I heard from Eric this week. According to his airgraph he is still stationed at the same port. I have not heard from Arthur yet. Tell him he is letting the R.A.F. down, being so late with his letters.

I shall have to close now dear, as I have to be driving very early in the morning, and my blankets have an inviting appearance just now. I am just patiently waiting for the time when I shall be on the road very early with my own vehicle, for the benefit of my own business. I hope that time is not to far distant for your sake. Just keep your chin at the usual angle and carry on.

All my love from your loving husband

Gerald X X X X X X X X X X X X X X X X X X X X X

P.S. Please remember me to Lucy and all next door.

25/12/1941 Benghazi is retaken by the British

Dec 25th 1941

Somewhere in the desert

Darling,

Just a few lines on this very appropriate day to let you know I am safe, well, and above all sober. I have kept my resolution, but believe me when I say the temptations have been many. It is morning now. About 11 a.m. I expect the latter part of this letter will be written tomorrow as there are to be great celebrations later in the day. I have had quite a lot of work to do for the festivities. One job included the decoration of the mess room, and it was no easy job. You cannot go to Woolworth's and get just the necessary articles so two other fellows and myself used our imagination and the job is completed. Christmas Eve midnight when we finished. We may be in the desert miles from home, but "Oh boy! Did things hum". As the Yanks would remark "I'll say they sure did". Reveille, On parade, lights Out etc have been sounding for hours. I think the buglers must have found a small bottle of beer or something equally good. Just at present the lads have got the Arabs and Egyptians etc in some sort of procession. They are doing all sorts of war dances as they march round the camps. They have rigged up a band and a drum major dressed like Lawrence of Arabia is doing all sorts of tricks with something that looks to me to be very much like a native boat paddle. I don't know whether our snaps will come out. I will let you know. The little Arab youth in our hut is staggering all over the show. The boys have been feeding him on "Johnny Haig". I cannot tell you all the things that happen as it would take all my wages in stamps.

One thing however was most unpleasant, at 5.30 a.m. we had a tropical storm, and barracks and desert were swimming with water. After the storm I went for breakfast. Had a grand feed too. As I came out I saw a very strange sight. Six men of Philip's unit came out with a bed full of what I imagined to be Army kit. It seemed full of blankets, overcoats over the top and two great fronds of date palm placed on top. They carried it into the desert, placed it gently in a great pool of water, and started to sing a hymn. Then they walked silently away. Imagine what my thoughts were when the blankets moved and a fellow who had no cares in the world (on the previous night I mean) tried to find a way of getting up and dressing in those circumstances. His clothes were still where they normally should be. I do not know what happened to him eventually as I had some jobs of my own to attend to.

The C.Q.M.S. has given me a very nice present. While I was on with the decorations he came across at about 11 p.m. and gave me a grand scarf made in Australia. The mornings here are rather cold and I can't think of anything more welcome just at the moment. Please don't start sending me those sorts of things now as by the time I receive them the weather will be getting very hot again.

Well darling it is Boxing Night now so I can let you know a little more of how I spent Xmas. To begin with, the dinner was one of the best I have ever tasted. For once the Army cooking really surprised me. Had real turkey too. The best bit of poultry I have ever tasted. We had Officers and sergeants to serve the meal and I am afraid the remarks I heard at times will not stand printing. They enjoyed every minute of it just as much as we did. It is the one day in the year when the men do and say what they like. After those celebrations were over I had to lie down on my bed for a couple of hours and then went for tea. Well darling to be perfectly honest the tea was as good as the dinner. The beer was plentiful but I have still kept my promise. Went back then and had the "pack out". I had quite a nice time thank you. I know what you will say, but it is Christmas and I enjoyed myself thoroughly.

I should be having a few more snaps to send you in a few days. Worked this morning and had the afternoon off. Plenty more revelry. Dressed our sergeant major up in Aussie uniform. He had already got a nose cut and a black eye in conjunction with a few medical dressings and the lads pulled his leg unmercifully. Still he took it all in good part. He came round the mess room to see that the lads were having a good time, (And I am sure he had one) and when he put his arm round anyone and asked "How are you doing" they usually barked out, "Stand to attention and take your "b" hat off when you speak to me". He is a Scot. If anyone wanted more beer they shouted "Where is the "B" Haggis". Tonight men of all Empire forces are mixed up and the desert is ringing with all sorts of weird cries. There is a brilliant moon and starlit sky, and at times when I look outside I see all sorts of strange capers. Yes dear for just a few fleeting hours the lads have "played hell". I am glad they are taking it like that for it is going to be more hard work towards victory from now on.

I have just seen orders. I have to work all day tomorrow and at "knocking off" time I start again for the night. It is my turn as duty driver. I have to stand by all night in case of emergency.

Well darling it is getting late and I shall soon have to close. Please remember me to Mrs Taylor and Billie. Also Lucy. Tell her I will write her another nice letter next week. I suppose you will have the poker or some weapon ready to tap me on the head when I get back, but I can soon square that. One of the fellows by me has just written to his wife. He tells me if he was at home now the bed would soon be needing new springs. What do you think? I suppose you will say the editors decision is final.

Well darling I really must close. (My ears were burning pretty well at 8.30 last night. I could imagine the party at Mrs Digger's) All my love dearest from your loving husband

Gerald X X X X X X X X X X
      X X X X X X X X X

Christmas Day in the Desert. Note grocery shop at side

Mess room at Christmas. Date fronds used as decoration

Xmas Day 1941

Xmas Day in the Desert

Monday Dec 29ᵗʰ 1941

My Dear Wife,

In your last letter you say you cannot understand why I have not received your letters and telegrams. Well dear, I have received all except the registered mail up to the present. I have already acknowledged receipt of them in previous letters and airgraphs but evidently you had not had delivery of them at the time you wrote. I expect they will have arrived by the time you get this letter. At least I hope so. Please let me know whether you have received all the letters I wrote while I was on the ship.

According to orders published here recently some unavoidable delay had arrived at that time, but it also stated that it had now been safely delivered. I hope mine was amongst it. While I think of it, my extra pay has now gone through and you will get 3d a day extra and I get the other 3d put to my credits. I have already mentioned it in an airgraph which I sent to Brook Street. I had already completed an airgraph to you and had no room left to inform you, so I am taking this opportunity. When you draw it, you will get the back pay from December 12ᵗʰ 1941.

Well darling, I hope you enjoyed Christmas. I wish I could have been with you, but it is the fortune of war, and I did manage to have quite a good time with the rest of the boys here. I have already written and told you some of the programme. Very surprisingly we had a terrific tropical storm which lasted from about 4 to 6 a.m. on Christmas morning. The desert was like a lake. Boxing morning we worked then had the afternoon off and worked all day Sat. had a miserable day. I was driving nearly all day in a "something" sandstorm. It was not too bad in the camp but out in the desert it was extremely unpleasant. My steed was swaying like a cork in water. I hope we do not get any more of that sample of weather for a long time.

Please remember me to Lucy. I hope she is still doing my job with efficiency. I know you will have the poker ready or should it be the rolling pin, but I can't help smiling about it all. Very pleased you let me know about the raids or the lack of same, as I often wonder where they take place. It eases my mind to know that you are safe.

Fancy writing a letter and calling me an old "so and so". That is fighting talk and I can't reach you. I shall have to save the beating up for when I get back. You would be surprised if you knew all the resolutions I have made for when that day arrives. Consider that as one of the pleasures to come.

I came out of my "shell" as the saying goes and all the lads in the hut swore I had been celebrating Christmas. I can feel myself changing in some ways. That was one of the occasions. I hope you will like the change. You used to say you wished you could see me in different ways occasionally. It will be a bit of a problem if I come back acting like an Arab or some other Eastern person. They sit on the sand to eat their food and I should be wearing a lovely dress too.

Well my darling I must finish leg pulling as space is nearly ended. All the best for the New Year to yourself, Lucy and all at 41. Just keep smiling and as I have said before, stay where you are. I want the same home to return to that I left.

All my love from your husband

Gerald X X X X X X X

Chapter 5
1942 BEGINS

> **01/01/1942** British forces take Bardia. They also took 8,000 Axis prisoners

January 9ᵗʰ 1942

Somewhere in the Desert

Darling,

I was very pleased to receive your letter of October 5ᵗʰ 1941. Somehow it seemed much nicer than airgraphs or telegrams. By that please don't think I want you to discontinue sending the latter. I certainly want you to write as often as possible, and by the quickest method, but the letters seem so much more like home. It may be just fancy, but there it is. I can't help it. It was just over three weeks since I had received any sort of mail from home, so it made me feel on top of the world! It rather took the polish off it all, when I was told I was to stand by as Duty Driver for the night. I am writing this letter in Company office while I am waiting for an emergency that may occur. The last time I was on this job I had to go out in the small hours for a special job that should really have been done by some other unit with similar initials. I got nearly frozen stiff driving a fast open wagon across the desert, but I came back 20 piastres better off, which, when interpreted into English money is about 4/-, so it was after all as the Arabs say "Tamaur Kiwi".

Well darling, since I wrote those few lines I have been floating about the desert for nearly three hours and it is now nearly midnight so I expect most of this letter will be written sometime in the near future. However, I will try and keep awake long enough to write a little more. First of all, please thank Mr Digger for the information he gave you, socks and handkerchiefs are just what I need. Food etc. I can get easily, and I can also obtain the above mentioned articles, but after all they are not like those from home. According to the letter from Roma, I am now an Uncle once again. There is nothing like perseverance. I certainly think it is persevering when I have to cover about 16000 miles of water to do it. Now smile.

By the way dear, have you heard from Africa yet? You have not mentioned it. I am enclosing

Hubbly Bubbly Smoker

*Midst the marvellous scenery of the
Middle East*

Two people

Native debugging his robes

Hubbly Bubbly Smokers

Six to eight people live in this hut

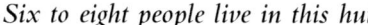

Mossie & Abdul.
These two Arabs look after 40 men.

another two snaps of myself just in case any of the others were unlucky. I have a few more to send next week, and I will also send you the negative. I am expecting quite a lot more snaps back tomorrow and more to follow next week so the album should be getting along quite well by the time you receive this letter.

I went with Fred Loman (we are still together by the way) into a local village recently to try and get some more pictures. It was a most awkward undertaking, but we got plenty of fun out of it. I managed to persuade a "hubbly bubbly" smoker to come out of his den and pose with his pipe. It is an affair about three feet long with a bowl about the size of a sugar basin at the end, and they are pretty tough customers when they are actually smoking the drug. I hope the prints are a success after all the trouble. I also got one of a fellow sitting on the corner of his hovel "de-bugging" his robes. After many attempts I have also got one of a local "belle" with her face uncovered. I can assure you they are very rare unless taken from concealment.

I got this one by genuine persuasion. I have just one print. I will send you one next week. I have seen the native men, women and children out here in their birthday suits, and I can say without any fear of contradiction that this lady would win a local beauty contest "hands down". Not that her morals are as good as her looks. Far from it. What did I hear you say? How do I know? That is a leading question, and you should know better than ask it. No dear, I have not fallen yet, and I am still confident that I shall not. I will tell you a little more of this particular lady. She approached me in a village one hot morning, with a bright smile and wonderful gleaming teeth.

All draped in a thin black gown as worn by custom. She was in a way inclined to a miniature Mae West figure. On her head the inevitable basket (similar to potatoe canes in England). She said "Sayeeda". I replied with a polite "How do you do". Then she spoke in few words of perfect English. I answered in the same language. Then came, "Sayeeda Whallad M'Sharr of Arabie". I looked at her without batting an eyelid. Those few words by the way mean "Greetings young man, do you speak or understand Arabic language".

I did not let her know that I did understand what she was saying. Then she called me a name I would not have stood from anyone in "Blighty". I gave no sign of understanding. She went on and on in level tones with that beautiful smile and pearly teeth for all the world as though she was saying the most flattering things to me. By this time quite a crowd of fellows in flowing robes had gathered round and added their smiles of encouragement. This went on for about five minutes. Fred did not understand a word. Then I got let down rather badly. A native who knew me turned up from nowhere in particular and told her I understood every word she had said. In a smart un-soldier like manner I immediately told her in the best swear words I knew exactly what I thought of her. Whenever I see her now we have a swearing match, but in my own mind I admit she knows more than I do.

Anyway I have got her photograph without getting my head smashed in. Some of the others I have sent to you show the women and girls, but they had their faces covered, and they all "cut up rough". I am going to try for some difficult pictures soon, but I have to be careful as the men folk can be pretty dangerous if I upset them too much.

I want to experiment getting a snap of a sandstorm. It is a difficult job as the sand usually spoils the negative, but I am hoping to succeed eventually. Of one thing I can assure you. They look much better on paper than a view from the middle of one. Ears, eyes, nose and teeth choked with particles of grit. It is a most unpleasant experience.

I think that is all for tonight my sweetheart, as I want to try and get an hours sleep before the telephone starts ringing.

Well it is now Friday and I have a few minutes to spare so I will continue my epistle. Please excuse the blobs etc. but the pen is at fault. However that is a minor detail as long as the letter is readable. From your letter I can just imagine how you and Lucy felt when you got my first letter. I can't decide which one it was you received as you give me very little information as to its contents, but as you seem to think I was in close contact with the enemy it must have been the second one I wrote. I sat down and wrote one immediately I went on board ship but as there was no information with regard to censorship at that time I posted it in time for the "destruction stakes". As far as I can remember I stated what a grand ship it was, and described the cabin I was lucky enough to have during the entire voyage. Well afterwards we were told we must not describe the condition of the ship. If you do not get the letter I shall be very sorry. I shall not make the same mistake again.

Fancy thinking all those queer things about me just because I sent a kiss for Lucy. Well here is another X. Tell her if I am like a long lost brother I shall be expecting a lot of service when I get back. Glad to hear Mrs Willetts and Molly are in good health. They deserve to be after the blitzes they have survived. Please remember me to all at Palfrey Rd. also Uncle Bert and all at Willow Cottage. Tell them I got an airgraph from Eric about three weeks ago, but as it is almost impossible to read his address I have decided to write to him at Norton. Glad to hear Mr Gretton has been industrious in the garden during my absence. Please give him my thanks and wish him all the best for 1942. You seem to have done very well out of the kidney beans. I think I should try some more in the same place if this letter is not too late in arriving.

Darling, while I am writing this page I have just learned a lovely swear word in Eastern Language. When I see you again I will try it exactly as it should be spoken. I am willing to bet that if I can preserve a composed countenance you will smile innocently instead of lashing out. That is of course always providing you are not learning a host of swear words in several languages. The boy who attends to my needs is sitting by my side and smiling at all this rapid "Engleese" writing. He is supposed to be one of the best natives in the area. I think that just about describes him too. I do not know why but he has a soft spot for me. He will do anything I ask and very often things I do not think of. He is extraordinarily intelligent. Some time ago he came up to me and said in his own language "You are my friend." It struck me as being most peculiar as I know quite a lot of his peculiarities.

He seemed very doubtful about something so I said "Come on! What's wrong Abdul". He pulled ten piastres out of his robes and handed it to me. I thought he wanted me to get some article or other for him during my travels. I asked him what it was. He replied "Inta" which means for you. Myself "Annah" or "for me". Abdul "Away" : yes: He then told me that I had no "feluse" (money) and no cigarettes for four days.

To be perfectly candid he was quite correct but how he knew is beyond my comprehension. He was quite upset when I smilingly handed it back to him. He looks at your photograph every morning and murmurs "Inois!" Inois Ketters" or -------- Well I won't print it or you will be getting a swelled head. He is annoyed just at present because the snaps I want to send to you have not arrived yet. Sorry I can't record his language but translated into English it is exceedingly bad.

The mail has just arrived. Still none for me. I cannot understand why I am not receiving any air mail or airgraphs. It is nearly a month now since I got the last.

After another spell of work I will resume writing by the dim light of a hurricane lamp. To begin with I have received some snaps mentioned in the beginning of the letter. Considering they were taken on a very cold dull day they have come out very well. I am enclosing a few in this letter and I will send some by airmail. I am expecting some more to arrive in the next few days, and I will send them on. One is of our mess room at Xmas. It is the best snap of all.

Darling I really must close now as I must get up early in the morning. All the best to both you and Lucy. Please remember me to all next door. All my love dear from your husband

Gerald X X X X X X X

12/01/1942 Sollum is captured by the British

January 18ᵗʰ 1942

Somewhere in the Desert

Darling,

I have already sent you several airgraphs in acknowledgement of the mail I have received recently but just in case they fail to reach you I will thank you once again. I am in the best of health at present. I hope you are keeping well too. Have just recd. a telegram which should have arrived in the middle of October last. Still, better late than never. I have sent you quite a lot of letters by sea in addition to air mail so you should be getting plenty of mail now. Most of them contain snaps of life as I find it now. I have also sent some to Brook St. and as I wrote previously I want you to start a joint album for me when I return. Some of the more valuable pictures will not be sent as I do not want to lose them. You can rest assured however that I shall keep you well supplied. Except for 2 x 10/- from Dad no further money or parcels have arrived yet. I suppose it will all turn up soon. Anyway, I have managed to carry on with my Army pay and I now have a credit of over £1. It is not a large amount, but it will all add to the total you are sending to enable me to achieve a certain ambition. I am sure that when I start to send to you a pictorial record of the places I shall be able to visit you will be more than pleased. I expect it will be a few weeks yet as I shall have to give several weeks notice for leave. I can go any time now, but it is just the £.s.d. The only thing that vaguely worries me is the fact that in the service corps you never know how long you will remain with a unit. I may be here for a long time, yet on the other hand I may move before I get the chance to visit the places I want to see. One thing about being on Active Service is that when leave is due there is usually very little trouble to get it.

I was with some of the lads recently. They told me plenty of stories. They had one grumble. You will never guess what it was. It made me laugh. <u>They had to lay their kit out for inspection once a week</u>. To them it must have seemed a terrible thing.

Darling, you will find a few seeds from a beautiful little desert plant I saw during my travels. I want you to give them to Mother and ask her to try and get them started in Uncle Bert's greenhouse. I shall be expecting good results when I get home.

I have already written in reply to Lucy's query. I will let you know more later on. One of the fellows is just changing his shirt. He can see me writing so he says "as he can't send a photograph can he send a hair off his chest". I won't tell you my reply. I'm sure Lucy does not want a gorilla.

I have just returned from an afternoon's driving in a very rough wind. The sandstorm has subsided after nearly two days, but the wind remains. It is pretty rotten while it lasts.

By the way what did George Calver have to say when he knew I caught that shark. Of all the places in the world that is one ocean in which I never want to fall overboard. It was simply infested with sharks and dolphins.

I am sending you a few local periodicals this week. As I think they will be of interest to you. Please excuse my writing as the letter is being composed under the most awkward conditions.

Glad to hear the garden has done well. Remember me to Mr Gretton and Mrs Taylor and Billie. I am patiently waiting for the day when I shall be with you all again. I expect you are getting all the news of the action out here. All I will add is that to my mind it seems to be one continual rumble of tanks, guns, aircraft and other military traffic. All day and night it goes on and at times it gets quite a strain driving amongst it all. Still I can manage my part alright. It is like music to the ears.

Everyone has been working all out and now we are being rewarded with one extra hour in bed on Sunday mornings. I am wondering whether I should get the day off if we worked a little harder.

I see that George has gone overseas. I hope he gets on alright. Anyway he is old enough to look after himself. Give my best regards to Arthur and Mildred. Tell them to get plenty of coppers ready, as I shall be in good form. I am not getting the chance to go stale like Arthur. That will make him smile or at least it should do. Have received an airgraph from Margery today. Peter wants me to send him a lion. I don't know what I can do about that. If it was a camel he wanted it would be simple. I think I shall have to wait and see if I ever get into lion country. Personally I hope not. The light is fading rapidly now and the desert blackness will descend in a few minutes so I shall have to close very soon. I think of pages to write to you while I am out driving, but somehow I have to write a little bit at a time and then I have forgotten what I wanted to say.

Well darling, just keep your chin up. All the best from your loving husband
Gerald XXXXXXXXXXXX

Sunday Jan18[th] 1942

My Dear Wife,

Many thanks for the letters which I have received during the last few days. I have had four from you, two from Roma and two from Dad so you see I have been doing quite well. Most of them are dated Sept. and October but they are just as welcome as the airgraphs so keep writing. Up to the present the only money I have received is from Dad. Two 10/- P.O's by airmail. I have already acknowledged receipt of these by airgraph. I intended writing you a long letter today, but I am afraid it will have to wait a day or so, as we have been having a terrific sandstorm for the last eighteen hours and my eyes are pretty bad from driving in it. The particles of sand cut like a whip. Anyway, I think I can manage to fill these few pages. First of all, tell Lucy I will see what I can do for her in regard to the correspondence. I showed that part of the letter to some of the lads who sleep near me and I think before I do any more in the matter I had better let the rivalry die down a little. Quite a number of poor old married men were trying to muscle in too. I showed them the snap and they were making their choice. Unanimous decision was number three. Of course they already knew No.1 was out of bounds. Those sorts of things are all we have to do to keep ourselves amused at night. It is surprising what fun we get out of it. We need it too. The lad next to me has received an intimation from his fiancée that she is marring someone else during his absence. Another one has just learned that his two year old baby has died. Yet a third has heard that his brother is believed drowned. He was in the navy. In spite of all this they say little of it, and to hear some of the sounds of revelry at night you would never guess their thoughts. They come in and start salaams to the sun god, and suddenly a boot or pieces of orange peel or in fact anything handy start flying about. It is usually some innocent soul who gets accidentally in the line of fire. According to your airgraph George is at last bound for the Far East. Well dear, although he pulled your leg pretty well, I wish him the best of luck. I can just imagine him telling you the tale of our meeting in the North. I wish I could have seen him again, but although we were so near each other, it was not to be. However we did have a nice quiet celebration. I hope your ears did not burn too much. By the way, I have just received a telegram. I really can't understand it. It was addressed in the proper way, and arrived in these parts on the 17th October 1941. Yet it only reached me today. It was simply signed "Milner", so you see I do not know who to thank. While I think of it please tell Mother I am sending her about half a dozen tiny seeds from a desert flower I happened to see one day. Perhaps Uncle Bert will start them in the greenhouse if they ever arrive. I shall expect to see a nice addition to the collection by the time I get home. At times I see some really beautiful little flowers, but I do not see seem to be able to find any seed pods on them. The next time I manage to get a weekend away from all this sea of sand, I intend to visit some Botanical gardens. I shall have to try my luck there.

Well darling, the storm has abated a little now and it is nearly time for bed so I am afraid I shall have to end very soon. I have sent quite a string of letters containing snaps and I have a few more to send this week. I hope the first ones have arrived safely. Please remember me to Mrs Taylor and Billie also all at Palfrey Road. By the way, Abdul asks after you every day. He thinks I should get a letter by every post. When I opened the registered letter from Dad he muttered "Abu" which means "Father". He immediately knew the different hand writing. I really must close now. All the best from your loving husband

Gerald X X X X X X X

20/01/1942 Benghazi. Is captured by the British

Jan 22nd 1942

Darling,

Many thanks for regular air mail which I received quite safely yesterday. Dated Nov 25th according to information contained in your letter I should have already read several previous letters, but I have no doubt these will turn up in the future. In any case you should know by the time you receive this letter as I shall continue to send airgraphs and letter cards as they are so much quicker. Still I know you like a letter so I send you one or two every week. You say you get very impatient if you do not hear from me for a fortnight. I wonder what you would feel like if you waited a total of sixteen weeks. I will reserve my thoughts on that subject until I see you in person. I hope that time will not be too long delayed. Very sorry to hear you have had a bad cold. Please give Dr. Eric Sinton my best wishes, but tell him I do not think much of his injections if people still get colds. Of course you would mention the £.s.d. to Father. I can just imagine you. I suppose you still retain your persuasive powers. I hope you have forgotten some of them by the time I get back. About counting those notes. You say I have "a cheek" to think such a thing. The only alternative I can possibly imagine is that you got Lucy to do it and save your conscience. Alright, I am a long way off so I do not know who you will throw the crockery at now. You say you can't imagine us getting leave out here. Well dear, all I can say is that we do get it occasionally as the chances occur, and I can assure you that after sticking in these places for a period, it is richly deserved. You say I can keep any surplus money until peace is declared and then see the places I want to visit before coming home. Believe me, the day I get my feet on the homeward trail I shall not ease up until I see you again. I can stick the life of a desert rat just as long as is necessary, but after that, as the Americans say "Just watch my smoke".

The weather has been much cooler lately and sandstorms have been quite frequent. While they last they can be most unpleasant. The mosquitoes however, have disappeared for the present. So you see I have something to be thankful for. Yes, I had got rid of all the bites when I had the snaps taken. I suppose you will have received some of them by now. I have sent them quite regularly by air and boat mail. What a coincidence. You did not know I had been dispatch riding, until you got my letter telling you I was off the "bikes", and now today I have been told I am going back on it again. I had intended giving up "two wheels" for good, but I feel it my duty to do any job I am asked to the best of my ability. Still you have no occasion to worry. I have a pretty fast open truck too, so I shall get plenty of fresh air if any of that is needed out here. I think you had better ask Arthur Perry to examine the springs in the mattress. I don't think a "little tick" like Lucy is a fair test. More crockery flying about I presume. You want to know whether I am still with Joe Booth. Well dear, he is not in my unit. There is only Fred Loman left of the old crowd, but he is quite close. I see him occasionally. I really do not know how you know he is near me as I do not remember mentioning his name. Perhaps it will be explained when I get some of the delayed mail. It is most awkward when I get a letter before the previous four.

Glad to hear all at Harts Hill are alright. Give them my kind regards. For your sake darling, the past is a closed book. I await your reply with great interest. Thank Mr Chapman for his advice but up to the present I have not seen or tasted any of his remedy. Perhaps they have altered it since he served out here. I am rather surprised to hear Mr Hancox has joined up. What is he in? Army or R.A.F. Hope he likes it alright. While I think of it, remember me to Arthur and Mildred. Tell him, if he wants a lovely sunburned complexion to come out here but if he will take my tip, he will stay where he is at present.

As soon as I receive a little more of the registered mail I intend to go to the Holy Land. I want to see the Garden of Gethsemane and the Mount of Olives, The Church of the nativity and all those places of Biblical interest. I shall be very disappointed if I can't go. I will send you all the snaps I can get hold of. I only wish you could go with me. It seems rather mean after always going everywhere together that I should have to see all these places by myself. Still darling, I know you would wish me to go, and I shall have to tell you all about it later on. Wherever I go I am thinking of you and all the happy times we have had together. Somehow I do not think the return of the old days is so far distant. For your sake I sincerely hope not. Must close now as it is almost midnight. All my love dearest

from your husband

Gerald

P.S. please remember me to Mrs Taylor & Billie, Also the many people you say have been enquiring after me. Give my love to Lucy too.

X X X X X X X X X X X X

January 29ᵗʰ 1941 *(The date on this letter is in error and it must be 1942)*

My Dear Wife,

Many thanks for three airgraphs which I have received during the last few days. I have already acknowledged two of them by airgraph and the other is the one I got today. I am very glad to know that you heard from the people I stayed with. Your guess was correct. You know the old statement "owing to unforeseen circumstances etc." You say all your customers are waiting to read my next letter. I am afraid I cannot tell you much about the happenings at this end of the world. I <u>could</u> write just as interesting letters as those previously sent, but that would involve military affairs, so I am afraid you will have to contain your curiosity until I see you again. I know exactly what you will say under your breath but there it is. I cannot alter it. Very pleased to hear the pigs have been killed. I hope they turned out alright. By the way I asked in a previous letter if you or Mother would send a nice cut off one of "the pictures on the wall" to an address which I enclosed. Just in case that letter failed to reach you please find the address repeated at the end of this letter. By the way news penetrates even to places like this. I learn that our friend "Blondie" has been relieved of £1 for a black out offence. I have also learned a lot about the Abel case, but I have no means of finding the verdict of twelve good men and true, so perhaps you will let me know. I am very interested in the case, and after all I bought those chairs off him. I do not know whether you have received the mail telling you about the stone and a half I have gained but I think you had better get all the furniture reinforced. I think it must be the comfort of all these tarmac "roads" which is making me gain all this weight. If it is, I think driving in "Civie St" again will soon be causing me to turn the 20 stone mark. Second George Lovatt in fact. I know you will be <u>most</u> concerned about this beautiful "middle age spread" I am developing. Still dear, if you really do not like it I think this splendid open air dessert complexion I have obtained should soon find me someone who will not mind the increase in weight. Yes I have already dodged the teapot.

By the way I have a bone to pick with you and Lucy. I recd a certain airgraph asking me to supper. Pigs fry, liver, scratchings etc. I think my supper on that night comprised a packet of biscuits. I could just imagine the old pot boiling and a scrap for the "sticky bread". Anyway the thoughts made the biscuits taste all the better. Anyway I can stick it for really the food is not too bad considering everything. While I think of it I will once again mention that business of addressing letters to Base Depot. I cannot understand what has made you start writing to that address again. The only conclusion I can arrive at is that you may have received a very badly delayed letter written while I was at Base, which probably led you to believe I had returned there. My address is still 2 HRS.

What has happened to Charlie Boxley. I have not heard any news of him for a long time now. Is he still in the army? And Mr Taylor. I have just heard he is home. Is it for keeps or just leave. And what of Arthur and Mildred. Darling I am not rebuking you for failing to let me know these things but between Nov 15ᵗʰ date and Dec 18ᵗʰ I received no mail with the exception of two from Dad (Nov 11ᵗʰ and Nov 18ᵗʰ date). So you see I have quite a lot of correspondence on the way somewhere. No doubt it will turn up later as I know you would not fail to write. I did not have any mail from Mother or Roma during those above dates. I suppose by the time you receive this letter it will be time for you to begin on the garden in real earnest. I hope you make a success of it again this year. I am very sorry I posted a letter for Mother & Dad in an envelope addressed to you. I knew immediately I had done it but in the dessert one has not got the means to rectify these slips of the pen so I just let it go.

And fancy "jumping down my throat" because I did not send you an air mail letter as well. I thought I had already explained that I was splitting the mail between you and Brook St as well as I could and to the greatest extent that my very shallow pocket permits. Altogether I spend in the region of 2/6 per week on mail. That is for writing pads, pens ink and stamps.

I'll try to send you 10d airmail every other week. In addition to that there is the cost of all those snaps I have sent you and I can assure you it is no easy thing to stay in this "perishing desert" in order to keep you all supplied with the letters I know you are so anxious to receive, when I could be spending my pay on a good time. As I have told you we can get family leave fairly regularly if we can afford it. Darling, please don't think I am annoyed with you. That is the last thing that will ever happen. But unless I do write like that I am sure you would never understand.

I am still patiently waiting for the "Filthy lucre" to arrive. I have as I mentioned received 2 x 10/- P.O.s from Dad and £1 from you. There is such a lot I want to do with it when it arrives. Of course if the majority of it is coming by sea that explains the delay. Some of the boys of Tobruk that I was talking to a few days ago told me that it is possible to get money through quickly by doing business through Cook's agency. So in future you will be able to make enquiries.

As I have already written there are plenty of places I want to visit, and also lots of things I want to send to you. I know that anything I can send will be appreciated. Some of the things I must retain myself as I do not want to risk losing them. For instance I have a tiny piece of **alabaster from one of the pyramids**. I have a little wooden image too. I know you would really like him, but I cannot make up my mind whether to take the risk of posting him. I expect I shall, together with other things as soon as the rest of the money arrives.

I am so glad you keep me informed in regard to raids at home. Of course I think of you after the previous blitz. I often look up at the old full moon and think of days or rather nights in the past two years. Honestly I think the enemy did his worst then and we survived it, so I have every confidence in the future.

Darling you will find enclosed another snap of yours truly. It was taken a few weeks ago in an orange grove side by side with the owner. It was a terribly cold and dull day. The coldest for many years according to a newspaper I read, so you will understand why it is not as clear as some of the others. I expect you will receive snaps on all kinds of paper. Some firms use ordinary post cards especially for enlargements, some with a very "official" photography looking crinkled edge, while others prefer the usual Velox paper. Anyway, as long as they print them, I don't mind.

While I think of it, please find enclosed numbers of regd. mail I have had up to the

Gerald in an orange grove with the owner

present date:-

From Dad :-   No. 0426

   "   "   " 0455

   "   you   " 9290

Well dear I do not think I have much more to write about just at present so I will conclude my letter. Please remember me to Mr & Mrs Taylor and Billie. Tell Lucy to behave herself, or I shall have to take drastic action when I return. It is very difficult when you have to speak to young ladies of 35 like that. Or should it be 40. All my love from your husband

Gerald

Address previously mentioned:- Mrs Chalk,

24, Birch Crescent, Hornchurch, Essex

Please send a nice little piece of the flitch, marked :-

With compliments from a friend of Dick in the Middle East.

For services rendered

Thank you very much

Gerald X X XX X X X X X X X X X X X

One for Lucy X

February 2nd 1942

Darling,

      Just a few lines in answer to an airgraph (or rather an airgraph and a continuation) which I received today. It was dated Dec 3rd 1941. I have already received 3 written since that date (Dec18th - 23rd and Jan 5th) but it is just as welcome. Glad to hear Roma received one of the parcels back. I have already told you I received one soon after arriving here. You say you are still waiting for the Pyramid snaps to arrive. Well they should be delivered by the time you get this letter. I have sent one or two snaps in every letter I have sent you and also to Brook Street. I thought that by doing that they would stand a better chance of getting through rather than chancing the whole lot together. And I am sure you will appreciate them all the more by waiting for the "next one" to arrive. You will of course understand that I can only send one snap in these airmail letters because of the weight.

Well darling it looks as though you got a repeat of last winter. I have been reading about it. I also note that yesterday's football had several postponements so once again I draw conclusions. In three or four previous letters I mentioned that I had not been receiving much mail. Of course that partly explains why. I suppose the other will turn up soon. By the way I am completely in agreement with Lucy. She has not had time to write me a line yet and I am sure it is because you are making her do all the work. And with regard to Christmas presents tell her I am still tea total but still willing to pay for a drink. I don't know how many she has had at my expense but the one celebrating a "very near squeak" should have been a "double". But that story is still a very long way off now, and I am on the verge of forgetting all about it. Did George get his too? You are very anxious to know why I was so angry on an occasion mentioned by me in an old letter. Well I expect your guess is entirely wrong. To cut a long story short I was trying to get back to camp before dark. I did not manage it. As we came through a native village we ran into trouble and that my dear is all I will say for the present. On another occasion I saw the East as it really is. I had been on a very long journey and I was on the way back travelling at a fast speed when suddenly there was an ominous splutter. The engine had "gone dead". After examination I discovered the trouble, and as they do not have wayside garages round here, I decided that yours truly had a job of work to do and pretty quickly too. I knew that in 1½ hours it would be dark. Well just as the

95

black African night was rapidly descending on the desert I got the engine going. Suddenly I heard the queerest music coming from behind one of the folds in the desert. I took a chance to investigate. There around a small fire were a number of Bedouins. One fellow was playing on a thin pipe affair and the sounds were beyond description. And yet although it sounded like a thousand souls in torment there was something very fascinating about it. All around him the rest of the party were on their knees making their "salaams" to the East. I stood for a few moments unobserved, and then remembering the affair mentioned above I decided to "make tracks". Eventually arrived safely in camp, had a good meal and off to bed to read your airgraph which was waiting for me.

The lads in my "abode" are still causing plenty of amusement. Two of them are on a new "stunt" now. Instead of the old tricks and "larks" I have mentioned they are pretending to be a courting couple about to buy their home and furniture. You never heard anything (or saw anything) like it. They stroll round arm in arm, talking in whispers to each other. The greatest laugh came when one said to the other with an expression I can't describe "And darling, what about er- er- baby's room. After that there was another great hesitation in regard to a picture on a wall. In due time it turned out to be a lavatory wall. I can't tell you all of it as I should be writing all night. While I think of it darling, have they started any schools for good swear words in Birmingham. If they have I would advise you to attend. Reason? The boys say I have started to talk in my sleep describing some of the things I have been through at various times. They say they are waiting for the next instalment of the story now. I don't think I have given away any secrets yet though. I know it must be true because I woke up one morning singing in Arabic. As long as I stick to that language when I get back home it won't be so bad. I suppose you will now be dying for me to get back and find out for yourself. Well I am afraid you will have to wait a little longer yet.

Another thing I will mention now which causes me a lot of amusement when I recall the incident. As I told you I was learning to speak in several languages. Well Abdul, who I have mentioned before, helped me quite a lot. However some of the lads got to work on Abdul. He made me practice various forms of greeting until I was word perfect. With a very confident manner I tried it out one day. The fellow started waving his arms and shouting La- La- La (No-no-no). I went back greatly puzzled. It was not for several days that I learned I had given him the best "cussing" he has had in his life. I can assure you I have been very careful to make further enquiries before I use unknown words now.

Another thing I must mention. I got an airgraph from you recently saying that you had planted a lot of BLUBS in the garden. What are those things? I have overlooked quite a number of minor mistakes but I really had to mention that one.

Well darling I think I have written nearly all I have to say for this time so I must draw to a close. Please remember me to Mr & Mrs Taylor & Billie. Also all at Palfrey Rd and Willow Cottage. Tell them I will write soon. It is such a job to remember all I have written to, but if I have already written I expect they will still want news from the desert.

All my love dear, from your husband

Gerald X X X XX X X X

One for Lucy X

P.S. Please find another snap enclosed.

04/02/1942 Derna is recaptured by Rommel's Afrika Korps.

February 7t**h 1942**

P.S. Have just rec'd a letter card (Jan 26ᵗʰ) in 10 days. Keep sending them.

Dear Youngster,

Many thanks for the reg'd letter No. 3480 which I received quite safely today. Also contents P.O £1. I am rather disappointed that the other money has not arrived (with the exception of that already acknowledged) I had already told you I wanted it to go to a certain place for leave. I have just learned that I shall be unable to go there for the present. But rest assured that there are plenty of other places I want to visit while I have the chance. I will let you know immediately the other cash arrives. Also please thank Dad for his contribution. It is all very welcome. Very pleased to hear the business is going on well. I hope you managed alright during your temporary management. I am afraid I shall be giving you your cards when I get back. Or will it be the other way round. It seems as though Charlie Mason is looking after you pretty well. Remember me to him and tell him to leave all he can at the shop. Try and get him to persuade Walter to open that store cupboard. I expect he will spin some fairy tale but do the same as I did. Worry him until he gives way. How I wish I could have the "gloves on" with him again. Yes you can tell him what I think. I know what he will say and he knows my reply. How are Palmer & Harvey's treating you now. From your letter you appear to be dealing with their a/c but you do not say what amount of goods they are allotting to you. I am still very interested in my business you know. Everything seems to be settled with regard to Webbs. I know they will look after you. I have often wondered what they had to say when they knew I had gone overseas. Well I suppose I had better leave business matters for the present or you will be writing back "Dear Sir".

One other thing you have not told me yet, unless it is in one of those letters which I have not received. I went on a long journey recently and by luck saw Edward. He is still at the same unit. You never said you had been in contact with his wife. According to letters from home she sees you quite regularly. He did not know where I was. Someone near me (I do not know who) wrote and told him my address but the censor decided to cross the address out so you see he was still "in the dark". It was rather unfortunate that I could not stay with him for many minutes as I had such a long journey back. Anyway we talked over old times and I hope your ears are not too badly burned.

I have sent mother another batch of snaps during the last few days. What about all those others. Have they arrived yet? I shall have to get busy and take some more soon, but I am afraid I have been too busy just lately. I am expecting to make up for lost time when I go on leave. What do you want me to send you for a present? Will a battleship do or would you prefer a camel.

Well dear I must close now and I will write again in a few days.

Please remember me to Lucy, Mr & Mrs Taylor and Billie and all my many friends. Just one other little item. In addition to the air mail and airgraphs you send please try the letter cards. They are very quick. Some of the lads are receiving them in seven days. All for now from your loving husband

Gerald X X X X X X X X X X X X XX X

07/02/1942 The Gazala line is a series of fortified boxes each of brigade strength running south for a hundred miles from Gazala to Bir Hacheim. They were protected by minefields and regular patrols.
Rommel's counter-offensive came to a halt in front of the Gazala.

Sunday February 7th 1942

Darling,

Many thanks for the (unlucky) No. 13 letter which I received safely today. I wonder what you thought when you put that number at the top of the page. The contents were very welcome. Most unfortunately however I cannot now go to the place I was so anxious to visit. I cannot give you any reason of course, but with the same amount of money there are a lot of other places of interest which I intend to see. I am sorry I upset you with the beginning of my letters. That will have to be altered. As you say I got quite a lot of interesting information during my visit to the pyramids but that was a long time ago. I have not been out of the desert since. Yes the "Seven Pillars" would be very welcome now, but it must remain at home. I can't risk losing it. You paint a glowing picture of that new house you require but as far as I am concerned the first love is the best. Treasures from my travels I may have and probably they will be a source of great interest, but the only treasure I am looking forward to is returning to my wife. The only part of your suggestions which interest me in the least is to sit by a good fire and tell the story of all I have seen. And darling, believe me I think I shall be able to keep on for ever. If I stay out here much longer I don't think I shall be able to remember it all. I reckon all that will set you off again. "Hurry up and get back". There is no one more anxious to do that than myself, but there is a pretty tough job to be done out here. Still, no one doubts that we can do it. All I can tell you is that the desert is a very hard task master.

How curious you are about that spell of anger I had a long time ago. Well I have already told you in a previous letter. It is not very pleasant to be the target of large stones and the necessary action had to be taken. That is all I will say.

Fancy calling me a beggar. Glad you did not have the courage to put a "u". I suppose that will be in the next letter.

Glad to hear you have tried your hand at managing the shop. I am waiting the next letter with great interest to know how you performed. Sorry you missed the staff party. I suppose Mothers "perm" was Roma's usual Xmas box. Glad to hear old Charlie Mason is still doing his stuff. It must have been pretty awkward without the car, but now it seems to be in good order. I trust it will remain so in the future. I am certainly pleased that your mind has been set at rest in regard to finance. I stuck it out for a long time, and I have never wavered in my opinion as to what the future held. And when I get back I have other ideas which I intend to carry out. It will involve hard work but I am quite prepared to see it through. I am not going into details at present. I must wait and see how the land lies when I return, but those ambitions will never be crushed. Your immediate thoughts are answered. "Yes you are in the scheme" You say you are keeping my clothes aired. By the later part of the letter you seem to be wearing them out. Still as long as they suit you it is alright. I should like to have seen you give the demonstration at Brook St. Very sorry if you have difficulty in reading this letter but it is being composed under rather awkward conditions and in between journeys. I have just been informed that I am to go out again in one hour so I shall have to pack up for the present. If I go on at this rate darling, it will be a week before I finish writing.

Well at the time I wrote the previous few lines I did not think it would really happen like that but anyway it is now Saturday Feb 14th. In between I have managed to send a letter card and an Airgraph. As you know the work has to be done at all costs, but I make up for lost time at every available opportunity. I am writing rapidly in pencil as I am again due out in a very short time. This week I have received a parcel from Mother a Regd letter from Dad and several other letters from you all at home. I am afraid I am just a little bit too busy to answer them all today but I will take them one at a time this week. After many weeks of hardly a word from home it has come as a very pleasant surprise.

I have already written to you about Roma's party. What a pity the weather was so bad. You say there were about 80 persons present including Curly. Well I know he would have to tap the barrel, but who could the other 79 be. I can think of friends but certainly not as many as that. Anyway so long as it was a success that is all that matters. Very sorry Roma did not get a line from me for her birthday but I can assure you I have written to her personally on one or two occasions, but as you know, after I put them in the post they are beyond my control. I have also sent wishing Mother many Happy Returns in one or two letters. I hope they get there alright or I shall have to wear my helmet when I come home.

Really I think your mail seems to be arriving fairly regularly. You can't expect one every day you know. Will you please thank Lucy for the book Bomber Command which I received in a parcel yesterday? It will provide me with many happy hours reading, especially as the evenings are lengthening now. It is light until about six o'clock and now after the terrific effort we put in through the winter, we are getting a readjustment of hours. Whatever the fortunes of war may be it can never be said that the boys of the Army of the Nile or as you may choose to call it the Eighth Army, have ever shirked a job. I cannot tell you the full story or even part of it but when I see you again I think I can explain quite a lot of my deficiencies.

While I have been writing I have been called out again to fetch the mail for the unit. A letter from Mother and an airgraph from you, also the first lot of papers. I was really pleased until I opened them and I am afraid I must confess my spirits sank to zero. I don't know whether I am being chastised three times for omitting the above mentioned prefix to my letter or whether I have missed it out three times in succession. Whatever the case may be I am sorry. I was going to write you a really nice letter but now I do not know what to write. You say the old feeling of taking second place has returned. Second place to whom or what? There is nothing I would prefer to being in your company once more. I have told you many times that past mistakes are to be altered. I have been in this desert for months, the number of white women I have seen can be counted on the fingers of two hands, and every available copper I have had has been spent on writing to you and my friends at home. For all that I stand rebuked.

Well my darling it is time for me to go now. Thank Lucy for the book. I will write her in the week. I must end up by telling you just what you want to know. My love for you remains the same as I always said it would. That is "unchanged". I only wish I were with you to prove it. One last word. Under no circumstances must you do what you say you want to do. Hard as it may seem I must remain alone and take my chance. Please do not think badly of me for putting it as bluntly as that but it is exactly what I mean. All my love my darling from your husband

Gerald X X X X X X X X X X X X X X X X X X X

Sunday February 15th 1942

Somewhere in the desert

My Dear Youngster,

Please accept my humble apologies for having once again missed out on the prefix to one of my letters but really I must blame the circumstances under which I often have to write. I have all the fooling about by the lads to contend with. I usually write by the light of a hurricane lamp. Many times I have started a letter, just completed the address and then been called out. Just try writing with interruptions at every few lines and see what sort of effort you will make of it. Well darling I now have that little lot off my chest, but if by any mischance I should make another slip you will know the reason. I will try hard to remember. Sorry to hear you have toothache. I hope it will be cured when you visit the dentist for your overhaul.

Darling, please don't think I am angry with you. Far from it. I only wish I could be with you if it were only for a few hours. I have steeled myself to the fact that it cannot be so and I have no illusions at all. The more we put in this job the sooner it will be over and the sooner I shall be able to prove to you my real feelings for a wife who tells me she is taking second place.

Glad to hear George is getting along safely. I hope he gets to his destination in one piece. I keep making enquiries about him but I may never hear anything of him unless he comes and finds me. I expect he knows my address. I am enclosing this letter with one I wrote during the week. I did not find time to finish it until last night and at present I am Duty driver for 24 hours. So I am trying to get everything fixed up during odd moments.

While I was finishing that letter last night I dropped off to sleep (no it is not an excuse for omittances). I had been driving nearly all day, and I must have been very tired. Some of the lads got a piece of card and wrote on it in large letters "Do not disturb the Sleeping Beauty" and stuck it on my battle dress. As luck would have it the Company Sergeant Major came in that afternoon, looking for one of the men. He saw the notice (so the boys say) looked at it from all angles and remarked "Cor Blimey, What a Bloody hero". I don't know what he will say when he sees me again. I expect he will be pulling my leg to get his own back for the day in the dim past when I towed him back on his motor cycle. He got a pretty bumpy ride that day, but he is a good sport and enjoyed it as much as I did. Recently he performed an act of great bravery and he will be remembered for a long time for it by the men. That story is just another incident that must be kept until after the war or a least until I come home.

There is a grand sandstorm blowing again and my eyes are none to good as I have been out in it for the last hour. I cannot think of anything more unpleasant. By the way darling I am off the motor cycles once again and I hope it is for good this time. It is strange how I have altered my opinions after so many years on them. I am very glad you are keeping my letters for reference in the future. They will bring back to memory things I may temporarily forget or things of which I must not write.

Well my sweetheart, I suppose I must close now as it is almost tea time. One thing I must mention. Instead of 3/6 per week 1/9 has been allotted to you and the remaining 1/9 to me. I have already mentioned this in two letters but evidently you have not received them up to the time of your last letter. Cherio darling and remember I still love you just as much as ever even if I don't always say so. Yes I know you want me to keep telling you. Alright, I will go quietly. Please remember me to all at home. God Bless you and keep you safe until I come home from your loving husband

Gerald X X X X X X X X X X X X X X X X X X X X

One for Lucy X

February 17ᵗʰ 1942

My Dear Youngster,

Just a few more lines to let you know that I am still in the best of health and behaving myself. At least I am trying to. I have written several letters and airgraphs just recently, but I know how you look forward to a letter from me and as these letter cards are reputed to be the quickest means of communication I thought I had better keep up my reputation as a dutiful husband.

Glad to hear you have been fairly free from raids. Have you had the windows replaced yet or are you still expecting them to be blown out again. I suppose you are suffering from the old complaint of cold feet. What a shame when the warm half of the family is in the tropics. Still darling, if you do as you say and use my "civie" clothes, get the windows replaced, a hot water bottle and a few blankets that should make a good substitute during my absence. I am still waiting to hear how you fared when you had temporary management of my business. According to previous letters the supply of goods seems to be better than expected. I somehow think it will remain so. You do not seem keen on my getting those letters after my name until after the war. Well darling, as it is obviously impossible for me to see Major Webb myself I must abide by your decision. After all, it would be no use at all to me here so as far as I am concerned I am prepared to let the matter drop for the present. However that will not alter my decision when I get back home.

You say in one of your letters that you have heard nothing of the extra pay yet. Well from Dec 12th 1941 you should receive 3d per day extra. The other 3d goes to my credit. I expect you will get it altogether as soon as the notification goes through.

Please thank Mrs Digger for the compass to help me find my way home. Tell her I have set it correctly but I now want her to send me the required permission. I think the beautiful smell of frying bacon from those four pigs you killed would guide me home in any case. I wish I could drop in for supper as you suggest. Still considering everything we don't get on too badly out here. When the efforts of the day are finished there is always the "skylarking" of the lads in the billet to keep us alive and believe me it is amazing what they do at times. The food is quite respectable. In fact it is far better than I really expected to get in the desert and as long as we work hard and conduct ourselves properly, there is very little interference from officers and NCO's. So you see although the desert is no picnic we have quite a lot to be thankful for.

Well dearest it is nearly time for me to turn in for the night. I wish it was on a feather bed at No. 43, but still that time will soon roll round again.

Please remember me to all next door. Also to Lucy. By the way, have you received any more of the snaps I sent. You have not mentioned them.

All for now. God Bless you and keep you safe, and may our reunion not be too far distant. All my love from your husband.

Gerald X X X X X X X X X X X X X

Saturday Feb 21st 1942

My Darling,

I am writing these few lines while I am sitting in my lorry with a few moments to spare. It is really a half day for me, but I rarely get one complete as there is always work to be done and I never mind turning out for an hour or two. Well darling I have a lot to write about this week, yet I suppose when it is on paper it will not look very much. To begin with I have been in and out of trouble all the week. I have still to face the more serious charge. More about that later. For three days this week I was really ill. I managed to keep going but only just. I could have reported sick, but it is such a performance that I decided not to bother. How I wished you could have been with me at that time. The cold weather we get at night has brought me a return of that cough I had last year. Played me up for several days but it is getting better now. Well you see I did not get a chance to write much yesterday so I must try to collect my thoughts and continue as I intended.

First of all let me thank you for the airgraph telling me the numbers of the Postal orders you have sent up to the present. It will enable me to check up as each one arrives. Only two of them have arrived up to the present, but I am not worrying as it is a big job sorting millions of letters.

Well my dear to return to the subject at the top of the page. I almost got into trouble through a bunch of prisoners I had in my charge. I managed to extricate myself from that lot and ran into more trouble in doing it. I got out of that fairly easily and then I received mail from you and Mother rebuking me for not starting my letters properly. I have already answered that and now I have removed the load from my chest I feel much easier in my mind. Now I have this other charge to face. I am not in the least bit worried about it. I do not even know what the charge is at present. I expect to be up before the O.C. in the morning. It is for a driving offence supposedly committed by me but when I tell you I am innocent I know you will believe me. Somehow I think the OC knows the truth, but if the case goes against me I shall take the punishment without grumbling. If I had been guilty I should have been worrying myself stiff, yet here I am in a light hearted mood. Tell Arthur that after this affair I have lowered my opinion of his crowd. I shall have to knock a few coppers out of him when I get to South Avenue again.

Sorry I have not been able to send quite so many snaps just recently. I expect it will be a couple of weeks before I am able to get any quantity again, as I have been very busy lately. I shall probably get plenty of opportunity later on. Please try and send me a copy of the wedding photograph. I often wonder what I look like in a blue suit. And of course there is always the constant female to bring back pleasant memories. I often wonder what you will think of <u>me</u> when I come back. Don't tell me "The same as before", because I am altering quite a lot. The law of the desert teaches us that we are all in it together and good comradeship is the order of the day. There is no room for pessimists in our crowd, and if thing look black at times, well, it just means trying a little harder. I am the only regular driver in our billet and I often have to drive motor cycles light and heavy vehicles or staff cars.

If as very often happens, I do not get in until midnight, I can usually rely on finding my bed made and my spare kit ready for dawn the following morning. If I am lucky enough to get an hour or two off I try to return the compliment. As for "back chat" or whatever you chose to call it, I think I can hold my own with anyone now. They think I am a very respectable sort of fellow and if I use one of their own expressions occasionally they tell me it sounds strange coming from me. I have had plenty to put up with this week. They say "Fancy you of all people going off the straight and narrow path and smiling about it". They are now speculating where my "crimes" will take me. I do not know whether crime is responsible for colour but I am gathering quite a lot of grey streaks. Hope you approve. It gives me a sense of noble old age you know.

Well darling I think the letter is going to be shorter than I intended. I am writing you an airgraph too. I will let you know how I get on about the other affair as soon as possible. You will be in my thoughts when I get on the carpet. Please remember me to Lucy and all next door. Look after yourself until I come home again. God bless you and keep you safe sweetheart. All my love now and for the future from your husband.

Gerald X X X X X X X X X X

Saturday Feb 28th 1942

Darling,

Since my last letter I have not heard from you again but as I am Duty Driver until 7 a.m. tomorrow I have a few hours to spare so I have decided to use my time in writing a few more lines to you.

First of all let me say how pleased I am that the snap got through alright. Seems as though you were satisfied with it. I have quite a nice little lot to send you in my next letters and I am expecting some more to arrive soon. I am enclosing one which should interest you. How do you like the fellow at the front of the picture? The one that is curled up I mean. I think that I am doing well with the snaps I am getting but I often say a few words under my breath when I see a grand opportunity and find I have not got my camera handy. Some of the things I see here would never be believed if I told people at home. Yet to us in the desert it is an everyday happening. Even troops who are stationed in towns have to look twice on many occasions when they have reason to come into the wilderness. I was driving steadily over a bumpy desert track recently when I saw a familiar sight. Native girls tending their sheep and goats. I believe I have sent you several snaps of them. I was amazed at the next part of the proceedings. One of the young ladies suddenly lay on her back and manoeuvred under a goat. To cut a long story short she got one of the goat's "fingers" in her mouth and proceeded to drink her daily milk ration. Just imagine that happening at home. I often wonder what stories the desert could tell if only it could speak. Perhaps it is just as well that it cannot. I do not know what the reason is but when one gets to know it and its people it holds a strange fascination and creates a desire to learn more of it.

Every day I find something new to arouse interest. Recently I have seen roses in bloom besides other strange tiny desert flowers. Marigolds do fairly well too. I have also found stocks that would make our most choice blooms look very second rate. Giant cactus of all varieties make wind breaks in place of trees and even the more common date palm holds great interest on examination. Then there is the skill of the native boatmen with their dhows. They are a never ending source of fascination for me. I have sent you quite a number of pictures of them but I have some you will not see until I get home. I think my snaps are worth every piastre I have spent on them. I have taken great interest in getting them just for your sake. I know how interested you will be when I am able to tell you stories <u>and</u> illustrate them.

Then there is my "lady friend" Izeeza. She says she will love me "bandin" (later). I am afraid the affections are not returned but I have a quiet smile when she ignores the rest of the boys and insists on talking to me while I sit at the wheel with a few spare moments. I have a little bunch of curios she has been wearing for a long time and later on I shall send them to mother. Oh dear no, I have not left you out. I have already sent you a few pieces of pure alabaster from the Pyramid and I have a lovely little fellow to send you later. I know Mother would much prefer the tiny curios especially if she knew how much persuasion I had to use to get them.

I have also sent a few seeds of an extremely pretty flowering bush I found in the desert. I posted them three weeks ago so I hope they arrive safely. Just at the moment one of the early Khamseen winds is blowing, and giving a warning of what is to come. Khamsa means five. Thus fifth month winds. They are like a fire searing and burning the flesh and the temperature gets up into the realms of 130. I cannot say I relish the thought. I had quite enough of that when I went through the Tropics of Cancer. One peculiar thing I noticed about it was the fact that a cup of scalding hot tea had to stand nearly a quarter of an hour before it became cool enough to drink.

Well darling I am still on the charge I mentioned previously, although by the time you get this letter you will probably have had an airgraph telling you how I got on. To begin with, I have been "pegged" by the police of Arthur's unit. My OC is not at all satisfied with the evidence, and from what he has told me it appears to be conflicting. He is on my side evidently for he says he believes me. Most remarkable thing is I was charged with this minor offence with a heavy vehicle at a time when I was miles away from the place mentioned and I can prove it. So you see they cannot even tell the time properly. I have not told the OC that yet. I am waiting the next inquiry before dropping the bombshell. Of one thing I am certain. With this OC I shall get a square deal. He has gone into the case most thoroughly and carefully, and given me some very good advice. He could have finished the case by giving me a "severe lecture" but he is not satisfied with the other side of the picture, so he is going all the way with the case. He has told me I am released without prejudice until such time as he requires me to appear before him. Actually I have never been "in irons". It is just an Army regulation that I am automatically under arrest. I have done nothing wrong so I have no fear for the future. Before I went up to him the first time I wondered what to expect. I was examining my chin for "undergrowth" with the aid of a mirror when I suddenly noticed that you were there behind me too. It was just a reflection of your photograph hanging above my bed, but I had to smile. I knew it would be alright then and it was. As I have said before he was like a Father to me. I hope he remains that way when judgement is delivered.

To get off that subject and return to others, I am in two minds with regard to my photography. There are some things that I do not think even you will believe when I tell you, and I am wondering whether the proof will bear print. How should you like to see a few snaps of native men and women boys and girls in their birthday suits. I can fill an album with those. All sizes shapes and varieties. I think I shall have to get some and keep a separate album. One of our lads sent one home and his wife wrote back "All the girls at work fell in love with him. How old is he?"

When I go amongst them they take no notice and I must confess I am getting case hardened. I often wonder what I shall be doing when I get back to civilisation. I suppose I shall be shocking someone. Of course in the towns and nearer civilisation these things do not exist to the same extent as in the desert. Here it is just primitive life and primitive methods. Brick making etc. by hand and ploughing with oxen and wooden ploughshares. I see it all and get used to it, but behind it all are thoughts of home and you dear. We have a job to do here and it must be finished beyond all doubt. To express a personal opinion one thing only will finish it and that is unremitting toil and believe me when I say super human efforts have been made and are still being made. The desert is a very hard task master and at

Transport in Eastern Egypt

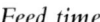

Feed time

Native making bricks

104

*Native
shepherdess*

*Native girls or
"bints" attend to
their flocks*

*Ploughing by
oxen*

times gives the impression of laughing at us puny beings but which ever way things have gone we never despair for we know in our hearts that Rommel can never beat us. I often wonder idly whether, when I come back, I shall head my letters the same as now just from force of habit. And whether I shall be rolling myself in my blankets and sleeping on "the deck". I think I shall have to reserve that one for any occasion when you annoy me. And then come thoughts of comfortable home, a good fire, a decent bed, and above all a wife who can never take second place. Yes darling, that little bit still sticks, and it is not true. I am confident I shall prove it before very long.

The desert has taught me a lot of things, patience, comradeship and thoughtfulness for others. I learn those lessons every day and it is amazing the instances to be seen. On one occasion some time ago I was in charge of a crowd of Libyan prisoners and each one had a native made carved cigarette holder. They had one cigarette between them and it was passed around until it had been in each holder and every man had had a chance a share. I have seen it happen many times since. Even now in their work they change round by an unwritten agreement, each having a spell at easy and hard work. So you see darling it is possible to learn lessons even from prisoners.

Of one thing I have no doubt whatever and that is there is nothing in the world I desire more than to return to you. When that day comes it will be the happiest day of my life. I know you will say "What about Aug 5th?" But even that will pale by comparison. I have dreams for that day. I want to find a place where we can go for a few days without seeing the familiar uniforms. No sand, no sea, no natives and Babel of tongues, no thoughts of war, just peace and solitude. I think I must be thinking of Utopia, but there it is and there it will remain. A gun, fishing rods, a farm, in fact anything you please. If you think those things sound too selfish, I don't mind. I leave it to you, but I am determined to have you to myself for a few days at least. That is all, my sweetheart. If I do not refer to it again you will know just what I think. So until that day dawns I must continue with my dreams. I must close now too, as I must write a few lines home. Give my love to Lucy and remember me to all next door. Goodnight sweetheart. God Bless you and keep you safe and grant that we may have a speedy reunion. All my love now as before from your husband

Gerald X X X X X X X X X X X X

one for Lucy X

Wednesday March 4th 1942

My Dear Youngster,

Many thanks for the mail which I have received this week. I have had a Regd letter from you No. 0716 containing P.O. for £1. Also 2 airgraphs dated Feb 8th and Feb 12th and on top of those a letter by boat mail written a week before Christmas. It has been a curious week altogether. Really darling I do not know where to start. I think I will first of all sympathise with you over the loss of a molar. I hope by now it has healed up. I can imagine what you felt like having to part company like that when you have never had any trouble from them before.

Next thing on the agenda is the subject of my past conduct. You say you often think of why I stayed with you when you had all your trouble and were lonely. I did that not only because I considered it to be my duty but because there was a far stronger call. That call still remains today. I have a job to complete at present but when that job is through I shall be back at your side at the earliest possible moment.

With regard to my mentioning the possibility of "getting a packet" you say you think I shall be lucky. Well my darling I wrote that because we never know what will happen on active service. Last night tragedy and death stalked very near. Some of the boys were sympathising over me because my name was not answered on Roll Call this morning. They thought I was one of the unlucky ones. As a matter of fact I had been out on duty long before dawn. The lads were very quiet this morning but tonight after a quiet discussion the same old revelry and laughter rings out. Out here the misfortune, work and laughter go hand in hand; The job has to be done and somehow we get used to taking whatever Fate chooses to hand out. It is the only way. The icy hand has clutched very near to me on several occasions since the war started but each time that Guardian Angel has been in the vicinity and all has been well. I have the same feeling as you that I shall be lucky now. For your sake I hope so.

Now for another subject altogether. I refer to the Charge I was on and which I have .already mentioned in previous letters. To set your mind at rest the case against me was dismissed. Quite a number of men in the Army have been of the opinion that a man who does as he pleases gets the same treatment as a man who behaves himself.

Well since I have been in the Army I have endeavoured to conduct myself as you would wish, and on this occasion, it was a great help to me: My conduct had evidently been noticed by the powers that be. I told you in a previous letter that I suspected that my OC was on my side. Well when I went before him for the final hearing I do not think anyone could have been praised more than I was. Coming from such a man I really think I blushed. In addition to hearing the case and giving the verdict he defended me right through. He tore the evidence against me to shreds and tatters. He told my accusers that I was the best driver in the unit, that I had given every satisfaction, that my conduct had always been exemplary (I seem to remember Dick Worthington saying that when I left the HG) that I was a very good and valuable man and above all, that he believed every word I had said. To be quite frank the evidence had been pretty black against me but in the face of all that I simply told the truth and that was my reward. I can honestly say that no one was more surprised than myself. What he eventually said to the men who had charged me had better be reserved for a date when I come home. I have grave suspicions that the Sergeant Major had been at work on my behalf too, although he denies it. Anyway he confirmed my character at the hearing. All these things boil down to the comradeship of men in the desert and even if I had the inclination to sit down and write it all and risk the censorship, it would take far too long to tell.

I have a lot off my chest now so I will endeavour to deal with all the correspondence I have received. I have already told you the story of my Christmas and that should have reached you by now. With regard to the dancing I am afraid I must disappoint you. Since the South African affair I have had no opportunity or inclination to resume my lessons. Glad it caused George to call out "Happy Days".

With regard to the fishing he mentioned I am afraid I shall have to keep you in the dark over that business. That little affair is just between George and myself. I think what I saw at the time would make anyone forget the fishing part. As he says it is very private.

You say the band was playing "When day is done I think of you" Well dear if you could hear the boys at night you would wonder whether it would be possible to forget. Some of them are remarkably good singers. We go through the whole lot some nights when we get to bed. Occasionally we end up by singing soldiers versions of "Desert Songs" If you ever hear those I am very much afraid it will only be by accident. They may be vulgar, but oh! How true they are. You mention "That is if I am not too shy" Just imagine that from my wife and on top of that you ask me how I feel about it. Well after due consideration I think the desert has made me immune from all shocks, and on the other hand I think I shall be embarrassing quite a lot of people in the future. To begin with the lads even now are talking of changing the name of our abode from "Dun Romin" to the "Virgin's Nest". I don't know what they will end up with, but that is only a tame example. Will you please give Lucy due warning and tell her to take the required precautions.

Since I completed that little piece two days have passed so I had better spend a few more moments in trying to finish my letter. I am most surprised at you telling me you had just finished the pork. I suppose you will be making my mouth water by telling me you had apple sauce with it in your next letter.

Fancy getting so excited about hearing the bells of Bethlehem. Personally Bow Bells would suit me. Many thanks for sending the piece off the wall to the address I gave you. If you should see fit to send a little bit more please mark it the same and add "for services rendered" I cannot tell you anymore at present except that it was to do with the anger affair.

Darling, you do not seem too pleased at the decision I gave you. You say it means you will have to remain in "Civie" street now. That is just what I want you to do. I want a home and a wife to come back to, and I want both of them to be there for me without having complications. I could never reconcile myself to anything otherwise. I think you will appreciate this eventually.

Another thing I must not forget to thank you for is the £25 you mention. Naturally I am pleased with your efforts, but sweetheart; I am sincere when I say I would rather be without my business or banking account if I could get back to you now.

No! I am not nursing any illusions. I am prepared for the worst while hoping for the best, but you wanted me to write like that, or rather my true feelings so now you know.

Once again I will resume after a two day interval. I have been extremely busy just lately. I went out at dawn today and now it is almost eight o'clock and the first chance I have had to write to you. Still darling I know you will forgive me when you get a nice long letter like this, even if it does have to be written at intervals. And in any case I always endeavour to write an airgraph or two either to you or Brook St to let you know I am keeping well. Received a letter from Roma yesterday written in December. Please tell her I am writing to her personally again in a day or two.

I tried to see Edward today but I think he was away for the weekend. How is his wife keeping? Are you still in contact with her?

By the way you ask in your letter and in an airgraph if that photo is still in place. The answer is "YES". It has even remained there for every one of the O C's inspections and he has never said a word, although the lads said I would have to take it down on inspection days. That is where it will remain until I am ordered otherwise. After all it is the only real treasure I have.

The story of my trial seems to be getting around now and the lads are quite enthusiastic about it. Yesterday I heard a voice behind me say "Ah the man to shake the ----- " It was the CSM. I don't know why but small troubles have followed me all this week. They have all turned out O.K. eventually.

Glad to hear Dad has had an airgraph from me. There are one or two more on the way. I expect he will have received some of them by now.

I have managed to get another pile of snaps today and I am expecting some more next week so you should be kept well supplied. You will find another two enclosed in this letter. I hope you will like them as much as the others I have sent to you. My own collection is beginning to get very interesting too. Some I have forwarded to you which I cannot repeat and I have no duplicate so I hope you will take great care of them. In any case I know you will.

Well my wife I suppose I shall have to close now as it is getting time for bed. Give my love to Lucy and tell her not to be so miserable. Fancy dishing it out in small portions like that. Also remember me to all next door, at Palfrey Road, Norton Road and Mildred and Arthur. When you see him, tell him I have a big score to wipe off with him. I'll tell him what it is when I see him, as it is very, very private. Good night my darling. God bless you and keep you safe until I come home. All my love from your husband

Gerald X X X X X X

One for Lucy X

Native's returning from a day's work

Natives holding a conversation

Places like these are rare. Trees are date palms at various stages of growth

Washing day

Native bazaar

Scenes often encountered on the outskirts of the desert

Notice how the lady covers her face. In the basket she will carry concrete on her head.

Objections to camera man

Family on parade

Scene in a park

March11th 1942

P.S. Please find enclosed two more snaps.

My Dear Youngster,

Well of all things I have wanted most I think a letter from you which I received on Monday was the most welcome It contained a 10/- PO Letter No. R2265. It has been badly delayed somewhere but I do not mind that now. You think I have changed since I left home. Well my darling I do not think, I know. And what is more I know it is for the better rather than worse. I have told you in previous letters some of the ways in which I have changed. One thing is that I do not care two hoots what other people think of me. I just go my own way and behave myself. If others chose the easier path that is their affair. One day I will tell you the story of that charge I was on and exactly what happened before I went before the OC. My comrades told me that if I had gone about it the right way I should just have been "choked off" and the case would have been ended. Well I went my own way, and told the truth at the same time risking the consequences. You should know from previous letters that I left the orderly room without a blemish on my character.

Glad to hear you have invested in a pair of warm boots. Whatever you spent on them is far better than suffering ill health. I suppose you thought I would not approve. Well I told you I had altered. I do wish you would not keep writing about cauliflower and melted cheese and roast pork etc. I really think if you persist I shall be jumping the Med and Atlantic or something like that. With regard to my billiard cue, I do not think there is anything else you can do. It should actually be kept in a warm dry place or it will warp.

Fancy writing and telling me you saw Mr tonight. You say he was surprised to hear I was out here. Who is this Mr. I seem to remember a reprimand for a certain omittance. Now what about it? And just fancy you getting the feeling that all you do is for the present only. I am confident that I shall be returning to you to share the future. I am gaining a wealth of experience and I have so much to tell you when I get back. And yet I have never lost patience. I know I cannot alter it and all I ask is for my home as I left it or as you see fit to alter it, and above all your presence. I have written a letter by boat mail which will surprise you, but I want you to treat it seriously. I mean every word that I have written in it. Call it a catalogue for our future if you choose. I am certain that you will be happy, but darling please write and let me know if you do approve.

Glad Lucy approves the celebrations, but I have told you before I don't ask you to celebrate for nothing. With regard to the other charge you mention, you have nothing to fear. You will be able to ask me that question at any time and I shall give you an answer without hesitation. Please remember me to all at home as it is time for bed now. Think I had better turn the light out or ----. Goodnight my darling. All my love from your husband

Gerald X X X X X

One for Lucy X

Another reg'd letter No. 1940 arrived yesterday.

Saturday March14th 1942

My Darling,

        I have a confession to make. Oh no! My dear it is not what you will immediately think. There is nothing like that about it, but somehow I cannot help having to tell you about it. For a long time now I have been looking at life as it should <u>not</u> be, both out here and back at home. I have seen death and destruction, the unknown peril overhead at night, and the deadly menace of the deep. Through all that I never felt more than a vague uneasiness which was forgotten when daylight came. But this week an indelible picture has been burned into my brain. And now for the confession. For the first time in my life I experienced the real meaning of the word fear. My darling you know I cannot tell you many things and this is one of them but I can at least tell you my feelings. I told the boys in my "mansion" of my experience and how I had the "wind up" and they just smiled and said "We have felt the same before today". Ten brief seconds which were an eternity. After that, well, I tried to breathe again. I must have succeeded otherwise I would not have been writing this. Some of my past came up before me. But most of all I thought of you. That I am certain is why I was afraid. I saw a picture of you the same as I saw you years ago. Bravely facing stark reality, yet still bewildered and wondering what you had done to deserve such misfortune. I may not say much about it but that is one of the old memories I think of most. I could see you still facing up to an empty future. For myself I would not have troubled. But for you and the future I know you would wish, I was placed in a desperate situation. Above all I felt I still had to keep up an appearance. The "Icy hand" was very near again, but at the critical second the Guardian Angel came, and you still have a future worth looking forward to. Many times I have told you that you are the only girl in my life. During the time you have been my wife you have believed it too. Well my sweetheart after those ten seconds in Hell itself I know beyond all doubt that it is so and always will be. If only I could see you for a few hours. My burden and hardships would be far easier to carry. I suppose most of the boys think the same. To see them at their duties they are a tough happy go lucky crowd, but when the toil of the day is over and the cool of late evening comes, they talk of home. The happy hours of the past are recalled, and often very quietly the tragedy of the present is spoken of. Can you imagine the feelings of a man on active service when he gets several airgraphs telling him that his wife is now recovering? Recovering from what? He does not know and then eventually gets the delayed mail telling him his baby is dead. That is only one instance I could relate. But in spite of everything the self made merriment goes on every night.

Unfortunately I am again Duty Driver so I do not know much about it at present. Anyway to cut a long story short, we have clubbed together and treated ourselves to a radio. It has cost us 10/- each in the billet but I think we have made a good investment. And among the subscribers we have first class electricians and radio men so we should be well away now. Whenever I am finished in time to hear the six o'clock news the time here is eight o'clock. I believe that is one of the questions you asked recently. By the way darling the letter you wrote on your birthday has now arrived. I had given up hope of several of them but when I check up I think I shall find only one is now overdue.

I told you I wanted to visit the Holy Land, but leave there has been cancelled temporarily so

I am just waiting patiently for a reopening. When that time comes I am going to look out for anything which I think will please you.

Another thing that may interest you is that I have started school again out here. It is a hard school, and it could be termed a school of experience. Actually it is a school of mechanics. There are about a dozen of us including three officers who attend after duties at night. Our instructor is a Mechanical Sergeant Major who knows the job inside out. I went to the first class last night and I am looking forward to the next one.

If I pass out at the end of the classes I shall be given a special certificate. I think I shall get it. I have also entered for map reading classes. Certificates are to be given there too, but the classes do not start until Monday. I will let you know how I progress. I have been asked to go as a tradesman in our own workshops on several occasions. I should like to go in, but I also know that workshops with a temperature around 130 degrees can be pretty unpleasant. And above all, while driving hundreds of miles I see sights that would be denied me otherwise. Of course there is always the risk I mentioned when I began my letter, so you see dear I am undecided. Don't be surprised at any news you may get but honestly I think I shall be staying as I am. In any case as far as the Army is concerned I have more or less to decide for myself. Much as I would like to I cannot ask your advice as you can have no clear idea of circumstances here.

How I wish I could get away for leave for a week. I could get it at any time. I have almost enough money, that is with what you and Dad have sent up to the present and also with my meagre savings, but if there is the slightest chance of going to the place I have always longed to see, then I think the waiting will have been worthwhile. Of course there are a number of places I travel through at various times but that is not like having plenty of time to wander as you please. And my camera has got to work overtime then, too.

Well darling I must end shortly. Give my love to Lucy. Remember me to all next door, and also those many friends who so kindly enquire after my welfare. In regard to yourself. I can only say that I love you now more than ever before. Just let that be a lesson to you. All the best darling. God Bless you and keep you safe until I see your smiling face again. I will conclude with all my love from your husband

Gerald X X X X X X X X

One for Lucy X isn't she lucky

(P.S. I think she had better have another drink after that escape.)

2 more snaps enclosed

March 21st 1942

I feel I must sit and write a few more lines to you although I have written several times during the last few days. I must of necessity write small because if everything goes well I have quite a lot to say. First of all I wrote you a letter about three days ago which I hope you will receive. It will tell you all about the time when I had "the wind up". But darling as we are only supposed to send a small number of Green envelopes I am purposely delaying that one until next week. I know darling that you would prefer to receive this one.

Well to begin with I am writing under almost impossible conditions. All morning the heat was almost beyond endurance. Afternoon was sultry. You can imagine what that was like in the tropics. And we are still wearing battle dress. Phew! It was hot. It is no good praying for rain as that is almost unknown. Anyway to cut the story short we know the worst now. A terrific sandstorm is "playing Hell" with everything. We can hardly hear ourselves speak. The lights keep blowing ----------- ----- ------- likely to move at---------- ------- ------ de is choked with------ ------ ------- --- you have quite a ------ ------- ----- ---- just my trousers---- ----- ------- ------ And now for the------ ------ ----- ----- e now deciding-- --- ------ ----- ------ the latrine.

Very awkward is it not. Now to come to more personal matters. Some time ago you wrote that Lucy asked me to find someone to write to her. Well the deed has at last been accomplished. I have written to her and also the person concerned has compiled a very nice letter. How it will all end I cannot say but there is one thing I want you to do for me. Dick Chalk is a true friend of mine and I don't want to let him down. No doubt Lucy and he in their exchange of correspondence will be saying to each other many things of mutual interest. But darling, we are in the desert together and only men living under such conditions know what that means. I could tell you a very long story, but I will have to leave that for him to explain in his own time. For the present all I will say is that he has been very, very badly treated during his two years out here. The person concerned was of course still in England and he could do nothing about it. But I must say this he took it like a real man. Oh! Curse this "B" storm. To continue I know both you and Lucy will reflect this confidence until such time as he should see fit to mention it. I have no doubt he will in good time. By the way he is 6ft 1½ is well built and quite good looking. Even through his troubles he has been -- --- -- billet. He is also v-- --- -- in all he does. So --- ---- - That is all I have to ------ you both. I have ----- ----------- too. I am more ---- ----- ---- in her reply ------ ------ -----that I have a very deep brotherly affection for her. If it had not been for that, every man in the M. E. F. would have been writing to her by now. Well youngster how are you getting on, on your lonesome? I wish I were with you now instead of being in this perishing storm. I intended to write pages but I shall have to pack up in a few minutes. That's how it is. Too hot to sleep tonight and out with the dawn this morning. I have sent you a complete list of Regd. Letter numbers in an airgraph this week. I have acknowledged every one as I have sent them and I am sending another complete list next week. Some of them should reach you. Well darling it's no use, I can't carry on.

Please excuse me,

Gerald X X X X X X

One for Lucy X

(Written later in pencil)

Darling, just a few more lines while I am lying in bed. You can see what happened last night and I do not feel inclined to alter any of it. The storms got worse and worse. I have been in a few storms but never anything like that, it raged hours. I was sick early this morning. I am afraid a great many men went without sleep. And this afternoon the heavens opened. There is plenty of water about just at present. If I still remain with this unit I shall be going on leave very shortly. I shall be thinking about you all the time. I am hoping to find something of interest to send you. I will let you know if I do. Well my darling it is time for sleep so I will close now. All my love from your husband,

Gerald X X X X X X X X X X X X X

(CONTINUATION)

Well my Darling,

I have a few more moments to spare and as I had not posted the previous few lines, I thought I had better write a little more. The heat has been terrific. The beginning of the real Khamsin's. There is no way of avoiding it. Steering Wheel is too hot to hold. Fine sand blowing everywhere. The heat from the sun and even the wind is red-hot. At times it becomes almost unbearable. We are however still working through it all. It's now eight o' clock and it is still scorching hot although the sun has gone down. Have not had any mail for a week now. I suppose it will turn up altogether as usual. Have not heard from George yet. I hope he got my letter. Well darling it is almost dark now so I shall have to close. All my love, from your husband,

Gerald X X X X X X X X X X X X X X X X X

Saturday April 5th 1942

My Darling,

Well to begin with I must tell you that I have recently returned from a most enjoyable leave. I decided to make the tour of the Holy Land and thus fulfil a longstanding ambition and now I propose to tell you something about it. Of the long and arduous train journey I will say very little. It involved crossing a few deserts, and heaps of discomforts with very little in the way of replenishments for the inner man, but nevertheless I survived it all. It also involved performances at customs and changing money of one country into the coinage of the country I was visiting. I managed it all quite well eventually and succeeded in crossing the border about 10/- better off as a result of bargaining for a favourable currency exchange. Most of the people travelling seemed only to get an equal exchange.

Eventually I arrived at a big junction in the midst of orange groves and changed trains for the final part of the journey. I had left the desert behind me and how I enjoyed the sight of something green and growing in a normal way, instead of isolated cases of struggles for existence. On the border of desert and fertility, I saw large plantations of fig trees just breaking bud. The farther I went, so the nature of the vegetation gradually changed. The fig trees gradually became replaced by lemon groves, then from lemons to grapefruit and finally to a hundred miles of closely planted orange groves. The price for best oranges was anything from 20 to 50 for a piastre (2½d English money) and I was rather sorry I could not send you any. I thought how welcome they would be at the shop. The strange thing about the orange groves is that while trees are covered with ripe fruit they are now in full blossom for the next crop. And the scent was grand.

Very sorry I am having to write in sections again, but I am Duty Driver once again and so liable to be called out at any time. However, I will endeavour to continue. First of all I would like to point out to you that I intend to cover my travels in several letters so please do not be disappointed when this one ends. The others will follow soon.

The last stage of my journey took me many miles through the mountains of Judea, and I must confess that the engineering feat to build a railroad under such conditions was considerable. It reminded me of some of the films I saw in England of the Canadian Pacific trains in the Rockies, simply a tiny ledge on the mountains for many miles.

Eventually I arrived in Jerusalem, very tired and weary but already filled with wonder. From that stage onwards, my conception of the Holy Land, as impressed on my childish mind

by a well meaning but evidently very badly informed teacher, was completely shattered. The more I saw and heard and read, the more I realised how vague are the teachings at home. I do not mean just in regard to the events, but to the places. And distance is all wrong too. Just as an example, try before you read any further to picture, absolutely honestly the place where shepherds watched their flocks by night. Picture the fields too. I am sending you a snap next week so that you will get a true picture, but I think I can disillusion you now by telling you that the place referred to consists simply of two medium sized fields in a valley surrounded by ancient houses. I had imagined something like Salisbury Plain.

And again the place where Christ went into the wilderness. It is an area of barren, hilly country similar to Clent or Kinver. So you see how an actual visit rapidly compels a readjustment of all former ideas.

Darling, how I wished you could have been with me. The place I stayed at reminded me of racing days at Brooklands except for an empty chair at meal times. Still I have kept my promise and spent many happy hours getting pictures for you. The boys here in camp can hardly believe that I have taken them with my camera, but just to convince them I have the negatives of most of them.

I am now reputed to have one of the finest collections anywhere in this area, and I am very proud of them. I intend to keep the negatives for a time while I get prints of each to send to you and to Brook St. As soon as you let me know which have arrived, then I will risk sending the negs, and you can get as many prints as you wish. Two of the finest examples of camera work I have ever seen are now in my possession. They are the Garden of Gethsemane and the Garden at Calvary.

I have an album too which I have inscribed with your name as a gift from me. I have not yet had time to complete it, but I will give you the details. It is made of red morocco leather at the hinge, or opening and closing part. The sides of it are of real olive wood, highly polished from the Mount of Olives. The front part is carved with a replica of Rebecca's tomb, while on the back is simply inscribed "Jerusalem". And now darling I am undecided. I have been offered

fantastic sums of money for it complete, but my answer is the same always. It is for you, and all the money in the world won't buy it. But much as I want you to have possession of it I can't make up my mind whether to risk sending it. It will take a week or two to complete it as I want to do it, so I shall wait for your reply. It is yours, and whatever you say I will do. If you tell me to keep it and present it personally, well my darling you know I will do it gladly. In any case I am going to send you a duplicate of most of the snaps.

I also have other little treasures for you all. A genuine olive wood cigarette case for Dad, a carved olive wood camel for you, brooches of Mother of Pearl made in Bethlehem for mother, Roma, Lucy and inscribed with their respective names. I could not find your name so I am sending two from the same place carved in the form of the Star of Bethlehem. I also have a soap (toilet) container made from stone hewn from Solomon's Quarries. And a brooch in the form of a butterfly, made in my presence, from silver wire thread. A fir or pine cone from the Church of St Peter where he denied Jesus Christ three times. And a candle from the Holy Sepulchre. Had also a camel made of olive wood, and beautifully carved. It is about 8 or 9 inches high. I have stones from the Dead Sea and curious little sea

shells from the various places I have visited. Also an olive wood pen (carved) with a tiny peep hole in the side, which reveals a good view of Jerusalem. A candle from Solomon's mines and a leaf from the olive trees in the Garden of Gethsemane presented to me by the high Priest. Now I have wetted your appetite I shall send just a few at a time and I sincerely hope they reach you alright. Please take care of them when they arrive as I cannot replace them.

By the way all the money posted by you and Dad up to January 25th or thereabouts has reached me safely. I am very much afraid the greater portion of it has now been spent on that leave but it was worth every piastre. I only wish I could see you to tell you about it. I think it will take me weeks to tell you everything when I do come back. I suppose you will be telling me to "dry up" and calling me an "old so & so". Still as I have told you before I have changed in many ways and I can stand it all. There is just one way in which I have not and never will change. That is my affections for you. And just before I close there is one other question. Has Lucy received that letter yet from the person I asked to write to her? I am sure he will appreciate a few lines for he only gets one letter a month from his parents.

As you can see, my space is ending, so I will write you another letter today and put it in the post for censorship. You should receive it soon after this one. Just had another airgraph from Mother saying she has rec'd several letters from me. It is a long time since I had one from you. Still they should turn up. Please remember me to Lucy and all next door. God Bless you darling and keep you safe. All my love from your husband

Gerald X X X X X X X
One for Lucy X

April 5th 1942

My Dear Wife,

           I have already written you one hurried letter telling you of the first part of my recent leave and I promised to write again so here goes.

First of all I will endeavour to describe the Holy City. It is built entirely inside the City Walls which are two and a half miles round. The Wall itself is intersected by seven vast gates each one having a special name. About a hundred yards from the place at which I stayed inside the City is Jaffa Gate. So called I believe because it is on the desert route to Jaffa. Like the entire Wall and City it is built on Mount Zion but I was unable to ascertain the exact time of the original construction. Two centuries ago a break was made in the wall and except for that it is a continuous structure.

Very close to Jaffa Gate is David Tower. In a few days I shall be sending you a splendid snap of the Tower itself. The base was built by David himself who afterwards became King when with 30,000 men he took the City by assault. The tower was later improved by the Crusaders and even more strongly fortified by the Romans during their occupation. From Jaffa Gate and David Tower I went to David Street. It is a very narrow terraced street paved with slippery stones and along almost the entire length it is shaded by numerous fashions in sun blinds which almost meet over the centre of the roadway. The street is about ¾ of a mile in length and the shops are very small affairs, side by side and include every art, craft or trade under the sun, Tinsmiths, blacksmiths, cobblers, merchants, rugs. Silks, cutlery, cooked foods, olives, fishmongers, butchers, tea & coffee blenders etc, carpenters, sweetmeat sellers, grocers, oranges, figs , dates, spring onions, matured onions, garlic, salad stuff, makers of fine jewellery, shoeshine boys, Hubbly Bubbly, bakers, watchmakers & candlestick makers etc. So you see what a strange mixture it is. But that is only a superficial appearance. Together with a pilot friend I took the trouble to investigate behind all these outward appearances. I think the wings on my friend's tunic were the "open sesame" to many places that we should not have otherwise visited. Behind the rather uninteresting looking exterior of one shop we were initiated into one of the great crafts of the country, Mother of Pearl work. An old man sat there as he has done for nearly five years on one article carving measuring and re-measuring. He is making an exact replica in shell of the Mosque of Cuiar. Five year's work and another five to complete it. The cost of the shell alone is £350 and when finished it is to go in the British Museum. I was told that money could not buy it. Behind other shops we saw the carving of olive wood, the hand painting of many souvenirs, the making of silk patterns, the art of brooch making with silver threads and the making of coloured glazed tiles. Looking on as a mere spectator the methods seemed very crude yet the output was considerable. Off this main street are many branching streets all very similar to the original. At one junction of roads is a dividing line of nationalities, one part each for Jews, Arabs, Armenians, Moslems and Christians. At the bottom of one of the side streets is what has been popularly described as the Wailing Wall. The correct name is the Wall of Lightening. It has a rock foundation and is the only remaining part of the Temple of Mahomet. He came 300 miles on his horse Lightening to see the destruction and since his death the Jews have used the remains of the wall as a place of prayer and lamentation. Thus it's present name. In another small street is a place known as the "Bad Market". It obtains its name from the fact that when the Crusaders occupied the City all food cooked for them by the inhabitants was bad.

Then I came to St Stephens Gate known now as "Flock Gate". It was the entrance through which Moses and his people brought all their sheep, and even today it is the traditional entrance for sheep being taken to market.

Then I visited St Anne's Church built over the Church of the Virgin Mary. It was Palm Sunday and I spent an interesting ¼ hour watching the service of the Greek R.C. The whole atmosphere was pervaded by a powerful scent of incense. Palm fronds were being carried and hymns sung. I had a dim recollection of the tunes but most of the words were beyond my meagre knowledge of their language. However it was all extremely interesting. I went below accompanied by a Sister of the Church.

We found the place where the Virgin Mary was born and a small Altar has been erected in commemoration. From there we proceeded through a large stone doorway to a chapel built over a courtyard. The chapel was filled with beautiful mosaic work. Again we descended, this time into a courtyard. It was here that Jesus Christ was tried by Pontius Pilate and ordered to carry his cross to Calvary. The place has like most other places of similar interest been well preserved through the centuries.

My friend and I, together with three officers of high rank were asked to kneel and pray for our victory, our home and families on this spot. When we arose I wondered what had been the prayers of those officers for they were men without a country. They turned around and shook hands with the pilot and myself and through the Sister who speaks six languages wished us luck and hoped our people and our country escaped the same fate as their own. In the circumstances I am afraid

David's Tower Jerusalem

Entrance to the Church of the Holy Sepulchre

Gordon's Calvary

118

it was very difficult to reply.

From there the two of us proceeded on what is known as The Way of the Cross. From memory I am rather afraid I shall be confusing some of these places for it was not until the second day that I started to make notes. I believe it is in 8 stages. Each stage marks a place where Christ fell under the weight of this burden. One place in particular I remember. That is where the Jewish women cried when they saw him and He said "Cry not for me but only for yourselves." By following these stages we eventually came to Calvary. There appears to be great diversity of opinion about this place but I will write of that in a later letter. The entire place seems to be covered by a Church and its precincts known as the Church of the Holy Sepulchre. As I have mentioned in a previous letter this was another place in which my childhood conception of the Bible were shattered. Calvary and the Holy Sepulchre within a mere 20 yards of each other. I had imagined a separation of many miles. It seems to be full of Altars and suchlike places. There is the spot where Christ was crucified together with the two thieves, also the place from which the Virgin Mary watched the death of her son. Over the latter spot is built an Altar decorated with treasures of fabulous price. There is also a case containing a figure of the mother and what struck us most was the expression in the eyes. They seemed to hold anguish, horror and – well it is beyond my powers of description.

And all down the ages contributions of priceless gems have been donated by successive monarchs of every nation in the world. The value of the contents of the case alone is £500,000. The ceiling is of Moorish mosaic and all candlesticks, chandeliers, pictures and hangings are of solid gold.

From there we went below to another chapel where Queen Helena discovered the three crosses. There are several stories each one vouched for as to how she discovered which one was carried by Jesus Christ. The most popular version seems to be that her son was gravely afflicted by some disease. On touching the first two crosses nothing happened, but when he touched the third one his affliction left him and he was cured. From there we went to see the strangest sight I have ever witnessed. The Holy Sepulchre on Palm Sunday and people of all creeds and denominations making pilgrimage and in their turn paying homage. Jews, Arabs, Americans, Greeks, Romanians, Catholics, Christians in fact people of every creed and country imaginable. And they were all dressed in costume of their respective nations. They marched reverently around until it came their turn to kneel and pray at the entrance to the tomb. We watched silently for an hour and then like a whirl wind the scene changed. As long as I live I shall never forget it. My friend and I unwittingly became the subjects of a very distressing incident. I am afraid I cannot give you the details until such time as I can see you personally as I am almost certain the version would not pass censorship. All I will say of it is that later we were both warmly thanked for our conduct by the powers that be, but I am afraid that cannot eradicate the memory from my mind. I will leave that unpleasant subject now and write a little of the procession itself. Everyone seemed to be carrying a banner on high or palm fronds and one or two were even carrying whole olive branches. I tried to fathom out the order in which they should be, but the more I watched the more confused I became. Old men , boys, Greeks and Jews and Abyssinians all mixed up in a throng of worshippers becoming more congested every moment and all singing a different tune with all the vocal power at their command. I suppose in England they would be called a cosmopolitan crowd of bohemians. Frankly I can't say what I would call them. We eventually came away with a gift from a priest which in normal circumstances would have been a source of great pleasure and pride. Now I have rather mixed feeling about it but I have kept it. It is a small candle from the Sepulchre itself and I have accidentally broken it. I have decided to keep one part and send the other part to you to add to the collection. As we wended our way slowly through the crowd outside an old Frenchman grasped us by the hand and whispered, "Strike a blow for France, my France". Somehow I think the fact it was Holy Week was rather stirring the emotions of a lot of people. Another surprising thing happened to me on Good Friday too.

I was standing at a certain place not in the least way connected with religion and I must confess that my thoughts at that precise moment were in England, when I felt an arm placed gently on round my shoulders. I turned my head to look over my right shoulder and saw a strong sunburned hand with a thick gold ring on one finger. I then looked over my left shoulder and from what I could see I felt a sense of embarrassment. Kindly blue eyes, bushy eyebrows, tremendous grey bristling mustachios while all the remaining part appeared to be gold braid and scarlet tabs. I immediately jumped to the conclusion that some mistake had been made. But his first words spoken in very broken English contradicted my thoughts. He told me that I was the first soldier in British uniform that he had seen since coming from some church service and that he would like to take the opportunity of wishing me good luck and God speed. Just a few other kind words, a handshake and we each went our own respective ways.

The pilot for whom I was waiting came up at that moment and asked if I was a friend of the officer concerned. He was most surprised when told him it was the first time I had ever seen him. He was just another man without a country and I shall always treasure the memory of his kind words and action. Yet another strange thing happened during my leave. A gentleman I have never seen before came up to us while we were watching a procession down a narrow street. He seemed to hesitate and then he smiled and asked us to accept a small gift from him. It was then our turn to hesitate. Eventually we accepted a small parcel each and looked at one another as much as to say, "What's this all about". The gentleman wished us luck and merged into the crowd. We decided to investigate and were very surprised at the contents. We each had a cross with a figure of Jesus Christ nailed to it. The cross itself was of beautiful mother of pearl and was strengthened by an olive wood structure at the back. I estimate it to be 8 or 9 inches in height and 5 or 6ins wide. I shall send it to you in the near future. Now I am back to my duties I am still wondering whether I paid a visit to dream land. Well darling it is nearly bedtime so I shall have to leave the remainder of the story for another day. Please remember me to Mr & Mrs Taylor and Billie, and all my friends at home. Give my love to Lucy although she is transferring her interests elsewhere. Tell her to have another drink too. I will write again soon. God Bless you and keep you safe until I return. All my love from your husband

Gerald XXXXXX

View of Jerusalem showing Mosque in foreground taken from the Mount of Olives. To left of Mosque is Garden of Gethsemane & church. Toe M Tower at summit. Ancient houses in foreground.

Weeping, Wailing and Gnashing of teeth.

*Tomb of
Lazarus*

Road to the Mount of Temptation

Palestine Good Samaritan Inn

(Published in the County Express Stourbridge in 1942)

IN JERUSALEM

Stourbridge Man's Interesting Experiences

An interesting letter, mainly a glowing description of Jerusalem has been received by his wife from Driver Gerald Milner of the RASC serving in the Middle East. Driver Milner is the son of ex-PC Walter Milner of Brook St. Stourbridge. In a previous letter, Driver Milner had written of the first part of a recent leave, and in his further written communication which is dated April 5th he describes the Holy City in much detail. He was accompanied by a pilot friend and says that he thought the wings on his friend's tunic were the "open sesame" to many places which they could not have visited otherwise. His description of the places visited is admirable and he mentions that at the spot where Jesus was tried by Pontius Pilate and ordered to carry His cross to Calvary his friend and he together with three officers of high rank were asked to kneel and pray for our victory, our homes and families.

He adds: "When I arose I wondered what had been the prayers of those officers, for they were men without a country. They turned round and shook hands with the pilot and myself and through the Sister, who speaks six languages, wished us luck and hoped our people and our country escaped the same fate as their own"

A SURPRISE

Among many interesting incidents recorded by Driver Milner was one which surprised him on Good Friday. "I was standing", he says, "in a certain place not in the least way connected with religion, and I must confess my thoughts at that precise moment were in England when I felt an arm placed gently round my shoulders. I turned my head to look over my right shoulder and saw a strong sunburned hand with a thick gold ring on one finger. I then looked over my left shoulder and from what I could see I felt a sense of embarrassment. Kindly blue eyes, bushy eyebrows, a tremendous grey bristling moustache, while all the remaining part appeared to be gold braid and scarlet tabs. I immediately jumped to the conclusion that some mistake had been made. But his first words spoken in very good English contradicted my thoughts. He told me that I was the first soldier in British uniform that he had seen since coming from some church service and that he would like to take the opportunity of wishing me good luck and God speed. Just a few other kind words, a handshake and we both went our respective ways.

"The pilot for whom I was waiting came up at that moment and asked me if I was a friend of the officer concerned. He was most impressed when I told him it was the first time I had ever seen him. He was just another without a country and I shall always treasure the memory of his kind words and action".

A GIFT

Another strange thing happened during his leave. "A gentleman I have never before seen came up to us while we were watching a procession down a narrow street. He seemed to hesitate and then he smiled and asked us to accept a small gift from him. It was then our turn to hesitate. Eventually we accepted a small parcel each and looked at each other as much as to say "What is this all about". The gentleman wished us good luck and emerged into the crowd. We decided to investigate and were surprised at the contents. We each had a cross with a figure of Jesus Christ nailed to it. The cross itself was of beautiful Mother of Pearl and was strengthened by an olive wood structure at the back. I estimate it at eight or nine inches in height and five of six inches wide. I shall send it to you in the near future.

"Now I am back on duties I am still wondering whether I paid a visit to dreamland"

April 7th 1942

Darling,

Just a few more lines adding further details of my leave to the letter I have already sent. I cannot really remember all I wrote in the other letters so if I should repeat myself please forgive me. In any case the weather is almost too hot to concentrate on letter writing, but I must keep my promise and let you have as much news as possible. There are so many things I could write about and so many phrases I could use to improve the descriptive parts of my letters but it is no use for they would only be censored.

Well sweetheart before I write any more of my travels I had better tell you that I have just received 5 air mail letter cards. 4 from you and one from mother, I will answer them in a later letter.

Now to continue the story of the holy land. I went from the city itself to Bethlehem. I stopped on the way and saw what is known as the Well of the Star. It has a stone rim with steel plating at the top. It is also the place where the three wise men first saw the reflection of the Star of Bethlehem which eventually led them to the manger. I estimate it to be one mile from Bethlehem. Just below are two fields in which the shepherds watched their flocks and on the hillsides all around are the houses in which they lived. Most of the places were very substantially built and a large percentage of them are inhabited today.

From there we went to the Church of the Nativity in Bethlehem. This Church struck me as having an entirely different atmosphere to the others and yet I cannot explain the feeling. It was just as though a sense of frustration and depression pervaded the atmosphere. That is the best way I can describe it. It was rather dark inside but I was feeling like "snooping around" and a poor light did not make much difference. The mosaic floor was just the same as in the church at Gethsemane. Were they laid by the same people and under each present day floor is the original. And in each case the top design is the exact reverse of the lower. After looking at the various and very valuable hangings I went below. I found a very small Alter on the floor of which was a gold star with a hole in the centre through which could be seen a portion of rock. This is reputed to be the exact spot where Jesus Christ was born. About two yards away is another small Alter together with a marble manger. This is to mark the spot of the original manger which is now in the Basilica in Rome. I am wondering now whether I shall ever see it.

I hope so. Next to that was the place where Joseph slept when he had the vision telling him to take the baby Jesus to the land of Egypt for safety from King Herod.

From there I went to the Mount of Olives. Climbed to the top of a tower and had a grand view of Jerusalem. Took several extremely good snaps. Shall send you some of them in due course. While there I went into the Church of the Ascension. There is a mark resembling a footprint complete with toes etc. which is hardened now and protected by a concrete rail. There seems to be a church for almost every event in this part of the world.

From there I went on to the British War Graves Cemetery. A fine memorial and neat rows of graves each marked with a cross containing name rank number and unit. My snaps of this place have been accidentally destroyed.

Darling I am writing this letter at odd moments and I think I shall have to end very soon. Please remember me to all next door, also give my love to Lucy and what of George. Have you heard from him yet? His people should be hearing from him now if he is in this part of the globe, but as you say you are not certain where he has gone.

Just keep smiling and pray for the speedy reunion of us both. I am always thinking of you and dreaming of the day when I can walk in and surprise you again. The time seems to fly out here. It only seems a few days since I last left you. I suppose you will say it seems years. What about that quiet place I asked you to find for when I come home. Have you had any

View of the Mount of Olives

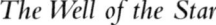
The Well of the Star

Inside the Church of Gethsemane

luck, or haven't you had the letter I wrote a few weeks ago. What I wrote then still holds good. If you don't know by now what I am writing about please write and let me know and I will write it all out again. And has Lucy received the letter I managed to have sent to her. It is almost time for me to close now, although I could go on writing for hours after the splendid holiday I had. By the way once again I will mention all the money you posted up to Jan 21st has reached me safely. And what service with one of those cards I had yesterday. Reply to airgraph written by me less than a month ago. I wish they would all arrive at the same speed. Am enclosing another couple of snaps. You say you have 20 up to the present. Well there are a lot more somewhere on the way. I have enclosed some in almost every letter sent.

Hope the weather is better for the gardening now. I wish I was there to help you. Still we will see what will happen about that when I come home. I know now the only place where I want to stay. Yes darling you are quite right in your first guess. I would like to tell you all I think about it now but that would spoil it for me when I come home. All my love darling, Keep smiling until we meet again. Once more, lots of love from your husband

Gerald X X X X X X X X X

one for Lucy X

Sunday Apl 12th 1942

Darling,

I received an air mail letter from you this week dated 22.2.42. Well darling when I received it I was very tired, and I think it is the only letter I have received which I felt like destroying. First of all there was no information about the return of the Christmas visitors, with visions of another visit in a few weeks. True to my old record of being blunt even if it is unpleasant I must say that I certainly do not like it at all. I know what you will say but that will not alter my opinion. I may perhaps be getting jealous or something. Anyway I have got it off my chest.

Then there is the subject of George. Have you no idea at all whether he really went for the place you mentioned or whether he went for another port. I sincerely hope he is safe. Please let me know as soon as you hear anything.

Then there was also the question of the money sent out by you and Dad. You do not seem to have received my letters. I have acknowledged every one at least twice. Once again I repeat that as far as I can ascertain <u>all</u> letters containing money, and mailed up to the end of January have reached me. There have been long intervals, and then perhaps four or five in as many days. However here is a list of envelope numbers which I have. I may have mislaid one or two. 0716 9290 3480 1940 2265 4864 3226 0426 0455 6568 0556 0638 2318 0916 5133.

So you see it was at that particular time a rather depressing letter. It did however contain its bright spots. For instance these trespasser's potatoes. By the way how is Uncle William keeping? In good health I hope.

Another thing was that £700. Please accept my congratulations for the present. I will deliver them in person one of these days if you have forgiven me for the first part of this letter.

Just one other thing I will mention while I think of it. I have a day free from all cares and troubles of state, so I shall utilise it to write you a long letter which will be sent by boat mail.

There is still such a lot I have to tell you about my tour of the Holy Land including the fact that I came back very much lighter in pocket. You will be pleased to know I have quite a lot of souvenirs for you all at home. The trouble is to find packing material. All we have is sand.

About this day off. Well dear we are to get every Sunday entirely free. Our OC has called for "Efforts reaching the limits of human endurance". I am not boasting when I say that my unit can win or lose this campaign in the desert, and just to show that it <u>will not</u> be lost we are packing 86 to 100 hours hard work into six days. And we are expecting more. We have been highly commended (as a unit) by HQ. Two of our fellows have been honoured this week at the command of His Majesty. But there is the other side to the picture. For the first time we have had a morning in bed. And were the boys amused when the Colonel sent a lorry round with fellows to dish out a cup of tea for every man IN BED. I began to wonder whether I was still in the Army. At eight o'clock the Arab boy came to work. Half the fellows jumped out of bed and ran him round the parade ground with shirt tails flapping in the breeze. Perhaps it is just as well there are no females in camp. I am sure they would have been most embarrassed.

Before I end my letter I have another request to make. As you know I am learning to speak foreign languages. The one I decided to concentrate on is Arabic, and as my trumpeter is m'feesh, I must say that I have surprised myself. My only real difficulty is obtaining good books on the subject. If you can find me a really good one, it will be the best gift you can make. I have several cheaper editions but they all seem to differ on various subjects and some words which are spelt and pronounced very similarly are of entirely different meaning for example. Malika (Queen) Malake (civilian) Malaka (What is the matter with you).

Well my dear, I must close now. All my love from your husband

Gerald X X X X X X X X X X X X X X

One for Lucy X

Sunday Apl 12th 1942

Darling,

I intend this letter to be more or less a continuation of the others I have sent telling you how I spent my leave in the Holy Land.

I will start with the Pool of Bethesda. It is divided into two parts and according to the Bible the first half was used by the people of David and his successors to cleanse their bodies of disease. They had to wait for the Angels to move the waters and after this had taken place the first person to wash in the pool was cured of all ailments. The Bible as you know tells the story of the sick man who had waited by the pool for 38 years. When Christ saw him he asked why he was not cured and he said that he was unable to walk. Christ said "Take up thy bed and walk". I am sending you a snap of the spot where the event was reputed to have taken place. The other half of the pool was used by the high Priests to wash lambs before sacrifice. For a number of years it was believed that a stone culvert affair was the dried up pool but a few years ago some person who would not be convinced of its authenticity decided to do a little excavating for himself. About 2 yards East and 5 yds down he found the original pool. Even today it is filled by rainwater trickling through from the street.

After that we went to the Church of All Nations in the Garden of Gethsemane. The

The Church of All Nations Gethsemane

The World's oldest Olive Trees

Church itself appeared to me as being very artificial if such a word may be used in that connection. The original floor is still preserved, but overlaid with a new one. The mosaic work in every detail is exactly the reverse of the original. A fine picture in mosaic over the Altar and a few other additions presented by various people comprised the remainder. One other notable feature was the ceiling of archways given and inscribed by almost every nation in the world. My personal opinion is that the Church looks far better from the outside. Perhaps it is the fine natural setting which creates that impression.

Very close to the entrance is the Garden itself. Shaded by the oldest olives in the world it makes a fine picture. Tiny beds of flowers neatly laid out and all in full bloom at the time of my visit. Once again I was surprised at the size. I should estimate it to be about 10 yds square. The name of the Garden means witness and the trees are reputed to have witnessed the suffering of Christ.

From there I went to the Inn of the Good Samaritan and proceeded through Jehricho to the Dead Sea. The inn is now merely a ruin. The Dead Sea had very little of interest except that it is full of minerals and it is impossible to sink.

From there I went on to Allenby Bridge over the river Jordan. I am sending you snaps in a few days. One side of the bridge is in Palestine and the other in Transjordan. Later on in the day we returned to Jehrico. Just a small Eastern town containing very little of interest. The name means City of Perfumes

Panoramic view of Jehricho taken from the hills near Apostle's Fountain

Mount of Temptation

The River Jordan

and was given by Mark Anthony to his sweetheart Cleopatra. What a girl she must have been. Just out of town is Elisa's Fountain or Pool. This is the place where the bitter waters were blessed and turned sweet. It struck me as being a pond full of exceptionally noisy frogs. Over the road is a small mountain. I climbed it to the summit and took several very good snaps. One was of Jehrico, with the mountains of the Amorites and Moabites in the background. Turning round I took a snap of the Mount of Temptation with a temple in the foreground. I could also see the Promised Land and the Wilderness of Judea. They are all very close together.

I saw during the return journey what my guide chose to call the pretended tomb of Moses. From the story he told it is impossible for it to be the real tomb although he confesses he does not know where the genuine one is to be found. Eventually arrived at Bethany where I took several very good snaps. I am afraid it is impossible for me to enclose them all in this letter so I am selecting six now and the others will follow at regular intervals. I saw the tomb of Lazarus also the place where once stood the house of Simon the leper. The spot is marked by a very old olive tree and a few fragments of stone remain of the original building. Standing between the above mentioned places is the house at which Christ usually stayed during his visits to Jerusalem. I refer to the house of the sisters Martha and Mary. Bethany itself is just a small village, built like all the other places of interest in that district on a small mountain. I think that almost concludes the sights of another day so I will end there for present.

Has Lucy received those letters yet? Please let me know as soon as possible. Just one other item before I end. All the money posted by you and Dad up to the middle of February has reached me safely. I have quite a number of souvenirs to send you in the near future. Please remember me to all my friends at home including all next door. Please let me know if you get any news of George. I know he was in a pretty rotten place but it is quite possible he got to some other port. I sincerely hope so. Must close now.

With all my love from your husband.

Gerald X X X X X X

One for Lucy X

YMCA Jerusalem

The Wailing Wall Jerusalem

On leave in the Holy Land

Inside the Latin Church Jerusalem

In front of Damascus Gate

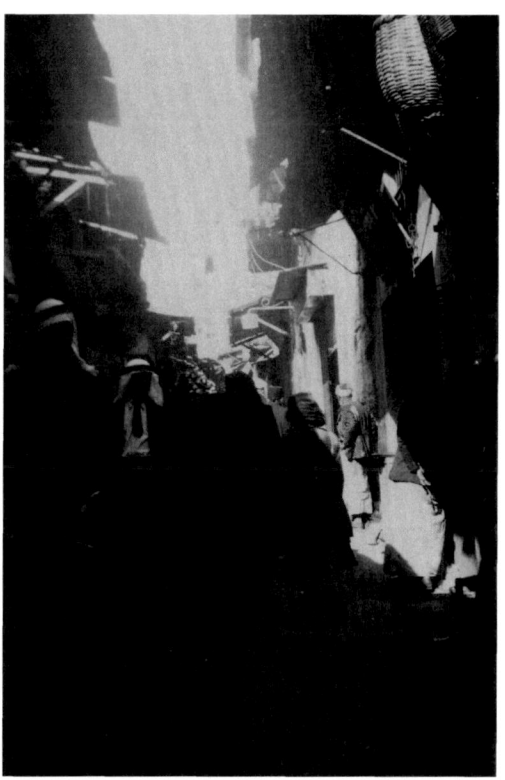

Part of David Street Jerusalem

Sunday Apl 19. 42.

Darling,

Once more it is my turn as Duty Driver, so I am utilising all spare moments to write you a nice letter. Had two letters or rather to be precise one air mail letter and a letter card yesterday. Card dated 26.3.42 and letter 2.3.42. All your letters are reaching me safely but I am afraid very erratically. I get one dated March and then probably the next will be December. On Tuesday I had five letter cards from you covering a period from January to 26th March. What I cannot understand at all is why you have not heard that I have received the money. I have sent several lists of Regd. Numbers but you still say you have not heard. Also every time money has arrived from you or Dad I have sent an airgraph and a letter to let you know. In your letter you ask whether I knew that Margery had a daughter. Yes darling I did know. I wrote to Norfolk Road twice and also referred to it in several lots of mail to you and Brook St.

Another thing I must mention before I forget. I have heard about George and I know where he is but oh! What a long way off it seems. From what I can gather he is alright and I should imagine in more favourable conditions than myself. I happened to meet a fellow who is stationed with him during my travels last week. I shall write this week. I was within a hundred miles of him yesterday during the course of a journey, but as it was I did not get in until midnight and I had to be on duty again at 5.30 today. As near as I can judge I shall need three days for the return journey and at the first opportunity I shall try and see him. As I have said before, the work our unit is doing is of primary importance and hard and long as we have worked in the past, efforts "up to the limits of human endurance" are now being asked of us.

You will realise that work must come first. So it will probably be a long time before I can find out various items of interest. I still have to ask him about that statement I am supposed to have made when I last saw him. What punishment do you want me to administer? Please think of something satisfactory.

Another thing in your letter you tell me I have not said what I thought of your visit to Shipley. Well darling, up to now that is the first I had heard of it but with that very scanty information I can imagine what your feelings were. Incidentally that is an indirect answer to several little puzzles.

Glad to hear the pile of snaps is increasing. What a cheek, not putting my snap in the front because you want to carry it about with you. You and Mother say you like the little girl with the smile. Well my dear it may interest you to know that she now has seven months in which to meditate on the sins she has committed. Yes even the natives have to obey a certain amount of law and order. From what I can gather, murder seems to be a secondary crime compared with theft etc. that is of course just my own impression but it is difficult to alter.

To change the subject I am sorry to hear that Webb's cannot supply the potato order. I wondered if that trouble would arise again. And how are you getting along with the garden. I hope it turns out as well as last year. I turn over a page of your letter, and really, darling it is most amusing. I am sitting here in a temperature about a thousand degrees above fizzling point (that is my own estimation of it) and you write "It is a bit warmer today. The sooner the ground thaws the better" Well I think that is one of the letters I am going to remember for a long time.

As I mentioned before I had a long trip yesterday and also a lot of rare opportunities of which I took full advantage. 12 lemonades, 4 ice creams, three fresh fruit salads and ice cream and about 4 or 5 cups of tea. Can you imagine it? Yes it was me alright.

Then at midnight hour I start to read a letter from you telling me it is a bit warmer. I'll say it is. Darling I will let you off lightly this time, but I shall still retain the right to smile when I think of those words.

Have just had an interruption. Had to fetch the unit mail from A.P.O. I am very impatient now as there is another Regd letter for me. Cannot have it until 1 p.m. and I don't know who it is from. More of that in my next letter. Shall also send an airgraph probably tonight. All money has arrived as I said in previous mail. That is of course allowing for any letters not yet due. I have also collected another lot of snaps. Am enclosing a few in this letter. I think you will like the one of Gordon's Calvary. It is the garden round the Tomb of Christ which was discovered by General Gordon. I am very proud of that snap and I shall always treasure it as my masterpiece of photography. Please don't be afraid to say if you think I have taken a better one. And I am to expect photograph and wallet in return. Thank you. Now I must wait patiently for its arrival.

So you wanted to broadcast to me. I know what you are thinking of, but please give up the idea. If I hear anything like that now, I think I shall be trying to jump a couple of oceans and probably be most unsuccessful. I know how a good many fellows feel about it. Very deeply engrossed in my penmanship when the Major walked silently in, looked over my shoulder, said "noot" and vanished. Perhaps he thought all the more. You speak of my place not being taken. No darling, I am not worrying much about that but in a precious letter I was very candid and in that respect I have not changed my mind. Xmas entertainment, yes. After that finish. If I am getting jealous, so much the better. And then again I am afraid you still have doubts about one or two things. First of all the promise I made to you has been kept. It will continue to be so. The next is after the show is over. You want to go somewhere with me. Well of all things. If that letter I wrote weeks ago has gone down I shall be most annoyed. It was full of nice things and also plenty of instructions for a holiday as you would desire it. I asked you to think of a place to go and also told you what type of place. I shall say no more now, but wait a little longer and see if the letter arrives.

Sorry to hear you have not received the increase in pay yet. Of course it naturally takes longer on Active Service as the records have to go to M E G H Q first and I presume after that London. 3d per day from Dec 12th you should receive. I guessed the money you have sent to me was your own. Well darling I have been reckoning up and I reckon I shall be getting too well off. I do not want to retire just yet, so I want you to buy something for yourself on my behalf to commemorate Aug 5th. I want you to have it from any account and if it costs a fiver, well that will be alright. Please let me know what you buy.

Sweetheart, please forgive the dirty page, but all the marks are perspiration as I write. The heat at the present moment is most intense. Yesterday I placed my bare arm on the window frame of the vehicle I was driving and it was very soon removed. I had a lovely blister from the burns. It is disappearing now. We usually place a cover over the steering wheels as they become "too hot to hold with the naked hands. I have a nice open air complexion just at present, but I suppose I shall look like "Bosambo of the River" in a week or two. We only wear shorts off duty and I think if it gets much hotter we shall be leaving those off. Please tell Lucy I will keep the camera handy. If it breaks then I shall want a drink off her.

About the "bust up" when I come back. That will be one evening and then you and I will be missing for a week or a fortnight. What people think of me does not worry me in the slightest now. Since I went on that charge I mentioned and cleared myself in every respect I know now that I can face anything. My sergeant could have persuaded my officer to let me off with a caution. I refused it. He told me I was all sorts of things, but in spite of that and the advice of the lads on my section I determined that there would be a clean sheet or a very black mark against my name. It was simply my word against two R.A.F. police N.C.O.s which could also have been substantiated by officers who were present. They did not however give evidence. When I went on with it I was told that if I was sentenced it would probably be Field Punishment. That did not alter my mind. Close inquiries were made into my Army record which was unblemished, and as you know I came away with a clean sheet, free and with the words from a Lt Colonel which I shall always remember.

I shall never forget the moment I walked back into our tiny workshop - office either. For 3 weeks the charge had hung over me. Each driver was looking at me silently with a look of enquiry on his face. After what seemed an hour or two one of them said "How did you get on". I told them. In the sudden rush I thought it was you greeting me on my return home. Anyway I knew at that moment what they all thought of me. No one is going to make me do or say anything now that will give you that old impression. I have an idea that when I come back to civilisation the boot will be on the other foot. I hope you will not have to make too many apologies for me.

For instance I went into a shop in Jerusalem. There were two very good looking girls were behind the counter. While examining an article one young lady said to the other "Here is a nice looking soldier for you". I think she was rather surprised when I interrupted "Yes but I look better still with my shirt off". So now you know what to expect.

Mothers carrying water (in British oil drums) Father: extreme right back row. Picture taken in the Holy Land

You say you hope your letter will not upset me. Far from it. The embarkation Cave was small fry compared to future ambitions. Just keep our home in trim, find that place for a holiday, tell other people to go to -- yes that's right, and wait for my return. You should get more news than I do, but I do not think it is going to last so very long now. I will just bet you a new hat to nothing that I am home within a year.

Reading a book

Please give my love to Lucy and remember me to all next door. And now dear, I must ask you to forgive me. I have written so much I shall not be able to send more than a couple of snaps. I really must close, or I shall be trying to bring you the letter myself. I wish I could. All my love darling from your husband

Gerald XXXXXXXXXXXX
One for Lucy X

PS Regd letter just arrived. No. R 1117 10/- from Dad many thanks

Entrance to the citadel Aleppo

Civic Transport

Poultry Farm?

Boulevard Baghdad Damascus

Mosque of Tekiyeh, Damascus

Window of St Paul's, Damascus
In Paul's time, the city of Damascus was surrounded by a wall with seven gates. On the southern side of Damascus is the above Bab Kisan Gate. It was dedicated to Saturn. It is close to the start of the Roman Road that St Paul would have taken and was where the Christians used to live. A window from which St. Paul was lowered in a basket and escaped from certain death was identified beside the Kisan Gate by the early Christians. **(2 Cor 11:32-33)**

Altar

Street Scene Damascus

Gateway at Jerusalem

Jidelph Street, Aleppo

The Souk Bazaar, Aleppo

Interior of the Temple of Bacchus, Baalbeck

Temple of Venus, Baalbeck

More ruins at Baalbeck

More ruins: Same temple

*The Great Mosque of
Zakaria Aleppo*

Eastern Ruins

Entrance to the Holy Sepulchre at
The Church of the Holy Sepulchre

Middle Eastern Town

The Sea of Galilee

The Wailing Wall, Jerusalem

Entrance to the room of the Last Supper
Jerusalem

View of Jerusalem

Shopping Day, Zion Hill, Jerusalem

Rachel's Tomb, Jerusalem

Sunday Apl 26. **1942.**

Dear Youngster,

First of all an apology for having neglected my writing for a whole week. As I have told you in previous letters, work up to the limits of endurance has been asked of us. Well darling all I can say is that it is being given willingly. During the last eight days I have worked between 120 and 130 hours so you can see now why I have had no time to write. Now I have a day off as a reward. I think this week has been one of the most remarkable I have yet experienced. Any way since I have been in the Army there are several ambitions I wished to achieve and quite a number of them have been granted almost together.

One of the first was to drive one of the biggest lorries in existence. I had looked at them as they went by me, and many times wondered whether I would ever have such luck. One morning I went to work as usual and before I got into the vehicle park or rather just as I went through the gates my Sergt. came up to me. "Right get in this one" he said. It was I should imagine one of the biggest ever produced and made some of the other ambitions look very small fry. I got up immediately, but oh! Dear, what a sensation. I knew absolutely nothing about it. Still I could not miss the chance. While waiting for the word go, I found out a few things and eventually got away. Anxious eyes watched me negotiate the difficult exit and away I went. After a few minutes I was feeling much happier. Now I think without boasting I can manage it as well as the other few. When I came back the OC came and asked me how it felt and what I thought of it. I climbed down and had quite an interesting talk with him. Since then quite a lot of fellows have wanted to go for a short trip just to fulfil their curiosity. I gave a chance to a young gentleman who has written to Lucy. He is learning to drive but he says he will stick to the type he is already using.

Then one morning I came back fairly early and as soon as I had climbed down from the dizzy heights of the cab, I was asked to go to the office. Someone handed me a pullover and belt with the words "Get these on quick". I won't tell you my reply. The answer from the Sergt was "Oh don't be a b fool, you have to drive the big staff car". I replied in Arabic "Yimkin" which means "Oh yes! Maybe." Anyway, much to my surprise it was true. A marvellous car and an equally marvellous trip. I think I shall have a car like that when I get back to civie St. and the officer, while conducting his business gave me about 5/- and the late afternoon and evening free. Well all I can say is that I took full advantage of the opportunity. My only regret was that I had not had a chance to get my camera. And darling I saw a chance of a lifetime for a snap. Whatever happens I am going to get it in the future if I have to wait hours for the exact moment. The subject of the snap is a tremendous pure white peacock. I saw it with tail feathers extended and I stood there fascinated for probably 10 minutes. Yes it must be added to my collection.

I arrived back somewhere about the time you would be handing out the jug to the milkman. I had several different trips after that with different cars. So you see that was another ambition fulfilled.

There are others of which I must not write. I think however that it is in order to tell you that some weeks ago I drove a tank for a small distance. I now have no ambition whatever to join a unit like that. I prefer something just a little more comfortable.

This week I have received quite a lot of mail from you. Mostly air mail cards. They seem to arrive fairly regularly. Also had one from Roma and a letter from Dad No. 1117. Glad to hear you received the telegram. You had it on the day I came back off leave. I suppose by now you will have received the letters telling you how I spent my time while on leave.

Up to the present, I have not had time to pack the presents up, but will make a special effort this week. I have decided to risk all of them so they will be contained in one parcel. You should receive them somewhere near a certain anniversary. I really hope they arrive on the exact date. Now I am looking forward to that present you have sent to me. Seems a long time to wait but

I must be patient. By the way, has Lucy received that letter yet? I am very pleased to hear that some of my letters are reaching you again. Must have been a welcome surprise to get that lot on Good Friday. Many thanks for the long letter I am to expect after all the mail you had. Fancy calling me an old so and so. And giving me two guesses what you will do to me. Well darling you say I would be wrong both times. I think you are wrong this time because you would be a pretty bad second at that game. I may be in the desert and perhaps getting a little uncivilised but still know how to greet my wife when I see her. If I should be wrong, please break the news gently, as I cannot stand too many shocks. So you see shortage of surplus crockery is no excuse at all. And what about that place I asked you to find for when I come home. Don't forget no uniforms, no thoughts or talk of war. Just a quiet place for two people with a lot of lost time to be made up. I think it is going to be for a couple of weeks too. And no other considerations are going to be allowed to stop it. I have made my mind up. So that my dear is that. I wish I could see you again for a little while but I would much prefer to be with you all the time. I suppose I shall have to wait for that. I often wonder what you think about during the evenings. When this war is ended I have decided that I am finishing with evenings at clubs or whist drives etc. unless accompanied by you. And if you do not want to go out well I stay at home. What a treat it will be to sit and talk to you, and perhaps afterwards a good book to read by a good fire in proper comfort, and without any chance of being disturbed by the calls of military duty. Or to turn to the humorous but uncomfortable side of life without having to stop and take your clothes off to find and destroy your closest friends. One of the things I miss most strange as it may seem is Sunday tea. That is a treat in store. And as to my civilian clothes I am glad to hear you are keeping them in good order. I shall have to be careful with them, or I shall be putting my shirt on over my suit or something similar. And I think a collar and tie will strangle me. And then again with long trousers I won't be able to show my beautiful, sun tanned knees. Or rather knee. For one is still enclosed by a bandage. It is a souvenir of a broken knee received by the slings and arrows of outrageous fortune. There is little inconvenience from it now, but the bandage gives it extra support. As long as I can walk alright and drive I am not worrying in the least.

Well my dear it is almost dinner time now and it has been grand to have a free morning. Had a cup of tea in bed too. You should hear the boys when it comes around. "Don't know what this Army is coming to. Now when I was in Poona in 1886 old boy" and then they try to think of a better one. And perhaps a voice will chime in "Oh! Were you with Cholmondby? Cholmondby of the Ninth. Now I remember _____" and so it goes on. One of the boys in our hut was very unlucky. He was detailed to help deliver the tea. I think the less I write about the remarks when he came in the sooner things will be mended.

Very glad to hear you are keeping fairly free from raids. I hope it will remain so. I think I have written all I can for the present, so I will end by sending you all my love. Look after yourself, and don't worry too much about me. Give my love to Lucy and remember me to all next door. Cheerio for the present darling and may we soon meet again. Once again cheerio.

Gerald X X X X X X one for Lucy X

PS Received one Card which ended :- God Bless you and keep you safe from your wife. (Have you become dangerous or something)

April 30th 1942.

Darling,

Once more I am Duty Driver so I am now about to occupy my spare moments in the usual way. I am already aware that I am about to get interruptions but I know you would rather have me write in stages rather than no letter at all. I have just noticed the date. How time seems to fly out here. It only seems a few days since I came out of that ship and got my first real view of the Middle East. And now all of us are waiting patiently and working hard for the day when we shall get our last view of the place. Can't say I shall be sorry anyway. Now to return to normal. Once more I will repeat all the money sent by both yourself and Dad has been received by me. I might also add "and spent". You see I went on leave but I have already written you several letters about that. I had a wonderful time and I did not mind coming back to the desert after such a wonderful break. I was extremely pleased with the results of my photography. I hope you like all those snaps I have sent you. Please let me know if you ever received the one of the native making bricks. If not I will get some more prints. All this reminds me of two air mail letters I have received from you today. One written on your 3 days holiday March 10th and the other one Feb 10th. Glad to hear you like the snap of me. You should have some more as I sent five or six at intervals just to make certain you received at least one. I am also sending the one of Gordon's Calvary at intervals. It is my masterpiece. By the way darling I sent the negative of that snap you treasure so much. About a month ago I think it was. Please let me know if you have received it.

You say you have sent a photograph of yourself. Well I shall expect it long before Aug 5th. With average luck, we get an air mail in six or seven weeks, boat mail is 9 or 10 weeks, airgraphs 3 or 4 weeks, but on the other hand I have had them in six days. On the whole mail is arriving quite regularly now.

You read of ships being sunk, but I really wish it were possible to say how many reached their destination. I wish someone would sink this perishing pen. Still I suppose Company Office have lost good ones before. I think I shall have to complain to the OC and he might lend me his.

Well darling three hours have gone by since I wrote that little piece. Have just persuaded someone to lend me a pen that is in fairly decent condition. Now for dealing with letter A. Sorry to hear Roma did not get the birthday letter. I have written to lots of people but I have had no reply up to the present with the exception of Dick Worthington and Charlie Stirk. According to your account of the snap you seem to like me a little bit. Is that just the same little bit you used to tell me about? I feel quite honoured to be placed by a bowl of daffodils. Wish I were there in reality. About those seeds I sent. I was hoping against hope they reached you. Please tell mother that one hour after I had your letter telling me of their safe arrival I saw the original plant. This was the first time since I obtained the seeds. What a picture. It was in full bloom and I cannot imagine anything more beautiful that is of course excepting my wife. I think they should turn out alright.

You say I would never admit that you ever teased me. Well I admit it now and when I come back, you will have to look to your laurels. I have learned quite a lot of things out here. Please give my sympathy to Syd, and tell Edna I have learned all sorts of Bedouin alternatives for those sorts of jokes. If you ever do the same then all I shall need is five boards, a blanket and as much livestock as it will hold, and I shall be waiting for reveille to sound. Now about that whiff of chloroform. Well my darling that is best left with you. If you think it will be better to see Eric Sinton now I shall not say anything against it. Do you think I ought to come home and be measured? All you have to do is wait until I come home and then by jingo things will be moving.

All joking on one side, I really think you should pluck up courage now if you definitely intend to go. You say you are still on the shy side. That will only be until a very short time after I cross the threshold. Really you are making me dislike having to stay in this desert.

Sorry to hear about the trouble at Veal's. Mrs Veal seems to get far more than her share. But sweetheart, about the house. My only wish is that our home remains as it is. It is the one thing in the world I treasure most. I can't imagine myself trying to tell you the story of my travels in some other house. No. 43 holds so many pleasant memories. Then you go on about that two stone. Well it is muscle, although I have lost a few pounds during the "heat wave". One day was

106 degrees inside with an electric fan going and it is only <u>warm</u> yet. So you can imagine what it feels like with a hot engine near you.

You had better hurry up and get in training. And Lucy putting on two inches all round. Is she getting prepared too? And has she received that letter yet. Seems as though I am too late. And the person concerned is such a nice fellow. I also notice the very tiny cross placed under supervision I presume, at the foot of the page. Well there is plenty of time for a larger one. I also hope she will send me that photograph. By the way I have given the one with five young ladies on, to the above mentioned young man. I hope you do not mind. I thought I had better let him see what he was in for.

Now for a few remarks on the second letter. Sorry to hear you have not had much chance to get in the garden, but very pleased to hear how well you are doing in the cookery line. You ask about the snap of the mess room at Xmas. Yes it was fruit. Oranges to be precise. I am now waiting for the snaps or photographs. Are there more than one? Abdul still thinks you should send me a letter every day. If more arrive he mutters Musk Kivoiss (no good). He usually adds a few pretty sound swear words. The Arabs seem to swear more than any other race. Of course I have purposely omitted those choice samples, or you will be wondering what the desert has done to your husband. But if you are very good I might tell you one or two that are no so bad.

Someday that is. When you lose your shyness. With regard to buying him something I shall have to wait until my finances are in a state to stand it. I have been on leave you know.

Glad to know Michael liked my shorts. My knees are getting quite a nice shade now. Have rec'd George's address and written to him. Am now awaiting a reply. You mention about sand storms. Yes, you have to be in one to know what it is really like and there is one blowing now. I hope I do not get called out. You ask when I am going to get some stripes. Well to be honest I am not bothered at present. I have a "lousy" job, with long hours and hard work, but as long as I am away from you I would not change it for all the money in the world. And promotion means just that.

What a big cross at the end of the letter. Thanks Lucy. Just what the doctor ordered. Must close now darling. All my love from your husband

Gerald X X X X X X X X X X X X
For Lucy X

Gerald Milner

Saturday May 2nd 42.

Darling,

Just a few more lines while I have a few moments to spare. I have already written twice this week, but I try to write as often as possible just in case I do not get a chance for several days when work is urgent. I know now that it will be five or six days before I have time to write again, so darling if you get a lot of mail one time and then have to wait a week for the next lot you will know the reason. We are working at full pressure now even through the heat of the day. I don't think you can possibly realise what it is like to work hard for twelve or fourteen hours in a temperature between 105 and 115 in the shade. And the hottest weather is yet to come. Trouble is we can't drink much or it causes a most uncomfortable rash in a most uncomfortable place. Anywhere from the pit of the stomach downwards.

Well darling I am in the very best of health at the present moment. Remember the time when I got angry. Well I had another affair like that actually. Came away with colours flying high this time. My knowledge of the native tongue is very useful now. I am getting on extremely well with it. In fact I have a working knowledge of several languages now, but my only trouble seems to be having to think which one I am using. Received another bundle of Picture Posts etc this week. They are arriving with fine regularity. Have already answered the letters I received this week. Well my dear, as I said at the start I have not much time to spare so I shall have to close. I still love you just as much as ever and I am praying for the day to arrive when I can be with you all the time. God Bless you and keep you safe until I return.

All my love your husband

Gerald XXXXXXXXXX

One for Lucy X

GERALD MILNER STORY

It was during times of such tremendous heat that we really learned what eyebrows are for. The slightest drink of liquid immediately pours out of the forehead and the eyebrows push the perspiration away from the eyes. The sun was often rising at 5 a.m. and setting at 7/8 pm. Many of us found that at sunrise we had a five minute fit of sneezing. After that we did not sneeze again all day.

Regarding what people at home thought of our life out there, one of our lads Johnny Shay, a small dour Yorkshire man, had a letter from his wife. It was accepted by all and sundry as a "classic". She asked "What do you do in your spare time? Dance or Hike?" To which there is no reply.

Wednesday May 5th. 42.

Darling,

For the last 10 days I have received no mail but I am still confident that plenty will arrive very shortly. It usually happens like that. The lull before the storm. But in this case, a storm awaited by everyone. We have a different kind of storm on just at present. A "b" sandstorm and the heat today. Well all I can say is "I shall never grumble again at a good English frost". You see darling there is absolutely nothing we can do here to keep cool. I can easily beat Charlie Mason's tea drinking record, but that only makes things worse. Honestly, I never thought it could be so hot, and the real summer is not yet here. I think the coolest spot in the camp today registered somewhere around 120 in the shade. And I have to drive in that temperature. Almost 90 in the shade at 7.30 a.m. I am thinking about leaving my overcoat off during the daytime. The worst part of the driving job is what I would call optical illusion. At times it actually amounts to a mirage, but with the intense heat being reflected from the ground everything becomes distorted and out of perspective. For instance you see a familiar object from a certain spot. It seems a long way off and yet from experience you know it is only a couple of hundred yards away. Then in the evening, objects a mile away appear to be only a couple of hundred yards away. It is all very deceiving unless one watches points all the time.

Darling I missed a great chance yesterday. I happened to be out of the camp when a driver was wanted to undertake a very long journey in quick time. My name came up but I was just two late to go. Another driver was sent, of all places, to within a stones throw of George. I have cursed my luck quite a lot since. Still I shall manage to see him one of these fine days. It is a most welcome relief to be able to write in the comparative cool of the evening. I do not think the temperature is any more than 85 now. That is equal to a day that calls for headlines in the newspapers at home.

I was to have gone out on a special job at midnight but my sergeant decided that I have worked hard enough recently so I am having about 10 hours in bed. I will not say sleep because of the heat, and other close companions. It is impossible to be separated from them. I think I shall miss them when I come home. Do you think I ought to bring a few with me? If they wake you up, so much the better. You know darling, I get roused at all sorts of unearthly hours, for all sorts of queer jobs, and I am sure you would not mind getting up at three or four o'clock, and perhaps going for a nice walk, or waking Lucy up. Or perhaps you can think of something better to do. I really must add that I have been given quite a lot of advice and I am determined as usual to try anything once. So look out. I get quite a lot of amusement from the natives out here. As you know I am rapidly learning to speak their language. I try to add to my list at least half a dozen words per day. Quite a lot of Arabs are anxious to help me. And now all sorts of people come to me to act as interpreter for various jobs. But in addition to this these people who live in the desert tell me all kinds of things. Some of them are almost unbelievable but I know them to be true. Just one small instance. Abdul was almost killed about a fortnight ago. A blood feud had to be settled. All his relatives from miles around marched to war against all the members of another family. Abdul had a terrible gash across his skull, but he survived. Those things are just incidents in their lives. Then there are all the strange customs of marriage of the various tribes. I think that had better wait until I see you personally. And the effect of various diseases. I more than ever intend to steer clear of them. All those snaps I have sent you represent the average everyday scenes out here, and not just isolated cases. And if I do not keep taking them I know I shall not be believed when I come home. Well my sweetheart it is getting dark so I shall have to conclude. Darling I still love you just as much and probably more than before. Shall be glad to get back to you. All my love darling from your husband

Gerald XXXXXXXXXXXX

One for Lucy X

Continuation

Well my darling, I have a few moments to spare, and as I had not posted the previous few lines I thought I had better write a little more. The heat today has been terrific. The beginning of the real Khamseens. There is no way of avoiding it. Steering wheels too hot to hold. Fine sand blowing everywhere. The heat from the sun and even the wind red hot. At times it becomes almost unbearable. We are however still working through it all. It is now eight o'clock and it is still scorching hot although the sun has gone down. Have not had any mail for a week now. I suppose it will turn up altogether as usual. Have not heard from George yet. I hope he got my letter.

Well Darling it is almost dark now so I shall have to close. All my love from your husband

Gerald X X X X X X X X X X X X

GERALD MILNER STORY

This brings me to the subject of light. When talk of the desert comes up, people say to me "Wasn't it very cold at night". This seems to be a common belief but the truth is very different. With day time temperatures often up to the high 120s and sometimes even 130s the body gradually becomes acclimatised and an evening drop of 40 degrees still leaves the temperature in the 90s. This is roughly equivalent to a drop from 80 to 40 degrees in this country, and of course it does feel cold. New arrivals in the battle area found it unbelievable that we should be sleeping with a blanket and an overcoat over us.

This great drop in temperature created another phenomenon, Distortion of light. Often for a couple of minutes the German soldiers appeared to be within hand shaking distance, features clearly visible and then as the light faded, fantastic sunsets turned the area into something no artist would ever believe. About five minutes and it was gone, returning the next evening often with yet even more fantastic colours. At about this time would come occasional mirages with palm trees beautifully arranged. Palm trees and water holes or oasis are popularly known as oasis.

I now turn my attention to the sandstorms or KHAMSEENS as they were known to the troops. The meaning of the word is "five days of hot winds". The sand is extremely fine and blinding, often bringing swarms of locusts. As they cannot be seen for sand we were often on the receiving end of some heavy bumps. When the Khamseen was blowing there was nothing anyone could do except place a ground sheet against the wheel of a lorry on the side away from the prevailing wind and lie "doggo" until it has passed. After losing a man who had merely gone 30 yards to a field toilet we invented the great idea of holding a piece of string tied to our truck so that we could wind it in and find our way back.

Here I should mention that "field latrines" were simply "three deckers" placed over a trench dug by the "Pioneer Corps" men. After a particularly severe Khamseen, just as the sun was rising the C.O. scanning the horizon with his binoculars called me quietly over to him. One lad was sitting on the wooden structure reading a letter from home. C.O. handed me his glasses and there basking in the early morning sunshine and at the other end from the soldier was a coiled snake. As I had won a number of shooting contests I was awarded the job of ending any danger from the snake. It was one time I dare not miss. The snake was duly killed and the soldier jumped up from his seat thinking he had been shot. He was very grateful when he knew what had happened. Whether or not it was correct I was later told that it was a "DIAMOND HEADED VIPER" and that death would be instantaneous.

In these conditions scorpions and spiders abound. In a patch of camel scrub we found a spider at least a foot tall. Our C.O. being a veteran of that part of the world told us that it was a scorpion eating spider. With his hands he picked it up and placed it in a medium sized galvanised bath and asked us to turn rocks and see if we could find any scorpions. We found over twenty and when they were placed in the bath a ferocious battle ensued. Scorpions were stinging the spider but his massive jaws crunched hem to pulp. When the slaughter was complete he ate his fill and then calmly stepped over the side of the bath and made for the camel scrub.

Saturday May 10th 1942

My Darling,

Two weeks now and no letters from you. I am wondering whether it is just another hold up in the mail or whether you don't love me anymore. Had one yesterday from Dad. 10/- in it too. Could not have come to a better place. It is marvellous what can be done out here with 10/-. A few instances of price at institutes at the desert. Ovaltine 3/3, cigs (5/9), St Martins Jam and mincemeat per 1lb jar 1/11, Fish Paste 6' size (1/3), Cads. Chocolate 2' size (about 6¼), Rolls of film 1/3 size (3/-). About 20 envelopes (1/-). So you see, when I have almost spent my wages I can't think of too many luxuries. It appears to me to be that everything is the same number of piastres here as it was pence at home. So you see again, that means two and a half times as much money. Still when I get detailed to go to any of the big cities I can suck an orange or ice cream or get a nice plate of eggs, chips and tomatoes for about 2/-! I do not know what is the matter with the hens round here, but their eggs are extremely tiny. Not much larger than the average pigeons egg. A conscientious English pullet would be disgusted at a result like that. However the eggs though small are quite good. We manage to get quite a lot of fruit in the mess room too. I am not grumbling about the food we are getting now as it is quite good for army rations. We had a new Sergt. Cook a few months ago and he has certainly made a great improvement. I hope it will continue so.

Once again I am detailed as Duty Driver. I think I must be doing the job too well for I seem to drop in quite frequently. The trouble is we are only a very small section all able to ride a motorcycle, I drive staff cars, lorries, articulators in fact everything, including tank carriers and I am not exaggerating when I say it is a mighty tough work at times, to handle such heavy vehicles in this climate. Sometimes a driver is late getting back, then the next in turn for duty is brought forward a day. It usually seems to be yours truly. The boys on this section have received the highest praises on several occasions, notably when one of our officers received an important promotion. He was an amazingly efficient officer, but he seemed a long way off from the men. Our tiny band of drivers had quite a shock when he came to our very small office and said he wanted all of us outside. He told us that no officer had ever had a better lot of fellows serving under him, and that if he had given an order he could forget all about it as he knew it would be carried out. He gave us the highest praise, and told us that he meant every word he said, and I think he did mean it. There were a lot of things we did during those hellish periods of waiting for details, and we knew he must have seen us, but he never interfered. On one occasion a long time ago we pinched his cakes. I think he must have seen us do it for he came across and said "see that you bloody well leave me one" and then turned about and walked away. He also mentioned the fact that he had occasionally had to give us a "bloody good raspberry" but no ill will was borne. Yes! We have quite a lot to thank him for. And then a fellow who is a fitter by trade wanted to drive. He had an interview with the officer who dismissed that previous case against me. He was told that everyone could not be drivers like this section. He said we were the few with the glamorous jobs and that it took a long time to get drivers trained like we are and someone had to do the other sorts of jobs. So evidently our work had been noticed. Personally it seemed more like hard work than glamour. I am always up by 5.30 am at latest, and for eight nights running I never got to bed before one o'clock am. I had reason to thank God for a pal like Dick Chalk. That is the fellow who wrote to Lucy. I always found my bed made and all personal necessities neatly laid out. And Abdul had "got cracking" too. All my washing done, socks darned and boots cleaned. I will omit his language about the hours I was putting in. Still if it will bring the end of the war one hour nearer I will gladly work harder.

The lads out here have had a mighty hard job to do and very little praise for it. In my travels I have been in contact with all sorts of people, and I only wish I were permitted to tell you some of the stories. Those will have to wait until I see you personally, but I am confident that when they are eventually told, the whole world will have a different opinion of the British troops out here.

One of my worst personal experiences was one very black night a long time ago when I drove a lorry into a gun pit. I had a Staff Sgt with me and he swears it is his record exit from a vehicle.

I have had to stand plenty of leg pulling, but I had a tremendous shaking up, and I am afraid I took rather a poor view of the jokes at the time. I can laugh with the rest now though. They wanted to know if the big lump on my head was part of the gun mounting. Then they tried to persuade me to lower my slacks to see if I had any more battle scars.

They said they could not let me come back to you until they had done their best to remove them. And so it goes on just like that. The Sergt comes in and says "An HRS driver. Can't see a ------- gun pit. Are you hurt". I replied "No". Then he started as one would say "to read the riot act, or lay down the law". I don't know whether any of the other drivers were listening but I certainly was not. I don't think we could find a better section Sergt in the British Army. Yes he is an old soldier with about 16 years service and a lot of fellows who do not understand him keep out of his way. He only laughs about it. A really burly fearsome fellow he looks, but we know from experience that he will go to any lengths to get us drivers out of trouble. One thing we all appreciate about him is the fact he rarely tells us to do a job, but always asks if we would like to do it. We never refuse, but if one driver has done more than his share. Then someone else usually comes up and says "Alright, I am going". That is all and the job is as good as done.

Well my darling I hope all this is not boring you too much, but there is little else to write about. Once again I will repeat that all the money sent by you and Dad has reached me safely. And what about the snaps. I hope they are arriving regularly. Please remember me to Lucy, and ask her about those letters. Has she received them yet? Also give my best wishes to all next door and all the other friends who so kindly enquire after my welfare. Must end in a few moments as I have work to do, and once again there is a sand storm blowing.

Sweetheart I am just waiting for the day when I can come home to you again. Seems such a long time since that embarkation leave and such a lot has happened. Seems as though the boys of the Navy are still on top of the job against the Jap fleet. According to the wireless they seem to be making a job of it this time. I hope our losses will be light. I told you a long time ago how thankful I am for the work of some of those men. Well, after the names of some of the ships lost were announced a few weeks ago, I know I can never thank them in person, but my thoughts will always be with them in a better world. I often wonder why fate deals such hard blows at such brave men, and then I realise that in war losses are inevitable. Darling I really must end now. All my love, with the overflow to be delivered in person later,

From your husband,

Gerald X X X X X X X X X X X X X X X X X   One for Lucy X

     X X X X Sorry no more ink left X X X

GERALD MILNER STORY

At this point I think I had better correct one or two impressions of people who were not in the thick of desert warfare. Firstly, there was no hiding place and all were subject to self imposed desert disciplines.

Secondly, officers N.C.O.'s & men were all together on one vast expanse of burning sand. Bombs and shells were no respecters of persons. On many occasions speaking to others, even soldiers who were not there, there seems to be an impression that barrack rooms, parades and drill were the order of the day, prior to a day's fighting. C.O. demanded that we salute him first time we saw him and that was enough for a day. He said otherwise it would wear out the peak of his cap, and he was too busy to go back to London to get a new one. Of course we all knew and respected each other. The rank of officer was respected but otherwise there was no difference.

Thursday May 14ᵗʰ 1942

Darling,

Just a line to let you know that I have this week received an airgraph from you. Although it did not contain much information except about the weather and asking me to send Mr. Gretton an airgraph I will certainly do that at the earliest opportunity. As you know or rather if you have received my letters, should know I have been working and driving for extremely long hours and so have had little time for writing. From now on darling I want you to understand this. You may be receiving my mail at very irregular intervals. I shall certainly write at every opportunity but I am expecting to leave this unit at any time now, and I am going to need all the luck you can wish me. I am not waiting for the reply. I am taking your wishes and the love you will send me, for granted right now. Darling, please don't worry over me. Without any attempt to boast (we don't do that around here) it is going to be a good German who gets our little crowd. If you are not worrying about it anymore than I am, then everything is going to be fine. I still retain my implicit trust in that Guardian Angel who has served me so well on many past occasions. Those stories will however have to wait for a long time to come. Before I go from here there is one thing of which I must write. It concerns my business. As you know I have travelled the world a bit since I last saw you and I have always kept my eyes open for anything that may be of use to me when the war is ended. Last night I was asked to take a staff car on a long journey. The officer concerned has known me for a long time. For some reason or other, on this occasion he asked me what my job was in 'Civie Street'. I told him. That started what may well prove to be a great opportunity for us both at a future date. As you know, very little fruit etc. is now being shipped home. But this officer owns vast orange, grapefruit and lemon groves in Palestine. He also has places in other countries where grapes, raisins and dried fruit (at Xmas time) Prime figs and dates and Egyptian onions all come into his sphere of business. He has made me an extremely generous offer to help my business after the war. I had several hours talk with him and he told me to let him know when the time arrives, whether I still wish to accept. The offer he made me was to supply all the fruit and articles mentioned at the same rate that he supplies five thousand cases to Covent Garden, or Francis Nicholls Ltd. He also made an additional offer. That is, if I can persuade a few tradesmen in my own area to buy from me wholesale he is prepared to appoint me as sole district agent, with an additional bonus of 5d per case, and also, on top of that a generous commission to be agreed upon later. If I can possibly persuade enough people to go in with me and I find it possible to accept his wonderful offer, he told me he is not bothering about my financial position with regard to paying in advance. He said he is used to judging the character of people and he is prepared to trust me. In short he said 'Sell the stuff I send and pay me when you have sold it'. The approx. Price of best Jaffa oranges will work out from 7/6 to 10/- per case according to the quantity in the case. What he requires me to sell is a total of approx. 500 cases. I suppose that seems a lot. Well, at first it did to me. But that includes oranges, lemons and grapefruit. All that is over a period of a year. It also includes Egyptian onions counting one cwt as a case. Also prunes, figs and other goods counted on the same lines. So you see that boils down to an average of ten a week. I am certain that between several shops, if it can be arranged, this should be quite easy. In any case I am under no obligation. Perhaps you can think of someone whom you think may have interest in this proposition. But darling when you tell them at Brook Street, please ask them to say nothing to Charlie Mason or he may get awkward. I know you are saving hard for me when I come home again. You have all my thanks and love for that. It seems as though I shall be glad to have the money available. Darling I am a long way off and I only wish I could

talk it over with you, but I hope you and mother won't be too severely critical. I know this officer and respect him, I have been with him on many occasions and I am certain he is not making me an offer that will lead me into trouble. When men are together in these sorts of places, miles from anywhere a great respect grows up between them. This is just one instance. Well darling I don't think there is much more else to write about of present, look after yourself.

Give my love to Lucy. Remember me to all my friends. Just give my best regards to Bert Wilkes and family. All my love darling, now as before. Yes even more than before, from,

Your Husband

Gerald. X X X X X X X X X X X X X

One for Lucy X

Continuation

Bert Wilkes owned a bicycle & shoe repair shop in Glebe Lane Stourbridge.

Well darling since I wrote those few pages I have been without a spare moment even to post them. So before I do go over with the letter I better do your favourite trick and add a little bit more. First of all I have not long received the last two air mail letter cards. One from you and one from mother. There are evidently a lot missing at present. According to the way you number them it is about five. It seems as though you have been to hospital although so far I do not know why you were supposed to go. You say the pain is easier but I cannot decipher the complaint. The price for the car seems pretty hot, but of course I do not know what has been done to it. If any money is required to square up I leave it entirely to you as the money is under your control. Sorry I cannot enclose a snap as it will make the letter too heavy. So returning to your health. Well my darling, I do hope you are better by now. I shall be getting a letter telling me you are better and probably one written a month earlier, telling me what the trouble was. One thing I must say is that with the exception of the last two weeks I write on every possible occasion. The boys say they don't know what to write about so I tell them they probably haven't a wife like mine or they would know. From now on however there may be longer periods between my mail. Darling, please don't worry but just pray for that Guardian Angel to keep me the same as in the past. There are pretty tough jobs to be done and up to the present I have never shirked anything asked of me. I am not going to start now. In any case the asking may never materialize. I write the above just in case, so that you will partly know the reason. I listened to a broadcast the other night. Dedicated to R.A.S.C. and called 'The heroes of the M.E.F.' Seems we are getting famous. Well we only do our best the same as everyone else. Shall have to close now as it is getting dark. Glad to hear you had luck with the chicks. Hope it continues. Give my love to Lucy and tell her I am going to ask for the first aid post to run a matinee when I come back. That is if you get awkward. Still I know now how to handle awkward customers. That is not a threat. Just a promise. Cheerio darling. God bless you. All my love from your husband,

Gerald X X X X X X X X X X

One for Lucy X

Sunday May 16ᵗʰ 1942.

T/271347
Driver Milner G
No. 2 Company
Base Depot
R.A.S.C.
M.E.F.

My Darling,

As you will see by the above address I have now left H.R.S. First of all I will ask you to continue writing to that address (I mean H.R.S.) until I can give you the address of my new company. You see it is just a kind of rest camp and transfer unit here at base. As you see I am in No2 Company today, yet tomorrow I may be in another part of the Base Depot, and then maybe in a day or perhaps even a month I go to the new unit. So if you send letters etc to H.R.S. I shall notify them as soon as I get to my new company and it will save all the time my letters would otherwise be following me around various camps.

Darling please excuse the writing, but it is being done under conditions of extreme difficulty. One good thing is I have not seen a sandstorm here yet, so that is something to be thankful for. They always seemed to blow up when I sat down to write a letter at the other places.

Well sweetheart, it was with very mixed feelings that I left the old unit. The scene of parting was one I shall not easily forget. By great fortune and a little wire pulling Fred is still with me together with most of the other boys of our little section. I have told you many times of the hours we were working, and what little spare time we were getting to write home. We did that work willingly, and when we left we reaped all the reward we needed. To begin with the OC himself came to work at a far earlier hour than usual, and made a small speech, thanking us for all we had done and wishing us luck in the future. I believe this is right when I say it the first occasion there when such a thing has happened. Abdul had tears in his eyes and disappeared when we left. Many fellows left their work to wish us Godspeed. My old Egyptian driver was broken hearted. I had the greatest job in the world to persuade him not to leave H.R.S. and he is a very valuable fellow. It was well known in the unit what affection this man had for me. Many officers and men have said he was one of those people you read of in story books who would have gone through hell itself for me. I knew they were speaking the truth. If I gave him an order, I knew it would be carried out in the shortest space of time possible. He started off with us but after a time I persuaded him that he would have to go back. The lorry stopped. Mosie got out. With tears in his eyes he grasped my hand and the last I saw of him was a picture of utter dejection disappearing on foot into the desert he knows so well. Among these people I had many true friends. Mosie taught me to speak the language, and because of that I was able to find out for myself many things which would otherwise be a closed book to me. So from that you can see that our work was appreciated. In the near future as I have already written I shall be on the move again. I have not the slightest idea where I shall end up but all I hope is that I get as square a deal as I had with my old unit.

There are always rumours and speculations in these sorts of camps with regard to where we will go next and so far the favourite is somewhere near Philip. I myself think the favourite will be an "also ran". Very strange that two days ago I received a letter asking if I would sooner be nearer Philip or another place in the best country in the world. Well darling that question needs no answer. Wherever you are is the place I want to get to as quickly as possible. I do not know how far off that day may be, but I am glad you are making good use of the machine oil. Even that will not stop the creaking of the springs when I get back. So now you know. At the present moment I am as fit as the proverbial fiddle. In fact I had another pretty stiff medical yesterday. The best I have had since I joined the Army. Still A1 with regard to the one thing you used to worry over, what other people thought if I did something unusual.

Well darling I have been in tough spots and awkward situations and extricated myself on each occasion. It has also given me great self confidence. I don't care a hang now what anyone thinks. In fact some of my pals here say they are going to walk down the street by themselves when they get home, just in case I do something to embarrass them. They say I have come out of my shell. I tell them I have no shell now. They say it must be just thick skin. One thing you have never asked me yet. That is what I miss most now. Well I will tell you. It is after the day's work is ended, and I have no one to tell the story to, or talk to, or discuss things with the same as in the old days of peace. Still darling I suppose those days will roll round again if I still have the same good luck as in the past.

Since writing the previous three pages I have been for a lovely dip in the briny but the heat of the sun was terrific. I did not stay long, but I shall take every opportunity until I go away again. The desert is a perfect Hell, yet somehow I would rather go up there again than to plenty of places that sound so interesting. It gives a fellow a feeling that he is putting up with something for the sake of his wife, his home his country and everything he loves most.

Darling, please don't mistake me when I say that there is one thing I should worry about other people thinking. That is if all my Army service had been at home. I have a feeling of having done my duty although when I do a little bit of heart searching, I know it is at your expense. Just at present there is nothing in the world I would like more than a week's leave to see you again. That is one of the penalties for serving overseas. Two leaves a year here. Four in England pay your own fare. Here travelling expenses paid. Above all we cannot see the people we love most. Still we must not grumble. Someone has to be out here.

Have just learned something that every soldier would like to know. How to fold two blankets to carry in the smallest possible space. Well it is amazing how they can be fitted into a kit bag. The Army has its own methods, but we are always exchanging little tips for the convenience of each other. Especially do we impart the knowledge to fellows with little experience out here. You can always pick out a man who knows the desert. There is no superior air when giving information. Just plain common sense. Yet there is always that air of devil may care. Then it comes to exchanging stories and stories of home too. Officers have yarned with me on many occasions too. They say little when duty calls, but sometimes when I have been driving a staff car or during a turn as duty driver they have lost that oyster effect, and told me many stories that I know to be true. Once during a raid, an officer was telling me his experiences in the Abbyurian campaign and some of the things he told me were almost unbelievable. Yet at a later date he showed me photographs which backed up his story.

Well my sweetheart, I think I shall have to close now, as we have no light at all here. Please remember me to all my friends. Give my love to Lucy. Ask her to write to Dick Chalk when she gets his letter. If she does not receive it please let me know and I will give you his address. Cheerio dear, Lots and lots of love from your husband

Gerald X X X X X X X X X X X X X X

One for Lucy X

Monday, May 18th 42

Darling,

Just a few lines to let you know that I have once more changed my address. As it is probably only a temporary address please do not send your reply here, but I will send you a cable as soon as I get to my new company. I have already sent you an air mail letter and the parcel of souvenirs I promised you. I hope it reaches you safely. Please let me know how you like the olive wood camel and other carvings. The cigarette case is for Dad. The camel is for our sideboard. With regard to the brooches they are named with exception of yours I could not find one with your name on. The sea shells are yours. Also the candles. The long white one is from the Holy Sepulchre. Presented to me as a memento of that special occasion I spoke about. Anyway I expect that will be of interest to all at home. I still have a few more which I did not have time to pack but I will send them at a later date. Then there is the snap album. Please let me know whether you want me to risk sending it. As you know it will probably be impossible for me to replace it if it gets lost. Darling you must please excuse the waiting but I am taking the opportunity while I can still write. I have just had a dose of the old needle and you know how it served me even in England. Still I am getting used to those little inconveniences now. If I never have anything worse than that I shall have few worries. I have just learned that George was stationed within a couple of hundred yards of me and I did not know. I think it is too late now for me to see him. I had already written to him at the address you gave me but he had left there. I thought he would have looked me up as he knew my address. Please remember me to his Mother and family. Also to all next door. Tell Mr. Gretton I will write to him as soon as I get settled down again. If I start sending too many letters from here I expect I shall have delay in later deliveries. By the way all the papers etc, you have sent me have all reached me safely. I can assure you they are welcome. Please continue to send them. Also ask 'Curly' when he is when is he going to <u>send me</u> a few lines. Glad to hear Philip reached his destination safely. Remember me to his wife if you see her. Also Edward's wife. I am expecting to see him <u>soon</u> I suppose we shall find plenty to talk about. By great fortune Fred has managed to remain with me again. It was a near squeak for being separated. The only job now is to continue together. I think we can manage that alright. I will let you know what happens. How is the shop going on? Alright I hope. And is the car alright now. I think it ought to be if the cost of repairs is any criteria. Give my best regards to Charlie Mason. One other thing I wanted to mention. An officer of my old unit has made me a generous offer for when business can be resumed. I have already sent you a long air mail letter giving full details. Just in case it is mislaid, I shall send a repeat letter in a week or two. I sincerely hope this proposal will meet with your approval although I have at present entered into no commitment. Well dear, I must close now as it is tea time. Give my love to Lucy. God bless you and keep you safe until I return. All my love from,

Your Husband,

Gerald X X X X X X X

One for Lucy X

26/05/1942 Rommel attacked and the battle for the Gazala line began.

27/05/1942 The Afrika Korps, pushed round the British defences and then moved northeast towards Tobruk. Both sides suffered many tank losses. The British armour became increasingly scattered.

28/05/1942 Rommel's forces began to run out of fuel because his tanks had moved too far from their supply lines. Rommel himself searched for his supply line and then guided it to his Panzer Divisions. Major Archer-Shee ,a POW complained about his lack of water rations. Rommel told him that the POWs were getting the same ration as the men in the Afrika Korps—half a cup per day.

29/05/1942 After a series of inconclusive battles Rommel went on the defensive and placed his troops near the Knightsbridge "box" on the edge of a massive minefield. His tactics were unconventional and the area that he placed his troops was afterwards known as "The Cauldron". German sappers began to clear a route through the minefield.

30/05/1942 German sappers continued tirelessly to clear a route through the minefield.

31/05/1942 The battle of the 'Cauldron' began as Rommel attacked the fortified keep or "box" in the Gazala line held by the 150th Brigade of the British 50th (Northumberland) Division.

01/06/1942 British 150th Brigade of the British (Northumberland) Division was commanded by Brigadier Haydon and was based at Got-el-Ualeb. They held out for 72 hours but were finally defeated.

After the war General Bayerlin of the Afrika Korps said, "It all turned on the 150th Brigade Box at "Got-el-Ualeb". If we had not taken it on June 1st, you would have captured the whole of the Afrika Korps".

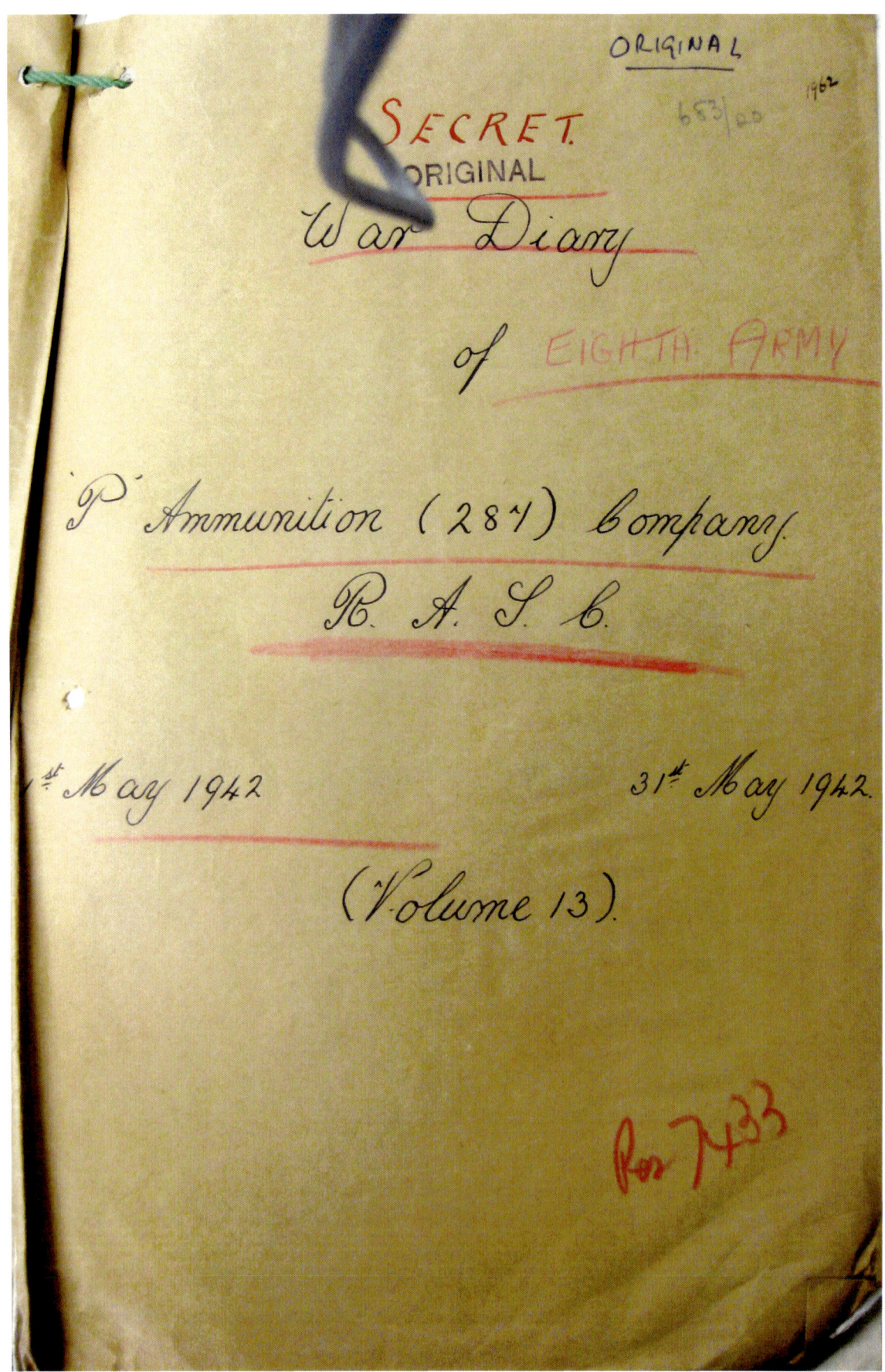

FROM THE ORIGINAL SECRET WAR DIARY of "P" Ammunition (287) Company RASC May 1942 (Volume 13)

LOCAL DEFENCE SCHEME (SOUTH AREA) SECRET

Information: Enemy air borne troops, paratroops or ground troops, are liable to attack Coys in this area.

Intention .   To defend Coy. Vehicles and personnel in the area.

Method   Company's under Command 2 L. of C. Tpt Coln, R.A.S.C. have been divided into North Area and South Area

North Area-	3 Water Tank Coy.)	
4 ,, ,, ,,	)	Under Command
4 ,, ,, ,,	)	Major R. Smith, 4 W.T. Coy

South Area-	286 Coy	)	
287 ,,		)	Under Command
346 ,,	(1 Pltn)	)	Major L.C. Smith, M.C.
168 ,,		)	"P" Amn (287) Coy
922 ,,		)	

For purposes of defence, 1 Pltn, 346 Coy is attached to 168 Coy. Will liaise with O.C. 168 Coy to co-ordinate their joint scheme.

Company defence schemes at present in operation, will continue to be implemented on sounding of General Alarm. In addition each Company will send to South Area Command Post (Officer's Mess Tent, 287 Coy, M.R.497381) a D.R. who must make a reconnaissance of the shortest route from his Coy to command Post and be familiar with it by day and night.

Each Coy will form an in-lying picket, to be made mobile, consisting of an Officer, a Sargeant and as many O.R.s as can be spared from essential defence and standing by vehicles.

Company Commanders know locations of all other Coys and on receipt of this Operation Order, will send to South Area Commander the map reference of their Companys.

The General Alarm will be given if any of the following events occur:-

(1). If warning by a responsible person is received of approach of the enemy

(2). If directly attacked.

(3). If enemy parachute troops are seen.

(4). If continuous small arms fire is heard in the area concerned.

Until otherwise notified, Companys will use a password:- "Whiteley" , which will be made known to all ranks.

Subject to Operational Duties, Companys will not move out of their present location unless directly ordered to do so by the competent authority of 2 L. of C. Tpt. Coln, R.A.S.C. or other competent senior authority (86 Sub Area, 30 Corps etc.) In this respect Company Commanders will, of course, use their discretion.

Companys will inform both South Area Commander and also HQ 2 L. of C. Tpt. Coln, of any attack, or landing, made in their area. The D.R. sold go to whichever of the two above report centres is nearer to his Company Location, and then on to the other report centre.

Dress on Alarm Steel helmets, arms and ammunition, Respirators at the alert.

Notes on above.

Paratroops are practically immobile when landed and rely on captured transport for quick movement. Therefore it is up to Companys to see that he does not capture their transport. As a last resort transport should be destroyed, rather than allowed to fall into enemy hands. This action will not be undertaken, except on the direct orders of Company Commanders.

It takes 60 seconds at least for a paratroop to become an effective fighter. That is the time to get him.

Fighting will not take place until the target has been DEFINITELY identified as enemy. Even then as much care as possible should be taken to avoid firing on own troops.

Coy Commanders must send reports to O.C. South Area, of any local action or landings in their Coy Location.

Owing to dispersion, unified control of fighting will be difficult, and all Commanders must use their judgement and initiative, as to the best course to adopt in any given circumstances.

Acknowledge

<u>L Colman Smith</u>

Major RASC

South Area Commander

Field 28.5.42

<u>Distribution</u>

H.Q. 2 L. of C. Tpt. Cln.

O.C. 287 Coy.

  ,,   286 ,,

  ,,   346 ,,

  ,,   168 ,,

  ,,   922 ,,

War Diary (2 Copies)

Chapter 6
"P" Ammo

WAR DIARY

Unit PAMMO (287) Coy RASC
Commanding Officer Major L.C. Smith M.C.

31/5/42	Coy HQ and W/shops ordered to move to El Adam area. On arriving it is learnt that our plns are forming part of "R" composite Coy a mobile FMC. Still under 4 L of C Tpt Cln For admin and 2 L of C Tpt Cln RASC for operations. This has proved most satisfactory
El Adam	
31/5/42	contd. From all points of view. Normal administration of Platoons Impossible as they are all under different commands. In addition one officer of this coy has been taken to act as liaison officer between 30 Corps and "R" Composite coy. The Coy is no longer a complete entity under one unified Coy Command but in series of small numbers, not necessarily from the same plns even, each under different commands. The ration question and water is very difficult to solve. "R" Composite Coy reports that reserve rations are being eaten. Do we draw for the whole Coy? If so where are the various parts of the Coy to distribute rations to? Lieut Williamson Act Capt For OC 287 Coy RASC
El Adam	
1/6/42	Coy settles in being under 4 L of C for admin and under 2 L of C for operations very unsatisfactory. Coy admin well nigh impossible.
2/6/42	Coy put under 2 L of C for admin as well as operations but the parts of plus forming R Composite Coy are being operated by 30 Corps direct. HQ still has no control over the majority of the Coy

T/271347
Driver Milner G
P.AMMUN Coy (287)
R.A.S.C.
M.E.F.
2.6.42. Somewhere in Libya

Darling,

Just a few lines in order to give you my new address. Any future letters etc that you send please use the above. Will you also please let them know at Brook St. You will in all probability receive mail with addresses at 2 or 1 Coy, Base Depot or 32 Station maintenance. Please ignore these. I mention all this because of the previous confusion caused by a badly delayed letter.

Well dear I have not enjoyed much spare time recently, so I am afraid my regular letter writing met with serious interference, but from now on I will endeavour to make up for the lost time. In fact I think it will have to be nearly all letters now as these cards and airgraphs are restricted to one of each per week from this area. I am writing this under very unfavourable conditions so if I should make any mistakes please forgive me. There is a pretty bad dust storm blowing and all I have is a bit of cover over a few supports, as shelter. Still I know what you would say "Never mind as long as I get a letter" Fred is still with me. We have had a lot of trouble to do it, but here we are, safe and well.

I have not had any mail from Brook St for a month, but that is of course owing to continuous travelling. Some of it should soon be catching up with me, and I will endeavour to reply immediately. I often wonder how you are progressing with the garden. Perhaps I shall know when I get some mail. Please let me know the results are as good as last year. With nothing but hundreds of miles of desert all around, even the thought of a nice garden and green trees makes me feel just a little cooler. It certainly gets very hot here at times when the Khamseen winds are blowing. That is when we are most thankful for our meagre water ration. I am afraid I shall have to admit that there have been occasions when a drink of water had to be balanced against a shave, and the drink usually wins. The worst periods are when we are on the move. Normally we get enough if we are careful.

Must conclude now darling as it is almost time for post. Give my love to Lucy. Tell her to a drink at my expense. One for you too. Tell Mr Gretton I will write to him in a few days. Also please remember me to Mrs Taylor and Billie and Arthur and Mildred. All for now. All my love from your husband

Gerald XXXXXXXXXXXX
One for Lucy X

June 3rd 1942. Somewhere in Libya

My Darling,

This is the first opportunity of letter writing I have had for nearly three weeks so I must try to make up for lost time. As you now know I left H.R.S. and went to Base Depot. You will probably receive several airgraphs or letter cards written from No1 and 2 Coy's at base. Also from No. 32 maintenance Coy. I was very unfortunate at that place but that story will have to wait until I see you. I was only there for a very short period, but during that time I went on a course of workshops. My job was to have been inspecting vehicles. I got on so well I was to have been promoted on Whit Monday. However that was not to be. Circumstances would not favour me and once again I moved back to base. The OC tried hard to keep me but it was no use. A misunderstanding had taken place and I was the one to be penalised. I want you to understand that I had done nothing wrong. Another thing to get off my chest darling. I came here of my own free will. Fred and I decided to risk it and here we are. We have both had our share of good luck and I only hope it continues. We take no undue risks, but at the same time we do all that is expected of us. I do not think we can do much more than that.

Our greatest trouble here is to purchase articles for personal use. To begin with I am using a pencil because I can't buy any ink just at present. We have a canteen lorry that goes back for supplies at regular intervals, but he cannot always get everything we need, and I think the nearest shop is about five hundred miles away. I have decided not to walk it as my feet may get sore. The food here is far better than at any other place I have been since I joined the Army, but that is counterbalanced by water being rationed. It was very hard at first. I am getting used to it now. I wonder how you would like to manage on 1½ pints per day for washing, a bath, drinking and also laundry. And you don't have to shave. I have made a resolution never to waste another drop of water, but I suppose when I get back to the plentiful supply at home my good intentions will be scattered to the four winds. You should have seen me in my birthday suit trying to have a wash down with a drop of water I had to spare. Hoping all the time that jerry would not come over looking for a good target for his machine guns. I eventually completed the performance and I feel quite clean again now. As you will realise from the first part of my letter, I have been moving continuously for some weeks now, and consequently it has upset my mail deliveries. It is just about a month now since I received a letter from home, but I am not worrying unduly. I expect they will all turn up soon. I will reply to all letters etc as they arrive. I have notified the responsible persons at each of my previous units, and all mail will be forwarded here. I am also sending you my address by telegram so you should have received it weeks before you get this letter. I hope you are getting my letters alright now. I shall write as often as possible, but airgraphs and letter cards are restricted to one of each per week. So I am afraid the greater part of my literary effort will be by the slower method of letters.

Still darling, I suppose you will not mind that as long as the contents are up to standard. You have not "told me off" lately. I must be getting better. And just another little item. I have a confession to make. Here it is, straight from the shoulder. I have had a drink of beer. In fact several drinks and no ill effects.

"After so many years" did I hear you say? Well I think two days with hardly any water warrants a drastic remedy, and as tinned beer was the only alternative, well my dear I ask you! We shall have to debate that subject when I see you again. I can assure you however that my conscience is not troubling me in the least. The other promise still remains intact and it will continue to do so. In any case I could not think of any really good excuse, except perhaps the sun.

Now to turn to the more serious side of life. Are you still putting plenty of machine oil on those springs? It is going to be just too bad if you are not, and you know I cannot be there to look after those sorts of jobs. Just remember to keep my suit in good order too. I am wondering whether to instruct you to cut the trousers off at the knees otherwise I won't be able to show my desert tan. I am sure you will be jealous when you see their beautiful shade. Tell Lucy if she is good I may allow her a view too. By the way has she received the letter from Dick Chalk yet? He is patiently awaiting a reply. And what about that place I asked you to find for when this lot is ended. Just in case the letters did not reach you. A quiet spot in the country away from all thoughts or talk of war, or armies, or "what I did when I was in ----- ". Just a place for us both to talk over the past and make new plans for the future. I have decided to give up all outside interests and make my home my sole hobby. So now is your chance to look around. I am afraid a lot of charities will be suffering but I feel now that I have done my share, and that there are others who can carry on.

With regard to my business and its future. I shall discuss that in the light of events when I can come back to you. I hope and pray that that day will not be too distant. Somehow I do not think it will be.

Well my sweetheart, I shall have to conclude as it is almost time to draw some pay. Give my love to Lucy, and please remember me to all my friends including Mrs Taylor & Billie.

All my love dear from your husband

Gerald X X X X X X X X X X X X X X X X

One for Lucy X

WAR DIARY

4/6/42   Odd vehicles seep back to Coy HQ. Permanent detachment with 4 L of C still out. Apparently they have difficulty in drawing rations and water.

Western Desert 4.6.42.

T/271347
Driver Milner G
H.Q. Platoon
P.AMMUN Coy (287)
R.A.S.C.
M.E.F.

My Darling

Once again I have fenced off my latest address for you just in case you have not already received it. You will probably be getting mail with all kinds of addresses on top of the page, but if any of them should turn up you will know by the dates that they are of <u>ancient</u> <u>calibre</u>.

Well sweetheart, <u>as you will know by now, we had to make a pretty hurried exit from</u> <u>Libya, but get this into the old brain box. We are far from being defeated. As far as I am</u> <u>concerned, a few hundred miles of waterless desert is nothing in comparison with the safety</u> <u>of an army. I suppose Parliament will have told you the story. I do not know what has been</u> <u>told so I can make no comment upon it. All I do know is that the boys here are worrying</u> <u>more about the "folks at home" than themselves. How many times I have heard the words</u> "What will Mother (or Mary of Joan etc) say. Wish I had a telephone for a few minutes". <u>I might add that</u> I have thought the same thing many, many times. <u>However, I have at last</u> <u>managed to dispatch a cablegram to you. I hope it arrives quickly although I have my doubts,</u> <u>as everyone is doing the same thing</u>.

Now to a more personal subject. Last night I received a letter card from you. Today I have had one from Roma and an air mail letter from you. I can assure you that nothing could have proved more welcome. And the letter contained a photograph of Aug 5th, or rather an event that took place on that date. You say you did not get any mail for 10 days, and it was such a long time. Darling, allow me to tell you that to be without mail from you for 10 <u>WEEKS</u> is like waiting a lifetime. <u>How many hundreds of miles I travelled in the desert during that</u> <u>time is beyond my powers of reckoning. All sorts of queer things happening, kit lost, blazing</u> <u>sun, worrying at times over water, in case the next water point was out of action, and above</u> <u>all, grimed with sand and dust. But we came through, as a unit. Organised, undepleted, spirits</u> <u>unbroken, but just hellishly tired. I think I have travelled at least five hundred miles on the</u> <u>front mudwing of a lorry. Desert all the way, too. And still I am here in one piece.</u> Lucky old hat with me too.

Then in the first letter I get from you are the words "Does my photo still bring back memories." The answer is most unfortunately "NO". I do not mean that I have forgotten you, but as you know my kit was lost, and I presume some dirty German is now the possessor of your photograph. Still he did not get this child and my thoughts were "Never mind I can always get another". That was just to console myself although I did not like it a bit. Well here I am a month later, and the first letter I open is in fulfilment of my wish. A photo taken on Aug 5th and the promise of more to come. One thing I was very pleased to know was that quite a number of my Palestine snaps arrived safely. As you know I lost all my others. And what about the parcel. Has that reached you safely? Please let me know as soon as possible so that I shall know what to try and replace at the earliest opportunity.

Please excuse the writing, but a pretty rough wind is blowing sand and paper all over the place. You see we sleep with the stars as a canopy here and the same conditions apply to everything. When the old moon is full I often lie awake and wonder where you are and what you are doing. I know it is too early for you to be asleep, for we have to turn in as soon as the sun disappears. <u>At this time of the year it is about 8.30 and your time is round 7.30.</u> Then I wonder why we all have to be out here, with homes broken up, and then I think of my past life. How I have done things in the wrong way, and how to put them right in the future. Always analysing myself, and usually finding myself wanting in various respects. One vice was smoking too much. So I gave it up just a month ago. I can save all that money now, and buy something for you when I see civilisation again. But do not be too anxious, for goodness only knows when that will be.

And now what about those cold feet you mention. You also say there are other things you prefer to a water bottle. Really darling as I have been in the desert for so long I am afraid I have lost touch with things, and I can't think what it could be. Still if it is anything nice I will let you whisper when I come home. I don't think that day is so far away either.

<u>We have had a rough time out here, but Jerry is more sick of it than we are. And the "Ities"</u>

just give themselves up. I know that because we brought a load of them down the line. They said the Germans quarrel with them and bully them. " ------ Germans" they said. Vacant space to be filled in as desired. And the way the boys of the R.A.F. are manhandling them will be making them quite ill. I have never seen anything like it. Attack after attack from dawn till dusk. Not just a few but 20s, 30s, 40s, 50s, every few minutes, all day long. And nearly all come back. The air belongs to us without any fear of contradiction. Wandering back to the war again. I wish I could forget it for a few moments.

Well let me try and make a picture of after the war. That seems to be a good topic with people who should have better things to do so why should I not do the same. Firstly, no smoking. Secondly, no going out at night. I have learned that in Libya. You can't go out there, only to visit Jerry and then you don't get back at all. But before those things I have missed out the most important. That is the holiday I proposed. Have you received those letters yet? Just a nice place to go. Then comes No. 3. Hard work and hard saving. And then, well, we shall have to discuss your part in it at a later date. It is no good me thinking of putting you like a peg in the ground. You will have quite a lot to do, but it is for you to decide when, where and how.

Sorry to hear about Roma's affair. Just for her sake I mean. Still I suppose it is her life. And just another word or two. Please don't be afraid to write and tell me anything you think I should know.

Well my darling, I think that is nearly all I can write for the present as this lousy sand storm still persists. Just keep the old chin up for a little longer. Give my love to Lucy. Also please remember me to all next door and anyone who may ask after my welfare. Cheerio darling. All my love from your husband

Gerald XXXXXXXXXX

One For Lucy X

05/06/1942 The Eighth Army launched a major counter-attack (code name "Aberdeen") against the Afrika Korps forces that are inside the 'Cauldron. It was badly managed and co-ordinated from the start and went disastrously wrong. 6000 British troops were killed or wounded. 150 tanks and 133 guns were lost and the Axis forces took 4000 POWs.

10/06/1942 The French, short of supplies having been totally cut off since May 26th 1943 and constantly attacked by Stukas finally withdrew from Bir Hacheim. Rommel had now destroyed 50% of the Gazala line.

12/06/1942 Rommel attacked the British positions between Knightsbridge and El Adem and trapped much of the British armour.

13/06/1942 German tanks and anti-tank batteries destroy 138 British tanks were destroyed by German tanks and anti tank batteries and left the Eighth Army with only 75 armoured vehicles operational. Rommel had total control of the "Cauldron" and therefore the coastal road that led to Tobruk as well. Lieutenant General Ritchie ordered a retreat towards Tobruk.

14/06/1942 Auchinleck sent an order from Cairo to Ritchie: "Tobruk must be held". Churchill was unhappy with the situation. The Eighth Army then held a line directly in front of Tobruk. It ran from the coast to Acroma, then southeast to El Adem and finally directly south to Bir El Gobi.

15/06/1942 Rommel launches an attack against Eighth Army's new defensive line, but is repulsed.

WAR DIARY

Unit 287 GT Coy RASC
Commanding Officer Major L.C. Smith M.C

5/6/42	R Composite Coy re names BAKOLL. Loads remain on wheels
9/6/42	BAKOLL ordered by 30 Corps to return to Coy HQ location because that many of our vehicles held in BIR HACKIM box having delivered Ammunition to the Free French Group. 1 NCO returns with 2 vehicles out of 8
El Adam	
11/6/42	Urgent orders received to vac immediately. Coy moves NORTH EAST by night.
12/6/42	All available vehicles to 4 Fwd Base to load 25 pdr & 40mm ammunition and move SOUTH to join 84 FMC.
13/6/42	Coy moves P.M. to MISCHEIFA. Role changed again. Now to fill 84A FMC from MISCHEIFA, Coy moves 1600 hrs loaded vehicles to 84A FMC direct
14/6/42	Coy still on the move. Arrive MISCHEIFA. Arrangements for POL, rations & water made. I move vehicle returns from BIR HACHEIM.
15/6/42	All coy locations changed. Coy moves 7 miles! Whole of Coy HQ & w/shop ordered to remain on wheels. Pltns, at 84A FMC still out. No idea where they are. Coy now had 4 moves in 5 days. Admin impossible. Weekly strength return impossible to render? Nobody knows where all the Coy is. Central control at Coy non-existent.
MISCHEIFA	
16/6/42	No. 3 Pltn returned to Coy lines with 14 V.O.R.

June 16th 1942.

Just a few lines to let you know that I am still alive and kicking although I am afraid I shall have to tender my apologies for infrequent writing. The reasons for that are many, the main one being, I suppose, the urgent job of giving constant attention to Jerry's sick headache. Last night I performed a most painful operation. Cold water and nearly a week's growth on my chin. What one would call a Western Desert shave. I have decided that in future if it is at all possible, a shave a day is to be the maxim.

I think I told you in a previous letter that I had broken a very old habit. That is that I had my first drink of beer for about fifteen years. And really I quite enjoyed it. I suppose that was because I was more thirsty than usual. I can't understand this water drinking business. Some days I never touch my water bottle, yet other days I could drink gallons of the life giving fluid. Since then however I have become an abstainer again. I know I have lost the coppers and I shall have to square up when I see you again, whenever that may be, but I have no conscience troubles.

Have had a nasty little affair happen to me recently though. I have lost my entire kit. Fred is in the same fix too. Sorry to say all my personal stuff has gone too. Will you please tell Mother that the gold watch she bought for my 21st was included in the loss? Also all my photographs of you and - well, in fact all I had. Have just had a reissue of all essential kit, so I shall be able to start off afresh now.

Well darling I shall have to conclude now. I will write as often as possible in the future but make no promises. Give my love to Lucy, and remember me to all my friends. God bless you and keep you safe until I return. All my love from your husband

Gerald X X X X X X X X X X
One For Lucy X

16/06/1942 General Norrie received permission from Lieutenant General Ritchie to withdraw 30 Corps past Tobruk and as far as Mersa Matruh in order to re-equip. Defensive positions on the Egyptian border were taken up by General Gott's 13. Tobruk was commanded by Major-General H Klopper, commander of the 2nd South African Division T but its defences were inadequate, having been allowed to deteriorate during the winter and left it exposed to another siege.

17/06/1942 The Eighth Army's withdrawal reached the Egyptian frontier. The 2nd South African Division to defend Tobruk with a 30,000 strong garrison.

20/06/1942 Rommel attacked Tobruk.

21/06/1942 Major-General H Klopper formally surrendered to Rommel. 32,000 prisoners, 2,000 tons of fuel, 5,000 tons of food and 2,000 vehicles were captured by the Germans.

WAR DIARY

Unit 287 GT Coy RASC

Commanding Officer Major L.C. Smith M.C

17/6/42	No. 1 & No. 2 Plns return still carrying loads of ammo. 34 x 3 tons ordered to rail head to off-load. Many of these vehicles off loaded tail board to tail board on to vehicles of other Coys taking the ammo straight back to 87 FMC
18/6/42	26 x 3 tons to HAMRA to take troops to SOLLOM. Final progress report rendered on re-organisation to 4 Pltn GT Coy.
20/6/42	Coy moves south to area 84 FMC
21/6/42	Coy HQ & w/shops cross frontier into Egypt. Vehicles with ammo remain at 86 FMC

June 21st 1942   *Somewhere in the Western Desert*

Darling,

      Although I have not received any mail from you for the last six weeks I thought I had better keep up my end of the bargain. I know quite well that you have not forgotten to write to me. It is owing to all my travelling through the Middle East that my letters have not reached me as quickly as before. Yesterday however my hopes were raised considerably. I received two Regd letters from Dad, posted respectively on Apl 4th and Apl 21st 1942. I have already acknowledged receipt of them, so he should have had my letter card by the time you get this letter. The good sign is that my mail has found me. It is something to know that. From now, the mail you have sent to HRS will be redirected straight to my present Company, so there should not be a great deal of delay. So you see all I have to worry about now is that lot that is following me around. I think it will arrive alright. What I want to know however is probably contained in one of those letters.

    That is how you feel after the visit to Sinton. As far as I could make out, it was a badly swollen face, but the writing in that particular letter was badly blurred. May have been rescued from the water. Anyway, please let me know when you receive this letter. You will never do wrong to repeat anything like that in later letters, just in case the original meets with bad luck. Have sent you an airgraph and a telegram today. Letter written to Lucy yesterday, too. Getting good don't you think so? I am still very curious to know whether she ever received that letter from Dick Chalk. I keep mentioning it as up to the present I have heard nothing at all about it, and there is always the possibility that the same thing has happened to it as to a lot of my letters.

   Well darling, how is the garden going on. I wish I could be there to see it now. It would make quite a nice change from this unchanging view of sand, sand, and still more sand. Even that would not be so bad if it were not for the merciless sun.

24/06/1942 The 8th Army evacuated Sollum and Sidi Barrani and the Germans advanced into Egypt .

25/06/1942 Sidi Barrani, Sollum and the Halfaya Pass are captured by the Germans. The 8th Army retreats to Mersa Matruh in Egypt. General Auchinleck relieved Lieutenant General Ritchie and took personal command of the 8th Army.

26/06/1942 Hitler made Rommel Field Marshal. Rommel launched attacks against Mersa Matruh.

27/06/1942 British start to withdraw from Mersa Matruh towards the El Alamein line as Rommel begins to outflank them.

28/06/1942 Fuqa is captured by the Germans. British units are increasingly confused.

29/06/1942 Mersa Matruh is taken by Rommel after heavy fighting. 6,000 prisoners are captured along with large quantities of supplies. Retreating British units mixed with German advance units.

30/06/1942 Rommel's forward units reached El Alamein. General Auchinleck tells a disorganised 8th Army, that 'He (Rommel) hopes to take Egypt by bluff. Lets show him where to get off.'

01/07/1942 Rommel lost 18 tanks leaving him with only 37. He also captured 2,000 prisoners from the El Alamein 'box' on the Gazala line.

02/07/1942 Rommel now only has 26 tanks and fails to take El Alamein from the British despite heavy attacks.

03/07/1942 Rommel suspended his offensive operations and began to construct defensive positions. His army was exhausted due to lack of supplies. He was very short of fuel for his armoured divisions

---

WAR DIARY

Unit 287 GT Coy RASC
Commanding Officer Major L.C. Smith M.C.

24/6/42	Coy moves SOUTH of Matruah
25/6/42	Coy moves 22 miles NORTH EAST. Going appalling.
26/6/42	"A" & "B" ration packs sent to 86 FMC
27/6/42	Coy moves to DABA. "C" ration pack t 86 FMC
28/6/42	Coy located 4 miles SOUTH of DABAA. Ordered to move 32 miles SOUTH EAST, 19 miles done before dark.
29/6/42	Coy on move
30/6/42	Coy arrives at El IMAYID. Very soft going. Nos. 1 & 2 Plns return to Coy. All V OR sent to AMYRIA to 13 Corps Group w/shops
EL IMAYID	
1/7/42	Coy ordered to Amyria
2/7/42	Coy at Amyria in ??? Plns still out.
3/7/42	Plns start dribbling back.

WL Williamson Capt
For O/C 287 Coy RASC

Continuation   July 3rd 1942

Darling,

Please forgive me for not having written to you during these last few days. I know what you have been thinking and wondering and saying. Let it be sufficient to say that after all my adventures since leaving home I am still safe, and above all lucky enough to be still in one piece. How I wish I could come home to tell you all about it. I suppose however that all the details will have to be reserved for another day.

I do not know a great deal of the story as told to you in the English newspapers etc but it certainly has been a mighty battle out here. I want to point out now, that anything I may write in this letter is entirely a personal opinion. I am not attempting to clear or blame anyone.

For days which seemed numberless, two mighty armies were locked in a death struggle. Rommel was confident and so were we. Rommel made certain promises which I think he will fail to keep. Still the struggle went on. Then suddenly something gave way. I am sorry to say it was our boys. But I am equally certain that it may just as easily have gone the other way. Our Major already has the MC. Well darling, if steady nerve in a tight fix is any criteria, I can imagine how he won it. For he certainly brought us through alright where a lesser man might easily have failed. But even among all the trials and dangers of war, there are spots of real humour. The funniest thing I have known is a story against Fred. He had his hair cut off completely about three weeks ago, because the sand was making it knotted. He now has a nice growth resembling a newly mown lawn. Well on the way down we picked up some Italians who gave themselves up. An officer looked at a lorry that was already heavily laden. He said "I think you can take ----" To complete the story, he checked up again and went away. It was only then that Fred realised that he was sitting in the back of the lorry with his hat off and had been counted as a prisoner. It will be a long time before he hears the last of that episode.

Just one request I have to make while I think of it. Please thank Mrs Digger for the present she sent to me some time ago. Tell her it has proved most valuable to me. Seems weeks since I heard from you. In fact I think it is over two months now. I know you have not failed to write, but I have been similar to a man on a draughts board. Moved all over the place. I am hoping now to be able to stay at my present home long enough to receive all my arrears in one big bundle. I am afraid it is a lot to wish for but still I may be lucky.

Have you heard anything of George? I have not been able to find out where he is, but I think he must have been farther down than I was. I cannot write to him again either as I have already told you that I lost all my kit and George's address with it. Your photograph too. I am sorry about that, but I can always get another you know. What about it? Hurry up. And tell Lucy to send one too. I do hope the Aug 5th parcel turns up safely. Please let me know if it was Regd and when it was sent, and also please ask Dad to let me know when he has sent a letter. I was religiously keeping a record of all Regd numbers of letters received, and now I have lost the lot. Still I am smiling. I have the money so Jerry is welcome to the numbers. But just to enable me to try and check up, will you please let me know what registered mail you have sent recently. I think it is pretty certain that I have had all you have posted up to Apl. 21st. So actually there is not very much I am expecting just at the time of writing, but I thought it might save a lot of trouble and delay at a later date. In fact I think if it boils down to hard facts, I would rather lose some of my mail than my freedom. I think those unpleasant visions are past for a while now.

I still say it is all because of my lucky hat that I am here. The boys laugh at me, but they never attempt to interfere with it. You remember the way I got it in Capetown, I suppose. How far away those days seem. Marching in column, when up came an old lady off with my hat, emblem fixed in it and the words "There you are my boy, take that and wherever you go good luck goes with you Keep it there, and no harm will come to you". I may add that it has been there ever since, and if I tell the truth I know I have had more than my share of luck. And I am confident it will continue.

Well darling, after that journey, I feel like a little rest so I will close now and probably write again tomorrow. Cheerio darling. Keep your chin up. I know how you feel but I certainly am not down

Gerald wearing his "Lucky Hat" with a friend

hearted and the tables are going to be turned before very long. You would think so too if you could see the R.A.F. getting to work. I am beginning to feel sorry for the enemy already. All my love sweetheart, from your loving husband

Gerald X X X X X X X X X

One for Lucy X

HOW FRED GOT COUNTED AS A PRISONER BY G MILNER
(See previous letter)

Sandstorms seemed to be getting more frequent but we were still eluding the forward enemy troops. As my Company had lost most of its equipment during the enemy onslaught the most urgent things we needed were food and rifles or machine guns. In one mighty sandstorm we came across a NAAFI which was packing up and clearing out in what one might call a "bit of a hurry". They need not have worried. We helped them by throwing as much as we could into our trucks.

Then we had a bit more luck. In the clouds of sand we ran smack into one of our own ammo dumps, which because of the proximity of the German advance column was to be blown up. The officer in charge, whoever he was, had his hand on the plunger. Our own platoon Captain, Micky Ridgway ordered the officer with his hand on the plunger to remove himself. With reluctance, and with a little help from an empty revolver he complied, whilst we four plundered the Bren Guns, 303s and as much ammo as we could get in the seconds available to us. We went off groping our way to the track and soon a mighty explosion was heard.

We had been just in time. Retreating steadily it became quietly obvious that we were <u>following</u> the leading German D.R.s (Despatch Riders) I quietly told Fred Loman who was for a time my spare driver what appeared to be the situation. Most of our vehicles had an "observation hole" in the cab roof. Fred stood on a seat and elevated himself through the cab roof, pointing a newly acquired Bren at the rider.

After a short burst in front of him the rider stopped. We took him prisoner. The same fate befell another half dozen before we regained our own outfit. I often wonder what the Germans made of a series of motor cycles strewn about the desert.

Here I must confess I have somewhat over run my story as before the real pressure was put upon us we stopped for a short break. All but three of our tanks had been lost in battle and or ack/ack were mostly silent. Fred Loman said he was going to lie down in the back of the truck. He was asleep in very quick time. Next came a German plane flying at a tremendous height. We were not sure if it was a bomber or a recce plane. The anti aircraft lads said they had only one shell left. They decided to give it a go. With careful aim and with us lesser mortals waiting for the bombs to drop the shot was fired. A mighty shout went up when one of the engines was hit. A bomb was released which fell well away from us. Next thing we saw the engine was on fire, the plane still at a great height was out of control. Fred had been asleep through all of this. As the plane neared the earth, completely out of control I could see we were likely to be in the next world at any moment. I grabbed Fred by the ankles and dragged him out of the truck to lie flat on the ground. Almost immediately came one of the biggest explosions I have ever heard and I assure you in 4½ year I have heard a few. The bomb load had blown the plane to smithereens. Debris was scattered over aprox 2 miles. One engine landed about 10 ft from my truck. Fred got his breath back and said, "That was close".

Resumption of retreat to the foregoing Ammo dump. By the time we reached our "sticking point at El Alamein we had collected a truck load of prisoners. Fred was the sole guard with a 303 rifle. In the sweaty heat, dust had adhered to faces, arms and in a few cases bare chests and legs (shorts , socks and boots were a familiar type of uniform) . Fred had the hair shaved from his head and like the prisoners looked as though a bag of sand coloured flour had been thrown over him. I mention this because he was so indistinguishable from the Germans that the receiving officer refused to believe that he was my spare driver. I was reporting to my C.O. at the time and did not know what was going on. It was with some difficulty that we obtained his release.

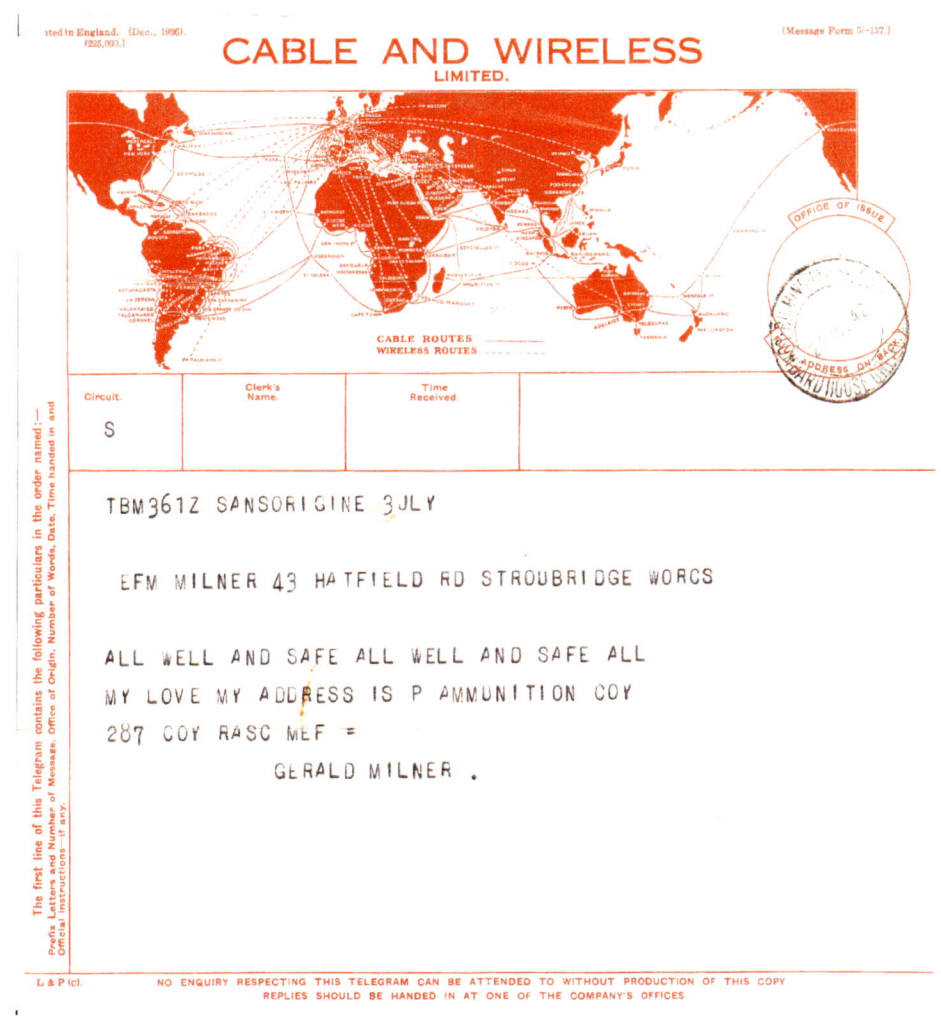

Post marked '21 JUL 42'. Dated '3 JLY'.

> **05/07/1942** Rommel's troops laid minefield in front of their defensive positions at El Alamein.
> **06/07/1942** Panzer Army Afrika held its position despite continuous attacks by the 8th Army.

WAR DIARY

Unit 287 GT Coy RASC
Commanding Officer Major L.C. Smith M.C.

4/7/42	Role now to fill 86 & 93 FMC. Apparently being held on wheels
7/7/42	01/&2 Pltn returns to report that 10 x 3 tons loaded 87 octane petrol have now been on wheels stationary at 86 FMC for 5 days.

July 7ᵗʰ 1942   *Western Desert*

Darling,

I have already sent you an airgraph but as I have a few minutes to spare I have decided that there are plenty of worse ways of employing them than writing to you. For one thing I feel I owe you as many letters or airgraphs as I can possibly send just to make up for any deficiencies similar to those that were absolutely unavoidable during recent world shaking events.

You see darling they do not provide many mail boxes in the front line and even if they did I am afraid I should not be inclined to stay and look around for them. We had some rather anxious moments at various intervals, and at times I began to wonder if we would ever stop Rommel's men. And then like a thunderstorm came the R.A.F. They have never failed in their support since the battle began. But darling, if only you could see them as I do now, you would never have any doubts who will eventually win out here. What great lads those pilots are. They come back over us, flying at times about 20 ft up and somewhere around 300 MPH. Dip their wings in salute and suddenly out shoots an arm with thumb vertical. All the time just a pure devil may care attitude. All day long they are going over us, and since they have been flying in such vast forces, Jerry has begun to realise he is in a pretty tough spot. Still by the time you get this letter I suppose a lot of changes will have taken place and the battle of El Alamein will have become history. My only hope is that I am alive to read the story. The battle has had one good point. It has left Jerry with water supply difficulties while we have come back to plentiful supplies. While we were making chess board moves in order to avoid being cut off in the dessert we learned what the possibility of water shortage means. Actually we were never in desperate need, but we did not know for certain when we could get any more. Our water bottle supplies had to last a long time and we dared not wash and shave sometimes for days. As I have already written, the farther back we came, so our chances of water increased. But I must say that I do not fancy another experience on similar lines. My lips were badly swollen, and when the swelling eventually went down they cracked and peeled and became ---- well never mind that they are in trim now for a visit home.

In fact, I am feeling fighting fit all over. Had plenty to make me feel that way. Clouds of R.A.F. still going over as I write. The only snag about all that is that we have to be very careful not to get caught. All day long we say "Another lot of ours". But one day I took a very poor view of things, when Jerry decided to blow my bread and jam out of my hand. Still that is just a minor incident. I think during my time in the Army, he has tried to "get me" by every known method, but I also think he will give up first. Yes there are times when I reflect on the escapes I have had during the past year, and the memories are not too pleasant. Still I <u>have</u> survived up to the present, and I am pretty certain I can carry on now.

There is a pretty severe sandstorm blowing again now, trying to interrupt my writing efforts but I think the sheltered side of my lorry will prevent that. And now it is also tea time, so I must go for food and sand. It simply has to mix on these kinds of days.

Well darling I owe you more apologies now. I thought I should finish this letter after tea, but it is now four days since I had that meal. You already know how Jerry came down, and of necessity work must come first. It has been extremely hard work during recent days, but I think an easier time is ahead in the next few days. And what is greater news still is the fact that we have just been promised regular trips to the sea for bathing.

Well my dear I have already written you an airgraph, but I will repeat the news that I received 20 letters and airgraphs in one day, so I have set to work to answer them. Have just received another from Dad Regd May 17th I think the date was, but I will write to him personally. Shall try to write as much as possible during the next few days. I have tried to write to you on every possible occasion especially since the fighting here. You and Roma seem very anxious to know exactly where I am. Well darling it is in the best interest both for yourself and me that I should not tell you. Please look at it like this. If I had for instance told you I was in Tobruk or Bardia or any of those places and the letters had reached you at the time of the fall of those places, what would you have been thinking? And while you would be worrying yourself to death I may be miles away. To put it bluntly, we may be here today and a hundred miles away tomorrow. I will just add a few other words. This company has always had a good name. Today after the enemy has been halted it has a reputation second to none. Very sorry to say I shall soon have to send this letter as it is almost time for post. And I must send my letters at every opportunity as we may move to a place where the mail situation is rather difficult. Just had some papers from you. Date-- well I hardly dare tell you. Feb 7. Still they will provide a little reading matter.

Give my love to Lucy. Tell her to be a good girl, and that I have quite a lot to tell her in my next letter. Well darling, I really must close or I will be too late for post. Cheerio darling. All my love, from your husband

Gerald X X XXXX X X X

One for Lucy X

P.S. Just a word about your work. If you take my advice you will stay where you are. I do not see why you should leave while there are A.1. men in the Army doing jobs as clerks in more or less safe areas. That is my personal opinion and after all, I can't think of any one who will turn round after the war and say "here is what you would have saved extra". I think my service and your voluntary work is quite enough from two people. Let them go on talking. All for now darling

Gerald X X X X X

GERALD MILNER STORY

What ever anyone may say there was always a certain amount of tension, which became broken in various ways. One of the most important things to us was reveille. About 5 a.m. all night patrols and guards would discharge their weapons in the direction of the enemy. This was a daily occurrence. Then iron rations breakfast.

Then if fighting permitted came the ritual. Someone, sometimes an officer, at other times a driver would walk away for a few yards. He would look at the sand and then observe that he was sure that he had seen that grain of sand the day before. Because of enemy "strafing", only one or two people at a time could go and have a look. Then came "serious" discussions. Some thought the grain of sand was slightly different in shape from yesterday's. Others would think it was more oblong or a deeper shade. The enemy usually reminded us that it was once again time for business.

I feel that I should briefly mention one of our lads, A.B. Taylor always known as Abe.

Previously to joining the Army he had been a member of the Salvation Army. Each evening at sundown he stood in front of he enemy, trumpet raised and the strains of well known hymns rang out across the desert. No one fired at him, and very soon the Germans could be heard joining in the singing. A.B. had such tremendous faith.

09/07/1942 Rommel continued to attack British defences at El Alamein but is slowed down by stubborn British resistance.

14/07/1942 The British attacked positions to the south of El Alamein but are repulsed by the Axis forces.

15/07/1942 New Zealander troops attack 'Kidney' Ridge was attacked by New Zealander troops in three days of heavy fighting. 2,600 prisoners were taken and 115 guns captured.

WAR DIARY

Unit 287 GT Coy RASC
Commanding Officer Major L.C. Smith M.C.

9/7/42	All available empties ordered to load ammo.
10/7/42	Coy ordered to move to ARH Burg-el-Arab. Role is wat ammunition only.

BURG EL ARAB

11/7/42	Coy in new location. Orders received to move all vehicles Coy HQ & w/shop to 93 FMC operate the replenishment at 93 FMC with ammo.
12/7/42	Coy on the move. Very bad going. Many vehicles stick in soft sand. 8 x 3 tons attached from 922 Coy
13/7/42	OC Coy takes over all ammunition details to 93 FAD 35 x 3 ton now attached to make up 2 days holding
14/7/42	Coy order to move entirely to pt 16 miles NORTH EAST. On arrival no signs of X L of C Tpt Cln
15/7/42	Guide marines from X L of C Tpt Cln to guide Coy to location which CR ASC had reconnoitred 7 miles SOUTH of original
16/7/42	Coy placed under Comd X L of C Tpt Cln f.a.p. Work continues filling 93 FAD

July 17th 1942   *Western Desert*

Darling,

Many thanks for all the mail I have received recently. I went ten weeks without a line from you. All the time the battle raged I was wondering if and when I would get a letter from you. And yet, through all those desperate days I had a most queer feeling. No darling you are entirely wrong in your guess. I had a sense of devilish satisfaction. Yes! Danger was there in plenty but all I thought of was just one thing. And what that thing was the fact that you had once and for all made up your mind about this child. You have always said there are times when you did not know what to think of me, and then the next minute! Well there is no need for me to write all that story over again. I am just waiting for your letters written at that time. I wonder whether I am right. And yet I am certain I am. I can almost imagine you pushing your chest out with pride when people asked after me and all the time muttering sweet words because you could not be there with me. Well darling, as you know it is not usually my policy to write of the war, but I will just say these few words. Still have confidence in the Eighth Army. We are not beaten yet and Jerry will come no farther. That is my own opinion and I stick to it. Glad to hear George is keeping well. I know as long as he can hold a pint glass there is not much wrong with him. I suppose he will be wanting to know all sorts of queer things when I come home. As I have said before, I think I shall be giving him some sweet shocks. Tell him to get in some practice with a trembling glass or he will be wasting good food. Especially when I give him the English interpretation of what I said to the Arab Gentleman. I think I shall have to take him out of your hearing. Very sorry if I put the wrong address on one of my letters. Especially as you had no letter for 3 weeks. Darling I can assure you I write twice every week so that you should have a letter of some sort.

But what I want you to try and realise is the conditions under which I have to write. At present I am perched in the back of a lorry with a strong wind blowing and several articles holding the paper down and the desert night rapidly descending. Can't make out yet where these authors get there Romantic East from. Desert Song seems to be just a fabrication to me. I will reserve a more lucid description of it until I get home. I think the paper might set fire. Well my darling I have already sent you an airgraph today, and a telegram which I hope arrives by August 5th just to show that I had not forgotten. So I shall soon have to close. Having difficulty to see what I am writing. Will write again tomorrow. Photographs in wallet and £1 rec'd this week. Also about 3 Regd letters from Dad. Pictures very good, but you are worrying. Your face looks pale. Cheer up darling. It won't be so very long now. Give a little love to Lucy. Will write to her this week. All my love from your husband

Gerald XXXXX XXXXX

One for Lucy X

WAR DIARY

Unit 287 GT Coy RASC

Commanding Officer Major L.C. Smith M.C.

20/7/42	Second section of W/shops ordered up from Amyria OC protests as it is much easier to get heavy work done in the rear areas.
22/7/42	Second section of W/shops orders cancelled. Allowed to remain at ARH. Additional pack for 4 Lt Armoured Bde taken on in 93 FAD. Only 287 Coy & 241 Coy employed on this duty. All other attached vehicles returned.

July 22nd 1942

My Darling,

What a to do. You say you have had no mail for three weeks. At one stage in this bit of a dust up out here I had none for 10 weeks. And that is a lifetime out here. You can go and look on the floor or in the letter box etc. but I know it is no good looking on the sand. You see, we have made this sandy place very useful. Sand for a bed pillow, chair, footstool, in fact everything you can think of. But it has its limitations. There are plenty of desert breezes but no lullaby. At least I have not found anything like that up to the time of going to press. And when the wind blows, instead of the English and perhaps one would say gentlemanly way of playfully swirling ladies skirts at a totally incorrect angle, it just blows steadily and strongly for a time and then with terrific force suddenly decides to throw sand in all directions. When it comes like that food and everything else is covered. We have no time even to move anything. And probably within the space of a minute it has passed. And that darling was a whirlwind.

Last autumn, during a visit near the Sinai Desert I saw columns of sand about 300 ft high coming toward me just like a great spiral staircase. Since then I have seen it on several occasions. It is also possible to follow the direction in which it is travelling. In a few moments it can change course completely. It has one great peculiarity. If I stand and watch it, it just goes in the other direction. But if I am endeavouring to erect a tent, well you know what happens. So much for sand storms.

Well my darling, I am afraid I am wandering rather badly from the subject of ten weeks and three weeks respectively without mail. Then all at once my supply of mail began to arrive more freely. Twenty in one day, and only two of them from you, and those were very badly delayed. All the same they are always most welcome. As long as I do not get one telling me to stay out here I shall never worry. I don't think I am liable to just at present. At least your letters recently seem to be calling me back.

I am at present endeavouring as suggested on the front of my pad to save paper so you will find it written rather erratically. Still, I suppose it will be just as welcome as long as it is readable. And just to make things as awkward as possible I am writing while sat on my vehicle. Almost like trying to compose a letter on the ship except for the rolling effect. And just about as much as I can tell you.

All the things that happened to me and all the places I visited, and yet I know if I wrote them they would be crossed out, so I must await a suitable time and place. Is it to be dear old Devonshire after all, or Midland country or Scotland? I can't think you have found a place yet. I can imagine you finding about 20 places then trying to decide which is best and all the time wondering whether you will come across a better one. Well I hope you do find a nice place and after that I should like mother to go away for a change. I think she has earned it.

Seems as though the car has been packed up too. Well if it applies to everyone the same it is a necessary sacrifice. Shipping space has to be saved, and the sooner it is not only realised, but put into practice, then the sooner the men serving overseas will be returning home. I often wonder what sort of reception we shall get when we return.

According to the radio our Army out here is redeeming itself. What did you think of it all during the anxious days that we have left behind us? I have been wondering quite a lot lately what your reactions were. I have already written and told you some of my thoughts at that time. I try to make my letters as interesting as possible but it is difficult to sit and write fluently and at the same time avoid everything liable to censorship. You will notice that I have obliterated a place at the heading of this letter.

New censorship regulations have just come into force so I suppose before long I shall just be telling you I love you, I am safe and so for the present goodbye. In any case it is a most difficult job to write a letter. Oh! And I may be able to tell you we are getting some fine weather. Still darling, when some more letters arrive I shall be able to write a little more freely.

Had a lovely surprise the other night. Real pickles and a tin of peaches for supper. A very good friend of mine and myself found them growing on a bush. It was an extremely luminous bush and can only be found after dark on rare occasions, and even then it takes a good soldier to pick them without damaging the tree. But it was a shame to see them just left there to spoil. Hoping to find some more one of these fine days. Well sweetheart, I shall have to close now as it is almost time for the post. Give my love to Lucy and please remember me to all next door. Cheerio! All my love, from your husband

Gerald X X X X X X X X X X X
one for Lucy X

22/07/1942   Having mustered 323 tanks against Rommel's 92 in the second battle of 'Kidney' Ridge, Auchinleck lost 131 tanks and 2,600 men.

July 23rd 1942

Darling,

Many thanks for the papers which I have received during the last few weeks. Have had four lots during the last five days. Always have a waiting list when I have read the pictures in them. Quite a lot of fellows from the County Express district near me. I always pass them on. Never be afraid to send reading material of any sort to me. The more the better, in fact.

Glad you had the letter about the goat. That was a long time ago but it still remains an interesting memory. There are many more similar affairs I have seen but I shall have to keep those stories for another day.

While I have been writing these few lines I have received three letter cards from you. Seems as though you have been having a mixed time, but I rather envy you the scenery through which you have been passing. Seems to me your chief concern is my whereabouts. Don't worry dear; I can still take care of myself. Must now wait patiently for the remainder of your cards telling me of your travels. Did you find the place you have been looking for? Somehow I don't think so. If you have not done so yet there is no hurry, but honestly I do not fancy the Severn. Something like the quiet at Himbleton, although I am not actually suggesting that place. I leave that to you.

Have just been listening to a most interesting conversation while I am trying to write. One of the fellows is asking or rather wondering what sort of quartermaster will be waiting to dish out the wings in the next world. And whether he will chant out in Army style "Wings - pairs - one". I do not know what they will find to discuss next. Anyway it all brings the end of the war a little nearer.

Heard from Dick Chalk this week. He is anxiously awaiting the letter from Lucy. Give her my love and I hope the massage proved satisfactory. Cheerio darling. All my love from your husband

Gerald X X X X X X X

one for Lucy X

23/07/1942 Fierce fighting continued along the El Alamein front.

July 25th 1942

My Darling,

Just a few more lines while I am patiently waiting to hear from you again. Since the first three letter cards posted on your holiday trip on July 1st I have had no more mail. And honestly darling I feel as though I want to write pages and pages to you but I know it is going to be a great effort. There is quite a lot I can find to write about but I feel almost desperate.

You have no idea what this sun is like. I can stand that alright, but oh! The flies. Simply millions of them. To sit still for a moment is a living torment. And there is no period of the day which is free from them. From dawn to dusk. And George had the same complaint in his letter. I told him in reply that I was very surprised to find he had some there. I thought we had the whole lot here.

Anyway sweetheart I will try and make my letter readable. To begin with you should be receiving another 3d per day from June 12th 1942. Sorry to hear you had rather a lot of trouble to get the other lot, but it was a nice little sum to pick up. As this lot was entered up in the field, it may take a little longer to get through, but you will get it alright. I shall also inform you in an airgraph. I can't remember whether I have already told you about it. If I have please forgive me as this is the same 3, but if I did not tell you, still forgive me.

I am now wondering to return to the subject of these --? .. x x flies. Why I did not grow a tail with a lot of hair, after the style of a horse. I am sure it would be most useful. What do you think?

Had quite a good night's entertainment yesterday. I was asked to arrange a knowledge Bee. Without access to any books I managed it quite well and after it concluded and darkness fell we just sat until someone started telling stories. Most of them were in true Army traditional style. The old moon was casting a pale white light over everything and I thought as the party broke up of days of long ago. Walks over the fields and back by nine thirty. How I wished I could repeat those days. But never fear they will roll round again.

I note from your letter cards that you are trying to find a place for us to stay when I come home. I have all the time at the back of my mind a picture of a stream full of trout and shaded with lovely green trees and I suppose just to shatter the dream and come down to earth a <u>few</u> flies. I should like to sit and fish, and at the same time tell you quite a lot of stories and plenty of other things too. The kind of things you have always wanted me to tell you. And I shall even be able to manage that. If you fail to find a place during your travels, as I have mentioned in a previous letter, I still have visions of the stream at Himbleton as an example. At the junction of the two parts of the brook. It is not just for the trout fishing, but for a place of quiet and peace. And there I can tell you stories of Africa and Egypt and Libya and Palestine and Transjordan. In fact all the places I have visited during my service out here. And if you should be sufficiently interested, I could relate some of the incidents that occurred during the great retreat of a few weeks ago. Not only stories of great courage but of wonderful physical endurance and strength in a hell of heat and dust and sweat. But my dear those tales will have to wait until I am sitting by your side on that bank by the stream. You say in your letter you wish you could transport a few of the green trees and country lanes over here to me. I wish the same thing could happen and happen pretty quickly. Still I suppose I can put up with it for a good while yet.

In fact I think I am getting pretty tough. Only myself who thinks so though. My sleeping partner, a corporal says I can't take it. That is because I have said wicked words about these flies. Says when I have been out here as long as he has, I shall take no notice of such things. He has been out here a month less than myself. I tell him one has to be in the soldier's language, brothel bred to stand them so over goes the petrol tin seat and me with it. Well sweetheart this corporal I am spending my time with is a very good fellow. I get on very well with him. Fred is on another job in the camp, so although I can see him I am camped 600 yds from him. You see dispersal of vehicles and men is essential. We have an exceptionally good officer too. To return to this corporal fellow. He is very witty in a "half soaked" way. In many ways similar to Curly although in outward appearances he is very different.

Plays me at crib when I am not writing to you. He has a board which I want to "lift" but he has a second sight. It is made from mica taken from a Jerry plane in the dim past. Similar material to that used by Arthur Milward for that ring. Someday I may be able to get one of my own. We play twice round the board for 1 piastre which is 2½d. After about 300 games (more or less) we are exactly level. When I lose I usually pay him with Palestine piastres which are not currency here, and if he loses he returns them. And if he loses more often than that he gives me a packet of ration cigarettes because he knows I have given up smoking. He also does a little hairdressing so I have an occasional haircut to square up. On one famous occasion he was just half a piastre short so he ran the clippers in a straight line up the back of my head and just left it until the following day. Sometimes we square up with postage stamps, in fact anything to amuse ourselves. Then we get down to discussions or talks on various things, such as letters to newspapers in England.

I am five miles from the nearest town and have no books. Could you send me a wireless?

Well we have none of the civilised amenities so I think we should write. No! We just make our own amusement. And we make quite a good job of it. My corp. nuisance says I am to send you his love. I told him you are not a Valentino fan. I won't tell you his reply about me. Well here is to the day when we can be together on that shady bank. Cheerio darling. All my love from your husband,

Gerald X X X X X X X X X X X X X X X X X X X X

One for Lucy X

26/07/1942 The 8th Army goes on the defensive after taking 7000 Axis prisoners. Churchill decided to replace Auchinleck after visiting the 8th Army.

NOTES BY GERALD MILNER

The line held and we returned to El Tahag to refit. After drawing new vehicles and equipment we retuned to the desert and were based at Burg el Arab just behind the forward area. Here we worked ceaselessly to get the required supplies to the forward area. Here violation of a given order became hilarious and I assure you that there was not much hilarity around at that time. A tent was erected to house a meeting of C.O. adjutant and a number of other officers. C.O. instructed me to see that no one approached the tent, and that the meeting was not to be disturbed in any way. Of course the inevitable happened. Urgent message from Command via radio truck. I was asked to go over to the truck. Radio operator said the instructions were to get the message to the C.O. at once. I took the envelope and decided to risk my neck. I told the C.O. that I knew my instructions but that this was an urgent message from Command. He said I was quite right and opened the envelope. He burst out laughing. He turned to the adjutant, Captain Brown and said "Here Dodger" read this. Dodger burst out laughing. The message went round the other officers with the same result. The C.O. then asked me if I had seen the message before delivery. I said that I had not, so he handed it to me. It may not seem so funny now, but under the circumstances it was a classic. It simply said, "C.O. 287 Coy R.A.S.C. urgent delivery required of map ref ★★★ 3 Q.L. Bedford loads of VITAMINS" signed ★★★. It should of course have been Bitumens for a new track being laid.

July 26th   1942

My Darling,

Yesterday was certainly an eventful one. First of all I was told by the post corporal that there was a letter for me. Chest out and head high I strode over for it. It was from Dick Chalk. Soon after that I was informed that there was a registered letter for me. That was from Dad. While I was opening that, more mail arrived and with it one from you. The one you had marked No.X Someone who saw it said "No kiss". I had to smile. Well darling it was a very welcome letter. In fact, I thought quite a lot of my literary efforts had gone astray, and I was feeling rather disappointed. All I am waiting to hear now is that the snap of Gordon's Calvary has arrived.

I have had some hard knocks, but if I lose that one it will be the hardest of all. I thought I should surprise you when I told you the size of various places in the Holy Land. It may interest you to also know that immediately after I took the view of Jehrico I turned round and took the one of the Mount of Temptation. That is of course if it has reached you safely. And Elishas' Pool where the bitter waters were made sweet is just about 300 yds away. I am very proud of some of those snaps and I said a few very wicked words when my camera was lost. But now I know you really appreciate my efforts I shall endeavour to obtain another one soon. Am

173

saving up very hard just at present. Still not smoking. Getting good don't you think? And I quite intend to take up photography as a hobby and take snaps of the various beautiful places we shall visit once more.

And now once more my sincere regrets. I did not really think you would attach so much value to the album. I endeavoured to complete it and I was going to send it to you on a certain day in the dim past, although I had not had any word from you telling me to do so. But for military reasons I obviously cannot give you full details of why I made that decision. The fact is I never had the opportunity to carry out my intentions and I know now that I shall never be able to. I do hope you will forgive me darling. When I first read your letter I almost began to think you had second sight. But your letter was written before the event. What is it called premonition? Afraid I must leave it at that.

When I see anything worth a snap now, I am endeavouring to borrow a camera. So you can still expect a few choice specimens. Although for the present is nothing like the same qualities as previously. In fact I am enclosing one now of quite a common sight in these parts. I don't really know whether to edit it "Happy Family" or just "Mother and Son". Don't you think the little boy looks pleased to have his picture taken?

I hope the parcel reached you safely. I believe I sent it direct to you. In fact when I changed companies so rapidly I had to get Dick Chalk to do the actual posting. I had it packed up and censored by my good friend Capt. Syme who made me the generous offer in regard to the fruit business. And then it was "away to the woods". The Mother of Pearl Cross is in that parcel too. Please let me know if it reaches you safely.

And what a lot of other things you want to know. If I keep telling all those little details I shall have nothing to tell you when I come home. Still I will endeavour to appease your curiosity just a little. First of all, my pilot friend. I met him in Jerusalem. He had 10 days leave after a particularly bad time of it. He had just finished telling me a certain little story when we heard the same thing told on the radio. Just a few days after. But we had little to say afterwards about the war. We were both interested in the same sort of things. Photography and poking

Happy family

our noses into all sorts of queer places. I think one or two of the interior snaps you speak of were taken with his camera. I used it on several occasions as mine was not fitted with exposure apparatus.

Then you want to know about the incident at the Church of the Holy Sepulchre. You asked me to answer simply yes or no. Well darling it was just another of those affairs between Jews and Arabs. Something happened to go wrong during the ceremony and the trouble developed as I have already told you. But that is now a very old story. My pilot friend who was about 5ft 7, quite good looking, with dark moustache and tremendously fit, just got cracking, and it was soon settled. More than that I will not say. Strange how I keep running into all the trouble there is going.

Have noted your remarks with regard to the business, but I think if the rumour does become fact, then you are in a better position to deal with it than I am. You see I get hardly any of that type of news here except from the papers you send me. And since my rapid movements those have not arrived as regularly as previously. They are just starting to catch up with me again.

Sorry to hear about Mr Maudling. Have not yet rec'd that County Express.

Well darling I think I shall have to dry up now. The heat is intense but there is also a very strong hot wind blowing too, and my paper takes flight every few moments. By the way the letter from Dick Chalk was to tell me the letter from Lucy has arrived. I won't tell you what he said. Anyway he was very pleased. And what about that wandering arm of yours. Well, Well, Well, WELL. And I thought you were so <u>cold</u> natured. Look at that "o" at the end of the previous "so". The nib went through the paper in excitement. Just to think of it. Can't imagine what it is like now. Even my pith helmet has taken flight amid all the excitement. Cheerio my sweetheart. Keep smiling. It won't be so very long before I come home now. I can feel it in my bones. Give my love to Lucy. Tell her I am still waiting for that letter. All my love from your husband

Gerald X X X X X X X X X X X X X

One for Lucy X

P.S. In that photograph you were quite correct in your surmise. It was wood I was carrying. In fact I had just come back from the Mt of Olives and they were olive wood logs. Dick Chalk has them and he is going to make some ash trays similar to those he made for himself and he will send one to you and one to Dad. That is if he has time now he has a letter to write. Glad you think I look well. That is nothing to how I feel now.

WAR DIARY

Unit 287 GT Coy RASC

Commanding Officer Major L.C. Smith M.C.

26/7/42	4 Lt Armoured Bde ordered to another sector. Ammunition pack transferred to 30 x 3 tons 287 Coy and sent to 86 FMC. Detached from Coy under 01/2 No. 3 Pltn
27/7/42	Capt R A Williamson posted to HQ X L of C Tpt Coln . Capt R A Brown RASC assumes duties of second in command 287 Coy RASC
28/7/42	Coy ordered to proceed for refit, as Ammunition build is handed over to 241 Coy RASC (XLC/R/L/88 30 ton

---

July 28th   1942

Darling,

Many thanks for your most welcome air mail letter. It certainly was a splendid effort. 12½ pages is I think the longest letter you have sent since I have been out here. Well there are quite a lot of letters on the way for you and all at Brook St. I keep writing to you and perhaps another to all those people who expect great literary efforts from me. I have written to Harts Hill also to Mr Gretton so I expect they will receive them in due course.

Sorry I cannot send the album. I have already told you about that but all the other souvenirs had already been sent. I hope they arrive safely. They were posted somewhere near May 15th as near as I can remember. They should reach you near the end of August. Your photographs in the wallet have been received by me. Also the few words to accompany them and the money. Saving up now to get another camera. Pretty expensive out here though. Yes I shall be quite willing to take up photography as a hobby when the war is over. But let us get that job done first.

I suppose you had all sorts of "blue fits" when you had the news from here a few weeks ago. Still I am still very much alive and kicking at the present moment. Had to spend £3.10.00 on a new watch. Keeps perfect time. Dick has received the letter from Lucy. Give her my love. Must close now as it is almost time for post. Cheerio darling. All my love from your husband

Gerald X X X X X X X X X X X X X

One for Lucy X

July 29th 1942

Darling,

Very pleased to let you know I have just received two telegrams. One from you and one from Lucy. I have also sent one to you for that special occasion. You should have received it weeks before you get this. But I am making this a special letter all the same. Just take a look at the snap of yours truly and tell me what you think of your husband now. You will of course observe that I am very different in dress to the original snap I sent last autumn. Notice for instance the pith helmet instead of the previous toupee. But the rest of the dress is just how we get to work out here. Often we don't wear that much. And at the back of me you will see the house belonging to myself and my corporal friend. Yes of course the snap was taken a little while ago but it is nevertheless interesting. You see how I look myself. Well you know how I lost most of my kit, and I think that was about all I had left at the time.

But darling that is an old story now and I suppose I must try and forget it for the present. The bowl in front is one I found growing on a big tree. We often find things like that you know. I think it is the sun. But do you think the camera is sun struck too. Yes! Darling I think I look just a little more tough than I did in Civie Street. What about camping, like that when I come back home. And I could show you how to make a quick cup of tea. By the way I had just washed my knees too when the snap was taken. Shall probably send another similar

snap in a few days and then after a little while I shall send you the negative. I have one or two more I have taken with a camera which I have recently borrowed for a few minutes.

Please excuse the writing but you can see my house or rather what it was like at that time. And flies and hot winds do not help matters. Well darling, I have already sent you an airmail letter card today and an airgraph yesterday, so there is not a great deal for me to write. And darling, I sent you quite a long letter the day before. I write now at every opportunity to try and make up for that time when I could not send to you owing to my rapid movements. Still it all goes to make a lifetime and the thing I am looking forward to most is the day when we shall be together again: miles from anyone and everyone. For the moment I look forward more than ever to receiving a letter or card from you.

There is one thing in one of your letters that rather sticks in my mind. That is that you

think you are in danger of falling in love again with your own husband. Well darling there is nothing I should like better. As I have told you in a previous letter all through that hell I came through there was a little devil inside me which kept saying "the worse the news, the more she will make up her mind". I have to admit it, but now I have to smile when I think of it all.

Well my sweetheart, I shall have to close now as the sun is going down rapidly. Please give my love to Lucy, or just as much as you think fit. Goodnight darling, God Bless you and keep you safe. All my love from your husband

Gerald X X X X X X X X X X X X X

One for Lucy X

Please remember me to all next door, also Mildred and Arthur when you see them. Glad to hear Arthur is still on the Island. Tell him from me to stay there as long as he can.

July 30th 1942

Darling,

Thank you very much for the telegram also the one from Lucy. I understand she has also sent a message for me in her letter to Dick. Hope to get it before very long. Well my dear I know I cannot walk in to celebrate the anniversary this year, but I shall still make a valiant endeavour to take advantage of anything the circumstances may permit. By the way the fellow in that picture I sent you was not Abdul. I think he would be most insulted. Still have not been able to find out where George is located. Edward Round gave me Philip's address just at the time I received a letter from you. Shall probably be dropping on him one of these fine days. Have written to Mr Gretton. Also to Harts Hill.

Now what is the great idea about these greenhouses? When and where do you propose to have them? I should like to know just a little more about them, and the proposed cost and where my F.R.H.S. will come in. Especially out here. Still I am steadily increasing my knowledge. That rose I saw a month or two ago was quite real and not caused by an overdose of sun. Very pleased to hear the seeds have germinated. Keep them in the greenhouse.

And now what about this beautiful trout stream you are looking for. To my mind, just the stream would be welcome without the fish. Must close now as it is almost time for post. Give my love to Lucy. Cheerio darling. All my love from your husband

Gerald X X X X X X X X X X X X X

One for Lucy X

GERALD MILNER'S DIARY

Aug 4th Bought note book & pencil. had picture taken on sea front. Result good. Took snap of Fred without his knowledge. . Breakfast. Picture bought. Arab scene. Bought snaps. Cpl Stone asked for clippers. Recd clipper cigarettes again later. Recd our clips. Had lunch in Maelecsh Bar. Very good. Woras again below standard. Bought ??? for Mother. ??? beer & lemon. ????

Second Page

Got swindled. Interval between pictures 1 hr. Met party for return. Charry through Alex by light of search lights. What an experience. Eventually reached camp very tired in small hours of my wedding anniversary.

Aug 5th Got into working order reasonably early. Felt very tired all day. Wrote letter to Eva and one to Mother. Indulged in memories. Took snap of Jack on donkey. Had one taken myself. Experimenting with special filter. Panchromatic Super X X . One of Jack at exercise silhouette 1. One second 2. 14 secs.

WAR DIARY

Unit 287 GT Coy RASC
Commanding Officer Major L.C. Smith M.C.
IKINGI- MARYIVT ORIGINAL

5/8/42	The following vehicles handed over as shown by order CRASC 1 Lafe Tpr Coln RASC
	To: SA RMT Coy Chev, 3 Ton 40; Bedford 15cwt 6; Willys Scout Car 1 Bedford Water Tanker 1
	To: 50 Coy RASC Bedford 15 cwt 1
	To: 163 Coy RASC Ford 15 cwt 1
	To: 56 Coy RASC Ford 15 cwt 1
	To: "A" Pack 10 VRD Chev 3 ton 3 Dodge Pll 5
	To: 309 Coy RASC Chev 3 ton 5
	To: 345 Coy RASC Chev 3 ton 4
	To: 462 Coy RASC Chev 3 ton 11
	To: I.L.AA Srt RASC Chev 3 ton 2
	To: 27/28 Battery 7th Med Reg RASC section Chev 3 ton 1
	On completion of above Coy ordered to proceed to TAHAG
TAHAG 8/5/42	Coy located in Camp 3 El TAHAG under command HQ Mobn Centre RASC. Intention to re-organises on a four Platoon basis with 1 R&I Local details performed for Tpt Officer TAHAG and have parties sent away. 50% of Coy at a time.

August 5th 1942

Darling,

Many thanks for papers which I received yesterday. Posted April 26th. All reading material is very welcome. Glad to hear you are going on nicely with the cycling. How many massages has Lucy received up to the present? as I better mention the fact in my next letter to Dick. He is a very keen cyclist too, but I do not think he allows massage to enter into his sport.

Went to Alexandria for a short leave recently. Had quite a nice time. Still prefer Jerusalem though. Bought myself a new camera. I shall be far happier now. I can carry on with my hobby. Look out for more pictures now. I shall send some in most of the letters I write to you, and you will also find a few at various intervals which I have purchased to replace some of the 400 I lost. Had a picture taken in Alex by one of these five minute fellows. Not too bad really, but I think there is room for improvement. However I am enclosing one for you. I shall abide by your decision. You will also find enclosed a couple of snaps of interest.

Wrote you a letter yesterday which I sent by boat mail. Hope it arrives safely. By the way I forgot to mention one thing in previous letters. Something about going to some gardens when this war is over. Well first of all, let us get all this foolery ended, and then I will go to any place in which you are interested. And if I can, as a result of my travels explain anything you wish to know then I shall be only too pleased.

Well my dear I shall have to confine my letter writing to this one piece of paper or it will be too heavy for air mail in conjunction with the photographs. Give my love to Lucy, and please remember me to Mrs Taylor & Billie. Also Mr Gretton. Must close now. All my love darling, from your husband

Gerald X X X X X X X X X X X X X X

One for Lucy X

The Brownie Box Camera

Fred gets down to an exchange of watches

August 5ᵗʰ 1942

My Darling,

You will see by the above that I have not forgotten you or the anniversary. So now I will try to write a few lines as I know you would like me to write them. First of all I must ask you to accept my excuses in regard to the writing. I am in a most uncomfortable position, and the heat affected my pen. Bakelite swelled and I could not unscrew it so I had to force it, I am afraid at the expense of the nib.

Well darling, how are you? Mail is very irregular from you just recently. I get one card and then go a few days and get one written previously. Still waiting for all those holiday cards. Had the first 3, but no more since. Yet I have had cards dated July 13ᵗʰ, which is a month later. Now just in case all my mail has not reached you let me once again thank you for the wallet and photographs. Have had a good gaze at them today and you have dressed you hair differently. I know that because I looked the wedding photograph. And really darling, I like the wedding method best. Now for a very stern reply. Alright, I am getting really hardened to the slings and arrows of outrageous fortune as Shakespeare calls them, and a few more will make no difference. But perhaps I am allowed to state these things without retribution being cast around my head now that I am also a very staid old married man. Anyway I wish that just for tonight I could be with you instead of lying on a bed of sand or possibly in a slit trench for the hours of darkness.

You see if we move rapidly, the camp has to be erected with all speed and often we do not bother to fix up our own tiny covers until the following day. But that is away from the subject. Whether my bed is in a comfortable barracks, or just five boards, or a bed of sand or even in the slit trench which at one time was fairly regular when we were in the danger areas, it is all the same to me. There is at the back of my mind always one thought, and that is you. In fact I think I love you more, (and miss you even more than that) than I have done before. And as I have said before I have altered considerably. Oh! Yes. I know that it is for the better. I have left behind me quite a lot of old ideas, and I have tried very, very hard to discipline myself in moderation. Before it was all or nothing. Now I have practically given up smoking, but if I feel like a smoke in the evening when some of the lads are having a chin wag, well I just have a smoke.

And as you know there has been a time past when I was extremely glad to get a tin of beer to drink. Since then I have had a drink if I have felt so inclined but know I could give it up again tomorrow. On one occasion only have I gone beyond the limits of moderation, and on that occasion I must confess, I tried to get in a state of drunkenness if that is the way to spell it. You see darling it is the first time so I can't be sure of my spelling. But you may be quite sure I had a very urgent reason for it. I had been stung by a scorpion.

Possibly that conveys very little information to you but it is an experience I would not wish even to my worst enemy. Strange to say, there are not too many cases of this type although the scorpion is very common out here. But anyone who has been stung will tell you there are few complaints more powerful while the poison is circulating. It was just like a million red hot needles running slowly oh! So slowly up my arm. And all the time the pain was increasing. And to make matters worse the sun was gaining more and more power every minute. So to try and clear the

poison I had about 2 or was it 3 bottles of beer at 1/10 per pint. Anyway heat or no heat, flies or no flies, I slept the sleep of the just, and when I awoke towards late afternoon, although the pain was still there it was bearable. But I shall never forget that poison gradually creeping up my arm, through my shoulder and into my chest. I was quite worried about it for a time. Anyway it is all over now, so I will just give you a little idea of what these scorpions are like by enclosing a picture I managed to obtain recently. Don't forget that these fellows crawl about where we have to sleep and I found one among my blankets today.

I much prefer fleas although I can manage without either.

Have sent you some pictures which are rather larger than snaps. Anyway dear, when they arrive please keep them with the rest of the collection. And I think I can promise you some more snaps in the future. I have treated myself to another camera and I hope I have a little better luck with this one.

Today I am also writing you a letter to be sent by air mail which will contain a photograph of myself taken by the sea wall at Alexandria while on leave. Had a lovely time while it lasted. Before I end darling I will once again thank you for the song "When the day is done". And now what do you think of my version of it on the picture enclosed. That is my reply.

Must close now my sweetheart. I shall still be thinking of you when the shadows fall. By the way I also like your new coat very much. But it is the person inside it I need most. Cheerio darling. All my love and lots of kisses from your husband

Gerald X X X X X X X X X X X X X

One for Lucy X

When the Day is Done

GERALD MILNER'S DIARY

Aug 6th Early to rise. Just discovered I have taken both silhouettes in the same position. Very annoying. Must trust to luck now. Wrote letter home. Snap enclosed. Took snaps in daylight. Results awaited. Went to bed after exercises on spring stretching.

Aug 7th Night extremely noisy and uncomfortable. Came the dawn. Took snaps. Had snap taken of HQ. Wrote to Roma, Michael and Eva. Airgraphs. Evening. 2 Lt Cantauch made Capt.   Celebrations ring out through the night.

Aug 8th Early to rise after guard. Packed and away with a ---. Had blow out. Changed wheel and had second "blow out" shortly after. Repair same and continued. Arrived safely.

Aug 9th Little work today. After lunch drew a few ackers and did an unshy Saw Dick and had a long talk. Arrived at camp. Half an hour to find my tent. Dive bombed by mosquitoes for a long time. Slept well eventually.

Aug 10th Little of note happened

Aug 11th Went after lunch to Ismailia with bathing party. Had nice swim. Cut myself in various places on raft. In conjunction with Cpl Strong dealt satisfactorily with native. Better off by one fly swat. Had tour of City. Showed Jack around a little. Arrived back at camp safely but very late.

Statue in Alexandria

Alexandria

Caught napping in Alex

Fred & Gerald in Alexandria

Street Scene in Alexandria

Chapter 7
Montgomery takes over

August 12th 1942

T/271347
Dvr Milner G
H.Q. Platoon
287 Coy
R.A.S.C.
M.E.F.

Darling,

       Just a few lines to let you know that I am still quite safe and in very good health. In fact I am having a fairly easy time just for the moment. That is just by way of a change from the stress and strain of the last few months. Instead of sleeping in the open I have a cover over my head once more and somehow I can't get used to it. Have quite a job to sleep some nights, but still it gives me the opportunity to lie awake and think of you. I have sent one or two pictures a short time ago as a small gift just to let you know the appearance of some of the scenes out here. I hope they arrive safely.

  Saw Dick Chalk a few days ago and had quite a long talk. Hope to see him again tonight. Taking advantage while we stay in this location. I am also expecting to go on leave in a few days. Afraid it will not be such a good one as last time, but I shall make the best of it. I know I shall have to go carefully with the odd coppers because it cost me quite a lot to replace all the things I lost. All my Army kit has been replaced free, but all my other articles reckoned up to quite a considerable total. One thing I am thankful for is that I can once more send you some snaps. Have another camera now. Am enclosing a snap and a negative of myself. I suppose you will still be entertained by gazing at my features. At least you told me in one communication that I was getting far too interesting to lose. Many thanks.

  Will you also please let me know if any of my letters came through from the danger zone? I wrote quite a lot out there, with all the musical accompaniments of battle as an aid to quiet thought, but up to the present I have no knowledge of whether they passed the censorship. I really do hope you get them as I am afraid I wrote them under rather a great nervous strain, and I may have written things you will appreciate. I am almost certain. I did get just a little bit sentimental when I thought my chances of ever seeing you again were almost nil. However, here we are, tough old veterans, talking often to fellows who have never been up there and telling them some fearful stories, which we know they don't believe, but which at the same time are absolutely true. The veterans of other companies can soon check up in their own mind whether the tale is accurate, and one very rarely hears of a contradiction. Yes, these boys certainly know their battlefield. Incidentally, I learned from Dick that I was a dead man, and that Fred was a prisoner. Very strange. Dead men writing letters. What rumours get around.

Well my darling, I must close now as I want to write you a letter card too. See how good I am. Cheerio dearest, All my love from your husband

Gerald X X X X X X X X X X X X X

One for Lucy X

GERALD MILNER'S DIARY

Aug 12 Informed just after Rev. that I was proceeding on leave to Cairo. Drew pay. Packed kit for a full marching order. Went miles with Fred to wet our whistle. Proved a great failure. Eventually went to bed

Aug 13 05.00 Train for Cairo. Arrived Cairo after monotonous ride. How many times I had done it before! Good digs at lucky Rest. Went out for a stroll with Fred. Met Johnny. Pal had left him to his own devices. Alone in City of everything. John tacked on to us. Ended up by going to Metro to see Dr Jekyll and Mr Hyde.

13/08/1942 Montgomery took command of the Eighth Army, two days early.

Cairo Station (right) Pulling in on leave. Kids on lines selling eggs (hard boiled) bread rolls and tomatoes

August 12th 1942

Darling

Have already written you a letter today so this will be rather brief. To begin with I have received a letter telling me of the delivery of goods to Mrs Chalk. Dick also received notification. Saw Dick for a few hours recently, and had quite a long chat. I expect you will hear all about it when he writes to Lucy next time. By the way, he gave me the letter to read.

Just tell Lucy she is most annoying. Fancy describing a beautiful tour in England and trips to the Channel Islands. Makes me feel like indulging in a little wishful thinking. Am expecting to go on leave in the near future. I will write and let you know all about it.

Hope to get some good snaps too. I am still unable to find where George is located. Seems as though he belongs to the "Order of Will o' the Wisps". I still have not given up hope though. I suppose I shall drop on him at some unexpected time or place.

Glad to hear the garden is doing well. Also the one at Brook St. From Mother's last letter, it appears that the new American Rose is a splendid sight. I am also anxiously awaiting the report on the progress of the plants originating from the seeds I sent to you. I shall try and get a few more of other varieties when I go on leave.

Please remember me to all next door. Also give my love to Lucy. Have sent you quite a lot of snaps photographs and pictures recently so you should be receiving them very soon.

Well darling I think that is all for this time so I will close with all my love from your husband

Gerald

One or Lucy X

Veterans

GERALD MILNER'S DIARY

Aug 14 Started out rather late to pay a visit to zoo. Arrived eventually after two crossings of the mighty Nile. Spent a most interesting day there. Took many snaps. Had one disappointment. White peacocks refused to display the glory of their tail feathers. Waited one hour but no luck. Came back and had a good meal and then went to pictures. Not to good a show, and atmosphere terribly hot. Arrived at Lucky Rest at Saar etnashar nw ncus. Slept like a log in ----- Well more of that when I get to England.

Aug 15th Rose reasonably early and had usual shower. What a luxury after the petrol can method of wash shave cum bath. Started out on Nile scenery snapshot expedition. Found many wonderful subjects. Results awaited. Approached by beautiful damsel, and she wasn't even in distress. Offer declined with many thanks. Fred told me I was slipping. Came back and had a meal in Shonia Abdul, Solimas Pasha. Later performed a very difficult but entirely satisfactory deal. After much bargaining came to a feluse decision with native to take us through the genuine bazaars. It is most difficult to find a fellow who will show you behind the scenes but once again our luck was in. I told him in his own language what I wanted and that was the open sesame to wonderful sights. Fred and John were a little worried at first because it was all a seething crowd of flowing robes etc and not a KD suit in sight. We carried on. Saw the marvels of ancient craftsmanship. Bought a necklace for 30pt after much argument. Had seen it made. Saw more examples of inlaid mother of pearl work on ebony boxes and tables. Very similar to the Jerusalem efforts. Went to Museum of Hygiene. Had already paid a visit but it was quite a memory refresher. Went to pictures. Saw coloured films of moon over Miami. That became stifling. Roof slid back and the welcome cool of evening descended. Back to Lucky Rest for an early evening. Suddenly had an urge that I had forgotten something. Then I remembered the date and the anniversary. Sat on the balcony high above the Babel of Tongues in Cairo to write these few words. Thought of Eva and, as on so many previous occasions allowed myself to indulge in memories. Stayed up until it was time for the milk. Self and one or two other fellows of various units taught Mary to sing English songs. What a marvellous voice she has. It is quite true, as her sister says "Wherever Mary is, there is always music". Own impression: – Beautiful singer, lovely girl. In features and voice reminds me of Shirley Temple but oh! So very much more grown up.

Aug 16th Rose early. Wash shave shower. Breakfast. Food good. Recd First snaps. Results only fair. Affected by shimmer from terrific heat of desert. Exposures of Jack not developed. Negatives appear to be OK Handed in more negs for development. Proceeded to Pyramids. Had already seen them on previous occasions. Found splendid specimen of alabaster from Pyramids to keep as souvenirs. Returned after taking snaps of Sphinx from various angles. Note: – Many excavations have been carried out since my last visit. Returned to Cairo eventually. Very tired. Had trouble with shoe shine boys/ police and my fist eventually decided the problem to our advantage. Found mine host had procured valuable specimens of Alabaster Art for me to send home. Very pleased with them. Viewed some splendid examples of Art collected by "mine host".

Six fifteen: time for an hour at the pictures. Pictures Mafish or should it be "ee". Came back to "mine host" heat terrific. Clothes reduced to minimum for sing song. Terrific tan of my knees shown up by white part of leg. Mary does not like white people. But she changed her mind because I have sunburnt knees. Mary decides to sing for me. First of all "My love for you is never ended" Can't think what she will end up with. Made rather a shocking discovery. Leave ends on Wednesday and not Thursday as I had originally believed. Mary sings spasmodically. Boys come in and evening ends up at 2 AM

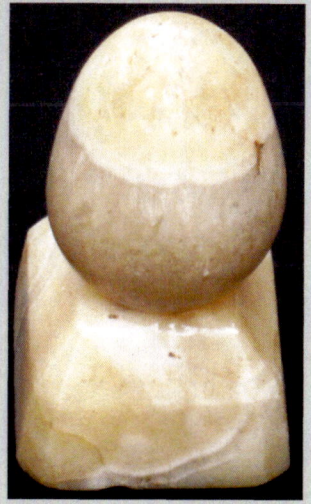

Aug 17th Up at 7.30 AM Greeted by Mary and Douv Breakfast shoeshine and the arrival of John. Went to see Old Cairo. Mosques everywhere every man of any

importance seemed to have had at least 20 wives. Son of Ismail pasha had 35. Saw various articles of great value belonging to the Royal family. Notes taken on all items of interest. Also several snaps taken but results will probably be rather unsatisfactory. Light bad. Guide proved to be very efficient. Had used him before. Went to Blue Mosque. Climbed to top of minaret. Tremendous height. Took several panoramic snaps. Rather a tough journey back down steps. Accomplished it safely however I went through some of those streets which it is better not to mention. Sights so sordid that even a veteran sightseer like myself was rather disturbed. Always pervading the atmosphere was the smell of broken glass. Houses in ruins with graves in the outer parts of the houses. Then to the native workers quarters. Not much difference in appearance yet quite a lot of the smell had vanished. Had already seen so much and taken so many snaps of these types of places that I decided not to take any more. Guide eventually brought us back safely to a good lunch with Greek people. My knee was letting me know of my climb to the top of the minaret. Received snaps taken at the zoo. Results highly satisfactory. Hope the remainder turn out as good. Returned to Lucky Rest for a hard earned shower. Felt much better afterwards although the heat was still almost unbearable. I wondered idly what fresh troops thought of the weather. Visited Citadel before returning, but this was omitted from the foregoing. Marvellous alabaster work but little else of note. Alabaster itself was a revelation of colossal pillars beautifully carved. Should estimate each piece to weigh at least five tons. Height of each piece approx. 3ft. height of mosque approx. 40ft Area of temple approx. half size of a football pitch. Or I may be under estimating its size. Just noticed a bowl of beautiful roses on the table. Went to picture which we saw a week ago. Came back to Lucky Rest early. Mary was wishing a number of men goodbye. The rest of the evening she devoted to singing for me. Went to bed just after midnight. Mary gave me her address. See back of note book

Aug 18th   Rose fairly early and had breakfast. Saw our trusted guide and he eventually took us to an Arab cattle market- Took several snaps. Usual bargaining over feluse. Camels, water buffalo, donkeys, sheep, goats, horses, pigeons, fowl, and many other smaller animals were being bargained for. General impression has of necessity had to be committed to memory. Those memories can never be erased. Later after much difficulty, gained admission to large tobacco and cigarette manufacturing building. Was taken by student lately passed out from Egyptian university all around the various departments. He certainly knew his business, and nothing was too much trouble for him. Had one of King Farouk's cigarettes in addition to many other excellent brands. Visit ended after approx. three hours. Came back to Cairo and had a good meal at Greek restaurant. Went all round Cairo to find a nice box of chocolates for Mary. Presented them to her and she was very pleased. Went to sleep and was later told that she came to offer me one of the chocolates. However I received it later. Mary's remarks committed to memory. Stayed in all evening. Mary was not in the mood for singing. At one o'clock she came and sat by me, placed her arm around my shoulder and sang Ava Maria. Never have I heard anything so beautiful. Wish Eva could have been here to hear it. At last welcome sleep.

18/08/1942 Montgomery's official appointment as C-in-C of the Middle East is officially announced as he replaced Auchinleck

Aug 19th. Rose. Shower Breakfast. Went for stroll and was soon back. Mary sat with me all morning. Kept looking at the clock and telling me how much longer I had to stay. She is trotting around now and singing snatches from Ava Maria. Hope she will sing it properly once more before I leave MO! She could not sing well this morning. Half an hour before I left she came in my room and helped to pack. Emptied the remains of my water bottle and filled it again with ice cold water. Sat down and talked to me. Told me she did not want me to go away. Family devout RC all knelt down and prayed for my safety. Mary told me the same as Eva has said so many times. She knows I won't be killed. I must send her the pictures I have taken. Sadly took my departure. Straight out into the wicked world and was unwittingly twisted. Paid Gharry driver and Fred had already parted with 10piastres without my knowledge. Shall square that account in the future. Long wait at the station. All the usual Eastern station accompaniments. After very tedious journey arrived back at camp.

August 20th Work did not go down well, but I managed to get through with it. Detailed for guard. Wrote very long letter home telling of all I saw in Cairo. Had previously sent airgraphs and a green envelope to Eva telling of Amaryka

August 20th 1942

My Darling,

      I hardly know how to start begin this letter and for me that is a very rare event. You see my dear, up till a week ago I had a certain picture stamped indelibly upon my mind, although I had never told you of it. And now, well I have two pictures. And the old contract of no secrets still exists at my end. When you read that I suppose you will be wondering whether the sun is affecting me. I will set your mind at rest by telling you that it is not. I will endeavour to explain. The first picture was of you standing on the doorstep as my train slid out of the station to carry me thousands of miles to see strange lands and peoples and also to the hell of war. That picture will always live in my mind. And then as the weeks lengthened into months and my travels and experience of war increased, I began to believe that I was getting what is termed as "case hardened". I was granted a short leave to Alexandria as you already know. To me it was just the same as all the other places I had visited in the past. I looked diligently for anything and everything that I thought would interest you and anyone else at home. Then I had rather a surprise.

Without my knowledge I was granted seven days leave in Cairo. And in the past I had, again as you already know, paid quite a number of short visits to this great Eastern city. So really I was not unduly thrilled. However it was just another chance of a spell away from the desert, so away I went. And it was there at the house at which I stayed that I met Mary. I really wish I could see your face now. Darling, Mary is just sweet twelve years of age and so very, very grown up. I have to call her Mary because Amazykha is too much for me to say. You see she is a little Greek girl. In the past I have heard a lot of people sing but I have never heard anyone sing like she does. When I first had a conversation with her she seemed to know from what part I had travelled. She asked me how I liked it there and I replied that I had just one week to try and forget the war, and occupy myself peacefully. She thought that was a very nice idea, and why didn't other soldiers think the same. And then she told me quite a lot of things I did not know. About religion and customs of the various tribes and races of people here. And all the other soldiers wanted her to sing all the time. Did I like to hear her sing?

Amazykha or Mary for short

Well darling after the great solitudes it was like being in another world to find someone who would speak to me like that. I told her I always liked to hear her sing, but that she must only sing when she felt like it. Almost every night when I came in she came to give me a song. And she could sing or speak in six languages. She liked to sing for me more than for the other soldiers, because she said I never got drunk. To be fair it was only natural that the lads on leave should have a few drinks but I never saw them "over the mark". However that was her opinion. Then the night before I was due to go back, I was sitting down in comfort talking of anything but war, and as the night was hot I stayed up very late. At one A.M. Mary came in. She came straight to me sat on the arm of the easy chair and said "I want to sing to you because you have to go away tomorrow".

She sang a song which she had refused previously, and which was most difficult. It was "Ava Maria". I believe that is the way to spell it. Never have I heard anything like it. And then I asked her a special favour. That was to sing the song you had sent me. She knew the tune but she did not know the words in English, so I found your piece of paper. She hummed it through softly twice, and then, I really think she equalled the previous effort. Then with a "Good night" in polite tone, to the company present and a special good night for me, she went to bed.

All morning before I left she hovered around. And just before I left she gave me rather a shock. She felt my water bottle and it was almost EMPTY. I had slipped up rather badly. Without a word she went away and filled it. And as I left she said a short prayer for my safety, and my speedy return to you. She thinks you must be a very nice person. And so to the second picture. A mere child, just twelve years old, standing at the top of the stairs, waiving a silent good-bye.

I have thought quite a lot about it all since my return. It seemed so fine to have just one ray of sunshine introduced into my life after such a long time from home. Well sweetheart no one will ever take your place but I shall await your comments with interest.

And now for a few words about my leave. I had a good look around and took quite a lot of snaps for you. I have had the first sixteen delivered and they are particularly fine examples of camera work. In fact one of my officers is a keen camera man, and we had been having a friendly argument with regard to photography out here. I shall be sending you snaps in every letter including two in this one. And now for the crucial point. All these sixteen snaps have been taken with the wrong type of film, and I must add this was done deliberately, just to prove my theory. The officer was amazed when I showed them to him. And also showed him the negatives just to prove I had taken them. I should like your candid opinion on them as they arrive from now on. You will also probably receive at some time in the future a few taken with just a background of sand. I want you to ignore criticism of them as they were taken in exceptional circumstances. You will probably find too that I have written odd scraps on the back of some of them. That was just for my own information. I visited Farouk's Museum of Hygiene, The gardens on the banks of the Nile, The Pyramids, The Citadel, The Mosques and minarets and the bazaars. As I have written so much already I am afraid I shall have to leave all those subjects for the present. I shall describe them in detail in letters home, but I shall also have a little information left just for your eyes only.

Well darling, I must close. Give my love to Lucy. Please take good care of yourself until I come home. God bless you and keep you safe. All my love dear, from your husband

Gerald X X X X X X X X X X X X X

One for Lucy X

Elephant at the Zoological Gardens, Cairo

Flamingos at the Zoological Gardens, Cairo

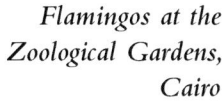

To My Wife

Think of me, dear, when I am absent
        Send me a message to cheer my way,
Tell me again I shall find you waiting
When I come back, dear, some happy day

I'm thinking of you now, dear,
                And send this just to tell
        A little word of love to you.
From one who loves you well.

Do you often think of me, I wonder?
Somehow in my heart I feel you do!
Send a little message just to tell me
If you miss me, dear, as I miss you.

God bless and keep you, - tenderly I pray
And this my earnest prayer will ever be
I ask his blessing for you night and day,
My own dear wife, so very dear to me*

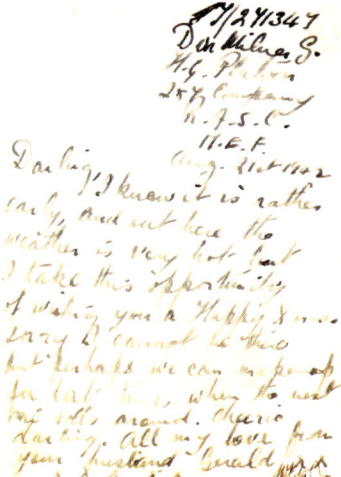

August 21ˢᵗ 1942

Dear mother, Dad & Roma,

Many thanks for mail received during the past week. I have already replied briefly by airgraph, but as I have just returned from a very enjoyable seven days leave in Cairo I thought perhaps you would like a letter giving more details.

First of all I went to the Zoological Gardens and I can assure you that the shade provided by the tropical trees was more than welcome. At first I had the feeling of being closed in, and this was even more noticeable at night when I had a room to sleep in, but it did not take long to get over that. The zoo itself was very similar to any other similar place, except that many species existed in the open instead of specially prepared cages as in cooler climates. But the thing that struck me as being most remarkable was the scrupulous cleanliness of everything. And above all there was an even greater blessing in the shape of comparative freedom from flies. I took some very fine snaps during my visit and I shall take the first opportunity of sending these home as I have learned my lesson from my previous experiences.

When evening came I went back to the house in which I was staying in what is known as Shania Malik Farida. Interpreted into English it means Queen Farida Street. Once again my luck was in. These people with whom I stayed were Greeks but that did not detract from the welcome they gave me. Nothing was too much trouble. And their youngest daughter Amazykha, whom I re-christened Mary, was a child with a voice like a nightingale. She is just twelve years of age, and I still think that Carol Levis has "slipped up" rather badly. I have in the past heard many "discoveries" over the radio but my personal opinion is that they were all quite moderate after Mary's efforts. And she can sing all these songs in six languages. When it began to get cool, which was usually in the small hours of the morning, or rather that was the time when it was cool enough to sleep, I retired for the night. It all seemed so strange to have a real bed to sleep on. And when I rose early in the morning there was the added glory of a cold shower. The food was excellent. Everything on the table spotless, while the atmosphere was pervaded by the scent from a bowl of roses. Incidentally that was one of the first things that surprised me when I arrived in the Middle East. I never expected to see roses.

Later in the day I wandered with idle curiosity around the main thoroughfares of the great city, looking for any items of unusual interest since you expect me to report so faithfully on all I see. One of the things that seemed rather strange to me was the positions of the various shops. Most establishments in the more modern parts of Cairo are built on similar lines to those of any English city. But for some unknown reason one finds a group of shops in close proximity to each other, all selling the same commodity. To give just one example, I wanted to buy a few chocolates to eat in the cinema. I had to walk round three busy streets before I came to a confectioner's. And everywhere, like a swarm of locusts, is found the British soldier's greatest trouble, the "Shoeshine Boys". I think every other boy in Cairo must belong to the "Shoeshine Union". Then almost as persistent are the dragomen, known at home as guides. They are a particularly untrustworthy species of humanity, and unless one is very determined he can soon be persuaded to part with excessive amounts of money in comparison with the service given.

And at times they have some unscrupulous methods of obtaining the money they demand. However we live and learn and we take necessary counter measures.

Then on another occasion I paid a visit to the native bazaars. There I found the strangest mixture of all. Walking down a reasonably clean but narrow street, I could see all the junk of the East displayed in shop windows. I judged the greater part of it to have been made in Birmingham or Manchester, and was at the time quite confident that my judgement was correct. But I got rather curious and after a little hesitation decided to investigate some of the places at the back of these premises. I had quite expected to find the real East there, and I suppose to a certain extend I did. But not exactly as I had imagined it to be. There were rows upon rows of tiny workshops, filled with craftsmen, carrying on their trade exactly as it was carried on a thousand years ago. Carpenters working swiftly, with wood shavings flying in all

Shoeshine Boys

Native Bazaar

directions looked up with idle curiosity and carried on with their work. Then there were the tinsmiths and coppersmiths, and the sandal makers, the painters, tile makers, and the men who make reed pipes. In fact almost every trade imaginable.

And then I wandered into a place where the activity resembled a bee-hive. This is the silversmith's shop. It was here that I received my first shock. Swarms of natives from the age of seven to seventy were making by hand all those necklaces and curios that I had previously been so certain had been machine manufactured in England. I was invited to go and examine the work closely. The tiny boys were shaping and cutting fine strands of silver wire, and the older craftsmen were placing them in position. No solder whatever was used while I was there, yet as a result of the slight springiness of the metal they were quite strong articles. I purchased a necklace to send home as a souvenir. It cost me twenty piastres or five shillings in English currency, and it had taken one man just half a day to produce it.

I was offered a drink of tea as brewed by the Arabs. I can assure you I was very dubious about drinking anything under the circumstances, and I am afraid all those "thrillers" I have read in the past came vividly before my eyes. But the generosity eventually became so overwhelming that I felt obliged to accept the offer. It was provided in a small tumbler, and contained no milk, but to be perfectly fair I must say it was a grand glass of tea and very badly needed. I am pleased to say I suffered no ill effects.

From there I wandered around for an hour, endeavouring to make my brain act as a sponge and absorb all details of interest. Eventually I came to an alleyway, the walls of which were hung with rich carpets and rugs and fine hardwood carvings. I decided to investigate once more, and no one interfered, although I saw several pairs of eyes keeping a very keen watch on the articles displayed. As I proceeded I came to a vast workshop once more filled with native craftsmen. But this place was different to most of the others. I learned later that it was what is classed out here as a factory, and the place adjoining was used as a wholesale warehouse. First of all I saw a huge wooden frame used for rug making. Four small boys, about six years of age, were working at great speed knotting and cutting the wool to the required pattern. An Arab, evidently of some importance in the business, came across to me and asked in perfect English if I would like to be shown around. I accepted the offer. He told me that the small boys had been working on the rug for over six months, and that it would take several months more to finish it. Their wage was 5 piastres per day, or 1/- in English money.

Then I was shown how the inlaid mother of pearl was done. The method and type of work was entirely different from that practised in Bethlehem. The carpenter had already made the hardwood boxes, but the mother of pearl in this factory was filed into tiny flakes of various shapes by the boys. A skilled man had the box in front of him, and a layer of gummy substance was placed in the required spot. He picked up a pair of fine tweezers and with unerring accuracy placed each particle in position. In a very short space of time his work was completed.

Then the box goes to another man who adds a further transparent layer of liquid. This in turn sets and then the polisher gets to work. The completed box is sold for £3-10-0. Very good imitations are sold for 5/-.

The there was the old man carving a table leg, on a most primitive device. A type of treadle machine which he worked with one bare foot. The other foot worked in conjunction with both hands to manipulate the wood he was carving. I am afraid his feet and hands moved far too rapidly for me to keep an accurate check on all his movements. All I can add is that it was just the result of a lifetime's experience. After a very interesting visit I left and after a little difficulty made my way back to more civilised parts.

I also spent a very interesting afternoon at King Farouk's museum of Hygiene. Much of this dealt with tropical diseases and their causes. As far as I could see the predominant cause of most of them was filth. From the view I had of the very realistic wax models it caused me to hope that I never contract any in the future.

On another day I went to visit the tombs of the Royal Family of Egypt. Large buildings with a rather dull exterior, but filled with large marble, stone and gold carvings over the grave of each person. And each King or Pasha seemed to have had innumerable wives and sons all of whom had a monument erected to their memory. I used my camera by special permission to take pictures, the results of which I am still awaiting. After a long tour of these rather melancholy places I went inside the Royal Mosque or Chapel which is used regularly by the Royal Family. I saw the Korans used by the King and Queen, all written in gold lettering and, I was told, costing £500 each, and encased in very fine silk. I was then conducted by the Keeper of the King's Silver to the silver room. Here were very fine examples of old silverware, but they gave the impression of not being cleaned for a very considerable period of time. Before entering any of these Eastern mosques or Minarets a very ancient ceremony has to be performed. The feet have to be covered by a type of canvas slipper. No one is allowed to enter without wearing them, unless it is bare footed. After that I went on to the Citadel. Many things I saw here I am not allowed to mention so you must be patient until I come home. I can however keep to safe ground by describing the mosque of Mohammed Aly which is approximately in the centre of the Citadel. It is also know as the Alabaster mosque. I should estimate its area to be nearly half the size of a football pitch and almost every particle of it is genuine alabaster. Actually there is little else worthy of mention, but it is a magnificent sight. Gigantic pillars and vast domes carved by hand hundreds of years ago and a floor that I judged to be marble. All these things seem truly remarkable when one thinks of the instruments at the disposal of the workmen in those far off days.

From there I decided to visit the Blue Mosque. To reach this I had to walk through streets of incredible squalor and poverty. I think I shall do well to forget that side of the story for the present. When I arrived at the Blue Mosque I had to go through the same procedure as the other places. That is, cover my feet. You see I am an unbeliever in the Islamic faith. Except that the walls were

coated with a type of Wedgwood china, I saw nothing else of interest. Perhaps that is an overstatement. There was the tower. I made a perilous climb up stone steps in almost total darkness until I emerged at the top with all Cairo spread before my eyes. I could pick out all the main buildings, and the pyramids were very distinct. I took a number of snaps which are now being developed and printed.

John & Fred study the view from the top of the Blue Mosque Cairo.

Another place of interest I visited was an Arab cattle sale. There again was a queer mixture. Camels and water buffalo, sheep, goats and poultry if it can be called such, donkeys, mules and a few horses. Plenty of filth and livestock of a very persistent variety, and in the middle of it all, ice cream vendors and sellers of sweetmeats. All noise and bustle intermingled with violent language with dealers rapidly concluding their business. I did not stay there very long as my nostrils are rather sensitive.

I spent the afternoon by making a tour of a large tobacco factory, which was working on fairly modern lines.

I also paid another visit to the pyramids, but I have already described those to you nearly a year ago. The excavations are however, continuing and many new tombs have recently been discovered.

This is all I have to write for the present, and so from a very welcome leave, back to the more serious job in hand. I know you will be interested in all I have seen, so I will end by wishing you all the best in the future

From your Loving Son

Gerald X X X X X X X X X X X

PS I am enclosing two more snaps with this letter.

Cairo from the top of The Blue Mosque

*Cairo from the top of
The Blue Mosque*

All eyes right

Two men talk business on a donkey

The Cattle Market

Camel & Master

Cattle Sale

August 22ⁿᵈ 1942

Darling,

Many thanks for the air mail letter card and the airgraph of July 15 & 22ⁿᵈ. Have received quite a lot of mail recently, but strange to say, very little of it came from you. Have not yet received any more news of your cycling trip, so I do not know if you have found that place I asked you to keep a look out for. And what about the parcel. Has it arrived yet? I hope I do not lose that too. I am expecting to collect some olive wood curios from Dick Chalk in the near future, and after my leave in Cairo I also have a few other odds and ends including one of the Pyramids, or a least the greater part of it, to use as a paper weight. I have also managed to replace those curios for Mother. As soon as I can get the articles from Dick I will send you a parcel. I also have a considerable amount of snaps I have taken recently. Quite a lot of them are already in course of post. You will find a few that have not been taken by me. These I purchased to replace some of those I lost in the dim past, and mostly represent scenes which I do not often see.

Heard from George again yesterday. I am beginning to get exasperated. Still can't find out where he is and I suppose he is most probably very close to me. I expect I shall be meeting him in the near future.

Mosquitoes are very busy today. Not affecting me quite so badly as last year, but plenty bad enough. By the way, thanks for the book of Arabic. Just what I wanted. Saw one in Cairo recently and the price was 10/6. Exactly the same as this one.

Well my darling, it is getting dark and space is dwindling rapidly so I must close. All my love dear, from your loving husband

Gerald X X X X X X X X X X X X X

One for Lucy X

Water buffalo in native cattle market

The Second Pyramid

The Pyramids

Show Garden in Cairo

Show Garden in Cairo

Show Garden in Cairo

On the Banks of
the Nile

Garden near the banks of the Nile

Garden near the banks of the Nile

Garden near the banks of the Nile

Palm Trees

Camel in the Zoological Gardens Cairo

Boatmen on the Nile

The Sweetwater Canal

Palm Trees

The Desert at Night

An everyday scene

*Sailing on
the Nile*

Nile Ferry Service

Fred takes a ride in a gharry

The Fruit Shop

Snap taken to demonstrate how natives ride on trams. It is rather worse than this on trains.

Exposure of Dome of the Tomb

Fine Grotto Work

Camel Train heads for the horizon

Crossing the stream.

Ship of the Desert

Group photo

Buying for lunch

Snake Charmer

Shepherdess

Fallaheen at work in the cotton fields

Middle East irrigation

Blindfold oxen turns primitive water pump

Water supply

Gerald & Camel   Taken in Cairo   Guardian of the Desert

Street Scene   More palm trees   Camel Ride

Sunset neath the palms   Street Scene   Child

Pagoda

Pagoda in a grotto

Outside grotto

Water Melons

More snaps

A snap taken in Cairo. The Coach was moving at great speed

Snake Charmer

Warrior

Native outside hut

Street scene Ismailia

Street scene Ismailia

Street scene Ismailia

Largest Oasis in the world

Sir Lancelot?

Arab Villager

Station Ismailia

> **GERALD MILNER'S DIARY**
>
> August 21st Guard ends. Letter posted. Also Xmas cards. Had siesta. Day ended rather quietly by sharing snaps in the guard room. Shall be glad when they have all been sent home as everyone seems to want to look at them. Had good nights rest.
>
> August 22nd Tent orderly. Little of importance to do. Wrote airmail letter card to Eva. Early to bed and a good sleep.

August 23rd 1942

My Darling,

Evening is here and bringing back those thoughts of when shadows fall, so I thought I had better write just a few more lines while I feel in the mood. First of all I suppose you want me to tell you once more that I still love you. My feelings in that respect have never changed darling, and I am certain they never will. As I have told you already I have changed but not in that respect. As a small example, I have recently returned from seven days leave in Cairo. While there I never had a drink of beer or anything else. Yet when I was in Libya I often had a drink. And on the other hand although I have practically given up smoking I had quite a number of cigarettes on leave, yet I have given it up again now. So you see I can do quite a number of things which I could not have done before. And as I have already said, I have not and never shall change in that respect. In fact I think I miss you far more now than I ever did. Don't know why but at times when the going has been heavy, I have gone to bed and felt just like a caged rat. You, thousands of miles away and I myself going through, to say the least of it, a rather uncomfortable time. And then I wonder whether it will all be appreciated after the war. Still dearest, the main thing is to get the war over, and then I can look forward to seeing you again.

And now I will tell you a little secret. When I went on leave in Cairo I stayed at a large house in Queen Farida Street. And do you know, I could <u>not</u> sleep in a room. It took me hours to go to sleep. So you can look out when I <u>do</u> get back. Do you think you ought to get some anaesthetic while you have the chance? To send me to sleep I mean.

Well darling, it is almost too dark to write now so I think I shall have to continue tomorrow. I expect, by the way that you will think I have been getting quite a lot of leave lately. My trumpeter is dead so I must speak up. You know already what happened to my kit and the narrow squeak I had myself. Well, after that I did anything I could see needed doing during the critical period. I was thanked by an officer, while on parade, for the way I had worked. After that I was given every opportunity for leave. Too dark for any more dearest. Good night. Lots of kisses. Wish I could deliver them in person.

Tomorrow has been and gone so now I will continue. About that leave question I was dealing with. First of all I do not know how to write without infringing military censorship so I will confine myself to saying some of the boys are having a period of rest. It is not exactly that but at least it is an easier time. And during that time I have been granted leave on three occasions, but only one lasting seven days. In fact I have already written a long letter to 52 Brook St, and sent it in for censorship and it is most probably well on the way now. And now I must ask you a favour. I know how you all like to hear the descriptions I write of the places I have visited and so am sending a number of them to Brook St. Please read them there and it will save me writing them all over again, and it will also allow me to use my precious green envelopes to write to you. I often wonder whether all those letters have reached you. On that day I went back to enemy territory to try and get my kit back. I found a camp and after a quick look around saw quite a bundle of the envelopes. And I have made good use of them.

Well my sweetheart I don't know what is going to happen to me now. For a long time now

I have been beneath blazing skies and on burning sands and I am wondering whether I am going to get a change of scenery.

The mail has just arrived. Has to be sorted now. Am wondering if there is any for me. Have not had a letter from you for days now. How I wish I could come and warm your feet for a little while. Saw Dick yesterday. Just "slid off" quietly for a couple of hours and saw some of my old pals. Very welcome they made me too. Dick wanted me to send his best wishes to Lucy and all you other people at home. Everywhere I went the old lads stopped me to know the real news of the great battle. Well I simply told them that the Eighth Army can hold Jerry any time and I really believe that to be true. Well I must get off this subject of war. No mail for me again. And the post corporal said he went in to the office with all his guns blazing. I suggested that next time he take 6" Naval guns. The book on Arabic arrived recently. Thanks very much. I have already sent you a list of the Reg'd letters that arrived. I think I have had all posted up to the end of May. Darling I think that is nearly all for this time. Look after yourself and think of me just a little bit. Cheerio dear. All my love from your husband

Gerald X X X X X X X X X X X X X
One for Lucy X

August 28ᵗʰ 1942

Darling,

Many thanks for airgraph of July 28ᵗʰ 1942. Very sorry to hear of the unwelcome visitors and the additional damage done. Still never mind darling, keep smiling. I am afraid this letter is going to be rather brief as I am also writing an air mail letter card and an airgraph. It is just a few lines to enclose with 36 snaps I have taken mostly while I was on leave at various places. You see, besides the seven days at Cairo, I also had a couple of days leave at other places. And of course I had to get a few more pictures for you. I am writing a very brief explanation on the back of each snap.

Please remember me to all next door, and also give my love to Lucy. Cheerio dear. All my love from your husband

Gerald X X X X X X X X X X X X X
One for Lucy X

GERALD MILNER'S DIARY

August 23ʳᵈ Once again very little of importance happened in the morning. Slipped away to see Dick in the evening. Saw number of fellows I knew. Left eventually at approx. 11.30 to the sound of wailing. Arrived back at camp at the midnight hour

August 24ᵗʰ 1942 Rose early. Went through the old gas chamber. Very strong dose this time. Arms tingled owing to the perspiration. Heat terrific. Had forty winks. Notified of guard duties again. Convoy arrives. Took over the old two wheels once again. Had (but I was not supposed to have been there at the time) the greatest compliment yet paid me. Overheard my old officer say "He was the hardest worker in the whole bloody company when the shit was flying". Wondered in amazement what it was all about. Anyway I know now although actually I should not. My name is one of three sent in by the officer with strong recommendation for promotion. Don't think I shall get it though. Personal opinion is that JL will get it. If he does I wish him all the best.

Aug 25ᵗʰ 1942 Rec'd from Eva (Airgraph) Dated July 28ᵗʰ contents memorised. Took over M/cycle once more in emergency. Called out at midnight hour.

Aug 26ᵗʰ 1942 took over duties as D/R. Plenty of rough work. Soft sand Pretty tough job

August 26th WR duties. All day and far into the night. Knew the ropes fairly well which made the job a little easier. Slept in O.C.'s office after a good bottle of beer from Captains "Batch"

Aug 27th Up before O.C. for enquiries. Gave satisfactory evidence. Plenty of work but still no mail.

Aug 28th We arrived for Court orderly and witness. Had surprise when Lieut. Cripps walked in. happy re-union Case went off fairly well.

WAR DIARY
Unit 287 GT Coy RASC
Commanding Officer Major L.C. Smith M.C.

17/8/42	0230 hrs 2 Platoons return having cleared petrol from 5 Fwd Base
	0730 hrs No3 Pl under Comd 2/Lt CFBE Cornall loaded and proceeded to PALESTINE, 1 offr, 65 ORJ, 38 x 3 tons, 1 15cwt, attached to 400 GT Coy RASC
	0930 Loss of Security Box discovered and search instituted
	1000 Mobn Centre and Stb informed of loss of box which contained War Diary (original' Aug 4 and duplicate for July 4) Secret file, War establishments and one prismatic Compass
25/8/42	2 platoons given the job of charming Petrol from 5 Forward Base MENA to a dump at GIZA. This was duly completed by 21.30 hrs
26/8/42	Captain Phillips joined Coy as w/shop officer
26/8/42	0530 hrs 2 platoons forced to clear petrol from 5 Fwd Base to Giza
26/8/42	Order received to send one platoon to PALESTINE to be attached 400 Gt Coy RASC FAP 2/8 Cornall sent with No3 platoon
27/8/42	Security Box stolen containing among other things War Diary, Original & Duplicate for August and Duplicate for July. S/B informed and Court of Enquiry held
28/8/42	0920 Comt of Enquiry Assembles to enquire into the loss of the Security box by order Command HQ Mobn Centre RASC
28/8/42	Normal local details and all vehicles
29/8/42	0730 Nos. 1 and 2 Platoons load and proceed to Kilo 4 Cairo Suez Road on detachment.
	Formation of Cadu for No. 4 Platoon now ready for return of leave party on Sept 3rd
31/8/42	being checked and modified.

August 30th 1942

Darling,

Many thanks for airgraph of July 28th. Looks as though things livened up a little around the old city. Have recently been for a very pleasant leave in Cairo. Spent a big percentage of my time under the shower baths. I think I have got through to clean skin again. While I was there I took quite a lot of snapshots and most of them turned out very well. In all recent letters I have enclosed at least two, and this week I despatched a registered letter containing thirty six. I decided to take just the one risk and send all I had left. I still have the negatives, so if they do not arrive I will send another lot to replace them.

The weather here is still quite hot although the' days are getting shorter. But I think the fly population is like Germany in need of Lebensraun! And when they quieten down at

Pyramid

Missing chamber for the Great Pyramid on the left

Excavations

Pyramid Carvings

Repairs to the Sphinx

A Relic

Pyramid Carvings

SOME OF THE 36 SNAPS SENT HOME

The Sphinx

night, then the mosquitoes and sand flies begin their activities. Shall be very thankful when the cooler weather of winter arrives. I regret to say that I have not been receiving very much mail just recently. Just the one airgraph in three weeks. Still, I suppose it will all arrive in one batch, the same as the last time. At any rate I sincerely hope it does.

Well darling, it is almost time to close my letter. Please give my best wishes to Mrs Taylor and Billie. Also Mr & Mrs Haywood, And as for Lucy, well she knows.

Cheerio darling. Please look after yourself until I come home. All my love dear, from your husband

Gerald X X X X X X X X X X X X X X

One for Lucy X

GERALD MILNER'S DIARY

Aug 29th Orderly room as escort. Police duties all day including a small siesta. Letters & photos sent home every day.

Aug 30th Took over two wheels once more. Can't say I was happy about it. Stick it for a time. Still no mail. Seems years since I had a letter from Eva. Slept in O.C.'s office last night. Dreamt I was back home again. What a hope!

Aug 31st D/R again. Plenty of rough riding. Soft sand much, much pivaiso.

31/08/1942   Rommel failed in his final attempt to break through the line at El Alamein in the Battle of Alam Halfa. His 15th Panzer Division lost about 30 tanks and suffered heavy casualties.

August 31st 1942

My Dear Youngster,

Sorry I cannot thank you for mail received as I have only had one airgraph from you in nearly three weeks. Seems like three years. No mail from Brook Street either. I know the mail problem is very difficult during war time, but out here it is all I have to look forward to. Still I must try and be patient. I suppose a whole pile of letters etc. will turn up one of these fine days. But I would sooner have a fairly regular delivery than the other method. I am wondering whether all the mail I sent during and after the Libyans affair reached you. I know that at least some of it must have done for you to get my address so quickly, but I send piles of letters, airgraphs, letter cards and two telegrams to let you know I was safe. Sometimes when I get a little bit ---- Well, when I wish I could see you for a little while I think of those terrible days and try to imagine what your thoughts were at that time. Have not had many newspapers either and I am quite anxious to read the news as it appeared in the papers at home.

Interlude: - Sergt Major has just had an airgraph and now he is telling large stories. Says he writes home regularly therefore he expects mail. And he says his Mother always writes with a "Good Morning my Son". I wonder what he thinks you begin with.

Now to continue. During that period I was referring to, I never saw a paper or heard the wireless, so it will all be very interesting. Times out of count, I thought of those words of yours "You won't be killed". And many times I wondered whether I would ever see you again. I cannot of course tell you all that happened to me, or where it happened except that we had a pretty thin time on various occasions. But I think the worst of all was the terrible thirst. That occurred to me more than the other fellows because of a certain job I was doing at the time. I don't want a repeat performance. For the time being I am back on two wheels again. Seems as though I am in great demand in emergencies. I have a grand bike too but

I can assure you it is no picnic riding on sand. I do not know how long it will be for but I have strict instructions to take care of myself. Had to do a special job the other day, and ran into one of my old officers. One of those who censored my letters on the boat. Had quite a long talk.

Please remember me to all next door and all those friends who inquire about me. Also give my love to Lucy. Tell her I am expecting to see Dick this evening. Please take care of yourself darling. It won't be so very long now before I come back to you. I can feel it in my bones. I am just waiting and praying for that day to dawn. And don't forget we are going away, whether or not you found the place I asked you about. Cheerio my dear. All my love from your husband,

Gerald X X X X X X X X X X X X X

One for Lucy X

P.T.O

Just a few more lines in great haste to let you know that I have just received two air mail letters. You will probably already have heard of this by airgraph. Just thought I would duplicate it.

Cheerio dearest. All my love

Gerald X X X X X

WAR DIARY

Unit 287 GT Coy RASC
Commanding Officer Major L.C. Smith M.C.
TAHAG

1/9/42	Ordered by HQ Mobn Centre RASC to hand over to 543 Coy 2 Platoons of non desert worthy vehicles in exchange for 3 Platoons of desert worthy vehicles. Surplus platoon on HD Vehicles to be handed back to "A" Park GVRD inc/108/266/Q of 1 Sept refers. To be completed in 48 hours.
2/9/42	1800 hrs All vehicles on charge handed over and 62 X 3 tons QL Bedfords drawn. 52 to these from 546 Coy remainder from 9 VRD, All of them require modifications.
3/9/42	1800 hrs Vehicles now complete from VRD. 111 x 3 ton QL Bedfords on charge. I Corv 4 , 6 x 15 cwt, Ling 6 x 30 cwt Water Tankers 1845 Hrs Workshop ordered to work all night ¾ Sept to complete modifications

Sept 3rd 1942

My Dear Youngster,

Well my dear, I am in receipt of your important A.M.L. Card of August 16th and I will endeavour to be brief and to the point. As soon as possible I will also write a covering letter. Firstly the date or year you require was I believe 1932 or 33. The figure inserted was a profit of £104 shown as wages. All other information I will give in the letter to follow. Anyway I think you have taken the right procedure during my absence, but I think the figure you mention is rather excessive. I leave everything in your hands as you seem quite prepared to take the job over. And do not hesitate, to use my bank a/c. Have also received the a/c of how the £18 was spent on the car. It appears to be very satisfactory, especially if it has received the approval of George.

And now to turn to other subjects for a few moments. I saw Dick yesterday, but he has not quite completed the olive wood carvings. Immediately I receive them I will send them to you together with a number of other odds and ends I have collected together. Very pleased to hear you received the parcel safely. Saw an airgraph from Lucy imparting that information. Some day I will tell you the story of that collection. I hope the next lot arrives just as quickly.

Still have not seen George, but I have had another letter from him. Also one from Capetown. Mrs George says she has written twice to you and Mother but as she has received no reply she presumes the letters lost. In one of your letters it appears that Lucy wrote to Dick in early July. Well the only airgraph he has received is dated Aug 6th or 7th. His age: - 28. Anything else you want to know just ask.

Well darling, I really must close now. Please remember me to all my friends, and please don't worry too much about me. Cheerio. All my love from your husband.

Gerald X X X X X X X X X X X X X

One for Lucy X

GERALD MILNER'S DIARY

Sept 1st 1942 Still on the old two wheels. Carried on gloomily wondering whether everyone had deserted me although in my heart I knew Eva was always thinking of me. What a surprise. Two letters and all explanations for lack of mail. Reasonable to expect it will arrive fairly regularly now. Still have not heard from Mother & Dad. Replied to letters.

Sept 2nd Days work completed early and Sgt Major's personal consent for a visit to Dick. Saw airgraph from Lucy. Oh! Joy. The parcel had arrived safely. A load off my mind after all I had lost in the desert. And another letter from Eva. Also a card which was not so welcome. All about finance at home. Had a nasty spill off the bike. Badly bruised ankle. Still carried on. Letter from S Africa too. Doing well now. Hope the good work continues.

Sept 3rd 1942 Usual routine work. Fellows up for tapes. My name not included. Keep trying. The day will come. Jim and Wally both had one. Best of luck to both especially Wally. He has really earned it. And he saved my life once too. A letter from Dorothy at 8A Vine St or rather an airgraph. Must reply to some very soon. Evidently they have not yet recd my letter written in Libya. Glad Eva had hers though and knows how I feel about it. Congrats from all sources on publication of my letters home. Still on duty. And so ends the third year of war and the fourth begins.

Sept 4th Still D/R Saw Dick for an hour. Nothing else of any importance happened.

03/09/1942 A record number of sorties were made by the RAF in North Africa. Heavy New Zealand pressure caused Rommel to speed up his withdrawal as the desert battle rages on.

WAR DIARY

Unit 287 GT Coy RASC

Commanding Officer Major L.C. Smith M.C.

4/9/42   0400 hrs All modifications to fans complete, all Vehicles handed over to platoon and tool kits checked. 45 Drivers, 1 Vulcaniser, 1 C/? arrived from RASC base depot. Coy now complete in strength to HQ, four Tpt Platoons W/shops (Serial 3) one RDI. One platoon (No. 5 platoon) being still on detachment to 400 Coy RASC.

Sept 4ᵗʰ 1942

Darling,

I have already written a considerable amount of correspondence on the financial matter you referred to in your letter of Aug 16ᵗʰ so now for a change I will endeavour to write of more intimate things.

First of all I will point out that I am compelled to write this letter at great speed as I cannot guarantee writing again for a few days. You can put your own interpretation on that and I will make no further comment. But darling I can assure you that just at present you have no need whatever to worry over me. Another thing I would ask. That is please excuse writing and any mistakes, as I shall not have time to check what I write.

First item is that I have had three letters in two days, also the A.M.L card of the 16ᵗʰ. And what memories that date on the card conjured up in my mind. I think you will remember what anniversary falls on that date. I seem to remember you making a fruitless journey one Wednesday afternoon. How I hated all that when I knew. Still it is now in the realms of memories. And then it starts me thinking of the past and then "When shadows fall". I think of my service out here and all that it has and will entail. And that terrible time through which the lads out here went and I try to compare it with other events. But I know of no other event which will stand comparison. And often I try to form my own opinion as to which was the most unpleasant part of it all. And yet I know. It was not all the work and loss that I sustained. No darling it was the waiting. Waiting for orders. Always waiting, and yet by the fingers of the clock we did not have to wait so very long. But certain indications and sounds at that time brought home with tremendous force the true meaning of the words "A thousand ages in Thy Sight is but an evening gone". I waited patiently studying the faces of the other men at times. They showed no sign of nerves or anything like that but at those times I would wager all I have that they were thinking of wives, sweethearts or parents. And then I fell to wondering what I would do if I were unlucky enough to be taken prisoner. I know by your letter what you would expect me to do. But now I am not so sure. I thought of you. If I tried to escape and got put out of action then once more it would be you who would suffer. And I had already made up my mind that you would have no more troubles if I could avoid them. But by the will of the Almighty that question never arose. And believe me my darling when I say I hope it never does.

And another thing I often think of and smile inwardly over was a sense of utter security when we crossed the line between Libya and Egypt. Why that wire should create such an illusion is beyond me but I have spoken to several other fellows and strange to relate they had the same feeling. Still that is another memory. I think I shall have to leave a lot of those stories until I see you. I shall just tell you the simple truth and you will I know be a very good listener. But a lot that I shall tell you not just of the hardship I myself suffered but also those of others related to no one else because I know that they will not be believed. And dear, I know that you will never doubt my word.

I think the place you mentioned in your letter is going to be ideal. The rods and lines, a quiet lake and you to talk to. That is all I want. You see, I am used to the great solitudes, and sometimes especially when there is a full moon making the eternal sand appear like snow, I go for a little stroll all by myself and imagine all sorts of things. At those moments I have the feeling of being in another world, and you are very close to me.

I ended there at midnight and now another day has passed and evening is here. You will notice the writing on one of the pages has become rather obliterated. That is the discomfort of the Middle East or rather just one of the minor ones. This letter has been in my breast pocket for a few hours and it is perspiration that has caused the writing to become dim. This morning we had a most unusual occurrence.

The real, genuine FOG. Lasted for at least half an hour. What a relief from the merciless sun. The night has gone and the mood I was in has also gone. I think if I had kept on in the same strain I should have been coming back to you. Still I know you like me to write nice things. I often feel like writing in that way but then we have no lights in forward areas. We just have to pack up at dusk except when the moon is casting its light upon the earth.

And now I am on a 24 hrs per day job on two wheels for the time being. I tried hard to get off it, but the Major said "No, I am keeping him on that job". So that was that. Now my old officer wants me in his crowd. You see this is a large company, divided into a number of Platoons. So far they will not release me from HQ Platoon. My officer went to another Platoon. Now he says he is going to try a big "wangle" to get me there. I did not ask him. It was the other way round. Fred is now in another platoon so I do not see much of him. Also nearly all the other fellows I got to know so well during those days in June when we were all up against it. And you have not yet let me know what you thought about our 8th Army during those days. Please don't be afraid to criticise. I do not, as you know, often mention anything in regard to military affairs out here. But there was just one thing heard repeatedly. "Oh if only we could have Archie Wavell here again. I think even now that the psychological effect of his mere presence would have had a tremendous effect. But he was badly needed elsewhere and we had to fight back with our new commanders. We stopped the enemy and I personally think his swan song has already been sung. You will probably think that I had written that before we came back. But I genuinely believed it then. Even more so now.

If you could have seen the morale and appearance of the prisoners you would never doubt who will eventually win. Oh! Yes I suppose it will be said "just another excuse". But I must also add that OUR desert men are treated as human beings even though the conditions are at times to say the least of it rather trying. And after all it is that experience that is going to be the deciding factor.

It is nearly midnight now and I will try and carry on with a few more lines. The mosquitoes are playing merry ---- with me. And when the dawn comes the flies turn out in their millions. I have a mosquito net for protection when I sleep, but I can't write under that so I have to suffer the indignity of lumps appearing in all sorts of odd places. No! There are none just there yet. Have just killed a beauty. I think by the dark red stain left on my arm I must have given him a blood transfusion. For some unknown reason there is a howling wind blowing tonight. Reminds me of a winter's night by our own fireside except for a different kind of heat.

Well my darling I think I really shall have to close. Just one item first. Have today received a Reg'd letter from Dad containing 10/-. Reg'd No.7149. I shall also write and inform him in an airgraph and give as nearly as possible a list of Reg'd no's up to the present. It is rather difficult as I lost the first list. I had taken the precaution of destroying almost all of my letters etc. and making a brief note of numbers of Reg'd mail and also addresses, but even those went. You do not even now seem to realise the extent of my misfortune. I came back with a field service cap (no topee) shirt, shorts, boots and socks. That was all. And I managed with those for far longer than I care to remember. At one stage, I managed to get a steel helmet belonging to someone who no longer required it. My conscience troubled me for a few moments, but sentiment has to be placed on one side at times like those. And so, here I am filling more pages. And now for the finish of my mind wanderings.

Please remember me to all at home including Mrs Taylor and Billie. Shall be very pleased to receive a letter from Billie. Now it looks as though I shall be filling this page too. I had an airgraph from Dorothy at Harts Hill. I will try and reply to it this week. I have already written to them once but this is not a reply to my letter so I presume it has not yet reached them. As I have already told you I am expecting my letter writing to go -- well I can't write in Army language so I will just say "to be erratis". And yet we are not certain. You see there are so many events that can happen to change everything in a few seconds. Well Cheerio my sweetheart. Take care of yourself until I come and warm your feet again. And have plenty of baths ready. You will be surprised how many I promised myself when I was in Libya. All my love and heaps of kisses from your husband

Gerald X X X X X X X X X X X X X

One for Lucy X

GERALD MILNER'S DIARY

Sept 5th Recd two letters from Eva. Replied to both.

Sept 6th Very busy day. Riding for hours. Saw Dick for a few minutes

Sept 7th Away once more on the old bike. Rode 15 hrs. Very tired and eventually sleep neath star spangled sky.

Sept 8th Away again. Going very tough. Made it though with all vehicles complete. Lovely view of Mediterranean. And so to bed.

Sept 9th Little to do. All day to rest. Needed it to.

06/09/1942 Rommel lost 51 tanks (out of 515), 70 guns, 400 trucks and 2,865 men. He was also back to the positions he held on the 31st August. The 8th Army lost 1,640 men and 68 tanks.

07/09/1942 Montgomery suspended the battle and stabilised the 8th Army position at Alam el Haifa.

WAR DIARY

Unit 287 GT Coy RASC

Commanding Officer Major L.C. Smith M.C.

4/9/42   0400 hrs All modifications to fans complete, all Vehicles handed over to platoon and tool kits checked. 45 Drivers, 1 Vulcaniser, 1 C/???? arrived from RASC base depot. Coy now complete in strength to HQ, four Tpt Platoons W/shops (Serial 3) one RDI. One platoon (No. 5 platoon) being still on detachment to 400 Coy RASC.

5/9/42   Modifications complete and unit sign being painted on all vehicles.

6/9/42   1800 hrs SA45156 of 6 Received from MIDEAST ordering coy to move to MARLOPOLIS on 7 Sept under instructors MIKEHAT MVTS. Coy to remain under command GHR

7/9/42   0045 hrs MIDEAST Move 6R/45286 of 6th received instructing 287 Coy to proceed Cowley 7th Sept to convey personnel of HQ 4 Ind Div to Kilo 179 Rd MENA – ALEXANDRIA. Further orders for onward move to be given to OC on arrival at COWLEY.

    0600 hrs Depart TAHAG and pass from command HQ Mobn Centre RASC MEF to command GHQ

On the move

    0900 hrs Held up at TREATY BRIDGE, bridge being open

    10.30 hrs Arrive COWLEY and contact CRIASC 4 Ind Div Coy HQ and w/shops sent ahead to refuel at KILO 12 platoon load up personnel and stores and under command of Senior Combatant officer for move. HQ RASC 4 Ind Div 239/ST of 6 Sept being movement order received.

    11.30 hrs Move off

    17.30 hrs Coy HQ and w/shops arrive KILO 170

On the move	
7/9/42	2130 hrs Remainder of column now arrived CRIASC 4 Ind Div orders move forward at 0600 hrs 8 Sept and all vehicles to be refuelled immediately. Petrol refuelling point AMYRIA ordered to supply petrol and all lorries filled up by 2350 hrs.
8/9/42	0600 hrs Coy HQ and w/shops ordered forward also by CRIASC 4 Ind Div and proceeds with column to Area S of El IMAYID
	0900 hrs Company unable to return to MAREOPOLIS as in 50 45156 as CRIASE 4 Ind Div orders Coy to stay in area to take HQ 5 Ind Div back to COWLEY area
	1200 hrs Loading of HQ 5 Ind Div Commences
9/9/42	1800 hrs Loading of 5 Ind Div complete

Sept 9th 1942

My Darling,

I feel I must write a few lines to you once more although goodness only knows when I shall be able to post them. You see, we refitted and had a rest for a short while and now we are back in harness with a vengeance. And today I feel really proud of myself. Yes, I know my trumpeter is already dead, but I have during the last few days earned for myself a reputation which will always be talked of by the men of my own and other companies. In fact to be brief I received congratulations from the O.C., the Adjutant Officers and all ranks. Of course I can't tell you all the story, but I acted as despatch rider on a very large, important and urgent convoy. It had to go through. Actually there should have been eight men to do my job, but I carried it out single handed without loss. It involved riding for miles at 85 M.P.H. Then would come the bad patches but somehow the old bike kept going. I had almost sole control of the convoy discipline and right well the drivers performed. And we reached our destination right bang on time. At times I thought it could not be done but each time fate took a hand and gave me help. On one occasion I had the front and back wheels out of sight in soft sand. I could not see the kick start or the foot change lever but once more I got going. I pulled in with the last vehicle, and the clutch lever and the air control fell off and the throttle wire broke. I managed to coast the last 20 yards. The Major saw that I had a good meal and ORDERED me to bed. Oh boy! What an order in the Army. And that my darling is just one of the things that happen every minute every day to enable the wireless to announce "The enemy retreated slightly westward". I have now finished with the bike for the present, and really I am not sorry.

And now I have just a little time off. I somehow suspect that I am being given a short rest but actually feel fit as a fiddle. After that experience I feel that I could now take you to Astley Hall again without giving any trouble. And I was so thickly coated with dust that I was given ½ gall of water to get myself clean. And for the fourth time I was recently recommended for tapes. I was unlucky once more but I think I have now put myself bang in the front for the next one going. I don't know how long that will be.

Sorry I can't write much now as my pen is full of sand, I am short of ink, and the conditions are very unfavourable. Will write again at the first opportunity. Shall probably have a lot of mail to post with this if we keep moving around. Cheerio my sweetheart. All my love from your husband.

Gerald X X X X X X X X X X X X X
One for Lucy X

NOTES BY GERALD MILNER

I had on many occasions acted as a Despatch Rider. In the Army this is a voluntary job and soon after the vitamin incident the C.O. said he would like me to meet a Col Perry of one of the Indian Divisions. He told me the Germans were making a very powerful thrust and were in danger of breaking through in the centre of our defence line. On the recommendation of my C.O. he wanted me to act as D.R to the convoy. I agreed but little did I realise the hazardous nature of the journey. Sandstorm blowing, bombs and shells occasionally flying around. The soft sand was several inches deep and the vehicles as well as myself had the utmost difficulty in progressing. 15 or 16 miles in two days. However I managed to get the convoy safely to its destination. I was totally exhausted and just lay on the sand at the side of my trusty "Matchless 500" Then the unheard of happened. The Colonel himself brought me a bowl of soup and personally thanked me for a job well done. I returned to base at a more leisurely pace.

GERALD MILNER'S DIARY

Sept 10th The journey through the Valley of Death. I could have named it otherwise. Worst sandstorm I have known even in this country. After hellish driving for many miles we at last emerged into calmer places

Sept 11th Away on the trail again. Drove for many hours. Arrived destination safely. Guard duty. Questioned by Platoon officer following morning. Cleared myself. Recd reg. Letter from Dad. Seems as though they had a letter telling of my escape from Libya.

Sept 12th Blazing sun all morning. In fact "Glorious Twelfth" Static. Did "Dhobie" Later expect to do a little writing. Did a little writing. Very little. Idle day still writing. Pining for action. Trying to decide whether to ask for interview with O.C. And so to bed. Bed made and had to move vehicle. A thousand curses.

WAR DIARY

Unit 287 GT Coy RASC
Commanding Officer Major L.C. Smith M.C.

10/9/42   0900 hrs Main HQ 5 Ind Div moves off for KILO

On the move

10/9/42   1200 hrs Rear HQ 5 Ind Div move off for KILO 170. Coy now clear of area. Heavy dust storm blowing. Route; "C" Track to KILO 179

1600 hrs Coy HQ & w/shops established KILO 179

1800 hrs Company completely refuelled. 22 x 3 ton carrying 5 Ind Div w/shops now found to have proceeded to COWLEY

11/9/42   0600 hrs Coy HQ and w/shops proceed to COWLEY in rear of 5 Div HQ

1400 hrs Coy HQ & w/shops located NE ½ mile, of Kilo 12 Rd MENA ALEXANDRIA

1730 hrs Off loading of 5 Ind. Div complete. HQ 5 Ind Div asked to give further orders. States they will ascertain Coys orders from GHQ by 1200 hrs tomorrow. Orders Coy to spend the night 11/12/Sept in present Location

12/9/42   HQ 5 Ind Div contacted by O.C. Coy Maj L C Smith. No orders for future move of Coy. HQ stated that S.T. Branch GHQ informed of Coy location and that detail completed, orders are to follow. HQ orders that Coy remains in present location at Kilo 12. Further orders will be transmitted to Coy by him.

Sept 12ᵗʰ 1942

Darling,

Just a line to acknowledge receipt of several letters and letter cards, and also two Regd letters from Dad. Perhaps you would let him know just in case my letters have not reached him. There are already quite a lot of letters on the way to all at home. As soon as I can find time to write again I will answer your letters together. Have been having rather a busy time just recently but I am in very good health and I always have the feeling that the more we all put into this job the sooner the war will end. I have already written an air mail letter card and letter in reply to the card of Aug 16ᵗʰ. The year was 1932 or 33. Profit £104 shown as wages. The rest of the information is contained in letters.

Many thanks for the picture of the lake. If the place suits you then it is good enough for me. In fact I think I should very much appreciate it if I were there now. Afraid I shall have to put those thoughts behind me though. Had airgraph from Miss Spicer. Shall reply in a few days. Am also preparing a small parcel of souvenirs to send in a few days. Have already sent quite a lot of snaps taken while on leave. 36 in one regd. envelope. Am still keeping a keen look out for George but so far have not found him. The M.E. is a very big place you know.

With regard to that other proposition you mention, I am afraid I cannot give you many details just at the present. My friend Captain Syme has now returned to England so he will probably pay you a visit. If he does you can trust him completely. His offer is quite genuine.

Well darling I am afraid I shall have to close now as it is nearly time to be on the move again. Please remember me to all my friends, and give my love to Lucy. Cheerio my darling.

All my love from your husband

Gerald X X X X X X X X X X X X X

One for Lucy X

WAR DIARY

Unit 287 GT Coy RASC

Commanding Officer Major L.C. Smith M.C.

13/9/42   0930 hrs No orders to hand yet.

14/9/42   0900 hrs S T Branch GHQ orders move to MAREOPOLIS. Go x 3ton loaded with ?

GERALD MILNER'S DIARY

Sept 13ᵗʰ Up early. Good breakfast. Very little hard work. Wrote letter to Misses Spicer. One to Eva. One to Mr Titley. Airmail card to Dad. Airgraph to Eva. Slept well.

Sept 14ᵗʰ Up with the lark and away to the woods. Lorry running very well. Arrived safely and soundly. And so to bed. Still no mail.

13/09/1942 Desert raids were made on Benghazi and Barer. An attack by combined forces was made on Tobruk.

Sept 14ᵗʰ 1942

My Own Darling,

I feel I must write to you and yet I am sure I do not know what I am going to write about. You see I have written quite a lot to you recently and all my movements since then cannot be explained on paper. Much as I should like to tell you and much as you would like to know the safety of British troops is at stake. All I can say is that all the boys out here are of the same mind. There is a certain job to be done. Everyone seems grimly determined that there will be no more trouble from the enemy. We all know the terrors and trials of desert warfare, but we are all anxious to "have another go". And I personally have a special reason. I partly got my own back a short time ago but the interest has still to be given. I wrote a special letter to you telling of that adventure. I received the thanks of all the company including the OC himself. And he gave me his cup of tea. That to a desert veteran is the crowning glory of all. As I write I can see him walking by and having a good look at an "emergency cover" I have erected. And now I have finished that job I feel miserable. And yet I suppose I am not really. But my bike. Well after the terrible handling I gave it on that trip it has a "few defects". Looks to me as though they will need drastic remedy. That is one of the queer parts about the Army. That convoy was essential and nothing was said about the bike. And yet if I had lost a spanner in quieter places, I would be expected to pay for it. Yet it was only fair to the driver.

And now I have no bike or lorry. And I am between dozens of fires. You see in those days when we had to do or die, I made a lot of friends. My officer at that time thanked me on parade for the untiring work I had done during those days. And now he is in another platoon belonging to this Company. And he wants me in his Platoon. And the officer who went back to try and recover my kit at the same time as I went back, also has a Platoon. And he wants me. And my old Sergt is in a Platoon. He wants me. My old friend who shared my tiny "Bivvy" for so long also has a section in a Platoon. And he wants me. But the fact remains that I belong to HQ Platoon. And I cannot make up my mind. And nearly all of those people I have mentioned have at some time or other recommended me for promotion. It has not yet materialised, and I can't decide what to do for the best.

Just at the present moment I am having a rest. I am sure I don't need it. I lived dangerously for a long time and I can't say I enjoyed it. But all the time I have a longing to get into the thick of it again and stay until the job is over. It is, in my humble opinion, the only way I can get back to you in the shortest possible time. And that is all I ask. In the meantime I shall still work for that first tape. And I can assure you that a tape in this company has to be really earned. They are certainly not thrown about to any Tom Dick or Harry. And it is usually a job to decide who merits it most. Every man is expected to pull his weight.

Well sweetheart I am wandering along and now I think I must conclude my letter. But before I end, I would give you just a word of warning. There may in the future be times when I cannot write for days. So if at times your mail becomes spasmodic please forgive me. If that happens I always try to make up for lost time at the first opportunity. Please remember me to all my friends including Mrs Taylor & Billie. And give my love to Lucy. Tell her I am still waiting for that letter. Cheerio my darling. All my love from your husband

Gerald X X X X X X X X X X X X X

One for Lucy X

P.S. You will find another snap enclosed. Have already sent about fifty in recent weeks. As soon as I hear of their safe arrival I will send the negatives as I do not want to lose this pile. Some of the snaps I cannot replace as I have earned quite a big reputation with my photography. Other fellows bring their camera and film and ask me to perform. Then if a particularly good one takes my fancy I get an extra print for myself. Otherwise, that "right reserved"

WAR DIARY
Unit 287 GT Coy RASC
Commanding Officer Major L.C. Smith M.C.
15/9/42   0730 hrs Coy completes move to MAREOPOLIS. Movement order MCR/213 of 14 Sept refers
1400 hrs Coy HQ w/shops 1,2,4 Rb established Camps G and 11 Mareopolis (GHQ 9Capt Morris) informed

MAREOPOLIS
16/9/42   Day spent in cleaning Camp which was stiff with Mosquitoes, and performing some small local details.

GERALD MILNER'S DIARY
Sept 15th Plenty of work on vehicle.
Sept 16th Still plenty of work. Lost lorry and detailed for bike.

Sept 16th 1942

My Darling,

Still have not heard from you for about 10 days. Seems like 10 years. How I wish I could get a few lines from you. And I have had no papers for ages. I suppose fate will give a helping hand before long. Today or rather tonight I feel particularly miserable but please don't worry. I am not in any trouble. It is just the fact that in my opinion, and also in the opinion of my N.C.O.'s I have had a pretty rough deal. What it is all about I cannot explain fully, but it boils down to the fact that I can do any job, and I always do my best in every case. And now I think that my willingness and hard work are being taken advantage of. So I am putting in the big kick that I am perfectly entitled to do. Rest assured that I have not run wild or anything like that. I have simply asked through the proper channels for an interview with my Captain in the morning, and if he cannot straighten matters out I shall ask to go before the Major. I know I shall receive due consideration if I go to him.

Well sweetheart it is almost dark now and we never get lights here so I shall have to close. Will write tomorrow and let you know how I got on. It is just at times like these that I long more than ever for your company, but I shall have to paddle a lone course for sometime yet.

Well darling morning is here again with all its heat and dust and flies. My interview has come and gone. I think I made out a grand case for myself. I asked for a transfer to one of our Platoons or to any Company in the M.E. I know I should be really sorry to leave such a Company as this but I told the Captain exactly what I thought. Gave him rather a shock in fact. Refused to post me, even to another part of our own Coy. Told me I was far too valuable a soldier for H.Q. to lose. I was quite blunt and told him I had heard that "Sob stuff" before. He went to great pains to emphasise that he meant just what he said. I told him straight out that my treatment did not uphold his statement. I have already told you about that convoy which went through. Well it appears I am the only fellow who can do the job I took on. I asked him what will happen if I get an unfortunate bullet. He would not tell me. However he has taken a couple of days to sort out a decent job for me. He now knows that if I get no satisfaction I shall ask for an interview with the Major. And that will write "finis" to HQ for me. I don't often write of my troubles because it is very rarely I have any but minor ones. But on this occasion I was ready to explode. In fact the Captain told me to go quietly away and loose off steam on any unfortunate individual who happened to cross my path. Well I have not got to that stage yet. When morning comes I usually feel better and fit for anything. But at night there are always the thoughts of home and you, and that makes it seem worse.

And on top of that at this time of the year, a plague of mosquitoes. And always the waiting and wondering whether the "Oompha, Oompha bird" will put in an appearance. Well my dear I think I shall soon have to end my letter. Please remember me to all my many friends at home, including Mrs Taylor and Billie. Also give my love to Lucy. Cheerio and a Happy Christmas sweetheart. Wish I could be with you. All my love from your husband

Gerald X X X X X X X X X X X X X X
One for Lucy X   Snap Enclosed

GERALD MILNER'S DIARY

Sept 17ᵗʰ Had interview. Not too satisfactory. Let off steam and received sympathy but little satisfaction. Probably try again later. Wrote airgraph to Eva. One to Mother. Letter to George Veal. Jim Hughes. Dorothy (Harts Hill) Green envelope to Eva. And so to a fairly peaceful sleep. Occasional interlude.

Sept 18ᵗʰ 1942 Still on two wheels. Little to do. Wrote more to Eva. Airgraph and green envelope while I had the chance. Shall post same tomorrow.

Sept 19th Very little of interest. Could not even settle to writing. Heat not too bad, but flies although in smaller quantities, determined to carry out nuisance raids. Went to bed very late.

Sept 20ᵗʰ Rose at the usual hour, with old shamesa just peeping above sahab. Another quiet day. Wrote A Ml Card to Eva re-songs to this Company. And so to bed.

Sept 20ᵗʰ 1942

My Darling,

A couple of days ago I wrote a letter to you Posted in a Green envelope. I want you to take little or no notice of what I wrote there. I was really at explosion state when I wrote that, but I know now I have cooled off that I should not have passed my troubles on to you. But recently sweetheart, you have no idea how this hell of heat and sand and flies and mosquitoes, snakes, lizards and scorpions, and every other type of creature can get on ones nerves. First time it has really got me. And that was only because I was definitely receiving treatment not exactly fair. The trouble arose over the fact that I had been on so many different jobs and taken off them to help someone else out on so many different occasions that I was beginning to sit up and take notice. I spoke about it in the proper quarters and was told they would remedy this. Well, to cut a long story short I was put on the bike for the convoy job I wrote to you about a week or two ago. I came off that terrible job with colours flying. For four days I was given a rest, although I did not need it. Then I was given a brand new lorry in H.Q. I drove it on one trip serviced it completely with great care and patience and immediately afterwards was taken off it. Not because of my inability, but because there is no one else can ride a bike like I can. Or so I was told. But there are quite a lot of men who have learned to handle four wheels.

POOR LITTLE BUGGER

He's been working again.
Oh Eva this desert's a wonderful land
To each blade of grass there's ten acres of sand,
The climate for camels perhaps is all right
But we roast every day and we freeze every night,
Our home is the desert; our roof is the sky,
With Heinkels and Stukes above as we lay
Mosquitoes, bugs, lizards, snakes, scorpions and ants
Creep into our shirts, socks, boots, hats, vests and pants
But when we're asleep we forget about these
Until we are wakened by millions of fleas
We scratch and we kill, then we strip to the core,
Longing to be back on old Blighty's shore

Anonymous

Well dear I can drive anything they can give me up to 15 tonnes and it is in my record too. But even that did not get me off the bike. So I am afraid I got into a pretty bad humour and let fly. And now I want to get my snap taken for you on this "B" bike. Sorry only had it taken by the side of a Jeep or desert scout car. Somehow I don't think it will come out too well, but still I will wait for the result and pass comment then. Really glad I made the camera my hobby. Actually I am not supposed to have one while in the "Field" but I think a lot of people are like Nelson. Perhaps as well they are too. I have told you of some of the hardships we have endured, but when I think of things, I know they could be made worse. For instance if things go a trifle wrong, and at times they are bound to do, well the Major never tears around crying "get this done, do that and why? And so on". Discipline is strict and yet there is great latitude. And the men appreciate it too. Moreover they rarely take advantage of it. I can honestly say that the men in this Company are about as tough a crowd as will be found anywhere. But I do not mean that in the slang sense. If a job has to be done, they never ask the terms or conditions or speak of the danger. They just do it. And they are a quite well behaved and decent lot of men. A type distinct from many other units. They make a point of writing to their wives and sweethearts at every available opportunity. They like an occasional quiet bottle of beer if the canteen lorry has been able to get any. But that is only after they have ascertained that their vehicle is ready to move at any time.

It has become almost a ritual with this Company that after a hard days run the vehicles are checked over for glaring faults even before meals are taken. Each man makes it his duty to see that the job is done. And so the work carries on. And the Company has a name that I am certain will go in the History books of the future.

We are now rested, refitted and once more ready for anything. And above all, I for one am ready to see the end of all this sand. Nothing but sand. But in spite of all I know in my heart that I am just another desert veteran and they cannot be made in a day. So any job is here unless the powers that be see fit to move us to other spheres of war. There are a lot of places I would like to see, but I try to put these ideas out of my head. I must be in the place where I can do most to speed the day of our re-union. It is not a very pleasant prospect but what we have done before we can do again. I remember one day going on a long trip with a lad who had never seen much of this country before except where the roads are. He was brimful of confidence at the start. But we ran into the worst sandstorm that even I have experienced. It raged for just about 10 hours. If another vehicle was within two yards of me I could not see it. I knew that when the storm abated I could pick up my bearings from the sun, but he was worried stiff.

As I say I was pretty confident I could find my eventual destination but it was more by luck than judgement that I found the exact spot first time. However he gave a sigh of relief and said he does not know how he will manage if he has to do it by himself, and he was sure his Mother would be very worried if she knew what it was like. I smiled at that and thought of my first trips, but I am certain he will be OK before long. You see there are laws in the desert that do not apply to any other place, and they have to be rigidly adhered to or trouble can be expected.

And now the sun is sinking rapidly. Night will be here in less than half an hour. And I have to try and find a nice smooth strip of sand on which to lay my two blankets. The stars will be my canopy, and all the creatures that crawl over the earth will be my companions. I shall have a couple of hours to lie and think of you before slumber finally claims me. That is if the Oompha, Oompha bird keeps away. And so my sweetheart I must close with those thoughts. No one will ever know how much I miss you. And that feeling increases as time goes on. But others have the same secret thoughts and we know we must finish the job. Then perhaps we can return to a country of thoughts of peace and ensuring that other countries think the same. We are just getting the news in papers from home of the battles out here. As a mere "spectator" they seem to be very faithful reports, but naturally there is a lot they cannot tell. Neither can I. But one day that story will be told, and the boys of the Eighth Army vindicated.

Please remember me to all my friends at home including all next door, and give my love to Lucy. Goodnight darling. Sleep tight and think of me. All my love from your husband

Gerald X X X X X X X X X X X X X

One for Lucy X

GERALD MILNER'S DIARY

Sept 21st Still on the bike. Nothing else.

Sept 21st 1942

Darling,

During the last three weeks I have not heard from you but I have continued to write regularly by the various Postal services available. I have no doubt your letters will turn up as usual. Probably seven or eight at a time as has often happened in the past. I am taking this opportunity of informing you that a broadcast by the BBC will probably be made to this Company some time in the near future. Some of the men have been asked to name their favourite tune, and I was one of the persons asked. I gave in your favourite "When day is done". I am not certain, but I presume that from the list submitted, the BBC will now select a limited number and fit it in with their programme. As far as I know at present the songs will be broadcast in the African Service of the Forces Programme. So perhaps you will learn a little more from your end. I suggest you ask Jan Berenska to find out further details for you at the earliest possible opportunity. It seems a long time since he played "Here comes the Bride". Ask him what he will play when I come home this time. Nothing about "Desert Songs" though.

And now for another small item. I have heard indirectly that the parcel I sent you early in the year has arrived safely. And now I am just waiting to hear what you think of the contents. I should have been most disappointed if that too had been added to my losses in the desert. I had a feeling that you would get it alright. I still have the carvings in Alabaster that I bought while on my last leave. I will send them in a few days. I am still waiting for that very special County Express you posted to me. I am anxious to read the story you mentioned.

Well darling it is now almost time for bed, so I shall have to close. Please remember me to Mrs Taylor & Billie. Also Mildred and Arthur. Give my love to Lucy. Cheerio. All my love from your husband

Gerald X X X X X X X X X X X X X

One for Lucy X

GERALD MILNER'S DIARY

Sept 22nd Same as 21st. late at night took over new vehicle. Or rather a fresh one.

Sept 23rd All day on maintenance

Sept 24th Once more all day on same job as 23rd. Still not satisfied. And so to bed.

Sept 25th After further search discovered the elusive trouble. Running beautifully now.

Sept 26th Same as 25th

WAR DIARY

Unit 287 GT Coy RASC

Commanding Officer Major L.C. Smith M.C.

17/9/42   1500 hrs Mid East So/49419 of 16 received, placing Coy at 24 hrs notice
to move forward under orders Eighth Army when required.

18/9/42   Local details only

19/9/42   Local details only

20/9/42 to 24/9/42 Local details only

24/9/42 to 30/9/42 Local details only

1/10/42   Local details as required by TD 65 Sub order are being performed daily

Sept 26ᵗʰ 1942

Darling,

As you can see my attention was taken from my literary endeavour, but I think I can now continue to write steadily. You will probably agree that the wheel of a lorry is not the best form of writing desk. However I will try and make the letter readable. First of all I would like to inform you that the long period without mail has ended. Had two cards and a letter from you also two bundles of papers including the account of Jerusalem. Looks good in print. I have also had a card from Mother and a letter, two cards and two Birthday Cards from Roma. Today there is another card and two Reg'd letters for me. One from you and one from Dad but I have not had delivery of them. Will write more of that tomorrow. You see when I sign for delivery of Reg'd mail the Post Corporal also collects the mail ready for censorship and that is why I am not waiting.

Sorry to hear you have been getting a few sleepless nights, but you seem to have had a very long spell of quiet. I have just had another lot of snaps delivered and they have turned out exceptionally well. I shall send one or two by letter, probably tomorrow. I shall also endeavour to answer all recent correspondence more fully during the next few days. Please accept my apologies for the letters about Devonshire. I have slipped up rather badly there. But I can easily explain. Since that disastrous night in Libya I have made a point of reading my letters and then destroying them. And for once my memory has let me down. But the place you mention will suit me admirably.

Must close now. Will send an airgraph tomorrow. Please remember me to Mrs Taylor & Billie. Give my love to Lucy. Just one other item. Dick has sent me the Olive wood carving. Shall have to send two parcels now. I know you won't mind that. Cheerio darling. All my love from your husband

Gerald X X X X X X X X X X X X X

One for Lucy X

GERALD MILNER'S DIARY

27ᵗʰ Sept Had game solo in Coy office. Plenty of maintenance. And so to bed after needle.

Sept 28ᵗʰ Arm very stiff. No other ill effects. Work as usual

---

Sept 28ᵗʰ 1942

Darling,

Once more I take the opportunity of writing a few lines as I sit at the wheel of my lorry. You notice that last word. I have come off the bike now. I don't mean fallen off. Just taken off. What a job I had to get off it. Had to go almost to the top of the tree to do it. Captain told me it was because I did the job too well. Best m/cyclist the company has had and all that stuff. Had a lorry soon after. Only had it a few days. Went back on the bike. Played Hell about it. Captain asked if I would do it. Told him I always obeyed orders and anyway he had 3 pips. So he ordered me to ride it. I told him I would carry out the order to the best of my ability although it went against the grain. A few days later he sent for me. I went prepared for another "bust up". Anyway, he told me he had made enquiries and received splendid reports of my conduct. Experienced desert man and all that sort of stuff. He asked me quite a lot of questions and I answered them all. He was more than satisfied. So now I have been given a lorry once again. It is I think the most important job in the Company. The water tanker. You can imagine what that means out here. It can be a heart breaking job too. When water bottles are empty and a fellow comes up "Can you spare a tiny drop" and I know he has had his ration. Well it is all part of the job. I think I shall manage to hold the job down alright.

I received your Regd letter of Aug 5th yesterday. Thank you very much for that. Also Regd letter from Dad. Yours No. 8328. Dad's No. 9822. As you know I lost my kit up Bir Hacheim way and I also lost all my records of Regd letters up to that date. I will however send another complete list of all registered mail received since that Hellish night. I cannot let you have it now as I am on guard, and I will also give you just a word of warning. It may be a day or two before I can write again. I have seen the Medical Officer about an hour ago and he still thinks I am a gramophone record. Anyway he put another needle in and pressed the trigger hard. And it happened to be the strong dose I was due to receive. Don't worry. I'll be alright in a few hours.

Have received another lot of snaps today. I am enclosing one specimen of yours truly caught by a fellow I have been teaching to use a camera the way I think they should be used. Catch 'em off their guard. He certainly caught me alright. I was looking up and wondering whether a steel helmet was just the thing to wear. And please don't think I had my tongue in my cheek. I was just finishing a meal while watching events. So now you can see what I look like when possible trouble is around.

Sorry to hear you have not yet been able to get a ring. I suppose you want me to have a say. My final words are "I told you what to spend and you are the sole judge of how you spend it. Suit yourself and I shall be quite happy". I am pleased to hear you liked the Cross I sent. Dad said everything else was put in the shade in comparison with that. And the camel too. And about the soap box for the nursery, well, it does put ideas into ones head. Shall have to wait a while yet. We have a sterner job to finish out here. When that is done then we can think of a lot of other things. Just think of me when you see the old full moon. The sand is bathed with its pale light and looks for all the world like snow. And that is always a time of expectancy out here. No one knows the terrible hardships the men put up with and yet they do the job cheerfully. I think the enemy think we are completely mad. We brought prisoners back with us a long time ago and they could not understand why we were all singing as though we had not got a care in the world. But after all, this Eighth Army DID hold Jerry. And it was just those singing British boys that pulled the fat out of the fire. One of these days I will send you a snap of the scores of camels and Bedouins. It was just their evacuation of El Alamein. It is the best I can do so take care of it for me.

Now for a few other items of interest. I have on several occasions told you I am sending you another parcel. I will endeavour to explain. This Company as you know is mobile. And during periods of waiting sometimes between battles we still work. And there arises the difficulty. Today I may decide to write or send a parcel. In a few minutes we may be ordered to a destination many miles away. That involves dismantling the whole camp and re-erecting same at new location. Then there is the job of finding an Army Post Office. And so you see that is how delay occurs. I am pretty certain I can manage a parcel tomorrow. I shall probably send an ash tray made by Dick Chalk from that olive wood log you saw in the snap. I brought it with me from the Mount of Olives for that purpose. Hope you will like it with its brass olive leaves. I shall also send a silver chain I had made in Cairo. That is for you. You will also find in the same box a little fellow with his dog. That was made in Alexandria when I was on leave. That is for Mother. Then in the other parcel which I shall send about a week later hoping that one of them gets there will be alabaster carvings. The Sphinx I had made, also the egg and stand for it. All native craftsmanship. There will also be two fairly large pieced of alabaster which I obtained from the top of the Second Pyramid. Please be careful with those as they are crystals and will easily crumble. As you can guess they are a day or two old. I am also sending in one of my letters a little book of pressed flowers I picked on one of the battlefields. And the wing of one of the fellows who trouble us out here. I expect "Curly" will be interested in that. Just a small fly. We have all varieties.

Well my darling I think I shall have to close after that effort. Will write again tomorrow if I feel fit. If not at the first opportunity. Have managed to obtain a few airgraphs above the ration so I shall be sending a few extra. Having some artistry put on some of them. Father Xmas in a tank etc. One of our fellows draws them as a hobby. Look out for them. Cheerio darling. All my love from

Gerald X X X X X X X X X X X

Lucy is getting very generous so here goes. XXX

P.S. 18 hours since I had the needle. Arm very painful but otherwise I have felt no ill effects. I don't think I shall now.

Love

Gerald X X X X X X

Sept 29th 1942

LETTER CARD

Darling Just a few lines to wish you Many Happy Returns and also at the same time a Happy Christmas. I know it is a little early but I shall write again in a week or two. And so I think at least one of the airgraphs should arrive safely. Today I have posted the first of the two parcels to you containing one olive wood ash tray one silver chain and a man and his dog for Mother. The chain for you. Father Christmas drawn by one of our fellows. Must close now. Aug 5th letter and contents received safely. Cheerio. All my love from your husband

Gerald

X X X X X X X X X X X X X

One for Lucy X

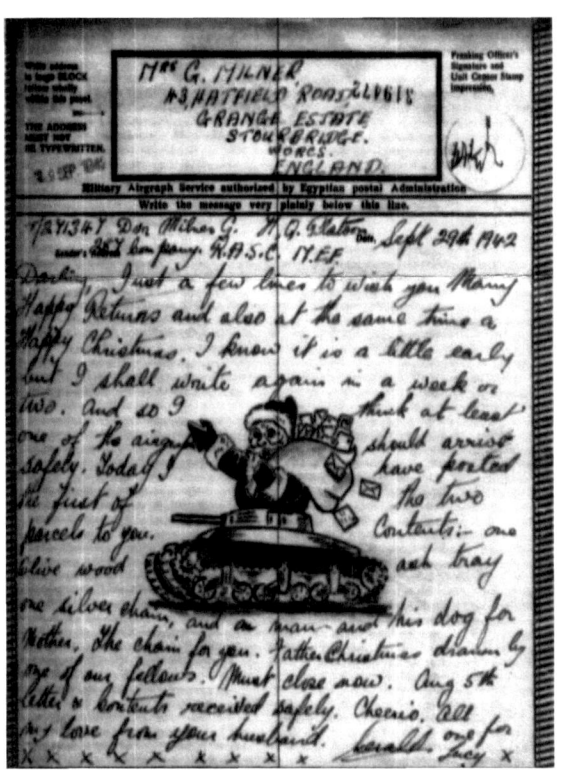

GERALD MILNER'S DIARY

Sept 29th Maintenance all morning. Afternoon as usual. Yesterday evening had musical accompaniment. Tonight another kind of celebration. Went off very well. Poem to PA very good.

Sept 30th 1942

Sept 30th Nothing special happened

Oct 1st Nothing

NOTES ON THE WAR BY GERALD MILNER

Drivers were quietly told what would be expected of them when the battle commenced. We had just about come to terms with the requirements when we were suddenly ordered deep into the desert for the battle at Alam Halfa which has been well documented. As soon as the battle was won quite a lot of timber and strips of metal and other odds and bobs began to arrive. With these we had to use our ingenuity to build skeleton tanks and guns, all to be covered with scrim or camouflage nets. We put up extra "Bivvys" and lines filled with washing and the Ack Ack gun situation was reinforced. When the Luftwaffe came to have a look they got a very hot reception to make them think the attack was to come from that quarter. The truth was that at nightfall we left the place empty except for the Ack-Ack gunners and moved back towards the coast ready for the big attack.

October 1st 1942

Darling,

Have just received your letter No. 14 telling me that you were not feeling well and had fainted when on duty. Have had all mail from number one to seventeen, but you never mentioned whether you were you were better in the last letters. Anyway I sincerely hope you are. Sorry I cannot convey your message about the flies to Cpl Jack Stone just at present as he is in a Platoon with Fred, and I am still in HQ. He is only about half a mile away but that is quite a long way when there is plenty of work to be done. Thought the joke about the lady going back for the oranges was quite "good". Also the fellow with the silk from Egypt. Think I can do the same. Or would you prefer the genuine article. And by the way, with regard to that soap container from Solomon's Quarries, I think your suggestion is quite good. By all means put it there, and how many more do you think I had better try and get. Sorry to hear you had little news from me during the Libyan affair. Of course, I myself know that hold ups in the mail were bound to occur. But I believe some very quick deliveries were made when they did get going. Sorry if I keep making mistakes. There is a burning hot dust storm blowing and the flies are a perfect pest. Shall not be sorry when winter is here again to reduce the number of pests.

Went to a concert last night. Not the kind you would probably imagine. Everything makeshift and the talent provided by my Company. Very good it was too. Quite a number of singers and comedians etc. but a corporal from our mobile workshops took most of the honours. Everyone knew him but still it was his first stage appearance and he took a few seconds to settle down. I have heard a few stage people in my time, but never anything approaching this turn. I would place max Miller well down the list. Just one of the stories.

Cow in one field. Large bull in the next. Cow and bull make eyes for a time. Ferdinand the bull walks to the other side of the field. Turns round, takes long run, mighty jump over fence and lands by cow. Cow all smiles, says "Well, aren't you the famous Ferdinand the Bull" Bull replied "Well just call me Ferdinand now, that "b" fence was higher than I thought".

Another one was about a lady who wanted to learn to ride a horse. Instructor asked if she preferred riding straddled or side saddle. She said she didn't mind. It was as broad as it was long.

He continued telling stories for almost an hour. He also composes his own poems. No nothing like the tales he can tell. One long one I want to try and get to send to you (if it will pass censorship) is dedicated to the work of P. Ammo. during retreat. It is true, it is well composed and indeed, after hearing it, I feel more proud than ever to belong to this Company. Some day the story will be told far better than I could tell it at present. Another was dedicated to the boys of our Coy. who made the supreme sacrifice in the service of their country.

And one day I will tell you the story of a lad who played his cornet and broke almost a life long resolution. He is in peace time a member of the Salvation Army. He would only play hymns etc. but suddenly he decided to play some of the good old songs. Night after night, amid the crashing of Hell let loose, I heard the beautiful notes ringing out through the desert almost defiantly. And last night that same boy was persuaded to appear, and he played "Mother Macree", "Last all clear", and one or two soldier's songs. Really it made a grand change.

Now you want to know whether I lost my money as well as my other kit. Well I did lose a bit, and toilet and other goods cost me quite a lot. Practically all my letters had been destroyed so you need lose no sleep over those. My camera was the loss I felt most of all, but I have another one now. The boys were very good to me. Had to borrow everything. Never shaved for about a week. Looked like the wild man from Borneo. Have received the picture of you in your new coat. It looks quite nice but then I think that of the wearer even without the coat. Well my sweetheart it is almost time to go on guard. I will try and write again tomorrow. Glad Lucy liked her brooch. Give my love to her, and remember me to all next door. Goodnight darling. Hope you are better when you get this letter. All my love from your husband

Gerald X X X X X X X X X X X X X

Ration for Lucy X X X

GERALD MILNER'S DIARY

Oct 2nd Same as 1st

Oct 3rd Busy on maintenance, refuelling etc.

Oct 3rd 1942

Darling,

Just a few lines to let you know I am still safe and in good health. Have got over the dose of the needle without much ill effect. Sorry I cannot make this a very long letter as I am rather pushed for time. The main reason why I am writing this is because I thought you would like the enclosed copy of a poem dedicated to the men of this Company. Please let me know what you really think of it. I heard it recited first at an extremely makeshift concert to celebrate a special occasion. There is another one too, but I cannot send you that just at present as it mentions a number of actions in which we were engaged. When time has disposed of the value of the information I can assure you it is better than the one enclosed.

Well darling I think that is about all. I have already written two air mail letters and three airgraphs to you this week. When we are stationery for a short time I try to write every day. You will understand then why there are times I cannot write. You see we are always liable to move at a few minutes notice. Even now, it is possible I won't be able to write again for a few days. Just look after yourself. God bless you darling and keep you safe. Don't worry about me. I can look after myself, and I know how to "rough" it. All my love from your husband

Gerald X X X X X X X X X X X X X

For Lucy XXXX

Burg El Arab Oct 1942. Jack, Sgt Nunn and Norman Payze outside their dug-out

"P.A." P. AMMO

'T'was the end of a day in the desert,
The sun shed a soft golden light.
She was sinking away in the West, there
Making way for a bright Starry night.

The gunners are doing their stuff now,
'Tis usual at this time of day.
A dull monotonous melody
Their twenty five pounders do play.

So I lay me down on two blankets,
My greatcoat under my head.
"At home" in the land where I live
They call it "Going to bed".

No beer will soothe me to sleep now
No loving "Good night" from the wife,
So my mind goes of in a ramble
Over things that can happen in life.

I started my life as a soldier
In the grime of smoky Sheffield
How a rifle should be at the "Port Arms"
How to dress a wound in the Field.

My experience was full and quite varied
After duty, there was dancing and song
Not to forget all the writing of letters
To the home I belong.

After months of waiting
For Para - troops -- They never come,
I found myself in "P.Ammunition"
Bound for a desert of fame.

For the name of "P.Ammunition",
It's convoys, and valiant men,
Are examples that Companies follow,
If they want to be in at the end.

We have our "Roll of Honour"
The names upon it are few.
But their devotion to duty
Has helped us, up in the "Blue"[1]

We take off our hat to our officers,
We acknowledge our brainy HQ
'T'is their Red Tape reading and writing
That helps us carry through.

Now I regret to record
The change that has just come about.
They call us "Two - eight - seven"
They've taken the "P.A.AMMO" out.

This is the end of my story
They can call us whatever they like,
But so long as there's a desert
Where convoys and supplies have to go,
NO Company shall claim the honour
Of being better than THE BEST P.AMMO

GERALD MILNER'S DIARY

Oct 4th Celebration of anniversary. Back to the trail again. Arrived in good time.
Oct 5th Found water after short circle to get bearings.
Oct 5th Plenty of work plenty of water
Oct 6th Out early. Filled tanker. Did arrears of Dhobie.
Oct 7th Thick fog. Found M.O. without to much trouble Afternoon: - found destination and returned to camp in terrific dust storm. Navigation by sun. Came back to find Dhobie completely ruined.
Oct 8th Routine
Oct 9th Work all day. Still no mail
Oct 10th Morning. Plenty of work. Afternoon similar.

06/10/1942 Final plans for the second battle of El Alamein are issued by General Montgomery to his senior commanders
08/10/1942 The Allied invasion of French North Africa was given the code name "Operation Torch". It was the first time the British and Americans had jointly worked on an invasion plan together. The final plans were issued on October 8th 1942

[1] "Blue" = Soldiers nickname for the Western Desert

Oct 10 1942

Darling

As I expected we were once more about to "hit the trail". Since I wrote that letter on Oct 3rd, I have had no opportunity of posting it. One or two airgraphs I had written were picked up from among my kit by the Post Corporal and he stamped them, put them in for censorship and posted them. Nice work. You should have received those by the time this letter reaches you. At present I am sitting in the cab in the midst of a sea of sand waiting to pick up one or two men. Have had a pretty tough job to do since we arrived here. The boys say I have true "direction instinct". Have to roam around for miles and find my way back. Can do it quite well though. Must end now. All my love darling, from your husband

Gerald X X X X X

GERALD MILNER'S DIARY

Oct 11th Same as 10th letter from Roma One from Mother Regd from Dad 2 Aml Cards from Eva.

Oct 12th Letter from Roma Nothing else.

Oct 13th Quiet day Plenty of work.

Oct 13th 1942

Darling,

Just a few lines thanking you for the two airmail letter cards which I received yesterday. You have not mentioned whether you feel properly well again after your illness. Glad to hear you are taking over the book keeping. Also pleased to hear you are receiving mail from me in record time. You say you cannot understand why I do not get letters from you more regularly. Well dear, I think if you moved your address as often as I do and got parked in the same outlandish places, then you would experience the same difficulties. Glad to hear you received the first of two snaps. They certainly did arrive quickly. At a guess they must have arrived in a week. Hope all the others arrive safely. About the negative of the Flamingos, I shall send it in a week or two. I want to get a few prints off it first. After I get one or two reprints I shall send you all the best negatives. Glad to hear the parcel arrived safely. Also that the letters from Dick are reaching Lucy.

And now, now, please don't tell me about it being very hot and having a thunderstorm. We have recently got rid of one, and it really was the genuine article. Many thanks for the parcel you have despatched also the one from Brook St. Hope it arrives safely. And what a thing to ask me. Come in and see the garden, and have some home fed ham & veg. Well perhaps it will not be so very long before I do that. Cheerio darling, and a Happy Christmas to all at home. Also "Many |happy Returns". All my love from your husband

Gerald X X X X X X X X X X X X X

One for Lucy X

GERALD MILNER'S DIARY

Oct 14th Routine

Oct 15th --------

Oct 16th What a birthday. Worst sandstorm ever. Followed by torrential rain at night. Navigation impossible.

WAR DIARY

Unit 287 GT Coy RASC

Commanding Officer Major L.C. Smith M.C.

2/10/42	1145 hrs 287 Coy placed under Comd. Eighth Army for immediate calling forward.
3/10/42	OC Reported to Eighth Army for orders. Placed under command CRASC 2 L of C Tpt Coln
	Ordered to move at 0700 hrs 4 Oct
4/10/42	Moved to Area 481903 under command CRASC 2 L of C Tpt Coln 90 x 3 ton loaded Pol
481903	
5/10/42	90 x 3 ton loaded. Pol sent Rd G of front to off load
1/250000	3 ton loaded ammo sent to G of Front Slut 15
6/10/42 to 10th	Platoons all engaged carrying petrol and Ammo Egypt Cryr)
10/10/42	to 97 & 97 Fmes
15/10/42	Lt. HCR Darnborough sent forward to control "X" pack "Y" pack being returned loaded in Coy hours
481903	
15/10/42	10 x 3 ton only involved carrying part of "Smalls" required for 13 Corps daily pack.

16OCT OVERSEAS   *Date stamped 21 Oct 1942*

Oct 16th 1942

My Darling,

       I don't know how to start this letter, but I will do my best. I have just returned to camp after driving for hours in a blinding sandstorm, and really, my eyes are like balls of fire. Sand working out in lumps. Still it is nothing fresh. In fact quite a regular occurrence. No one other than the men serving in the Eighth Army will ever know the hell of the conditions in which we work. I will try to give a small illustration of what is involved. Try and imagine the entire midlands area, without a house, road, tree or even a blade of grass. And then if you can get that picture fixed in your mind try and find your way to a given point say for instance, Stourport Electric station or any other place a similar distance away. And then on top of that add a thick fog, and you begin to get some idea of how we navigate. I have the small compass sent by Mrs Digger and it is certainly an assistance for a periodical check on the bearings, but I always use the sun for direction. It has not let me down yet. Visibility is often the front part of the vehicle and no more. Still darling, it has to be done, and we are going to lick Rommel. We know what is involved but every one is determined on that. I know we went down in the estimation of a lot of people and I shall not try to make excuses. But when the day dawns that tells of the defeat of the "Afrika Corps" I hope our name will be vindicated. And I know that my own Company will uphold its name as the most famous Service Corps Company out here. I am proud to belong to it. The men have just come in from a hard day, and the storm has abated somewhat, and I can see them now, playing a football match. Then will come a meal, sleep and away again at dawn to whatever fate holds in store for them. It is the only recreation possible.

    And now darling to other things or you will think I am making myself a martyr. When I came in letter No. 18 and letter cards 23 & 24 were awaiting me. Also a birthday telegram. Well when I read them honestly I did not know what to think. First of all I read the letter. I know I deserve all you wrote. But the letter cards. Whatever have you done to have blood poisoning like that? I was worried about it but the worst was taken away by the telegram saying "Health improving". Thank God for that. I hope you are feeling better now sweetheart. I don't know what I should do if anything happened to you. I feel just the same as you must have done when Bir Hacheim and Sidh Resegh and Messa Matrick fell. All the time I knew what you would be thinking, and wondering, and there was nothing I could do to spare you the worry. Time after time we, with the major's unerring leadership, extricated ourselves, but even though I wrote there was no way of despatching the letters. And so I had to be as patient as possible until we held the enemy in his present positions. And then everyone wanted to send mail at the same time, so I do not know how long it was before you received news from me.

    Darling, please look after yourself but never try to keep anything like that from me. I would far sooner know, wherever I might be. So you see there is just a slight difference. I could not write, but you can.

    Now about the other affair. Darling, you thought I had a business head. Keep thinking that, because I think you are right. But the one thing I could not grasp was how to show on paper, capital spent, received in takings, paid back, borrowed again and so on. But with straightforward capital to trade on I know I can do it easily. I know you have taken the best course and all you have done is for me. I am not afraid to start again and I know you are not. Whatever has to be paid, pay it cheerfully from MY account. And just one word of advice. Any gratuities you receive and all you save for me, save it at home. It will mean the loss of interest, but attempts may even be made to tax your "tips". After my service and experiences out here I feel I can face the world with a clear conscience, especially now that matter is being cleared up. Whatever it costs, I know I shall feel happier. Please let me know full details as soon as possible. And now let me thank you for all you have done.

Since I have been out here I have altered myself considerably. I am not boasting when I say that. I have known my faults. But I determined that the "tomorrow will do" attitude should not be allowed to enter into the scheme of things. I have had all kinds of jobs to do where a reliable man was needed, and I have never let anyone down. And I know also that I shall continue in that way.

Well sweetheart I think I shall have to close now. Oh! Thanks for the hydrangea snap. It was grand. Plenty more snaps to follow. Am now anxiously awaiting the next letter. Cheerio darling. All my love from your husband

Gerald X X X X X X X X X X X X X

One for Lucy X

Oct 16th 1942

Darling,

Just a few more lines hoping your health is improving. Sorry I put the wrong date on yesterday's letter. This is the sort of birthday to have. Sitting in the cab with the lorry trying to do acrobatics. I think I am underestimating when I say it is one of the worst sandstorms ever. My two companions in distress are crouching down in a "Bivvy" five yards from me and it is only at infrequent intervals that I can see them. And the wind is blowing with gale force. I am sure you did not mean this when you wished me "Happy Birthday". It will be a day or two before I forget it. I never thought it possible, but while I have been writing the storm has got worse. Just at the moment I cannot see the end of my lorry.

Now to turn to other subjects if I can give my attention to writing. Thank you so much for the snap of the hydrangea. It must have been a splendid show. I am glad now that I persevered with it. Just try and keep the roots protected with dead leaves if possible during the winter. And those desert flowers are perennials so look after those too. Thank you very much.

Had a letter from Dick yesterday. With his usual good nature he has sent me a very nice collection of snaps to replace those I lost in Libya. The Palestine collection I refer to. And the olive wood ash tray I have already sent on to you. I shall very shortly be sending you the other parcel. I have it already made up, but I believe the regulations do not permit two parcels to the same address at close intervals. This may only apply to food but I did not risk it. I think it is quite in order for you to send socks etc. to me but please do not send anything you require for yourselves. I can buy practically all my requirements out here. That is of course on the very rare occasions when I reach some semblance of civilisation. Had a letter from George too, about ten days ago. He has not been in very good health recently. Old stomach trouble returned. Can't write any more now as I can hardly see. Cheerio darling Hurry up and get well again. All my love from your husband

Gerald X X X X X X X X X X X X X

One for Lucy X

Oct 16th 1942

Darling,

Many thanks for letter cards No. 23, 24 and air mail letter No. 18. I am afraid they all contained rather bad news, but I am glad you let me know. How are you feeling now, and where and when did the injury take place? And above all however did you come to let the blood poisoning get to that stage? Up to the time of this card I have only had those two communications with the exception of a birthday telegram of Oct 9th saying "Health improving". The cards were dated Sept 13th & 14th so that makes at least a month that you have been ill. You say you have a "plug" through your right thumb. What is that for? I suppose

I shall be hearing more about that in further letters but it will just about be my luck to have them delayed again. Still that Oct 9th telegram has eased my mind a little. I think I am feeling now just as you felt when all those battles in Libya went against us. So far away and so helpless. If you are fully recovering when you get this card please take things very quietly and do as Eric Sinton says. He is a good doctor and friend to us both and you must take his advice.

I am sending other mail to you today, hoping that one of them will reach you quickly. Cheerio sweetheart, and once more please take care of yourself. All my love from your husband

Gerald X X X X X X X X X X X X X

One for Lucy X

CHAPTER 8
THE BATTLE OF EL ALAMEIN & BEYOND

GERALD MILNER'S DIARY

Oct 17th Almost as bad as Oct 16th. Navigated by sun. L/Cpl Marlow rather worried on return trip, but very surprised when I pulled into camp in one hour. 3 cheers for yours truly.

Oct 18, 19, 20 All routine

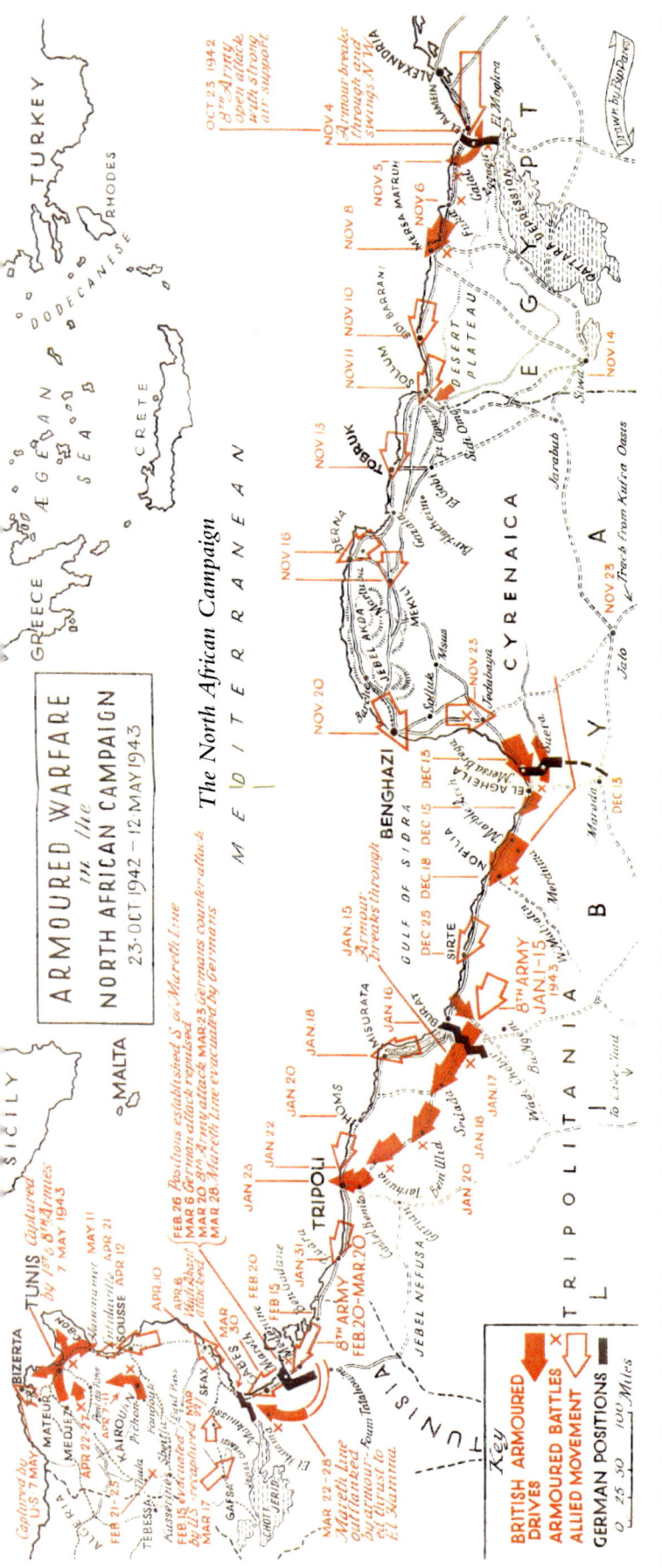

Oct 20ᵗʰ 1942

T/271347
Dvr Milner G
H.Q. Platoon
287 Company
R.A.S.C.
M.E.F.

Darling,

Just a few more lines hoping your health is improving. I have not received any further news since the letters, cards and telegram came altogether. I suppose I shall now be experiencing one of those periods without mail. It usually happens like that. Just one thing I will ask. That is if anything else as serious as this illness and the other financial business you wrote about happens in the future please do not hesitate to let me know immediately. I think Lucy is right when she says you should inform me at once.

By the way I have received the letter containing the snap of the hydrangea. It has made a fine picture. Hope you will send me more to remind me of the old places. I seem to be getting out of touch with quite a lot of things. One of our Sergeants is endeavouring to start a knowledge contest, and I have to provide a few "teasers" Well we have already had one or two contests during the past year, so the questions and answers which I can memorise and be sure of have almost been exhausted. However it appears that the "Powers that be" want a few questions fired at them and they will give the answers. I am writing quite a nice little list of questions. One question I would like you to try and get answered correctly and pass on to me. It is causing quite a lot of friendly argument. I say Gordon Richards was up before the Jockey Club Stewards and "warned off" in I believe 1927 Cesaerowitch for foul riding involving W. Stephenson who was given the race. The other 99% say he was not. Hurry up with the answer.

Have just read Ken Bolton was promoted in the field for bravery near

Tobruk. Captain in the H.A.C. now. Can you possibly let me have his correct address and I may be able to find him in my travels. Well my darling, I think I shall have to end this letter of requests. I hope you will soon be in good health again. Cheerio. All my love from your husband

Gerald X X X X X X X X X X X X X

One for Lucy X

GERALD MILNER'S DIARY

Oct 20, 21, 22. All routine.

GERALD MILNER STORY

Here I should point out that the various advances and retreats were known as the "Benghasi Spring handicap" and the big retreat was known as "the Flap".

One occasion which will never be eradicated from my mind was during the advance at Alamein. The terrain was mighty rough, with telegraph poles shattered everywhere. Among all the debris, from behind a broken telegraph pole stepped a German soldier with sub machine gun pointed straight at me. Before he could pull the trigger a bomb dropped, killing him outright. His body and face were black and swollen from the blast. I could not help wondering what his mother would have thought if she could have seen him then.

However the battle had to continue. Here I think it is time to inject a little humour. A well known and oft repeated little story in the desert. There were three storks in Cairo and Tunis. In the evening they met half way between the two cities. Mummy stork asked what Daddy stork had been doing during the day. Daddy replied "delivering baby boys in Cairo" "And what has mummy stork been doing?" "Oh, delivering baby girls in Tunis. And what has baby stork been doing?" Reply :– "Flying low over Tripoli giving the WRENS a shock!"

WAR DIARY

Unit 287 GT Coy RASC

Commanding Officer Major L.C. Smith M.C.

18/10/42	6 x 3 ton 25 per sent forward to increase "X" pack
19/10/42	26 x 3 tons have returned Forward for "X" pack "Y" pack now increased to 12 x 3 ton. ALL "Smalls"
20/10/42	I section w/shops sent forward to maintain "X" pack vehicles
23/10/42	"X" pack now complete with 57 3 ton vehicles
	"Y" pack holding in 36 x 3 ton vehicles
	Capt Fitzjohn sent forward to control "X" pack, Lt C R Darnborough remains with the pack also.

Oct 23rd 1942

Darling,

During the past week I have received no further news of your progress after your serious illness, but I have continued to write a few lines each day. Once again I wish you a speedy recovery. I was in a difficult position today as I have written so many letters recently that I was at a loss what subject to write about. And now All Highest of the military sphere have relented and made concessions. I am allowed to write and tell you some of my personal experiences up to the defence of that line that is now swiftly becoming history. I refer of course to the battle of El Alamein. All that has happened since is of course "Taboo". And you will realise too that what I write now is subject to censorship so I will try and make it as clear as possible without giving away details that even now may be useful to Adolf and his satellites.

To begin with I will tell you of just one thing that I remember most. I don't know why, but. After many days of hard work, driving under conditions and over territory that presented one continuous obstacle, we reached a point that made me think "Ah! Safety". It was just the wire boundary that separates Libya from Egypt. As I have already written I don't know why I should have had that feeling, but foolish as it now seems I had an idea at that time that Jerry could never break through that wire. On quite a number of occasions other men who were there at the time have told me they had the same feeling. But I can assure you the illusion did not last very long.

The second memory that still persists was the night before Bir Fuka aerodrome fell. A Jerry plane was endeavouring to press home his attack when what appeared to be every Ack Ack gun in the whole world opened up. Heavy and light stuff, flaming onions, flares and very lights together with tracer bullets from ground fire. And the plane was comparatively low. He kept a straight and very even course and to us watching the sight it appeared for all the world as though he was going to get away with it. How it stuck up there so long is beyond me. Then after what seemed ages, and still keeping a straight course, he came lower and lower, and his days work was done. Later the same night another one came over but what a difference. A shall burst set one of his engines on fire. And then his machine guns and ammo caught fire. He got out of control and what a display of aerobatics we got. At one period it looked like a crash coming to our camp. But with a sudden twist he went the other way in an uncontrollable dive, hit the deck and blew up in true Hollywood style. Once again we got safely away just in time.

Then we come to the hardest task of all. Soft sand. More like quick sand. Every time we tried to dig our wheels out so they seemed to get deeper. We worked for hours to get over the brow of the hill just as the convoy moved off. And then our engine packed up. After a short period of temporary repairs we got going again, only to get plug trouble. All we knew was that the Company was travelling North East when we last saw them. And all the time the guns were getting nearer. Once more we got going and once more bad luck overtook us. A very ominous choking spelt finish to our petrol supply. A lorry came rumbling by and helped us out to the best of his ability. And so we started off North East. After a time and certainly more by luck than judgement we found the Company.

After that we came along reasonably well. There is one thing however about which I was and still am puzzled. That was the apparent lack of Jerry aircraft. He certainly had a go at us on a number of occasions but there were times when I personally thought he could have blown us to pieces yet at those times we never saw anything but British planes. I might add that those kind were all we were keen on seeing.

And now to change the subject for a moment. I have just received another letter card from you, written just before the two I received last week telling me of your spell on the operating table. The more I hear of it the more I wish I could be at home with you. Still darling the telegram makes things just a little easier. Just keep on the improving side. And now it is almost tea time so I shall have to close. Please remember me to Mrs Taylor and Billie, Arthur and Mildred and give my love to Lucy. Cheerio darling. Hurry up and get better. All my love from your husband

Gerald X X X X X X X X X X X X X

One for Lucy X

Oct 23rd 1942

Darling,

Just a few brief moments to spare so I once again occupy them in writing to you. First of all I hope you are well on the way to complete recovery from your illness. Have just received a letter telling of the three hour operation. And then you say you were in terrible pain all that night and wondering where I was and what I was doing. Well, I suppose it is only natural that you should think of those kinds of things. You will realise that it is impossible for me to tell you where I was on that particular night, but I have very good cause to remember it. I had just ended a pretty stiff motor cycle "tour" and bed was the only thing I longed for. I can stand any amount of that sort of thing though. Anyway I am almost back in "Civie" street again. At least I have an engine and four wheels instead of two, even if the rest of the vehicle differs slightly from a saloon car.

Have not seen much of Fred just recently. I think he is out on convoy while I work more or less alone. Very pleased to hear you got the photograph I had taken in Alex. You did not say what you thought of it though. I suppose that will be contained in the next letter.

And now about this business of keeping my chin up. Well, well, well! I never knew it had been down. Yes, I know we gave you a bit of a shock and certainly plenty of personal worry, but have a good look at the map and see how much Rommel has actually gained. Just a strip of sand fit for neither man nor beast. But he is still a long way from taking his dearest objective, Alex. And I go so far as to say he will never get it. I have never heard anyone express the opinion that he has any chance at all. There is no room for pessimism here. And as for me personally, you have no need to worry. I can still take care of myself. So, I return your greeting "Chin up", and darling, hurry up and get better.

Have sent you a letter this week telling of some of the impressions I gained during our retreat. Censors are allowing us to give personal experiences now. You should get it soon after this letter. Must close now as night is fast approaching, and the old full moon is just peeping over the horizon. Cheerio darling, and once again "Many Happy Returns". All my love from your husband

Gerald X X X X X X X X X X X X X

One for Lucy X

GERALD MILNER'S DIARY

Oct 23, 24, 25, 26, 27, 28. All routine. Battle started 23rd.

23/10/1942 The Second Battle of El Alamein began with a 1,000-gun bombardment.

25/10/1942 Montgomery switched his attack to the North. Rommel who was on sick leave returned to take charge of the critical situation that his forces were in.

26/10/1942 The Eighth Army started to re-group it's divisions at El Alamein.

27/10/1942 The 21st Panzer-Division counter-attacked trying to push the attacking British forces back into the German minefields. They failed and were left with just 81 operational tanks.

WAR DIARY

Unit 287 GT Coy RASC

Commanding Officer Major L.C. Smith M.C.

29/10/42   Warning Order (CARASC 2 L of C Tpt Coln F3 of 29) received.
Company to be prepared to move forward to 96 FMC under command

	CRASC 5 L of C Tpt Coln Lt HR Darnborough takes up duty at ARH EL IMAYID to supervise loading of convoys.
31/10/42	Entro "Y" pack holding sent forward to G6 Fine
	2000 hrs Company ordered forward under command 131 Bde for troop carrying (RASC 2 L of C Tpt Order F9 of 31)

Oct 29ᵗʰ 1942

Darling,

Just a few lines to let you know that I am quite safe and well. First of all, I hope your health improvement is being maintained. Had two letter cards from you yesterday telling how you had progressed. Must be getting better if you do not have to bathe it every hour. Also I had a card from Mother. I will answer that tomorrow as I have only just reached camp, and the time is now 5.30 p.m. and it will be dark before 7. In that time I also have to feed the inner man.

Well I suppose by now you will know the news of our attack. We have been sitting pretty here for a long time now and working like hell to get this thing going. Have a new General in charge and he does not hesitate to tell us about what is going to happen and when. We knew when this lot was coming off, but darling can you imagine what the last few hours of waiting are like. But Oh! When it came I think we must have loosed off every gun and bomb in the whole world at the same instant. Anyway, that was what it sounded like. And I think the

BBC can describe the RAF better than I can. All day long they have been blasting a way through Jerry lines. Even as I write the sky is filled with clouds of returning aircraft and everyone is there. Most remarkable! Hardly any losses at all. Yes, it is the doom of Jerry alright this time. He can never stand up to this lot for long. I suppose you will think "Oh! I have heard all that before" Well, just listen to the news, and then recall the time lapse from when I wrote this letter.

All our aircraft returned. Fred in the plane.

And darling, please don't worry about me. I shall be alright. There is only one thing troubling me just at present. I have the bottom of my lorry sand bagged as a protection against mines. That means driving with knees up, legs wide apart, a good draught in the wrong place, and shorts fluttering in the breeze. I told the sergeant if it goes on much longer I shall have to ask for home leave. What do you think?

And now, how do you like the snaps of your black husband that I have sent on one or two previous occasions. I think some of them should have arrived by now. Hope you like them alright. Very pleased to hear how quickly my mail got home. 4 days and 6 is certainly getting a move on. Afraid it is hardly so swift at this end, but then we are always making moves so there is bound to be certain delay.

Glad to hear that Lucy got the letter from Dick. Seems ages since I last saw him. He would give his ears to get up here. By the way, you ask again how old he is. I have already told you in previous letter that I believe he is 28 or 29. May be a trifle more than that. Seems as though those letters have gone to the bed of the briny.

Well darling TEA time. More tomorrow. Cheerio

Well darling another day has dawned and it is fast approaching lunch time, so in my haste you must excuse writing and any possible spelling mistakes. At any rate, I will try to make the letter readable. Dinner or lunch over, and about ten minutes to spare. Still have not heard from George again. May get a letter tonight. Who knows? Sorry to hear Roma has hurt her back. Hope she is better by now. I wrote to her yesterday.

Just one little word of explanation now. During the last six or seven weeks you will probably notice that I sent you quite a lot of sea mail letters. Please forgive me. You see I could not tell you that I knew or expected this attack of ours. But I tried to do what is known in the Army as "Use my loaf". I have been in difficulties like that before. Can you see what I mean? All or rather, most of my air mail letter card and airgraph issue I saved when things were quiet. Now I have about 30 of each in reserve.

They will be far quicker to let you know I am safe now the battle is on. As time progresses they will be even more difficult to obtain. But don't worry; I shall still continue to write letters at frequent intervals.

Sorry Mr Gretton and Auntie Edith at Harts Hill have not received my mail. Should have arrived by now. I had the airgraph from Dorothy and have also replied to that. I will write again as soon as time permits. Getting grand weather now. Just like the English summer day. I suppose actually the temperature is quite high but after the blazing heat of the desert it is easily bearable. Hope it will keep like this now until we have Jerry running like an Olympic champ.

Almost time to go for the mail now, sweetheart, so I will close. Will write regularly, a few lines each day to one or other of you at home if possible. Cheerio my darling. All my love from your husband.

Gerald X X X X X X X X X X X X X

One for Lucy X

GERALD MILNER'S DIARY

Oct 29, 30, 31. All routine. Battle started 23rd.

31st after dark had accident to ribs. This slowly improving.

Extract of a letter sent to Gerald from Norman Payze also of 287 Coy

I was in Coy HQ at the start, and once we were up in "the blue" all I had to do was to take down the 10 a.m. news bulleting (in shorthand), type out a copy for each Platoon, and do nothing else for the rest of the day. I soon got fed up with that routine, and asked our C.O. Major "Battler" Smith as he was known to the rest of the Officers, for a transfer to one of the working Platoons. Within a few days he found me a job in Workshops Platoon under Capt Wally Slatter, and I was given the job of looking after the Stores and Spares truck in Staff Sgt. Bob Stuart's section. Bob hailed from Leatherhead. Others were Sgt Boyd Fuller Cpl Jack Brier from Leeds, Sgt Bert Slater, Fitter "Titch" Medley from London, Cpl "Bunny" Austin also from London, Fitter Eddie Best from Rotherham, M.S.M. Vic Knowles from Liverpool and his cousin C.S.M. Knowles H.Q. to name but a few.

Peter Broadhurst recalled picking up the 1st/6th Queens. Just before that we had been standing by, some miles behind the guns, waiting for the barrage to start, and, believe it or not, you may remember, loaded up with ammunition! We dumped it where we stood and reported back to "Beachy Head" to pick up the Queens who we carried to Tunis with a slight detour to join up with the 1st Army for the last drive. Then back to Homs for a break before embarking at Benghasi.

WAR DIARY

Unit 287 GT Coy RASC
Commanding Officer Major L.C. Smith M.C.
Beachy Head
444895
01/11/42   0600 hrs Having travelled all night company located at Beachy Head, less vehicles of "X" pack
0800 hrs Company now complete 131 Bde contacted
1000 hrs 30 vehicles allocated to each of 1/5, 1/6, 1/7, Queens Platoon. Commander in charge of each 30 vehicles.

Nov 1st 1942

Darling,

Just a few lines to let you know that I am quite safe and in very good health. Have not received very much mail from you recently, but as you have already told me your illness prevented you writing as frequently as before, I was expecting a period like this. Well dear, I hope by now you are well on the high road to complete recovery.

Just at present I am the dejected subject of a very large "leg pull". A week or so ago, one of the fellows who shares my abode accidentally washed one of my towels in mistake for his own. Well we thought he would never hear the last of that. But now I have had a wash day and unwittingly returned the compliment. So I shall have to remain very quiet for a time.

And now for a contradiction. I have just received 2 letter cards and an air mail letter from you. Very welcome they were too. Very pleased to hear that all the snaps arrived safely. But once more you have failed to pass comment. The exception seems to be the flamingos. You say you want the negative. Well there were three of us on leave together when I took all those snaps and of course we only had just the one print of each to see how they turned out. Now the other two men want one of each so I want to try and supply them. The main trouble now seems to be to get to a place where prints can be obtained, and stay long enough to collect them. You know what happened to all the others and I certainly do not want a repeat performance. However as soon as I can fulfil my obligations, I will post all the negatives on to you.

And what about the letter telling of my leave in Cairo. Have you received it yet? Seems as though a fair amount of my mail has gone astray. Don't give up hope. It may turn up yet. You also ask about your mail reaching me. Well, it has practically all arrived, although there are often long periods in between. I will send a complete list in a letter I will write probably tomorrow.

Well my darling I must close now as there is a job to be done. Cheerio, and keep up that health improvement. And just to end. Happy Xmas to you all at home. All my love from your husband

Gerald X X X X X X X X X X X X X
One for Lucy X

GERALD MILNER'S DIARY
Nov 1st Midnight never to be forgotten. On the trail again ever Westward. Arrived safely

---

WAR DIARY

Unit 287 GT Coy RASC
Commanding Officer Major L.C. Smith M.C.

El Alamein

2/11/42   Bde moves from Beachy Head to Area East of EL ALAMEIN. OC Major L C Smith MC 2 ½ Capt L A Brown RASC moves with Rear Btn HQ in back with Staff Capt, wireless set. Coy HQ & w/shops remain with Rear CRASC 7 Armoured Division in wireless communication with Bde. Capt A J Batchelor l/c Coy HQ & w/shops.

02/11/1942   Operation 'Supercharge', the breakout at El Alamein started today. Rommel had only 32 Panzer's left intact.

Letter No. 1. Nov 2nd 1942

My Own Darling,

      MANY HAPPY RETURNS

I can just imagine you now, wondering where I am and what I am on this special day. And it really is a special day. More than that I cannot say at present. But please my darling, don't worry about me. As I have told you before I can look after myself. There is one point you mention in one of your letters. That is the fact that I praised up the RAF out here. Well if that did you good, I will now add that they have in this battle now raging, absolutely exceeded all the expectations of the serving soldiers. Instead of driving and wondering where the next hail of bullets are coming from, we can be almost certain when we say, "Oh! A couple of dozen and all ours". That is happening all day long.

    And the tanks! Well this desert is a hell of a big place, but all afternoon I have been trying to pick a track through a seething mass of armour. And really darling, I somehow can't fancy trying to shove a Grant out of the way. I make no predictions. I will just let history redeem this Army of ours.

    And now for a further item of interest. I myself have been the victim of a pretty nasty accident. I am quite alright now, although I have a "man size ache". In the blackness of an African night I tripped up and fell, full force on my ribs. Unfortunately for me there was an iron peg just where my ribs landed. You can imagine what that was like. I thought it was the end of my career and so did my Sergt. and corporal who carried me into their so called office. I have now been told that I was black in the face, my eyes were hanging out and altogether I was in a bad way. Somehow I knew I would have to carry on. I was due to drive westward all night and eventually I recovered fairly well, and everything went according to plan. Except for the bruise I am fairly recovered, and ready for anything.

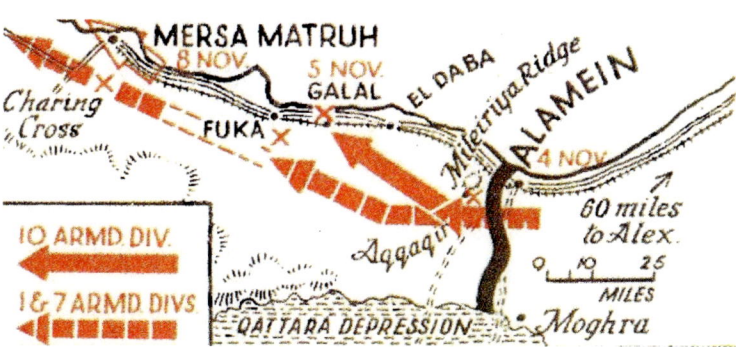

And now for a straight form the shoulder for the gent from Freetown or White Man's Grave as he prefers to call it. I have seen the place if only for a short time. I suppose by saying this place is far better than there he speaks from school days knowledge of the desert. Well if he would like to try it here there are probably many fellows who would be glad to change places, do their time on the Gold Coast and get their months leave. Does he realise that this desert is somewhere in the region of 1000 miles long. That you steer by the sun or the stars or the moon. That is if you are not choking for your very existence in the hell of a blinding sandstorm. And if the day or night has been clear, (in the old days I mean) Jerry was able to cast aspersions on us in the form of machine gun bullets and bombs. Then again, a heat, almost as great as Freetown with little or no water. Sun absolutely merciless. Daylight in the summer at 5 o'clock and dark at 9pm and us driving all day.

I have many times had the experience of watching my temperature gauge go one complete circle and then try to register on the oil gauge. We sleep "on the deck" at night. And this particular deck is littered with many varieties of insect life. Fleas, flies, bugs and beetles in a Keating's advert, but what scope for trade improvement they miss by not having a representative in these regions. We get in addition to the above mentioned, gigantic bats (half bird half RAT) wild desert dogs known as pieards, scorpions, (And I can tell you from personal experience that one dose from those is quite sufficient for any person) lizards, chameleons, centipedes, ant eaters and well I think that is enough to go on with. And just to clinch the deal, we get malaria carrying "mossies" and plenty of other insects of similar nature. So if anyone wants to come and try it, irrespective of the job we have to do, they can come with my sincere sympathy.

To be perfectly fair however, there is another side to the picture, but it is greatly in the minority.

Sometimes I get a job where I get a glorious run down the side of the beautiful waters of the Mediterranean. The intense blue of the water against a foreground of pure white sand is a sight one must see to realise its true value as a picture. Then comes leave. Cairo or Alex occasionally, and on just the one occasion, the Holy Land.

But think of the days and

El Alamein Front line view

nights for months on end with the dark side of the picture before you, and don't you think we earn those few precious days. To stick it out here there is one great factor in my favour. I am with the best RASC Company in the MEF and that says a lot. There are times when I think our Major should have been called Nelson, for he shuts one eye to many things. His one order is Work, Work, Work. He asks for no spit and polish. No boot cleaning or button polishing or anything like that. Rags and tatters do not matter much so long as they are clean. What more can we ask. If anyone does run a little wild, well we are in the Field and its Field Punishment for them. The cases are very rare though. He is a good listener, if it is the truth, but he has eyes that look through you and seem to be able to see the fellow behind as well. If an attack has taken place on us in the distant past, he just waits calmly for each man to do his job and then report. No wild tearing around giving stupid orders and "I'm in Command". No my darling, he trusts every one of us, and he will never have a word said against us. And when a new man comes to the Company he just says briefly, "Work and no one will interfere with you". He lives up to that. And now for a few words about this HQ Platoon. I don't think I have told you very much about it in the past. Well it consists of men practically all "old sweats" in the desert. I don't think I am boasting when I say that what we don't know about this campaign, between us is not worth bothering about. There are such things as ropes out here even, and if we did not know them it would be a much worse life. We have learnt the great lesson of comradeship in hardship. I get on well with all the men. At night I can go for a stroll and a chat in any "bivvy" and know that I will be welcome. That out here is a lot to be thankful for.

The two fellows I usually bed down with are cheerful north countrymen. Both 38 years of age. We get in terrific arguments after dark, but we never fall out. They will ride only on my lorry, and I have overheard words of praise from them, but at night they tell ME that I ought to get a couple of "L"s. Then there is the post Corporal. He rides with me almost every day, and we usually manage to find a little bit of mail.

By the way I have now received all letters numbered up to 23 and since that 27, 28, 31, & 32. They all seem to arrive, but in bunches with long periods in between. And now while I think of it, Happy Christmas and Prosperous New Year to you and all at home. This Corporal I was writing of, a good natured man from Reading, 6ft 1in serious expression, but Platoon humorist. Always "letting me in the cart" Still I can stand a few leg pulls.

Well sweetheart I know I shall have to close as there is stern work to be done. Hurry up and get better. I will write to you every day if possible, but please excuse scribble. Cheerio my darling.

All my love from your husband
Gerald XXXXXXXXXXXXXXXXXX Birthday X
one for Lucy X

P.S. Dick is about 29 or 30

The Gap, El Alamein. British column can be seen on the horizon

On guard

Monty questions enemy commanders

Gunners wonder whether the PBI will make it

The Lucky leader

7th Armoured looking for trouble

7th Armoured bofors move up

A brief halt

*Another push
forwards*

GERALD MILNER'S DIARY

Nov 2nd Back and forth to the old places with L/Cpl F M. Eva's birthday

Nov 3rd Barrage started again. All good news

Nov 4th Crack of dawn or first light. What a sell

Nov 5th Slightly noisy night. Slept well though. Jerry well on the homeward path. Still waiting orders. Nothing happened. Dinner time. Once more away to the wood. Daba & Fuka surs. Atta boy. 35 new planes captured. Just the job. Slept the night west of the Gap. What a night too. Patterns in the sky. Bonfire night too. Certainly well kept up in traditional style first by us then by Jerry.

WAR DIARY

Unit 287 GT Coy RASC

Commanding Officer Major L.C. Smith M.C.

3/11/42 Bde moves to GOLA 3-5 miles west of TEL-EL-EISA. Rear Bde & B echelon sited in the Gap in minefields. Much movement of MT and AV's dispersion difficult owing to dangerous ground. Area surrounding Gap shelled by enemy.

4/11/42 Same location. Shelling very light but closer. No casualties within the company.

TEL-EL-EISA

5/11/42 Coy HQ & w/shops moved up to Area West of TEL-EL-EISA. Rear Btn HQ moves forward 20 miles along 7th Armoured Div Axis. Replenishment takes place and a further 60 miles is covered. Bde now in Area 10 miles South of SIDI HANEISH. Heavy rain all day and many vehicles bogged down.

NOTES ON EL ALAMEIN BY GERALD MILNER

The German line was almost broken when a rather strange "permission" came down from Monty. In battles like this days and weeks seemed to merge and the message reminded us that it was November 5th. We were told that we could fire anything we liked for half an hour, so long as it was in the direction of the enemy and we were just about in the middle of that lot. Bofors and flaming onions, rifle and machine gun fire with tracers, shells from twenty five pounders and a few bombs and machine gun bullets from overhead made a sight never to be forgotten. That night we were ordered to park as close as possible without touching. Then came a follow up order. In the event of an air attack no response was to be made. We thought we were for an early visit to the next world but the search light did a marvellous job blinding the air crews. We did get one nasty event when a bomb dropped on an ammo truck not far away, but when they tried to capitalise night fighters were up there giving protection. As dawn began to break (or a false dawn) one of my colleagues began "gibbering" because two Germans had the barrel of a machine gun pointed at him. He said he was going to be killed. I had to take very strong action with him. Then did a belly crawl and found a gun pit with two dead Italians looking down the sights of a machine gun pointed directly at the aforementioned soldier. Daylight came and we finally broke the German line.

We took many prisoners and one who could speak English asked me what all that had been about. I told him it was to celebrate Guy Fawkes night. He said, "Who the Hell is he?" We live and learn.

The final break came and we got behind the German lines and drove deep into the desert. Darkness came and we heard a lorry load of Germans come into our midst demanding "Benzino" not realising that they were caught. My revolver and that of our C.O. and others soon convinced them they were taken as prisoners. Water was not plentiful but we managed a cup of tea for them. Surprisingly a number of them could speak English. I said to one of the officers that he must feel let down by German Intelligence finding themselves in their present situation. He would not have it under any circumstances. I said that if I had been caught like he was I would feel rather peeved. His reply was astonishing. He said "If the British High Command doesn't know what they are going to do next how can German Intelligence interpret it". To which there was no answer.

GERALD MILNER'S DIARY

Nov 6th Away again. Westward. Nightfall and just a little quieter night.

Nov 7th Westward again then south and what a trip. Swamp, swamp, swamp. Stopped the night. Quiet.

03/11/1942 Rommel was ordered by Hitler to stand and fight.

04/11/1942 The Italian 20th Motorised Corps were destroyed. Rommel only had 12 tanks left and re-issued his orders to retreat. The British captured 9 generals and 10,724 Axis prisoners.

05/11/1942 Battle of El Alamein was won

06/11/1942 The 8th Army continued to progress and took another 20000 Axis prisoners.

WAR DIARY
Unit 287 GT Coy RASC
Commanding Officer Major L.C. Smith M.C.

6/11/42	Very rainy. Bde very scattered and commandment difficult owing to mud. Coy HQ and w/shops moved to EL DABA.
7/11/42	Bde moves to and occupies ALGS at BIR–ALI–OMAR (751324 1/250000 Shut 14 EL DBA) Coy HQ w/shops at ALAM-EL-HALIF.
8/11/42	Coy HQ & w/shops move to BIR-EL-GARRARI 758317
9/11/42	Bde moves to QUAREA-EL-KANAYB for replenishment.

GERALD MILNER'S DIARY

Nov 8th Away again. Even more swamps. Terrible driving conditions. Eventually came to rest for a brief period. On again for a short distance. One attempt made to sleep. Could not sleep for the bitterly cold wind.

Nov 9th On again. Still SW

Nov 9th 1942

Darling,

Well my dear youngster, here we are again back in the old places. It seems a long time ago since I made a prophesy and it seems that the day of its fulfilment is at hand. In short we have Jerry on the run. But this time we are making no boasts. The job is going to be finished.

Incidentally I am sitting at the wheel of my lorry, waiting for the order to push on, and at the same time utilising the brief moments to fill this sheet of captured official Axis notepaper. So please excuse the writing, and just a word of warning in a very tiny voice. Take no notice of the date on top of the page as it may be days before I drop on an Army Post Office. Still I keep trying to get a line or two ready for the first opportunity.

A lorry with us now has a wireless running off the battery. The news is now on. What praise it gives to all the boys of the Army. But now I am going to be very straightforward and say "We deserve it". Just that and no more.

Now for a word about the defeated Army. Still traces of the old German arrogance. But they seem quieter. One sergeant of an airborne division paid our lads a great compliment. He says, "When we have taken them prisoner "THEY WON'T TALK". He hoped we would not punish him for not giving information involving the safety of his comrades. Well, that is for other people to decide. Some of them thought German food (Army) was good, but after a meal with us they all agreed ours was better, but "Where was our "Am and Heggs".

I suppose the English newspapers will have given you vivid stories of the great achievements of the Eighth | Army. But there are still quite a lot of details they will not be able to give. They will not tell of the incredible amount of work and hardship involved. Pushing Westward ever Westward, driving day and night through soft sand, then perhaps lumps of stone in patches, miles wide, or swamp where vehicles sink up to the axles. I have had some of each and I know all about it. Then "What of the Night" as the old poem says. Just a ground sheet and a couple of blankets placed on the sand at the side of the lorry. Come what may, wind rain or a hail of lead from above we have carried on. The work is even harder than in the June retreat, but we have the sure knowledge that the result will be reversed. No more El Alamein to keep the world on thorns. That place today is just a memory, with a tremendous litter of wrecked tanks, guns, aircraft and other pretty grim sights as a monument. As we broke through the sights we saw were at times remarkable. Batches of the enemy everywhere being unable to work out what it was all about, coming in and giving themselves up. A Jerry said he was glad to be a prisoner. "Spitfire, Hurricane". All day pop-pop-pop-pop was his idea of our air force.

And now my darling Cheerio. God Bless you and keep you safe. All my love from your husband

Gerald X X X X X X X X X X X X X X

one for Lucy X

WAR DIARY

Unit 287 GT Coy RASC

Commanding Officer Major L.C. Smith M.C.

9/11/42	Bde moves to QUAREA-EL-KANAYB for replenishment.
10/11/42	Coy HQ move to BIR-EL-THALATA, w/shops remain to effect engine damage and repairs
11/11/42	Guards left at BIR KHAMSA for w/shops. Bde moves forward to TOBRUK
13/11/42	Bde contacted in TOBRUK. Coy HQ following along TRIGH CAPUZZO
14/11/42	One 3 ton lorry found blown up on ruin outside TOBRUK. Arrangements made for evacuation.
15-16/11/12	Company concentrated at B403 (418408 1/250000 SALUM TOBRUK shut 3) 85 x 3 ton loaded for M'SUS.
17/11/42	1600 hrs Convoy leaves for M'SUS
19/11/42	1500 hrs Convoy arrives M'SUS and offloads under orders CRASC of Comd Div
20/11/42	20 x 3 ton left at M'SUS to offload Tpt planes remainder returns to TOBRUK

GERALD MILNER STORY

After that brief encounter we turned parallel with the coast line and moved swiftly towards Fort Cappuzzo. We hoped to get there quickly and then get behind the enemy retreating in some disorder along the coast road and thus end the war in Africa. It was not to be. We had almost reached our target area when we ran into the father & mother of all thunderstorms. The desert was flooded to a depth of roughly 2 ft and nothing could move. The Germans went steadily towards Tobruk but although we could not move we pumped plenty of lead into their flank. The irony of the situation was that it had not rained for the previous 13 years. Eventually the water faded away and the tanks did a good job in getting us out of the slushy sand.

Our next aim had to be Bir Hacheim, El Adam and Tobruk. On the way we saw a refreshment vehicle "manned" by two very brave titled ladies whose names I have forgotten. As in the desert there was nothing to spend money on we rarely had a pay day so of course we were virtually "broke". Five of us searched our pockets and just one piaster was found so our tame comedian asked for a cup of tea and five saucers. The good ladies smiled and gave each of us a cup of tea which was received with gratitude. We reached Tobruk and took many prisoners. One Italian was making his escape with a heavy lorry. I could see it was no use chasing him in a lorry so I "borrowed" a matchless motor cycle, stopped him and had a look at his load. I was amazed to find a load of brand new boots. Back to Tobruk he had to come. Our boots were badly worn as we had outrun supplies. In fact a day or two before our C.O. had been asking various men about the condition of their boots and explaining the supply situation. Our comedian said that if he trod on a penny he could tell whether it was heads or tails. C.O. said the lorry should be unloaded and everyone could try to find a pair of boots that fitted. Needless to say yours truly was the only one without a pair to fit.

And so to Benghasi. Our stay was brief but fairly eventful. We then moved along the coast road, "Bomb Ally" as it was known towards the salt flats at El Agelico. A way through the salt flats had been found by Major Gardener and my old friend Corporal Tommy Hallow. The 7th Armoured Div slipped quietly through and behind the enemy. For two days it was a bit ferocious. I gained the impression that the enemy did not like us being there without his prior knowledge. In fact the London Gazette Supplement summed it up brilliantly by reporting that "for 2 days the situation was somewhat confused". Because of the salt flats the Germans had thought it impossible for penetration to take place and consequently the number of troops in their forward area was not great. We captured a fair number and in retrospect I formed the personal opinion that at that point the German soldiers realised they had little chance of surviving the onslaught from our side.

GERALD MILNER'S DIARY

Nov 10th Carried on all day. Jerry seemed to have 7 league boots.

Nov 11th Cigarette issue at dawn and away again. Driving all day.

Nov 12th Away at dawn. Short break and away again until nightfall. Monument passed. Libyan border miles behind us.

Nov 13th Dad's birthday Wonder what he is thinking now. Away again but welcome relief. Just a bit of a break again. May be able to get a wash at last.

Beyond El Alamein

Tobruk, 13th November 1942

10/11/1942 The British captured Sidi Barrani

12/11/1942 Sollum and Bardia are retaken by the 8th Army.

13/11/1942 Tobruk is retaken by the 8th Army. Montgomery said: 'We have completely smashed the German and Italian armies'.

20/11/1942 The Eighth Army reached Benghazi.

Nov 20th 1942

My Darling,

Well dear, at last I can find a few moments to write a little more than an airgraph. But at the same time I realise you still want those quick short messages to let you know that I am safe. Just at the moment I am sitting at the wheel of my lorry with all doors and windows closed as protection against a terrific wind which looks like ending up in a blinding sandstorm.

I suppose you will now want to know something of what we have been doing out here. I will try and tell you some of my personal experiences without giving away any vital information. First of all we knew this lot was coming off. And what a time it was. Waiting. Always waiting. How we used to make preparations in the old days, just when the moon was getting full. And this time, how long it seemed before full moon. Every day was like a year. And then the hour arrived. Zero hour. And what a din. I shall never forget that barrage we slung over. The majority of the Axis army will never know what it was that hit them. Yes! When we went through what has now become famous as the El Alamein Gap, it was a pretty grim sight. But I can assure you that where there was a British tank knocked out there was always a swarm of knocked out Panzers all around. Yes! They gave a grand account of themselves before they went under.

And what a mess the entire desert has been ever since. I have travelled over many hundreds of miles, in many directions but nowhere had the enemy escaped the vengeance of the Fighter Boys above. And it is still going on. All these stories on the wireless are perfectly true, but I am sure you cannot even then get an accurate picture of the destruction. If you went from home to where Arthur is stationed, back again, in fact do about five or six return trips there, and never lost sight of at least one or two burnt out tanks, lorries, guns or planes you would still only be getting the Coast road and area in something like true perspective. If it were not for this sandstorm which as I anticipated has blown up I could see from my cab at least forty wrecks. It is the same everywhere.

Plenty of good Germans too. We buried quite a lot of them. Somehow I felt no sympathy whatever. I must be getting callous but I always remember that it was them and theirs which caused this war.

If death on the battlefield was their peace time ambition then that ambition has been fulfilled. I also think at times like those that their mad ambition is the cause of my being separated from the best wife in the world. I mean just that. And since this Hell began again, I have been thinking more than ever of you. Wondering what you are doing and <u>knowing</u> what you are thinking each time you hear the news. And here was I unable to lift a finger to ease your mind. Except to pursue this broken flower of the German Army to the end. Well we did that, and no one can ever know the sacrifices the Officers and men made.

The stories will undoubtedly be told in due course. But one must actually experience the hardships to realise to the full extent what they mean. If you want to get just a small idea of one part alone all I can advise you to do is to get a rubber ground sheet and a couple of blankets, and spend your coldest night somewhere in the garden. I think I have had several scores of nights like that. Of course in the summer the nights are warmer, but now. Oh! Dear. What a difference. Still we carried the job through. There is one crowning glory however and it really means a lot to us out here. Sometimes we listen to the BBC news and hear of the fall of some particular place. Red hot news just arrived. And we have already left the place, probably a day or perhaps two days before. Still it is better to give the truth a trifle late rather than premature rumours.

Major overhaul

I suppose now you will think this is a tale of self pity. Well my darling far be it from me to tell any other than the truth, and at the best only one small fraction of it. The thing I remember most and I know it will live in my mind always was actually coming through "The Gap". I did not know what to expect, or where the danger may be. Broken down barbed wire everywhere. And all those wires had enclosed minefields. The Gap proved to be quite a fair width, nothing but churned up sand, bomb and shell holes, Thousands of vehicles all trying to find a safe way through, shoulder to shoulder, midst blinding dust thrown up by the wheels.

Somehow we got through and then days on end of ceaseless driving over country, now like Kinver Edge, now like one of Guy Butler's ploughed fields after a week of heavy rain. Then we would come to miles of white stone, and the trip was just one big jump. And all the time the sky was black with the RAF. Can't imagine where they raked up so many planes.

We had quite a lot of prisoners, all German. The poor old "Ities" had been left to "hold the baby". Had a talk with quite a lot of them. One of them told me "British prisoners never talk. I hope I will be respected if I act in the same way." One blonde youth of 20 had over three years service as a paratrooper had been in the landing on Crete. He won't land anywhere else except in "clink". Another was quite pleased in fact joyful to be out of the way of our fighters. I can quite appreciate his exuberance too. They are not so certain now though. They seem as though they will be satisfied if they can get the whole of Europe. There is <u>nothing like being ambitious is there.</u>

Just a small selection

Well my darling, I suppose I must get on to other subjects than war. I started to number my letters etc and now I have written quite a lot in between so I can't think what number this should be. Anyway as long as they reach you, that is all that matters. And then you must wait patiently and one of these fine days I shall be turning up and delivering all messages, numbers as well in person. How will that suit. That is all I am longing for now. To see you again and tell you how much I love you. And when the great day arrives I hope it will be the end of our parting.

We have work to do yet, but it will be done alright this time. And now my own sweetheart I must close. At 6.30 it will be pitch dark. (4.30 in your time) And I shall be crawling between my two blankets to lie and think of you. Cheerio my dear. God Bless you and keep you safe for me. Please remember me to all at home, and give my love to Lucy. All my love and lots of kisses from your husband

Gerald X X X X X X X X X X X X X X
one for Lucy X

*287 Company
entering Benghazi*

Darling,

Just a line to
let you know that
I am safe and well. Don't worry
about me. Telegram letters and airgraphs
following. Love to you and all
at home. Just to finish.

A Happy Xmas
to everyone.
Cheerio. All for now
from your loving
husband
Gerald
x x x x
x x x x
x x

T/241547
Dvr Milner G.
H.Q. Platoon.
287 Company
R.A.S.C.
M.E.F.
NOV 14th 1942

Nov 23rd 1942

Darling,

      Just a few lines once more to let you know I am safe and well. Still have not received any mail from you, but am expecting all arrears to arrive any day now. I think this speed record we have been setting up has a lot to do with it. When it does eventually turn up I suppose I shall have a special size in headaches trying to answer it all. Still I will do my best. Now about that place you mentioned in Wales. Well I have already replied to that letter but you do not appear to have received it. I repeat it will suit me nicely. That is of course when the day arrives for me to set foot in good old England once again.

And now I am waiting to hear whether you eventually purchased the greenhouse. I certainly hope so if the price was alright. I shall need one or two of those when hostilities cease, and personally I believe now is the right time to buy. And by the way it can be a wise time to sell, too. If you think you have any of those prizes to dispose of, I would advise you to take the chance. There should be quite a number in duplicate.

Sorry to hear you have had bad luck with the garden this summer. Hope to be there to show you a thing or two when next harvest comes around. And about that rabbit pie. Well, I think I could swap you a couple of desert rats for it. Or would you like a nice genuine knocked out German tank. Just say the word and it will be done. We are giving dozens out with every packet of cigarettes now.

Well darling it is time to do a trifle more work now, so I must close. Please remember me to all my friends and give my love to Lucy. Cheerio. All my love from your husband

Gerald X X X X X X X X X X X X X X X

one for Lucy X

Nov 23rd 1942

Darling,

      It is just a week since I was last able to write to you, so I will endeavour to make up for lost time. Shall send a letter and also airgraphs tomorrow. Incidentally this is a free postage letter in place of special Christmas Greetings which have not yet caught up with us. Anyway, a Happy Christmas and Prosperous New Year to all at home. Sorry to say I still have not received any mail. The Middle East is a fairly large place and we keep finding all kinds of odd corners to settle for a night so it may be days before we get any more mail. I shall however keep on writing to you.

Saw Fred today. He is quite safe and well. Had a pretty hard run up here, but the scenery was grand. Quite a lot of it was similar to England. Saw real grass. Must be the first for more than a year except for in the Cairo gardens. And instead of the familiar water buffalo, there were small herds of cattle and flocks of sheep, all of English type. But some of the country over which we travelled was at times like tearing headlong down the Welsh mountains. And strange to relate, just at the present moment I am parked up in a field of wheat. Not yet December, wheat 7 or 8 inches high, due for harvest in early May. One of our drivers shouted for me to get out of his cornfield this morning. And the weather here at the moment is like a June day at home. But give me home every time.

Well darling must close now as there is work to do. Please remember me to all my friends and give my love to Lucy. Cheerio, and hurry up and get better. All my love from your husband

Gerald X X X X X X X X X X X X X X

one for Lucy X

GERALD MILNER'S DIARY

Nov 13th - 30th Nothing but work and driving. Tobruk, Der?? Bengasi and all the wonderful country in between. Mountain passes and dangerous ledges all accomplished safely. Mines everywhere but again safely negotiated Today took snap of Magrum. First another native village but certainly far cleaner than some I have seen in Egypt. Ex German and Italian camps in dirty state compared with British sanitation in the desert. Late in the year but thousands of flies breeding in the filth. Still nothing but wrecked Axis planes tanks guns and vehicles of every description. Listened to Winston Churchill last night. Onto Magrum. Back again to a grand spot for camping. Had quite a nice time there. Then Chemines and that place of salt El Agheila and so to Marble Arch.

WAR DIARY

Unit 287 GT Coy RASC
Commanding Officer Major L.C. Smith M.C.

TOBRUK

21/11/42	Convoy returns to Coy location less 20 vehicles and reports to CRASC for orders. 13 Corps informed that Coy is concentrated
22/11/42	1750 hrs Orders received to rejoin Btn in TOBRUK
	1900 hrs Btn contacted and a platoon sent to each of the 1/5-1/6 Queens. 11 x 3 ton sent to 507 Coy RASC for second line duties. 4 x 3 ton remain for collecting stores. 20 x 3 ton rejoin Coy from M'SUS
23-4/11/42	Loading up Infantry and POW
25/11/42	Move to BENGHASI
27/11/42	Arrive BENGHASI Coy HQ & W/shops concentrated Area (S) R9357 (1/250000 Shut/Benghazi)
28/11/42	Coy HQ & w/shops move to Area (S) R 9810
30/11/42	Orders received to move Ana (S) S 0477

BENGASI

1/12/42	Coy HQ W/shops and No. 4 Platoon located Bx BENGAZI – BENINA Map Ref (S) S 0374 (1/250000 Shut / Benghazi) No. 1 Platoon with 1/5 Queens, No. 2 Platoon with 1/6/ Queens. Role being to carry rubble from Benghazi at the docks to the rebuild mole. No information received as to location of No. 3 platoon which was attached to GT Coy RASC.

Pressed Wild Flowers from around the Tobruk Area

Dec 1st 1942, Somewhere in the Field

My Darling,

At last I have a short period in which to write you a little more than an air mail letter card. All the time I have been thinking of you and knowing that you have had further worries in regard to the welfare of my humble self. Some time before Oct 23rd I knew this affair was coming off, and all I could do in fairness to the men whose lives were in danger was to keep writing letters, airmail letter cards and airgraphs every day until the actual attack began. I knew you would receive some of them at a time when it would help to ease your mind.

And then came the Grand Slam. Well as you know the German line just fell to pieces and after that well, to put it very mildly, we have not known whether we have been on our head or our heels. Tearing along in all kinds of weather and through heartbreaking country at anything from 50 to 100 miles a day. Some day when we can sit together again by the old fireside I will tell you in detail what that meant to the men. Personal sacrifices were made by all, and made cheerfully too. Two nights ago I was lucky enough to hear Winston Churchill speak. He said "We have to think back over the last 3 years to realise what we have escaped". Well darling I do that sometimes, over the past year, and I shudder to think of what might have been. I mean of course to myself personally. It is not so good to see companions become casualties. Perhaps to see tiny pin points leave the belly of aircraft and come in my direction, growing larger and gathering momentum every second. And then the crashes maybe 50 or 100 yds away and you instantly wonder who is in that particular spot. More often than not it is just another near miss.

And then, before Tobruk fell to the Germans I have seen beautiful patterns in the sky, all made by incendiary bullets from enemy aircraft and perhaps some of our night fighters, and every one seeming to come in my direction. Most of that has altered now and those things are rebounding with greatly multiplied interest on the men from Berlin and Rome. But I have learned from experience to watch for the lone raider. And darling, rest assured I shall carry on watching. My sole ambition is to get the job over and get back to you. How I would like to be with you now. There is one consolation though; I am much closer to you now than I was a few short weeks ago. For months now I have asked you to have faith in the men of this Army in the desert. As I write in the cab of my lorry, which has almost become my home, I can see the twin domes of a mosque and the great minaret of a mighty city. Or should I have said "Once mighty". And behind me are a range of mountains which look very beautiful in the afternoon sun. Again I shiver to think of the trip down that mountain pass. About ten times as long and winding and far steeper than the one at Knightwick. And of course the retreating enemy did not leave it in the best of repair for us. Still it will all form an interesting subject for me to give you a lecture on when I get back. Very nice don't you think. Just a friendly description of a trip from the most battered city to the graveyard of ships. What a spectacle that port is now. Just like a place of death. Burnt out hulks of ships everywhere, all black in the brilliant sunshine, with the intense blue of the Med as a background and no sign of movement on them.

Then there was a grand run through the valleys and mountains which at times reminded me very much of England. In places there were native farmers most of them hurriedly evacuated by Italian and Libyan farmers. Herds of cattle, flocks of sheep and quite a lot of poultry. I was rather surprised to see a considerable number of splendid horses too. And strewn everywhere among all this beautiful countryside was the wreck of Axis ambitions.

Honestly I think from what I have seen if Musso had confined his aims to road making and development of agriculture he could have made a far more honourable name for himself. But as we know that fine road had as its final achievement the conquest of Egypt and the produce of the farm land was to save food export to his troops. How badly his dreams have been shattered. And all through this tremendous journey I have had as travelling companion a L/Cpl. who is in rather a poor state of health. So you can see I have had my hands pretty full. He has the same ambition as I and most of the men in the Army. Tripoli. And I don't think it will be so long if that Guardian Angel continues such faithful watch over me.

As soon as we have "packed in" for the night after "before dawn until after dusk driving", you should see the drivers get cracking ready for morning. Filling up fuel oil etc. Adjustments, tightening, in fact every conceivable job to get the old truck going again. But, hard as we have worked, and whatever sacrifices we have made, most of the praise must go to the boys of the RAF. They have been magnificent. How they have kept such a vast number of planes in the air all the time is more than I can explain.

And now I think I shall have to close my darling. We have travelled so fast I have had no mail for 5 weeks, but when we get to Tripoli I am hoping the lot will arrive and I can sit down and have an hour's enjoyment reading of home. By the way you should have seen me when I had not had time to wash and shave for 10 days. Well darling I really must close as the sun is fast disappearing over the City. Cheerio. Keep smiling. And give my love to all at Brook St and to Lucy. One big squeeze, lots of love and heaps of kisses for you from your loving husband

Gerald X X X X X X X X X X X X X

WAR DIARY

Unit 287 GT Coy RASC

Commanding Officer Major L.C. Smith M.C.

2-3/12/42   No change in role, local details only.

3/12/42   2000 hrs Ordered by 30 Corps to revert to Command CRASC 7 L of C Tpt Coln RASC for approximately 10 days to carry Amn from BENGAZI Area to 106 Fmc. Coy remain under command CRASC 7 Armd Div for admin. In the event of 131 Bde moving Coy returns to Bde forthwith.

Dec 4th 1942, Field

My Darling,

In beautiful scenery and warm sunshine I half recline in my bed to write just a few more lines. Sorry to say I still have not had any more mail from you or from Brook Street. But I think you will really understand when I say we chased the Axis in almost every direction and this is the aftermath of our efforts. We are not the rule but just the exception, or, if you will, just another unlucky Company in regard to news from home. Still we can put up with that for a little longer yet. My only worries are whether you are getting my mail (very few letters in the last month though. Mostly airgraphs etc.) and your blood poisoning. How is it progressing? The last news I had of that affair was dated Oct 9th. What a lot of water has passed under the bridges since then.

And I suppose you are wondering where I am. The Middle East is of course a pretty big place, and I only occupy a tiny part of it at any given time. But if you wanted to know where I have been during my long spell out here, you could place your finger on almost any part of the map of these areas and I don't think you would be far out. But this is undoubtedly the best location I have stayed in so far. With regards to the view and vegetation I mean.

The Feurker (or however you like to spell the lousy name) can still create a bit of disturbance if he likes to pay the price asked by the RAF and AA men. But he has quietened down considerably of late. Only this morning I passed by one of his old dromes. There was supposed to be grass on it but had a job to see any, for it was just one mass of tangled aircraft wreckage. And in what were once upon a time his ports, I have yet to see a building left intact. Yes those regular news bulletins at 6 o'clock telling of our aircraft raiding XYZ ports never gave a true reflection of the havoc created. Somehow when I look toward this great mass of masonry I cannot realise that it is in such a state. It certainly looks magnificent. And today I managed to buy a very small loaf of bread. What a luxury and above all what a price. It was a kind of milk roll, but nothing near the quality of peace time in England and it cost me (in English money) one shilling and a half penny. When I say milk roll I mean in appearance only for the size of it was perhaps a trifle over Bach cake calibre. But remember this since (I believe I am correct in this) Oct 23rd I have tasted bread on two occasions. Plenty of good food, but always the old dry biscuit. Really I can't say I dislike them but they do get a little monotonous after a few weeks.

Now for a little of my locality. A yard from my bed are a number of leaves which I fondly believe are the fore runners of a mass of golden daffodils. Mind you I'm not certain but they have that appearance. Just in front of me wild crocus. And as Ripley would say believe it or not, I have found one or two occasions REAL mushrooms, and no one has pegged out from the after effects. As I am becoming something of a vegetarian in this theatre of operations, I get quite a few chances of looking around. As you know my present job is very important out here. Water. I can always get the necessary ration allowed in the particular locality in which we happen to be situated. But if it is possible to augment that supply with what is popularly known as "Buckshee" then I am usually given permission to wander about. The boys rely on me and it is not often I have to let them down. They have been known to say that I can smell water miles away. Well that is a bit exaggerated, but luck has been on my side quite a lot recently. But you see, most of them do not know that I can speak quite a bit lot of the native language and that is the secret! A week or so ago I managed by the above mentioned method to get 300 gallons of crystal clear water. Went back inwardly excited but outwardly calm, and offered the water at the rate of 1gal per man. Everyone, officers included asked the same question. "How many days has this to last me?" When I told them "Just today" Well darling the clean faces were my reward.

My sweetheart, I hope I am not boring you with all this, but really I don't write a lot about what I do so I thought it would come as a change. You see, this Company is liable to move always at a quarter of an hour's notice. I very much doubt it, but it is always possible that we may have to move before I can end this letter. Many times it has been like that during the past few weeks. And we lose count of days and dates very often. Still we have shown the Axis what British lads can do but they don't appreciate it at all. Musso does not like us using his pool, but he can't do much about it.

Now just another little item. During the June retreat I saw a score board made by our workshops. It was made of mica taken from a German plane. I have wanted one ever since. Now I have "captured" a lovely piece of mica from the Axis twins and I think it will in due course make two. So I shall on completion of same send one for you and one for Dad. Another thing I have to personally bring home if I can manage to get it through is a scarlet Fez with a long silk cord and a large blue tassel at the end. I think Mother will be claiming that.

Well my darling there is more work to be done immediately, so I cannot write anymore. Very sorry. Felt like writing for hours. Give my love to Lucy. Cheerio. All my love from your husband

Gerald X X X X X X X X X X X X X
one for Lucy X

WAR DIARY

Unit 287 GT Coy RASC

Commanding Officer Major L.C. Smith M.C

4/12/42	Coy moves to Area Kilo 24 Rd BENGAZI-CHEMINES. 1,2 & 4 Platoons load 25 pdr and proceed to FMC 106
5-8/12/42	Three platoons still carrying Ammun to 106 FMC
9/12/42	Released by CRASC 7 L of C Tpt Coln to rejoin Bde (Righal 16/44 of 9 ex 7 L of C) 1600 hrs 4 Platoon rejoin 1/7/ Queens

Dec 10ᵗʰ 1942

My Darling,

Just a line in haste to let you know that I have now received a pile of mail from you, mother, Roma, Mrs Watkins, Dick and George. So you see I have a big job on now to answer that lot. Anyway I will do my best during my very rare spells of spare time. Firstly let me say how glad I am to hear of the improvement in your health. But I cannot understand why, in your letter you say you are better, and then one written a month later comes from a convalescent home. Did you have to wait for admittance?

And by the way I have just received a letter from Dick telling me that Lucy has improved her Saturday night habits. He does not know what it is all about, but it rather knocked me off my balance. Has she been in the sun too? The periodicals she sent to Dick have now been passed on to me. Please thank her very much.

Sorry to hear about the green house. Thought the people were anxious to sell. Still if you hear of another don't hesitate to buy it. Sorry this letter has to be very brief, but I will write more fully in a later epistle. Seems as though you are going to have a grand show in the garden this spring. Hope I can come and see it. I wonder!

Glad to hear Mr Gretton and your Aunt Edith got my letters. I thought Adolf had been spiteful again. I will write to them very shortly. Must close now as I have more work to do. Please remember me to all my friends at home, and tell Lucy I will still send her a bit of love. Cheerio my darling. All my love and best wishes for a complete recovery from your husband

Gerald X X X X X X X X X X X X X X

one for Lucy X

WAR DIARY

Unit 287 GT Coy RASC

Commanding Officer Major L.C. Smith M.C

10/12/42	1000 hrs 2 Platoon rejoins 1/6/Queens, 1 Platoon rejoins 1/5 Queens
12/12/42	Move forward of Bde. Coy HQ & W/shops moves in rear of B Echelon and maintains contact with OC "B" Echelon 131 Bde.
Area "MARBLE ARCH"	
17/12/42	1500 hrs Platoons all concentrated with Bn in Area "MARBLE ARCH" 2000 hrs No. 4 Platoon reports to Coy HQ with 25 x 3 ton released for transport of Petrol. Warning order received from CRASC 7 Armd Div through BRASCO (verbally) that 2 plus will be required to carry petrol forward from El AGNEILA. 2100 hrs No. 2 Platoon reports to Coy HQ with 3 x 3ton
18/12/42	0900 hrs CRASC 7 Armd Div contacted and orders received that maximum

	numbers of vehicles to report this afternoon to 21/c RASC 7 Armd Div Area El Agheila. There to await loading and delivery instructions.
	1200 hrs Remainder of No. 2 Platoon Vehicles report to Coy HQ
19/12/42	0900 hrs 2 Platoons Capt Fitzjohn 7c. working with 21/c CRASC 7 Armd Div

Dec 19th 1942

My Own Darling,

I was very pleased to get your letters and cards. Seemed years we had to wait for mail but quite a lot has arrived recently. All through that great advance I was wondering how you were but I felt you would be getting better. What a time we had. Danger everywhere yet we came through in fine style according to the news. It's a grand feeling to listen to the accurate reports of the BBC and when the fall of a certain place is announced think to myself "Well, well, well". On several occasions we have already got beyond those places. But Jerry is a rotten loser. Sticks mines all over the place without charting them, and plenty of booby traps. But even those things did not and will not stop us. I have always told you to have confidence in the lads out here and we would do the job when the day of reckoning came. And during all that time we knew what was about to happen and could say nothing, so I tried to time lots of mail to reach you at the anxious period. Seems as though it did.

Roma and Steve on their wedding day Dec 12th 1942. St Thomas' Church, Stourbridge

Got a grand snap today of one of Musso's archways of marble. Queer place to put it. Hope all these snaps turn out OK Goodness knows when I shall be able to get them developed. And now a tiny souvenir will just about make the weight. So cheerio my sweetheart. I will write again shortly. All my love from your husband

Gerald X X X X X X X X X X X X X X X

one for Lucy X

Dec 20th 1942

Darling,
Just a line to let you know I am safe and in good health. I know you will be wondering where I am and what I am doing, but you have little cause to worry. I have sent you an airgraph at every opportunity so I thought I would send a card as a change. First of all let me inform me that my mail is arriving in fine style now. All your letters numbered from 1 to 32 have arrived. Also no's 36 - 38.39.40.42.43 and 44 so the post people seem to be on top of their job. I sincerely hope they keep it up.

Very pleased to hear the pictures arrived. Have you had them framed? Another parcel was despatched to you a fortnight ago. Including the pictures that is the third sent since August.

Have spent a quiet hour tonight placing the contents of your parcel and the one from Mother in something like order. Picked up a very convenient ex-Italian wooden box and it is now packed to the brim. Medical kit is very useful, as I am always knocking lumps off my knuckles on the engine.

Have just heard the news on the radio. Seems as though the Eighth Army is still doing very well thank you. Am wondering now whether we shall find any turkeys floating around next Friday. Hope you enjoy your Christmas, and may it be the last one you have to spend by yourself. Are you going to the same place as last year or shall you be staying with Ella? I suppose that information will be in one of my next letters.

I received your letters telling me of the sapphire ring. You seem to like it very much so that is all that matters. But you have not told me how much lighter my bank balance is. Now I suppose you will tell me it is all for a good cause. Well, I agree. Cheerio Darling. All my love from your husband

Gerald X X X X X X X X X X

Dec 21ˢᵗ 1942

My Darling,

Just a few more lines while I have a chance to write. Have just been told I am on guard tonight too. Still I have not done many turns during all these operations. We drivers have had enough on our plates, and the men who do not actually drive vehicles regularly have had extra turns. Very pleased to hear you have recovered from the poisoning. I could not understand why you had been to work and then gone to a convalescent home. However the explanation has now arrived. Very sorry I was not able to answer all your letters in detail, but you know the hurry we were in for weeks. However I did endeavour to write at every available opportunity. Usually sitting at the wheel waiting for a few moments while some obstacle was negotiated or cleared. And so in due course I had quite a number of letters & cards written. Then came the problem of posting them. It is only natural that the APO must be out of reach of forward enemy troops, but the difficulty was soon overcome. In fact at times I received many surprises with regard to the organisation not only of fighting units but also every type of supplies including NAAFIs. One place we had occupied and passed on. The following day I had reason to go back alone for a certain job. And there was a NAFFI and all sorts of other places opened up. Great work. And the farther we go, the more speedy becomes the organisation.

Watched the RAF take off almost immediately they had occupied a drome. And they were carrying bomb loads. Their work seems to get better every day. Compared with this campaign, now we have plenty of arms etc Jerry's so called flair for organisation is not in the first 1.2.3. Not according to what he has left behind. I can assure you I have seen some of his evacuated aircraft repair shops and they would not (or rather the accurate pictures would not) go down very well with the German people. Hundreds of wrecked aircraft of every type in a pitiful endeavour to make one airworthy out of many. Ammunition was everywhere. And with regard to his transport they must have been in a great haste for some of our boys got a number of them going in a few minutes and are now giving good service. Plenty of companies have done the same.

Now then with regard to this matter of your seeing Dr Sinton. You say you are still --- but why bring all that up again. You won't be any more when I get back. That is a promise. Still take your time if that is how you feel.

While I think of it please thank Edna and Syd for the Xmas card. I do not know their address so I cannot write direct. Have written to quite a lot of people recently. Hope they all arrive this time. Sorry to say George is not too well according to his last letter. And he wants to know when you are going to answer the letter he sent to you six months ago. Says he has not been getting much mail for months and he does not seem too happy about Lily. Still that is not our affair. She says she has written regularly. I have had 82 letters in succession arrive safely from you, yet George has not received his with an occasional reception. So I leave you to draw the same conclusion as he does.

Got your card about the auditor's fee. Am now awaiting the letter. Hope everything is OK now. Shall feel far happier when I know. Once again thank you for all you have done. I shall make amends for all that when I get back and in the only way I know you will want. Still have not altered my mind about that. My sweetheart first.

Sent you a very small souvenir in a recent letter and I trust it will reach you safely, and I hope you will like it. I think you will. One for Mother to follow in a short time. Sorry I could only get two.

And now my darling I think I shall have to close. I must again thank you for the parcel and Xmas card. I have asked you to cease sending bundles of papers. It is just to help the shipping effort. Quite a lot of men have done the same. As you know, our mail was delayed for a time, and when it came there was about 2-3 cwts of papers just for this Coy. Most of them all the same dates and copies. Reckon that up for every Company out here and see what can be saved. It all means a small sacrifice, but a speedier return home for us. Cheerio my darling. Look after yourself. All my love from your husband

Gerald

X X X X X X X X X X X X X X

one for Lucy X

WAR DIARY

Unit 287 GT Coy RASC
Commanding Officer Major L.C. Smith M.C.
23/12/42   2 Platoon return to Bde and proceed to Bn locations.

Dec 23rd 1942

My Darling,

A lovely day, an hour to spare, so what better than a letter to you. I have written heaps of mail during the last two months, just to let you know that I am safe and well. I knew you would be wondering. At the moment I am sitting on the German officer's bed I "collected" with a Primus we "won" and a drop of water that came from a good friend, and in a few minutes tea will be ready. Would you like to call in? The water is very good indeed. Just two cup full's in an Italian Dixie "won" by the above method. Yes! The water is excellent. I cannot see the bottom of the Dixie, but it will go down well just the same. Oh! It has gone down. Just the job. Lovely sea breeze too. Not so lovely at night though. Mighty cold.

No mail again today. I expect I shall get it all in a huge pile again one of these days. That is one of the slight differences in Active Service and "In the Field". Don't think there is room for many more "Fields" in the "place paid" column of my pay book. Still it all goes to make an old soldier. Hope I never get to one of those although I have often been called an "old sweat" in the desert. "Dessert" we call it, or "Up the Blue". That was in the old days. Strange how one falls into the habit of nicknames out here. Almost Christmas, blazing sun in the daytime and thoughts "What shall we get for the 25th". Not expecting much as we have "a wee bit job" to do. And Jerry has to be kept going. He seems to be on his last legs, but we take no notice of that. He still has to be kicked out of Africa <u>and</u> we can do it. Saw some of his prisoners two days ago. What a difference in them when they have not got the upper hand. I thought they were going to burst into tears. I confess that if they had I would have been inwardly jubilant. Crimes returning on their own heads. They can't even fight clean so I have no pity. That story will be told another day. When scores of our fighters swooped down to land on a drome, they cringed down. Can't take it. It was very nice when things were the other way round. Different now though.

Well if we don't get much for Xmas I have a few good things religiously stored away. Suppose I shall have to open them. You once asked when I was going to get stripes. Well darling I can't say, and it's really a long say and one of the few real grumbles we have out here. If an NCO is killed or injured or leaves the Company, another man does not get promoted. An NCO at Base, probably just out from England is sent to us and he has to learn from our experience. But he draws the pay. So it seems as though I'll have to come to England first. I have been on the verge of it about six times and strongly recommended for it on other occasions, but there always seems that one snag. Still, I get on well with all concerned, so except for a little extra pay for you, I am not worried. Must close now dearest as I have work to do. Cheerio my darling. All my love from your husband

Gerald X X X X X X X X X X X X X X

one for Lucy X

Well my darling I had ended my letter but I have just learned that there will be no post tomorrow so I will write a few more lines. One of our officers has given a L/Cpl & myself a small tent, so we have rigged up a travelling home. Hit camp 20 mins & Hey Presto. All OK 15 mins notice and we are ready to travel forward. We have the Primus stove a small lamp and a few other odds and ends, and so I can write instead of going to bed at 6.30 p.m. Only trouble just at present is grave shortage of ink. Don't send any please. I expect we shall get some forward very soon.

You don't think I like the photos. I like any photograph of you darling but I still think you do not look so well as you did. And while I think of it, thanks to you, Lucy and Mother for the calendar. I have just one wish. That is that I shall not be out here long enough to strike Dec 31st. What do you think about it?

Very pleased to hear you have the garden laid out for the spring. Hope I shall be able to see it. Well sweetheart I think that is all for this letter, so I will close. Please remember me to all my friends including Mrs Taylor & Billie, and Mildred and Arthur and all at palfrey Road. Cheerio darling. All my love from your husband

Gerald X X X X X X X X X X X X X X

one for Lucy X

GERALD MILNER'S DIARY

Dec 24th Moved again. Sit 2 min sea The C laid on, but only in weather.

Dec 25th Good time. Letters sent home describing Xmas.

Dec 25th 1942. Somewhere with 8th Army

My Darling,

Thank you very much for your letter number 37 which I received at lunch time today. Very welcome and very revealing. Really sweetheart I am glad you wrote "that letter". Today is a day of goodwill so I will endeavour to answer it to the best of my ability. I sincerely hope you will be able to read this letter, but just at present I am feeling ---- well you know, the 8th Army has just given me the strongest tot of rum it has been my fortune to get. First drink of intoxicant since August so I had it gladly. I felt I had earned it. Long service man said it was the strongest and best they had ever tasted, so you can imagine what it was like. Of course under battle conditions we could not expect too much but we did better than expected.

The L/Cpl who travels with me at present, had two parcels from Durban, and we cooked a grand meal. Invited a tent full of the lads and I was feeling fit "to bust". As I have told you before, I being an old hand in the desert, or so the officer concerned described me, I am in charge of the water lorry. I have usually managed to augment our water ration one way or another but I don't know this end of the world like Libya and Egypt. So immediately after lunch I volunteered to go deep into the desert for water. Found water and could not get at it. Too deep. Got back safely and slept for an hour. Must try again tomorrow if we are still here. And then I had another great dinner. Cooked in the open desert, by the sea, but none the worse for that. In fact it was very good. We had the rum, a bottle of beer each, and 60 cigarettes. Now for a confession. I SMOKE. You do not appear to have had my letters telling you I had started again. Kept me awake to drive single handed in the chase across a continent. Someone had a bottle of whisky; someone else had a bottle of Gin. I did not take any, but they managed to make our young sergeant, a grand lad, quite happy. I laughed until the tears rolled down my cheeks. When he got really going, he wished us a Happy Xmas, told us we ought to be at home with our wives, that we did not appreciate them or we would be there. Then we pulled his leg and told him he ought to be with his "Mummy" (He is single) so he shouted "alright you shaver I hope you "b" well get to Bir Hacheim or Alamein for next year". Then he burst into song "When the sheets are short, the bed seems longer". All this without a care in the world. Lights were of no object to us. We took the chance of Herman coming over. And here it is almost midnight and everything in apple pie order. So now you know what Xmas on the battlefield can be like.

A driver cook volunteered to serve in the Officers Mess. Pitch dark. No moon up. He had two or three drinks. To the OC "Your dinner Sir", caught his foot on a guy rope, and went in on his stomach. The OC politely "Good evening, Driver Davin". That is the story as told to me. I believe it is true.

Actually I am lucky to be able to recount these stories. I was in a pretty tight spot recently. Too recently for my peace of mind. Drove into an uncharted minefield. I have told you before Jerry can never fight cleanly. My opinion of him as a great fighter is getting lower every minute. Those gallant but little praised lads of the Royal Engineers cleared a path for me to get out. I have nothing but the deepest respect for their great courage. I think I shall soon be minefield champ. Five or six times now since I have been out here. Still darling I have learned a lot of lessons, and you have little cause for worry. Mines or no mines he is going to get a complete hiding out here. Probably before you get this letter.

Another item of interest. Had a shave today. I knew you would not like me with a beard on Christmas day. And now I have all that off my chest I will get back to your letter. Thank you very much for all you have done at the shop. If you had any alterations made I know it is all for the best. And please thank Mother for the scales. I will write and thank her personally at the first opportunity.

With regard to the purchase of the property, I was rather surprised, as it is the first intimation I had received that any such thing had been contemplated. So you see, some of my letters have not yet arrived. I know that some sea mail on certain dates which I will not give for security reasons has been lost. I cannot say yet whether mine was amongst it. I will write more of that in a week or two. Property is bound to be a high price now and for a long time after the war. So many houses will be needed. But darling although I knew I could not afford it for a long time I have always cherished an ambition to buy the shop premises. But as you say, more of that when we go on that holiday and may it be soon.

There are a number of things I think about when the cases of state allow me a few moments but the future always comes uppermost. And your part in it. There will be one main thing that will concern me and that is continuous work. I am determined on that. Work all day and then you work when the days work is ended. With regard to our wedding, the remarks you made in your letter have received a lot of thought, and somehow that is why I asked you to choose the holiday spot. I don't care a damn whether there's any fishing shooting or anything else so long as I can talk to you, and try to make the future very happy for us both. I have always been happy when I have been with you. But I know we can make many improvements. Yes darling, I mean WE. You should have told me your thoughts when, and after we were married. You still should. It is only by doing that, that I can fall in with your wishes. I think I can fall in with anything now. Service out here has taught me many things.

Fortitude or don't care attitude come alike as the situation demands. On one occasion some time ago, I watched a shower of bombs coming straight for me. There was nothing I could do about it except wait for the end. And in those few seconds I was not afraid. I would have been at one time. But I distinctly remember kneeling against the side of my lorry and praying to God to ease your burden when I had departed. But by the wish of the Almighty it was not to be. Once again they were far too near to be comfortable, but I was unhurt. All the boys thought my time had come. Just a few words of congratulations and away again. I am not boasting about near squeaks. I have had too many in the past and I want to forget them. But it does reveal to me what I really think of you. I have always had faith in your belief that I shall come back to you. I too think you are right. When this job is over I shall remember what you have done for me. I still remember all you have done in the past. But I shall make amends for it. And there is Mother and Dad and Roma too. I wish I could see you all now.

Well my sweetheart it is almost Boxing Day now, and bed is calling, so I shall have to close. God Bless you and keep you safe. Sleep tight. Oh! By the way, I am glad to hear about those warm feet. Think you can keep the temperature up a little longer? Then I can really enjoy going to bed. And now cheerio and here's to Tripoli early in the New Year. All my love my darling from your husband

Gerald X X X X X X X X X X X X
one for Lucy X

Musso's Marble Arch.   *A Postcard for Xmas*

GERALD MILNER'S DIARY

Dec 26th Itla Oudem Static et nein June

WAR DIARY

Unit 287 GT Coy RASC

Commanding Officer Major L.C. Smith M.C.

26/12/42   Bde moves forward and Coy HQ & W/shops take up position 10 miles West of SIRTE

GERALD MILNER STORY

Now for a few words about a Christmas Day at Marble Arch. Not London but a great Archway over the coast road leading from nowhere to nowhere. It simply marks the spot where one of Mussolini's athletes dropped from exhaustion after a call for stamina testing. Rather close to the archway and on the coastal side was a strip of very hard ground. This had been used by the Germans for servicing their fighter planes. We captured what to us was a very valuable air strip. Our fighters landed, bombed up and were away again looking for targets. Christmas Day duly arrived and we were told that a temporary truce had been arranged. It was an understatement to say that the troops were very wary of placing much reliance on the outcome. However it worked out alright. The incident which I personally can never forget was when "Banksie" came to me and said, "Bring a truck over to the R.A.F.". I took a 3 ton "Chev" wondering what was going on. I soon found out. Chains were produced, a Spitfire was on tow, "Banksie" was in the cockpit and the pilot was sitting beside me. Slowly and somewhat gingerly we edged towards the Germans. All was quiet until some of the "enemy" came towards us and shook hands. Then a small "miracle" happened. "Banksie" produced a bottle of the very best "Scotch". Where he obtained it was a mystery and to this day I do not know where it came from. Tin mugs were produced and the liquid shared round as far as possible. No clinking of glasses, but clanging of metal mugs was the order of Christmas Day and it seemed totally unrealistic at that time that we could resume killing each other in the morning. Such however was the case.

Now I arrive at what I truly believe to be bordering on the ridiculous. After several days at "battle stations", with little sleep and seemingly even less food and drink the admin sergeant would suddenly say, "Look chaps, the War Diary has to be made up. What the "bloody 'ell" were you doing at 1.30 PM last Friday". And so amid the sound of shells and bombs the War Diary was duly completed.

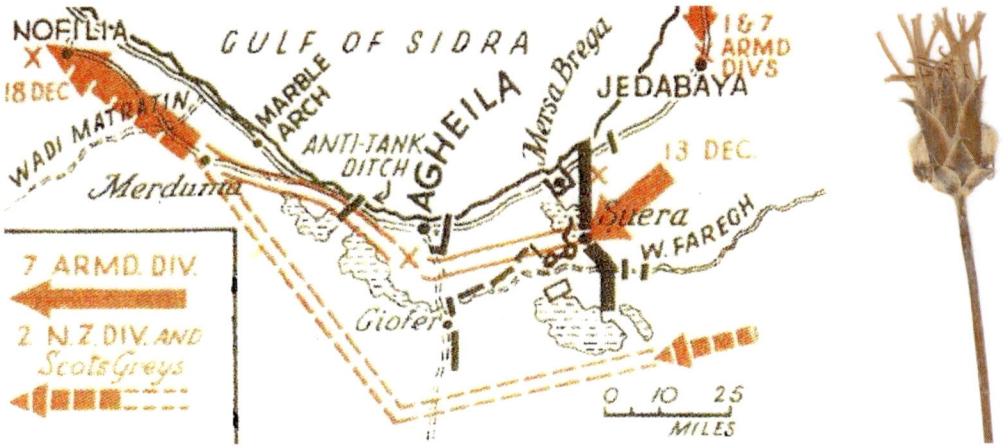

Dec 27ᵗʰ 1942

Darling,

  Just a few more lines before I go to bed tonight. Sorry I could not get the letter posted yesterday but we made another advance and so all my best laid plans went astray. My time at the Platoon radio was welcomed with the news of the fall of Sirte. Well, it is all very nice. Little nearer home every time we go forward. Had a very tiring day today. These advances can be very trying to a driver. There are so many things one must keep a weather eye open for. It was only natural that the enemy would place obstacles in our path but there are plenty of other things besides that. Water is a fluid load, and if my lorry is on the desert instead of the road it can easily overturn. The tracks are at times very similar to Clent or Kinver Edge. A thousand miles of that is no child's play. Never mind, Jerry is still going in the right direction.

  Tonight it has rained like you know what. And strange to relate our camp is in the middle of a solid mass of wild flowers in full bloom. Millions of them. Just as thick as blue bells in England. Only they are about two feet high so you can imagine what that is like when we

walk amongst them. Have just eaten a nice supper. As you know we have our tent and the utensils we "won" so a hot meal was exceptionally welcome. Had a tin of peaches too this afternoon. Medium size, cost in English money 1/5. Robbery but very welcome. Plenty of that kind of stuff in the NAAFIs nearer base or rear areas. Don't see much of it up here though. Probably as well at the price or I should have no filthy lucre left at all. Have got a copper or two in credit now. Hope to keep increasing it until I get leave or come home. There is very little we can buy in the battlefield areas except necessities and those are usually a high price. Beer cannot be obtained and cigarettes are about the only reasonably priced article. 6d for 10 Players. And those are pretty severely rationed. Still if I do not draw any wages for a week, that money goes to my credit. I can draw it at any time.

  The L/Cpl with whom I share this tent is a very dry person. Asks me every night if I have put the cat out. Saturday nights he asks me if his best suit is aired. I usually tell him that you are at the First Aid Post and that I am not to be disturbed. In fact I have bolted the door. And after Lucy reforming too.

  Well my darling I think I shall have to close now as it is nearly midnight and we shall probably be advancing again, so cheerio, God Bless you and keep you safe. All my love from your husband

Gerald X X X X X X X X X X X X

Saturday night one for Lucy X

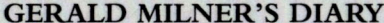

GERALD MILNER'S DIARY

Dec 29ᵗʰ Itla Oudem again. Grand location overlooking sea.
Dec 30th Itla Oudem.

Dec 30ᵗʰ 1942

My Darling,

  Thank you very much for your AML card No. 47. Very pleased to hear you have now fully recovered from your illness and feel fighting fit. You also mention that you are staying at Bridgnorth Road. Well dear I hope you will take things steadily and not get

269

overworking again. I understood from previous letters that you were not going there until December. I suppose you will be getting ideas during your stay there. By the way what is Lucy doing during all these spells away from home? I think I shall have to come and keep her company.

I must also thank you for your efforts re the Jockey question. Sorry the Mirror could not give a definite answer, as we have had quite an argument about it. Still, perhaps your letter will clear it up sufficiently to satisfy us all. Those are the sort of things that crop up regularly and we have no means of finding a correct answer. It does however while away the hours of darkness.

Had a Regd letter from Dad today. He says a month elapsed without even an airgraph from me. Well darling I can assure you that I write at least twice a week, whatever the circumstances. There was of course, a period during our rapid advance when I could not post what I had written, but about a dozen letters etc were dispatched then. Last night I wrote 4 letters etc. Tonight will be at least 3. So you should get a good supply. But somehow it does not seem to work out like that.

And now what about those feet. Are they still warm because mine are not? It has been a glorious day, and once again we have a grand camping site. I am at present on top of a rise. Can see the deep blue of the Med from my tent. Miles of densely packed spring flowers. Millions of night scented stocks (or flowers very similar in appearance and scent) and numerous other flowers. Only trouble is that with very heavy dew they are mighty uncomfortable to walk through. Hence the cold feet. And in the socks you knitted too. Got Mother's pair wet through last night. Have dried them in the blazing sun today. Same again tomorrow.

Well my sweetheart I think I shall have to end now as it is getting late. Cheerio darling. All my love from your husband

Gerald X X X X X X X X X X X X
one for Lucy X

WAR DIARY

Unit 287 GT Coy RASC
Commanding Officer Major L.C. Smith M.C.
SIRTE
30/12/42   Orders received from CRASC 7 Armd Div that all transport is to be concentrated in Coy Lines by 1500 hrs 31 Dec
31/12/42   1500 hrs All three platoons concentrated except 15 vehicles.
1600 hrs Order to proceed to 110 FMC to load Petrol to from Dump forward for supply 4 Lt Armd Bde. Coy to move complete at daybreak.

GERALD MILNER'S DIARY
Dec 31 Static wahed June

Dec 31ˢᵗ 1942

My Sweetheart,

Do you like that beginning or would you prefer Dear Eva for the New Year. Do you remember words similar to that? Well darling the former will suit me very well. Somehow I feel really fed up tonight and I shall be glad to see the back of 1942. Feel better in the morning. I think I have been working a little too hard lately, but that is nothing to do with how I feel now. Since lunch there has been so much to do, and yet I have been able to do so little and I hate to waste even one hour of daylight. But as I say that will pass off.

And then I had your AML card No. 52. That did not make things much better. I was glad to hear you have recovered from your illness but from the tone of your letter you did not seem too pleased with the job at Wollaston. I hope you do not do too much and make yourself ill again. I suppose if I really weigh up the day as a whole, I have little cause to grumble. I went out in search of good water to augment our ration, and got back with about 600 gallons. Never heard of so much water. So the boys got the old Bengasi's going all round the camp for a "brew up". In case you do not understand that is Eighth Army for fires and a cup of tea. There are two kinds of "Brew ups" though, the second a direct hit on an Axis tank causing it to burn out.

Now for a few words about those snaps. Up to the present I have not received letter No. 33. I will repeat those I have had up to this afternoon. Nos. 1-32. 33-4-5 not arrived. 36-7-8-9-40 arrived. 41 not arrived. 42-43-44 here. 45.46. not arrived. 47 and 52 arrived. So if there is any reply you are expecting and have not yet received, perhaps that will explain why. However I take it you like the snaps. I have quite a number of films when I can get somewhere to have them developed. Hope it will not be too long. You tell me you have written a rather sentimental letter. No. 52 arrived in 3 weeks so I think I have a little longer to wait for that one. Shall be glad to get it though. I feel that way myself quite often but it is no good. I have a pretty tough job to complete and when it is done goodness knows what will happen to me. I often wonder whether I shall be able to come home and see you or whether I shall get sent to another theatre of operations. Personally I think we deserve to come home if only for a short time. But that is another story and some day (perhaps I will tell you on that holiday) I will give you the full details. It is quite a long story and involves quite a lot of bad luck in regard to a number of us. But to tell it now would possibly give away valuable information so we will take it on the chin and "say nowt" for the present. Anyway, we are keeping up the glorious record of the Company. I shall be very glad to come home though. I suppose when I start telling just the plain truth you will be thinking this is the only Company out here that has done anything. Well darling, just think (if it bears thinking of) of the time I have been out here and a death struggle all the time. Something simply has to happen. But we have the upper hand now, and I think we shall retain it.

And fancy telling me about Charlie getting 10 days leave. Just tell him from me some people get all the luck. Perhaps it is as well he is not out here. I can do quite a lot of things with half a cup of water, but I would certainly be puzzled if I had to wash napkins as well. Just had a few interruptions and now I have dropped my pen in the sand. Seems as though I ought to go to bed and call it a day. My L/Cpl companion who shares my tent at present is busily engaged sketching on airgraphs. I think he is drawing a few for me so look out for them soon. And now darling, it is getting really late and I still have to fill my petrol tanks up, so I will do that, and then for shut eye. Cheerio my darling. Chin up and keep smiling. All my love from your husband

Gerald X X X X X X X X X X X X
one for Lucy X

Index of photographs: Part 1